# Memoirs of
# Extraordinary Popular
# Delusions
### and the
# Madness of Crowds.

Volume I

**Charles MacKay**

First published in 1852

Ockham Classics

contents

page 4        Preface

page 7        Chapter 1 - The Mississippi Scheme.

page 60       Chapter 2 - The South-Sea Bubble.

page 108      Chapter 3 - The Tulipomania.

page 119      Chapter 4 - The Alchymists.

page 277      Chapter 5 - Modern Prophecies.

page 301      Chapter 6 - Fortune-Telling.

page 325      Chapter 7 - The Magnetisers.

page 365      Chapter 8 - Influence Of Politics And Religion On The Hair And Beard.

page 375      Footnotes

## Preface

In reading the history of nations, we find that, like individuals, they have their whims and their peculiarities; their seasons of excitement and recklessness, when they care not what they do. We find that whole communities suddenly fix their minds upon one object, and go mad in its pursuit; that millions of people become simultaneously impressed with one delusion, and run after it, till their attention is caught by some new folly more captivating than the first. We see one nation suddenly seized, from its highest to its lowest members, with a fierce desire of military glory; another as suddenly becoming crazed upon a religious scruple; and neither of them recovering its senses until it has shed rivers of blood and sowed a harvest of groans and tears, to be reaped by its posterity. At an early age in the annals of Europe its population lost their wits about the sepulchre of Jesus, and crowded in frenzied multitudes to the Holy Land; another age went mad for fear of the devil, and offered up hundreds of thousands of victims to the delusion of witchcraft. At another time, the many became crazed on the subject of the philosopher's stone, and committed follies till then unheard of in the pursuit. It was once thought a venial offence, in very many countries of Europe, to destroy an enemy by slow poison. Persons who would have revolted at the idea of stabbing a man to the heart, drugged his pottage without scruple. Ladies of gentle birth and manners caught the contagion of murder, until poisoning, under their auspices, became quite fashionable. Some delusions, though notorious to all the world, have subsisted for ages, flourishing as widely among civilised and polished nations as among the early barbarians with whom they originated, — that of duelling, for instance, and the belief in omens and divination of the future, which seem to defy the progress of knowledge to eradicate them entirely from the popular mind. Money, again, has often been a cause of the delusion of multitudes. Sober nations have all at once become desperate gamblers, and risked almost their existence upon the turn of a piece of paper. To trace the history of the most prominent of these delusions is the object of the present pages. Men, it has been well said, think in herds; it will be seen that they go mad in herds, while they only recover their senses slowly, and one by one.

Some of the subjects introduced may be familiar to the reader; but the Author hopes that sufficient novelty of detail will be found even in these, to render them acceptable, while they could not be wholly omitted in justice to the subject of which it was proposed to treat.

The memoirs of the South-Sea madness and the Mississippi delusion are more complete and copious than are to be found elsewhere; and the same may be said of the history of the Witch Mania, which contains an account of its terrific progress in Germany, a part of the subject which has been left comparatively untouched by Sir Walter Scott in his Letters on Demonology and Witchcraft, the most important that have yet appeared on this fearful but most interesting subject.

Popular delusions began so early, spread so widely, and have lasted so long, that instead of two or three volumes, fifty would scarcely suffice to detail their history. The present may be considered more of a miscellany of delusions than a history — a chapter only in the great and awful book of human folly which yet remains to be written, and which Porson once jestingly said he would write in five hundred volumes! Interspersed are sketches of some lighter matters, — amusing instances of the imitativeness and wrongheadedness of the people, rather than examples of folly and delusion.

Religious matters have been purposely excluded as incompatible with the limits prescribed to the present work; a mere list of them would alone be sufficient to occupy a volume.

# Chapter 1.

Money Mania - The Mississippi Scheme.

*John Law*

*Some in clandestine companies combine;*
*Erect new stocks to trade beyond the line;*
*With air and empty names beguile the town,*
*And raise new credits first, then cry 'em down;*
*Divide the empty nothing into shares,*
*And set the crowd together by the ears. – Defoe.*

The personal character and career of one man are so intimately connected with the great scheme of the years 1719 and 1720, that a history of the Mississippi madness can have no fitter introduction than a sketch of the life of its great author John Law. Historians are divided in opinion as to whether they should designate him a knave or a madman. Both epithets were unsparingly applied to him in his lifetime, and while the unhappy consequences of his projects were still deeply felt. Posterity, however, has found reason to doubt the justice of the accusation, and to confess that John Law was neither knave nor madman, but one more deceived than deceiving, more sinned against than sinning. He was thoroughly acquainted with the philosophy and true principles of credit. He understood the monetary question better than any man of his day; and if his system fell with a crash so tremendous, it was not so much his fault as that of the people amongst whom he had erected it. He did not calculate upon the avaricious frenzy of a whole nation; he did not see that confidence, like mistrust, could be increased almost *ad infinitum*, and that hope was as extravagant as fear. How was he to foretell that the French people, like the man in the fable, would kill, in their frantic eagerness, the fine goose he had brought to lay them so many golden eggs? His fate was like that which may be supposed to have overtaken the first adventurous boatman who rowed from Erie to Ontario. Broad and smooth was the river on which he embarked; rapid and pleasant was his progress; and who was to stay him in his career? Alas for him! the cataract was nigh. He saw, when it was too late, that the tide which wafted him so joyously along was a tide of destruction; and when he endeavoured to retrace his way, he found that the current was too strong for his weak efforts to stem, and that he drew nearer every instant to the tremendous falls. Down he went over the sharp rocks, and the waters with him. *He* was dashed to pieces with his bark, but the waters, maddened and turned to foam by the rough descent, only boiled and bubbled for a time, and then flowed on again as smoothly as ever. Just so it was with Law and the French people. He was the boatman, and they were the waters.

John Law was born at Edinburgh in the year 1671. His father was the younger son of an ancient family in Fife, and carried on the business of a goldsmith and banker. He amassed considerable wealth in his trade, sufficient to enable him to gratify the wish, so common among his countrymen, of adding a territorial designation to his name. He purchased with this view the estates of Lauriston and Randleston, on the Firth of Forth, on the borders of West and Mid Lothian, and was thenceforth known as Law of Lauriston. The subject of our memoir, being the eldest son, was received into his father's counting-house at the age of fourteen, and for three years laboured hard to acquire an insight into the principles of banking as then carried on in Scotland. He had always manifested great love for the study of numbers, and his proficiency in the mathematics was considered extraordinary in one of his tender years. At the age of seventeen he was tall, strong, and well made; and his face, although deeply scarred with the small-pox, was agreeable in its expression, and full of intelligence. At this time he began to neglect his business, and becoming vain of his person, indulged in considerable extravagance of attire. He was a great favourite with the ladies, by whom he was called Beau Law; while the other sex, despising his foppery, nicknamed him Jessamy John. At the death of his father, which happened in 1688, he withdrew entirely from the desk, which had become so irksome, and being possessed of the revenues of the paternal estate of Lauriston, he proceeded to London, to see the world.

He was now very young, very vain, good-looking, tolerably rich, and quite uncontrolled. It is no wonder that, on his arrival in the capital, he should launch out into extravagance. He soon became a regular frequenter of the gaming-houses, and by pursuing a certain plan, based upon some abstruse calculation of chances, he contrived to gain considerable sums. All the gamblers envied him his luck, and many made it a point to watch his play, and stake their money on the same chances. In affairs of gallantry he was equally fortunate; ladies of the first rank smiled graciously upon the handsome Scotchman — the young, the rich, the witty, and the obliging. But all these successes only paved the way for reverses. After he had been for nine years exposed to the dangerous attractions of the gay life he was leading, he became an irrecoverable gambler. As his love of play increased in violence, it diminished in prudence. Great losses were only to be repaired by still greater ventures, and one unhappy day he lost more than he could repay without mortgaging his family estate. To that step he was driven at last. At the same time his gallantry brought him into trouble. A love affair, or slight flirtation, with a lady of the name of Villiers,[1] exposed him to the resentment of a Mr. Wilson, by whom he was challenged to fight a duel. Law accepted, and had the ill fortune to shoot his antagonist dead upon the spot. He was arrested the same day, and brought to trial for murder by the relatives of Mr. Wilson. He was afterwards found guilty, and sentenced to death. The sentence was commuted to a fine, upon the ground that the offence only amounted to manslaughter. An appeal being lodged by a brother of the deceased, Law was detained in the King's Bench, whence, by some means or other, which he never explained, he contrived to escape; and an action being instituted against the sheriffs, he was advertised in the Gazette, and a reward offered for his apprehension. He was described as "Captain John Law, a Scotchman, aged twenty-six; a very tall, black, lean man; well shaped, above six feet high, with large pock-holes in his face; big nosed, and speaking broad and loud." As this was rather a caricature than a description of him, it has been supposed that it was drawn up with a view to favour his escape. He succeeded in reaching the Continent, where he travelled for three years, and devoted much of his attention to the monetary and banking affairs of the countries through which he passed. He stayed a few months in Amsterdam, and speculated to some extent in the funds. His mornings were devoted to the study of finance and the principles of trade, and his evenings to the gaming-house. It is generally believed that he returned to Edinburgh in the year 1700. It is certain that he published in that city his *Proposals and Reasons for constituting a Council of Trade*. This pamphlet did not excite much attention.

In a short time afterwards he published a project for establishing what he called a Land-bank,[2] the notes issued by which were never to exceed the value of the entire lands of the state, upon ordinary interest, or were to be equal in value to the land, with the right to enter into possession at a certain time. The project excited a good deal of discussion in the Scottish Parliament, and a motion for the establishment of such a bank was brought forward by a neutral party, called the Squadrone, whom Law had interested in his favour. The Parliament ultimately passed a resolution to the effect, that, to establish any kind of paper credit, so as to force it to pass, was an improper expedient for the nation.

Upon the failure of this project, and of his efforts to procure a pardon for the murder of Mr. Wilson, Law withdrew to the Continent, and resumed his old habits of gaming. For fourteen years he continued to roam about, in Flanders, Holland, Germany, Hungary, Italy, and France. He soon became intimately acquainted with the extent of the trade and resources of each, and daily more confirmed in his opinion that no country could prosper without a paper currency. During the whole of this time he appears to have chiefly supported himself by successful play. At every gambling-house of note in the capitals of Europe he was known and appreciated as one better skilled in the intricacies of chance than any other man of the day. It is stated in the *Biographie Universelle* that he was expelled, first from Venice, and afterwards from Genoa, by the magistrates, who thought him a visitor too dangerous for the youth of those cities. During his residence in Paris he rendered himself obnoxious to D'Argenson, the lieutenant-general of the police, by whom he was ordered to quit the capital. This did not take place, however, before he had made the acquaintance, in the saloons, of the Duke de Vendôme, the Prince de Conti, and of the gay Duke of Orleans, the latter of whom was destined afterwards to exercise so much influence over his fate. The Duke of Orleans was pleased with the vivacity and good sense of the Scottish adventurer, while the latter was no less pleased with the wit and amiability of a prince who promised to become his patron. They were often thrown into each other's society, and Law seized every opportunity to instil his financial doctrines into the mind of one whose proximity to the throne pointed him out as destined, at no very distant date, to play an important part in the government.

*The Regent of France*

Shortly before the death of Louis XIV., or, as some say, in 1708, Law proposed a scheme of finance to Desmarets, the comptroller. Louis is reported to have inquired whether the projector were a Catholic, and on being answered in the negative, to have declined having any thing to do with him.[3]

It was after this repulse that he visited Italy. His mind being still occupied with schemes of finance, he proposed to Victor Amadeus, duke of Savoy, to establish his land-bank in that country. The duke replied that his dominions were too circumscribed for the execution of so great a project, and that he was by far too poor a potentate to be ruined. He advised him, however, to try the king of France once more; for he was sure, if he knew any thing of the French character, that the people would be delighted with a plan, not only so new, but so plausible.

Louis XIV. died in 1715, and the heir to the throne being an infant only seven years of age, the Duke of Orleans assumed the reins of government, as regent, during his minority. Law now found himself in a more favourable position. The tide in his affairs had come, which, taken at the flood, was to waft him on to fortune. The regent was his friend, already acquainted with his theory and pretensions, and inclined, moreover, to aid him in any efforts to restore the wounded credit of France, bowed down to the earth by the extravagance of the long reign of Louis XIV. Hardly was that monarch laid in his grave ere the popular hatred, suppressed so long, burst forth against his memory. He who, during his life, had been flattered with an excess of adulation, to which history scarcely offers a parallel, was now cursed as a tyrant, a bigot, and a plunderer. His statues were pelted and disfigured; his effigies torn down, amid the execrations of the populace, and his name rendered synonymous with selfishness and oppression. The glory of his arms was forgotten, and nothing was remembered but his reverses, his extravagance, and his cruelty.

The finances of the country were in a state of the utmost disorder. A profuse and corrupt monarch, whose profuseness and corruption were imitated by almost every functionary, from the highest to the lowest grade, had brought France to the verge of ruin. The national debt amounted to 3000 millions of livres, the revenue to 145 millions, and the expenses of government to 142 millions per annum; leaving only three millions to pay the interest upon 3000 millions. The first care of the regent was to discover a remedy for an evil of such magnitude, and a council was early summoned to take the matter into consideration. The Duke de St. Simon was of opinion that nothing could save the country from revolution but a remedy at once bold and dangerous. He advised the regent to convoke the states-general, and declare a national bankruptcy. The Duke de Noailles, a man of accommodating principles, an accomplished courtier, and totally averse from giving himself any trouble or annoyance that ingenuity could escape from, opposed the project of St. Simon with all his influence. He represented the expedient as alike dishonest and ruinous. The regent was of the same opinion, and this desperate remedy fell to the ground.

The measures ultimately adopted, though they promised fair, only aggravated the evil. The first, and most dishonest measure was of no advantage to the state. A recoinage was ordered, by which the currency was depreciated one-fifth; those who took a thousand pieces of gold or silver to the mint received back an amount of coin of the same nominal value, but only four-fifths of the weight of metal. By this contrivance the treasury gained seventy-two millions of livres, and all the commercial operations of the country were disordered. A trifling diminution of the taxes silenced the clamours of the people, and for the slight present advantage the great prospective evil was forgotten.

A Chamber of Justice was next instituted to inquire into the malversations of the loan-contractors and the farmers of the revenues. Tax-collectors are never very popular in any country, but those of France at this period deserved all the odium with which they were loaded. As soon as these farmers-general, with all their hosts of subordinate agents, called *maltôtiers*,[4] were called to account for their misdeeds, the most extravagant joy took possession of the nation. The Chamber of Justice, instituted chiefly for this purpose, was endowed with very extensive powers. It was composed of the presidents and councils of the parliament, the judges of the Courts of Aid and of Requests, and the officers of the Chamber of Account, under the general presidence of the minister of finance. Informers were encouraged to give evidence against the offenders by the promise of one-fifth part of the fines and confiscations. A tenth of all concealed effects belonging to the guilty was promised to such as should furnish the means of discovering them.

The promulgation of the edict constituting this court caused a degree of consternation among those principally concerned, which can only be accounted for on the supposition that their peculation had been enormous. But they met with no sympathy. The proceedings against them justified their terror. The Bastille was soon unable to contain the prisoners that were sent to it, and the gaols all over the country teemed with guilty or suspected persons. An order was issued to all innkeepers and postmasters to refuse horses to such as endeavoured to seek safety in flight; and all persons were forbidden, under heavy fines, to harbour them or favour their evasion. Some were condemned to the pillory, others to the galleys, and the least guilty to fine and imprisonment. One only, Samuel Bernard, a rich banker and farmer-general of a province remote from the capital, was sentenced to death. So great had been the illegal profits of this man, — looked upon as the tyrant and oppressor of his district, — that he offered six millions of livres, or 250,000l. sterling, to be allowed to escape.

His bribe was refused, and he suffered the penalty of death. Others, perhaps more guilty, were more fortunate. Confiscation, owing to the concealment of their treasures by the delinquents, often produced less money than a fine. The severity of the government relaxed, and fines, under the denomination of taxes, were indiscriminately levied upon all offenders; but so corrupt was every department of the administration, that the country benefited but little by the sums which thus flowed into the treasury. Courtiers and courtiers' wives and mistresses came in for the chief share of the spoils. One contractor had been taxed, in proportion to his wealth and guilt, at the sum of twelve millions of livres. The Count * * *, a man of some weight in the government, called upon him, and offered to procure a remission of the fine if he would give him a hundred thousand crowns. "Vous êtes trop tard, mon ami," replied the financier; "I have already made a bargain with your wife for fifty thousand."[5]

About a hundred and eighty millions of livres were levied in this manner, of which eighty were applied in payment of the debts contracted by the government. The remainder found its way into the pockets of the courtiers. Madame de Maintenon, writing on this subject, says, — "We hear every day of some new grant of the regent. The people murmur very much at this mode of employing the money taken from the peculators." The people, who, after the first burst of their resentment is over, generally express a sympathy for the weak, were indignant that so much severity should be used to so little purpose. They did not see the justice of robbing one set of rogues to fatten another. In a few months all the more guilty had been brought to punishment, and the Chamber of Justice looked for victims in humbler walks of life. Charges of fraud and extortion were brought against tradesmen of good character in consequence of the great inducements held out to common informers. They were compelled to lay open their affairs before this tribunal in order to establish their innocence. The voice of complaint resounded from every side; and at the expiration of a year the government found it advisable to discontinue further proceedings. The Chamber of Justice was suppressed, and a general amnesty granted to all against whom no charges had yet been preferred.

In the midst of this financial confusion Law appeared upon the scene. No man felt more deeply than the regent the deplorable state of the country, but no man could be more averse from putting his shoulders manfully to the wheel. He disliked business; he signed official documents without proper examination, and trusted to others what he should have undertaken himself. The cares inseparable from his high office were burdensome to him. He saw that something was necessary to be done; but he lacked the energy to do it, and had not virtue enough to sacrifice his ease and his pleasures in the attempt. No wonder that, with this character, he listened favourably to the mighty projects, so easy of execution, of the clever adventurer whom he had formerly known, and whose talents he appreciated.

When Law presented himself at court he was most cordially received. He offered two memorials to the regent, in which he set forth the evils that had befallen France, owing to an insufficient currency, at different times depreciated. He asserted that a metallic currency, unaided by a paper money, was wholly inadequate to the wants of a commercial country, and particularly cited the examples of Great Britain and Holland to shew the advantages of paper. He used many sound arguments on the subject of credit, and proposed as a means of restoring that of France, then at so low an ebb among the nations, that he should be allowed to set up a bank, which should have the management of the royal revenues, and issue notes both on that and on landed security. He further proposed that this bank should be administered in the king's name, but subject to the control of commissioners to be named by the States-General.

While these memorials were under consideration, Law translated into French his essay on money and trade, and used every means to extend through the nation his renown as a financier. He soon became talked of. The confidants of the regent spread abroad his praise, and every one expected great things of Monsieur Lass.[6]

On the 5th of May, 1716, a royal edict was published, by which Law was authorised, in conjunction with his brother, to establish a bank under the name of Law and Company, the notes of which should be received in payment of the taxes. The capital was fixed at six millions of livres, in twelve thousand shares of five hundred livres each, purchasable one fourth in specie, and the remainder in *billets d'état*. It was not thought expedient to grant him the whole of the privileges prayed for in his memorials until experience should have shewn their safety and advantage.

Law was now on the high road to fortune. The study of thirty years was brought to guide him in the management of his bank. He made all his notes payable at sight, and in the coin current at the time they were issued. This last was a master-stroke of policy, and immediately rendered his notes more valuable than the precious metals. The latter were constantly liable to depreciation by the unwise tampering of the government. A thousand livres of silver might be worth their nominal value one day, and be reduced one-sixth the next, but a note of Law's bank retained its original value. He publicly declared at the same time, that a banker deserved death if he made issues without having sufficient security to answer all demands. The consequence was, that his notes advanced rapidly in public estimation, and were received at one per cent more than specie. It was not long before the trade of the country felt the benefit. Languishing commerce began to lift up her head; the taxes were paid with greater regularity and less murmuring; and a degree of confidence was established that could not fail, if it continued, to become still more advantageous. In the course of a year, Law's notes rose to fifteen per cent premium, while the *billets d'état*, or notes issued by the government as security for the debts contracted by the extravagant Louis XIV., were at a discount of no less than seventy-eight and a half per cent. The comparison was too great in favour of Law not to attract the attention of the whole kingdom, and his credit extended itself day by day. Branches of his bank were almost simultaneously established at Lyons, Rochelle, Tours, Amiens, and Orleans.

The regent appears to have been utterly astonished at his success, and gradually to have conceived the idea that paper, which could so aid a metallic currency, could entirely supersede it.

Upon this fundamental error he afterwards acted. In the mean time, Law commenced the famous project which has handed his name down to posterity. He proposed to the regent (who could refuse him nothing) to establish a company that should have the exclusive privilege of trading to the great river Mississippi and the province of Louisiana, on its western bank. The country was supposed to abound in the precious metals; and the company, supported by the profits of their exclusive commerce, were to be the sole farmers of the taxes and sole coiners of money. Letters patent were issued, incorporating the company, in August 1717. The capital was divided into two hundred thousand shares of five hundred livres each, the whole of which might be paid in *billets d'état*, at their nominal value, although worth no more than a hundred and sixty livres in the market.

It was now that the frenzy of speculating began to seize upon the nation. Law's bank had effected so much good, that any promises for the future which he thought proper to make were readily believed. The regent every day conferred new privileges upon the fortunate projector. The bank obtained the monopoly of the sale of tobacco, the sole right of refinage of gold and silver, and was finally erected into the Royal Bank of France. Amid the intoxication of success, both Law and the regent forgot the maxim so loudly proclaimed by the former, that a banker deserved death who made issues of paper without the necessary funds to provide for them. As soon as the bank, from a private, became a public institution, the regent caused a fabrication of notes to the amount of one thousand millions of livres. This was the first departure from sound principles, and one for which Law is not justly blameable. While the affairs of the bank were under his control, the issues had never exceeded sixty millions. Whether Law opposed the inordinate increase is not known; but as it took place as soon as the bank was made a royal establishment, it is but fair to lay the blame of the change of system upon the regent.

Law found that he lived under a despotic government; but he was not yet aware of the pernicious influence which such a government could exercise upon so delicate a framework as that of credit. He discovered it afterwards to his cost, but in the meantime suffered himself to be impelled by the regent into courses which his own reason must have disapproved. With a weakness most culpable, he lent his aid in inundating the country with paper money, which, based upon no solid foundation, was sure to fall, sooner or later. The extraordinary present fortune dazzled his eyes, and prevented him from seeing the evil day that would burst over his head, when once, from any cause or other, the alarm was sounded. The parliament were from the first jealous of his influence as a foreigner, and had, besides, their misgivings as to the safety of his projects. As his influence extended, their animosity increased. D'Aguesseau, the chancellor, was unceremoniously dismissed by the regent for his opposition to the vast increase of paper money, and the constant depreciation of the gold and silver coin of the realm. This only served to augment the enmity of the parliament, and when D'Argenson, a man devoted to the interests of the regent, was appointed to the vacant chancellorship, and made at the same time minister of finance, they became more violent than ever. The first measure of the new minister caused a further depreciation of the coin. In order to extinguish the *billets d'état*, it was ordered that persons bringing to the mint four thousand livres in specie and one thousand livres in *billets d'état*, should receive back coin to the amount of five thousand livres. D'Argenson plumed himself mightily upon thus creating five thousand new and smaller livres out of the four thousand old and larger ones, being too ignorant of the true principles of trade and credit to be aware of the immense injury he was inflicting upon both.

The parliament saw at once the impolicy and danger of such a system, and made repeated remonstrances to the regent. The latter refused to entertain their petitions, when the parliament, by a bold and very unusual stretch of authority, commanded that no money should be received in payment but that of the old standard. The regent summoned a *lit de justice*, and annulled the decree. The parliament resisted, and issued another. Again the regent exercised his privilege, and annulled it, till the parliament, stung to fiercer opposition, passed another decree, dated August

12th, 1718, by which they forbade the bank of Law to have any concern, either direct or indirect, in the administration of the revenue; and prohibited all foreigners, under heavy penalties, from interfering, either in their own names, or in that of others, in the management of the finances of the state. The parliament considered Law to be the author of all the evil, and some of the councillors, in the virulence of their enmity, proposed that he should be brought to trial, and, if found guilty, be hung at the gates of the Palais de Justice.

*Palais Royal from the garden.*

Law, in great alarm, fled to the Palais Royal, and threw himself on the protection of the regent, praying that measures might be taken to reduce the parliament to obedience. The regent had nothing so much at heart, both on that account and because of the disputes that had arisen relative to the legitimation of the Duke of Maine and the Count of Thoulouse, the sons of the late king. The parliament was ultimately overawed by the arrest of their president and two of the councillors, who were sent to distant prisons.

Thus the first cloud upon Law's prospects blew over: freed from apprehension of personal danger, he devoted his attention to his famous Mississippi project, the shares of which were rapidly rising, in spite of the parliament. At the commencement of the year 1719, an edict was published, granting to the Mississippi Company the exclusive privilege of trading to the East Indies, China, and the South Seas, and to all the possessions of the French East India Company, established by Colbert. The Company, in consequence of this great increase of their business, assumed, as more appropriate, the title of Company of the Indies, and created fifty thousand new shares. The prospects now held out by Law were most magnificent. He promised a yearly dividend of two hundred livres upon each share of five hundred, which, as the shares were paid for in *billets d'état* at their nominal value, but worth only 100 livres, was at the rate of about 120 per cent profit.

*Law's house; rue de quincampoix.*

The public enthusiasm, which had been so long rising, could not resist a vision so splendid. At least three hundred thousand applications were made for the fifty thousand new shares, and Law's house in the Rue de Quincampoix was beset from morning to night by the eager applicants. As it was impossible to satisfy them all, it was several weeks before a list of the fortunate new stockholders could be made out, during which time the public impatience rose to a pitch of frenzy. Dukes, marquises, counts, with their duchesses, marchionesses, and countesses, waited in the streets for hours every day before Mr. Law's door to know the result. At last, to avoid the jostling of the plebeian crowd, which, to the number of thousands, filled the whole thoroughfare, they took apartments in the adjoining houses, that they might be continually near the temple whence the new Plutus was diffusing wealth. Every day the value of the old shares increased, and the fresh applications, induced by the golden dreams of the whole nation, became so numerous that it was deemed advisable to create no less than three hundred thousand new shares, at five thousand livres each, in order that the regent might take advantage of the popular enthusiasm to pay off the national debt. For this purpose, the sum of fifteen hundred millions of livres was necessary. Such was the eagerness of the nation, that thrice the sum would have been subscribed if the government had authorised it.

Law was now at the zenith of his prosperity, and the people were rapidly approaching the zenith of their infatuation. The highest and the lowest classes were alike filled with a vision of boundless wealth. There was not a person of note among the aristocracy, with the exception of the Duke of St. Simon and Marshal Villars, who was not engaged in buying or selling stock. People of every age and sex and condition in life speculated in the rise and fall of the Mississippi bonds. The Rue de Quincampoix was the grand resort of the jobbers, and it being a narrow, inconvenient street, accidents continually occurred in it, from the tremendous pressure of the crowd. Houses in it, worth, in ordinary times, a thousand livres of yearly rent, yielded as much as twelve or sixteen thousand. A cobbler, who had a stall in it, gained about two hundred livres a day by letting it out, and furnishing writing materials to brokers and their clients. The story goes, that a hunchbacked man who stood in the street gained considerable sums by lending his hump as a writing-desk to the eager speculators! The great concourse of persons who assembled to do business brought a still greater concourse of spectators. These again drew all the thieves and immoral characters of Paris to the spot, and constant riots and disturbances took place. At nightfall, it was often found necessary to send a troop of soldiers to clear the street.

*The Hunchback.*

Law, finding the inconvenience of his residence, removed to the Place Vendôme, whither the crowd of *agioteurs* followed him. That spacious square soon became as thronged as the Rue de Quincampoix: from morning to night it presented the appearance of a fair. Booths and tents were erected for the transaction of business and the sale of refreshments, and gamblers with their roulette tables stationed themselves in the very middle of the place, and reaped a golden, or rather a paper, harvest from the throng. The boulevards and public gardens were forsaken; parties of pleasure took their walks in preference in the Place Vendôme, which became the fashionable lounge of the idle, as well as the general rendezvous of the busy. The noise was so great all day, that the chancellor, whose court was situated in the square, complained to the regent and the municipality, that he could not hear the advocates. Law, when applied to, expressed his willingness to aid in the removal of the nuisance, and for this purpose entered into a treaty with the Prince de Carignan for the Hôtel de Soissons, which had a garden of several acres in the rear. A bargain was concluded, by which Law became the purchaser of the hotel at an enormous price, the prince reserving to himself the magnificent gardens as a new source of profit. They contained some fine statues and several fountains, and were altogether laid out with much taste. As soon as Law was installed in his new abode, an edict was published, forbidding all persons to buy or sell stock any where but in the gardens of the Hôtel de Soissons. In the midst, among the trees, about five hundred small tents and pavilions were erected, for the convenience of the stock-jobbers. Their various colours, the gay ribands and banners which floated from them, the busy crowds which passed continually in and out—the incessant hum of voices, the noise, the music, and the strange mixture of business and pleasure on the countenances of the throng, all combined to give the place an air of enchantment that quite enraptured the Parisians. The Prince de Carignan made enormous profits while the delusion lasted. Each tent was let at the rate of five hundred livres a month; and, as there were at least five hundred of them, his monthly revenue from this source alone must have amounted to 250,000 livres, or upwards of 10,000l. sterling.

*Hotel De Soissons.*

The honest old soldier, Marshal Villars, was so vexed to see the folly which had smitten his countrymen, that he never could speak with temper on the subject. Passing one day through the Place Vendôme in his carriage, the choleric gentleman was so annoyed at the infatuation of the people, that he abruptly ordered his coachman to stop, and, putting his head out of the carriage window, harangued them for full half an hour on their "disgusting avarice." This was not a very wise proceeding on his part. Hisses and shouts of laughter resounded from every side, and jokes without number were aimed at him. There being at last strong symptoms that something more tangible was flying through the air in the direction of his head, the marshal was glad to drive on. He never again repeated the experiment.

Two sober, quiet, and philosophic men of letters, M. de la Motte and the Abbé Terrason, congratulated each other, that they, at least, were free from this strange infatuation. A few days afterwards, as the worthy abbé was coming out of the Hôtel de Soissons, whither he had gone to buy shares in the Mississippi, whom should he see but his friend La Motte entering for the same purpose. "Ha!" said the abbé smiling, "is that *you*?" "Yes," said La Motte, pushing past him as fast as he was able; "and can that be *you*?" The next time the two scholars met, they talked of philosophy, of science, and of religion, but neither had courage for a long time to breathe one syllable about the Mississippi. At last, when it was mentioned, they agreed that a man ought never to swear against his doing any one thing, and that there was no sort of extravagance of which even a wise man was not capable. During this time, Law, the new Plutus, had become all at once the most important personage of the state. The ante-chambers of the regent were forsaken by the courtiers, Peers, judges, and bishops thronged to the Hôtel de Soissons; officers of the army and navy, ladies of title and fashion, and every one to whom hereditary rank or public employ gave a claim to precedence, were to be found waiting in his ante-chambers to beg for a portion of his India stock. Law was so pestered that he was unable to see one-tenth part of the applicants, and every manœuvre that ingenuity could suggest was employed to gain access to him. Peers, whose dignity would have been outraged if the regent had made them wait half an hour for an interview, were content to wait six hours for the chance of seeing Monsieur Law. Enormous fees were paid to his servants, if they would merely announce their names. Ladies of rank employed the blandishments of their smiles for the same object; but many of them came day after day for a fortnight before they could obtain an audience. When Law accepted an invitation, he was some-times so surrounded by ladies, all asking to have their names put down in his lists as shareholders in the new stock, that, in spite of his well-known and habitual gallantry, he was obliged to tear himself away *par force*. The most ludicrous stratagems were employed to have an opportunity of speaking to him. One lady, who had striven in vain during several days, gave up in despair all attempts to see him at his own house, but ordered her coachman to keep a strict watch whenever she was out in her carriage, and if he saw Mr. Law coming, to drive against a post and upset her. The coachman promised obedience, and for three days the lady was driven incessantly through the town, praying inwardly for the opportunity to be overturned. At last she espied Mr. Law, and, pulling the string, called out to the coachman, "Upset us now! for God's sake, upset us now!" The coachman drove against a post, the lady screamed, the coach was over-turned, and Law, who had seen the *accident*, hastened to the spot to render assistance. The cunning dame was led into the Hôtel de Soissons, where she soon thought it advisable to recover from her fright, and, after apologising to Mr. Law, confessed her stratagem. Law smiled, and entered the lady in his books as the purchaser of a quantity of India stock. Another story is told of a Madame de Boucha, who, knowing that Mr. Law was at dinner at a certain house, proceeded thither in her carriage, and gave the alarm of fire. The company started from table, and Law among the rest; but, seeing one lady making all haste into the house towards him, while every body else was scampering away, he suspected the trick, and ran off in another direction.

Many other anecdotes are related, which even though they may be a little exaggerated, are nevertheless worth preserving, as shewing the spirit of that singular period.[7] The regent was one day mentioning, in the presence of D'Argenson, the Abbé Dubois, and some other persons, that he was desirous of deputing some lady, of the rank at least of a duchess, to attend upon his daughter at Modena; "but," added he, "I do not exactly know where to find one." "No!" replied one, in affected surprise; "I can tell you where to find every duchess in France: you have only to go to Mr. Law's; you will see them every one in his ante-chamber."

M. de Chirac, a celebrated physician, had bought stock at an unlucky period, and was very anxious to sell out. Stock, however, continued to fall for two or three days, much to his alarm. His mind was filled with the subject, when he was suddenly called upon to attend a lady who imagined herself unwell. He arrived, was shewn up stairs, and felt the lady's pulse. "It falls! it falls! good God! it falls continually!" said he musingly, while the lady looked up in his face all anxiety for his opinion. "Oh, M. de Chirac," said she, starting to her feet and ringing the bell for assistance; "I am dying! I am dying! it falls! it falls! it falls!" "What falls?" inquired the doctor in amazement. "My pulse! my pulse!" said the lady; "I must be dying." "Calm your apprehensions, my dear madam," said M. de Chirac; "I was speaking of the stocks. The truth is, I have been a great loser, and my mind is so disturbed, I hardly know what I have been saying."

The price of shares sometimes rose ten or twenty per cent in the course of a few hours, and many persons in the humbler walks of life, who had risen poor in the morning, went to bed in affluence. An extensive holder of stock, being taken ill, sent his servant to sell two hundred and fifty shares, at eight thousand livres each, the price at which they were then quoted. The servant went, and, on his arrival in the Jardin de Soissons, found that in the interval the price had risen to ten thousand livres. The difference of two thousand livres on the two hundred and fifty shares, amounting to 500,000 livres, or 20,000l. sterling, he very coolly transferred to his own use, and giving the remainder to his master, set out the same evening for another country. Law's coachman in a very short time made money enough to set up a carriage of his own, and requested permission to leave his service. Law, who esteemed the man, begged of him as a favour, that he would endeavour, before he went, to find a substitute as good as himself. The coachman consented, and in the evening brought two of his former comrades, telling Mr. Law to choose between them, and he would take the other. Cookmaids and footmen were now and then as lucky, and, in the full-blown pride of their easily-acquired wealth, made the most ridiculous mistakes. Preserving the language and manners of their old, with the finery of their new station, they afforded continual subjects for the pity of the sensible, the contempt of the sober, and the laughter of every body. But the folly and meanness of the higher ranks of society were still more disgusting. One instance alone, related by the Duke de St. Simon, will shew the unworthy avarice which infected the whole of society. A man of the name of André, without character or education, had, by a series of well-timed speculations in Mississippi bonds, gained enormous wealth in an incredibly short space of time. As St. Simon expresses it, "he had amassed mountains of gold." As he became rich, he grew ashamed of the lowness of his birth, and anxious above all things to be allied to nobility. He had a daughter, an infant only three years of age, and he opened a negotiation with the aristocratic and needy family of D'Oyse, that this child should, upon certain conditions, marry a member of that house. The Marquis D'Oyse, to his shame, consented, and promised to marry her himself on her attaining the age of twelve, if the father would pay him down the sum of a hundred thousand crowns, and twenty thousand livres every year until the celebration of the marriage. The marquis was himself in his thirty-third year. This scandalous bargain was duly signed and sealed, the stockjobber furthermore agreeing to settle upon his daughter, on the marriage-day, a fortune of several millions. The Duke of Brancas, the head of the family, was present throughout the negotiation, and shared in all the profits. St. Simon, who treats the matter with the levity becoming what he thought so good a joke, adds, "that people did not spare their animadversions on this beautiful marriage," and further informs us, "that the project fell to the ground some months afterwards by the overthrow of Law, and the ruin of the ambitious Monsieur André." It would appear, however, that the noble family never had the honesty to return the hundred thousand crowns.

Amid events like these, which, humiliating though they be, partake largely of the ludicrous, others occurred of a more serious nature. Robberies in the streets were of daily occurrence, in consequence of the immense sums, in paper, which people carried about with them. Assassinations were also frequent. One case in particular fixed the attention of the whole of France, not only on account of the enormity of the offence, but of the rank and high connexions of the criminal.

The Count d'Horn, a younger brother of the Prince d'Horn, and related to the noble families of D'Aremberg, De Ligne, and De Montmorency, was a young man of dissipated character, extravagant to a degree, and unprincipled as he was extravagant. In connexion with two other young men as reckless as himself, named Mille, a Piedmontese captain, and one Destampes, or

Lestang, a Fleming, he formed a design to rob a very rich broker, who was known, unfortunately for himself, to carry great sums about his person. The count pretended a desire to purchase of him a number of shares in the Company of the Indies, and for that purpose appointed to meet him in a *cabaret*, or low public-house, in the neighbourhood of the Place Vendôme. The unsuspecting broker was punctual to his appointment; so were the Count d'Horn and his two associates, whom he introduced as his particular friends. After a few moments' conversation, the Count d'Horn suddenly sprang upon his victim, and stabbed him three times in the breast with a poniard. The man fell heavily to the ground, and, while the count was employed in rifling his portfolio of bonds in the Mississippi and Indian schemes to the amount of one hundred thousand crowns, Mille, the Piedmontese, stabbed the unfortunate broker again and again, to make sure of his death, But the broker did not fall without a struggle, and his cries brought the people of the *cabaret* to his assistance. Lestang, the other assassin, who had been set to keep watch at a staircase, sprang from a window and escaped; but Mille and the Count d'Horn were seized in the very act.

This crime, committed in open day, and in so public a place as a *cabaret*, filled Paris with consternation. The trial of the assassins commenced on the following day; and the evidence being so clear, they were both found guilty, and condemned, to be broken alive on the wheel. The noble relatives of the Count d'Horn absolutely blocked up the ante-chambers of the regent, praying for mercy on the misguided youth, and alleging that he was insane. The regent avoided them as long as possible, being determined that, in a case so atrocious, justice should take its course. But the importunity of these influential suitors was not to be overcome so silently; and they at last forced themselves into the presence of the regent, and prayed him to save their house the shame of a public execution. They hinted that the Princes d'Horn were allied to the illustrious family of Orleans; and added, that the regent himself would be disgraced if a kinsman of his should die by the hands of a common executioner. The regent, to his credit, was proof against all their solicitations, and replied to their last argument in the words of Corneille:

"Le crime fait la honte, et non pas l'échafaud:"

adding, that whatever shame there might be in the punishment he would very willingly share with the other relatives. Day after day they renewed their entreaties, but always with the same result. At last they thought, that if they could interest the Duke de St. Simon in their favour — a man, for whom the regent felt sincere esteem — they might succeed in their object. The duke, a thorough aristocrat, was as shocked as they were that a noble assassin should die by the same death as a plebeian felon, and represented to the regent the impolicy of making enemies of so numerous, wealthy, and powerful a family. He urged, too, that in Germany, where the family of D'Aremberg had large possessions, it was the law, that no relative of a person broken on the wheel could succeed to any public office or employ until a whole generation had passed away. For this reason, he thought the punishment of the guilty count might be transmuted into beheading, which was considered all over Europe as much less infamous. The regent was moved by this argument, and was about to consent, when Law, who felt peculiarly interested in the fate of the murdered man, confirmed him in his former resolution to let the law take its course.

The relatives of D'Horn were now reduced to the last extremity. The Prince de Robec Montmorency, despairing of other methods, found means to penetrate into the dungeon of the criminal, and offering him a cup of poison, implored him to save them from disgrace. The Count d'Horn turned away his head, and refused to take it. Montmorency pressed him once more; and losing all patience at his continued refusal, turned on his heel, and exclaiming, "Die, then, as thou wilt, mean-spirited wretch! thou art fit only to perish by the hands of the hangman!" left him to his fate.

D'Horn himself petitioned the regent that he might be beheaded; but Law, who exercised more influence over his mind than any other person, with the exception of the notorious Abbé Dubois, his tutor, insisted that he could not in justice succumb to the self-interested views of the D'Horns. The regent had from the first been of the same opinion; and within six days after the commission of their crime, D'Horn and Mille were broken on the wheel in the Place de Grève. The other assassin, Lestang, was never apprehended.

This prompt and severe justice was highly pleasing to the populace of Paris. Even M. de Quincampoix, as they called Law, came in for a share of their approbation for having induced the regent to shew no favour to a patrician. But the number of robberies and assassinations did not diminish; no sympathy was shewn for rich jobbers when they were plundered. The general laxity of public morals, conspicuous enough before, was rendered still more so by its rapid pervasion of the middle classes, who had hitherto remained comparatively pure between the open vices of the class above and the hidden crimes of the class below them. The pernicious love of gambling diffused itself through society, and bore all public and nearly all private virtue before it.

For a time, while confidence lasted, an impetus was given to trade which could not fail to be beneficial. In Paris especially the good results were felt. Strangers flocked into the capital from every part, bent not only upon making money, but on spending it. The Duchess of Orleans, mother of the regent, computes the increase of the population during this time, from the great influx of strangers from all parts of the world, at 305,000 souls. The housekeepers were obliged to make up beds in garrets, kitchens, and even stables, for the accommodation of lodgers; and the town was so full of carriages and vehicles of every description, that they were obliged, in the principal streets, to drive at a foot-pace for fear of accidents. The looms of the country worked with unusual activity to supply rich laces, silks, broad-cloth, and velvets, which being paid for in abundant paper, increased in price four-fold. Provisions shared the general advance. Bread, meat, and vegetables were sold at prices greater than had ever before been known; while the wages of labour rose in exactly the same proportion. The artisan who formerly gained fifteen sous per diem now gained sixty. New houses were built in every direction; an illusory prosperity shone over the land, and so dazzled the eyes of the whole nation, that none could see the dark cloud on the horizon announcing the storm that was too rapidly approaching.

Law himself, the magician whose wand had wrought so surprising a change, shared, of course, in the general prosperity. His wife and daughter were courted by the highest nobility, and their alliance sought by the heirs of ducal and princely houses. He bought two splendid estates in different parts of France, and entered into a negotiation with the family of the Duke de Sully for the purchase of the marquisate of Rosny. His religion being an obstacle to his advancement, the regent promised, if he would publicly conform to the Catholic faith, to make him comptroller-general of the finances. Law, who had no more real religion than any other professed gambler, readily agreed, and was confirmed by the Abbé de Tencin in the cathedral of Melun, in presence of a great crowd of spectators[8]. On the following day he was elected honorary churchwarden of the parish of St. Roch, upon which occasion he made it a present of the sum of five hundred thousand livres. His charities, always magnificent, were not always so ostentatious. He gave away great sums privately, and no tale of real distress ever reached his ears in vain.

At this time he was by far the most influential person of the state. The Duke of Orleans had so much confidence in his sagacity and the success of his plans, that he always consulted him upon every matter of moment. He was by no means unduly elevated by his prosperity, but remained the same simple, affable, sensible man that he had shewn himself in adversity. His gallantry, which was always delightful to the fair objects of it, was of a nature so kind, so gentlemanly, and so respectful, that not even a lover could have taken offence at it. If upon any occasion he shewed any symptoms of haughtiness, it was to the cringing nobles who lavished their adulation upon him till it became fulsome. He often took pleasure in seeing how long he could make them dance attendance upon him for a single favour. To such of his own countrymen as by chance visited Paris, and sought an interview with him, he was, on the contrary, all politeness and attention. When Archibald Campbell, Earl of Islay, and afterwards Duke of Argyle, called upon him in the Place Vendôme, he had to pass through an ante-chamber crowded with persons of the first distinction, all anxious to see the great financier, and have their names put down as first on the list of some new subscription. Law himself was quietly sitting in his library, writing a letter to the gardener at his paternal estate of Lauriston about the planting of some cabbages! The earl stayed for a considerable time, played a game of piquet with his countryman, and left him, charmed with his ease, good sense, and good breeding.

*Law as Atlas.*[9]

Among the nobles who, by means of the public credulity at this time, gained sums sufficient to repair their ruined fortunes, may be mentioned the names of the Dukes de Bourbon, de Guiche, de la Force,[10] de Chaulnes, and d'Antin; the Marechal d'Estrées; the Princes de Rohan, de Poix, and de Léon. The Duke de Bourbon, son of Louis XIV. by Madame de Montespan, was peculiarly fortunate in his speculations in Mississippi paper. He rebuilt the royal residence of Chantilly in a style of unwonted magnificence; and being passionately fond of horses, he erected a range of stables, which were long renowned throughout Europe, and imported a hundred and fifty of the finest racers from England to improve the breed in France. He bought a large extent of country in Picardy, and became possessed of nearly all the valuable lands lying between the Oise and the Somme.

When fortunes such as these were gained, it is no wonder that Law should have been almost worshipped by the mercurial population. Never was monarch more flattered than he was. All the small poets and *littérateurs* of the day poured floods of adulation upon him. According to them, he was the saviour of the country, the tutelary divinity of France; wit was in all his words, goodness in all his looks, and wisdom in all his actions. So great a crowd followed his carriage whenever he went abroad, that the regent sent him a troop of horse as his permanent escort to clear the streets before him.

It was remarked at this time that Paris had never before been so full of objects of elegance and luxury. Statues, pictures, and tapestries were imported in great quantities from foreign countries, and found a ready market. All those pretty trifles in the way of furniture and ornament which the French excel in manufacturing were no longer the exclusive playthings of the aristocracy, but were to be found in abundance in the houses of traders and the middle classes in general. Jewellery of the most costly description was brought to Paris as the most favourable mart; among the rest, the famous diamond bought by the regent, and called by his name, and which long adorned the crown of France. It was purchased for the sum of two millions of livres, under circumstances which shew that the regent was not so great a gainer as some of his subjects by the impetus which trade had received. When the diamond was first offered to him, he refused to buy it, although he desired above all things to possess it, alleging as his reason, that his duty to the country he governed would not allow him to spend so large a sum of the public money for a mere jewel. This valid and honourable excuse threw all the ladies of the court into alarm, and nothing was heard for some days but expressions of regret that so rare a gem should be allowed to go out of France, no private individual being rich enough to buy it. The regent was continually importuned about it, but all in vain, until the Duke de St. Simon, who with all his ability was something of a twaddler, undertook the weighty business. His entreaties being seconded by Law, the good-natured regent gave his consent, leaving to Law's ingenuity to find the means to pay for it. The owner took security for the payment of the sum of two millions of livres within a stated period, receiving in the mean time the interest of five per cent upon that amount, and being allowed, besides, all the valuable clippings of the gem. St. Simon, in his *Memoirs*, relates with no little complacency his share in this transaction. After describing the diamond to be as large as a greengage, of a form nearly round, perfectly white, and without flaw, and weighing more than five hundred grains, he concludes with a chuckle, by telling the world "that he takes great credit to himself for having induced the regent to make so illustrious a purchase." In other words, he was proud that he had induced him to sacrifice his duty, and buy a bauble for himself at an extravagant price out of the public money.

Thus the system continued to flourish till the commencement of the year 1720. The warnings of the parliament, that too great a creation of paper money would, sooner or later, bring the country to bankruptcy, were disregarded. The regent, who knew nothing whatever of the philosophy of finance, thought that a system which had produced such good effects could never be carried to excess. If five hundred millions of paper had been of such advantage, five hundred millions additional would be of still greater advantage. This was the grand error of the regent, and which Law did not attempt to dispel. The extraordinary avidity of the people kept up the delusion; and the higher the price of Indian and Mississippi stock, the more *billets de banque* were issued to keep pace with it. The edifice thus reared might not unaptly be compared to the gorgeous palace erected by Potemkin, that princely barbarian of Russia, to surprise and please his imperial mistress: huge blocks of ice were piled one upon another; ionic pillars, of chastest workmanship, in ice, formed a noble portico; and a dome, of the same material, shone in the sun, which had just strength enough to gild, but not to melt it. It glittered afar, like a palace of crystals and diamonds; but there came one warm breeze from the south, and the stately building dissolved away, till none were able even to gather up the fragments. So with Law and his paper system. No sooner did the breath of popular mistrust blow steadily upon it, than it fell to ruins, and none could raise it up again.

The first slight alarm that was occasioned was early in 1720. The Prince de Conti, offended that Law should have denied him fresh shares in India stock, at his own price, sent to his bank to demand payment in specie of so enormous a quantity of notes, that three wagons were required for its transport. Law complained to the regent, and urged on his attention the mischief that would be done, if such an example found many imitators. The regent was but too well aware of it, and, sending for the Prince de Conti, ordered him, under penalty of his high displeasure, to refund to the bank two-thirds of the specie which he had withdrawn from it. The prince was forced to obey the despotic mandate. Happily for Law's credit, De Conti was an unpopular man: every body condemned his meanness and cupidity, and agreed that Law had been hardly treated. It is strange, however, that so narrow an escape should not have made both Law and the regent more anxious to restrict their issues. Others were soon found who imitated, from motives of distrust, the example which had been set by De Conti in revenge. The more acute stockjobbers imagined justly that prices could not continue to rise for ever. Bourdon and La Richardière, renowned for their extensive operations in the funds, quietly and in small quantities at a time, converted their notes into specie, and sent it away to foreign countries. They also bought as much as they could conveniently carry of plate and expensive jewellery, and sent it secretly away to England or to Holland. Vermalet, a jobber, who sniffed the coming storm, procured gold and silver coin to the amount of nearly a million of livres, which he packed in a farmer's cart, and covered over with hay and cow-dung. He then disguised himself in the dirty smock-frock, or *blouse*, of a peasant, and drove his precious load in safety into Belgium. From thence he soon found means to transport it to Amsterdam.

Hitherto no difficulty had been experienced by any class in procuring specie for their wants. But this system could not long be carried on without causing a scarcity. The voice of complaint was heard on every side, and inquiries being instituted, the cause was soon discovered. The council debated long on the remedies to be taken, and Law, being called on for his advice, was of opinion, that an edict should be published, depreciating the value of coin five per cent below that of paper. The edict was published accordingly; but failing of its intended effect, was followed by another, in which the depreciation was increased to ten per cent. The payments of the bank were at the same time restricted to one hundred livres in gold, and ten in silver. All these measures were nugatory to restore confidence in the paper, though the restriction of cash payments within limits so extremely narrow kept up the credit of the bank.

*Lucifer's New Row-Barge.*[11]

Notwithstanding every effort to the contrary, the precious metals continued to be conveyed to England and Holland. The little coin that was left in the country was carefully treasured, or hidden until the scarcity became so great, that the operations of trade could no longer be carried on. In this emergency, Law hazarded the bold experiment of forbidding the use of specie altogether. In February 1720 an edict was published, which, instead of restoring the credit of the paper, as was intended, destroyed it irrecoverably, and drove the country to the very brink of revolution. By this famous edict it was forbidden to any person whatever to have more than five hundred livres (20l.) of coin in his possession, under pain of a heavy fine, and confiscation of the sums found. It was also forbidden to buy up jewellery, plate, and precious stones, and informers were encouraged to make search for offenders, by the promise of one-half the amount they might discover. The whole country sent up a cry of distress at this unheard-of tyranny. The most odious persecution daily took place. The privacy of families was violated by the intrusion of informers and their agents. The most virtuous and honest were denounced for the crime of having been seen with a *louis d'or* in their possession. Servants betrayed their masters, one citizen became a spy upon his neighbour, and arrests and confiscations so multiplied, that the courts found a difficulty in getting through the immense increase of business thus occasioned. It was sufficient for an informer to say that he suspected any person of concealing money in his house, and immediately a search-warrant was granted. Lord Stair, the English ambassador, said, that it was now impossible to doubt of the sincerity of Law's conversion to the Catholic religion; he had established the *inquisition*, after having given abundant evidence of his faith in *transubstantiation*, by turning so much gold into paper.

Every epithet that popular hatred could suggest was showered upon the regent and the unhappy Law. Coin, to any amount above five hundred livres, was an illegal tender, and nobody would take paper if he could help it. No one knew to-day what his notes would be worth to-morrow. "Never," says Duclos, in his *Secret Memoirs of the Regency*, "was seen a more capricious government—never was a more frantic tyranny exercised by hands less firm. It is inconceivable to those who were witnesses of the horrors of those times, and who look back upon them now as on a dream, that a sudden revolution did not break out—that Law and the regent did not perish by a tragical death. They were both held in horror, but the people confined themselves to complaints; a sombre and timid despair, a stupid consternation, had seized upon all, and men's minds were too vile even to be capable of a courageous crime." It would appear that, a one time, a movement of the people was organised. Seditious writings were posted up against the walls, and were sent, in hand-bills, to the houses of the most conspicuous people. One of them, given in the *Mémoires de la Régence*, was to the following effect: — "Sir and madam, — This is to give you notice that a St. Bartholomew's Day will be enacted again on Saturday and Sunday, if affairs do not alter. You are desired not to stir out, nor you, nor your servants. God preserve you from the flames! Give notice to your neighbours. Dated, Saturday, May 25th, 1720." The immense number of spies with which the city was infested rendered the people mistrustful of one another, and beyond some trifling disturbances made in the evening by an insignificant group, which was soon dispersed, the peace of the capital was not compromised.

The value of shares in the Louisiana, or Mississippi stock, had fallen very rapidly, and few indeed were found to believe the tales that had once been told of the immense wealth of that region. A last effort was therefore tried to restore the public confidence in the Mississippi project. For this purpose, a general conscription of all the poor wretches in Paris was made by order of government. Upwards of six thousand of the very refuse of the population were impressed, as if in time of war, and were provided with clothes and tools to be embarked for New Orleans, to work in the gold mines alleged to abound there. They were paraded day after day through the streets with their pikes and shovels, and then sent off in small detachments to the outports to be shipped for America. Two-thirds of them never reached their destination, but dispersed themselves over the country, sold their tools for what they could get, and returned to their old course of life. In less than three weeks afterwards, one-half of them were to be found again in Paris. The manœuvre, however, caused a trifling advance in Mississippi stock. Many persons of superabundant gullibility believed that operations had begun in earnest in the new Golconda, and that gold and silver ingots would again be found in France.

In a constitutional monarchy some surer means would have been found for the restoration of public credit. In England, at a subsequent period, when a similar delusion had brought on similar distress, how different were the measures taken to repair the evil; but in France, unfortunately, the remedy was left to the authors of the mischief. The arbitrary will of the regent, which endeavoured to extricate the country, only plunged it deeper into the mire. All payments were ordered to be made in paper, and between the 1st of February and the end of May, notes were fabricated to the amount of upwards of 1500 millions of livres, or 60,000,000l. sterling. But the alarm once sounded, no art could make the people feel the slightest confidence in paper which was not exchangeable into metal. M. Lambert, the president of the parliament of Paris, told the regent to his face that he would rather have a hundred thousand livres in gold or silver than five millions in the notes of his bank. When such was the general feeling, the superabundant issues of paper but increased the evil, by rendering still more enormous the disparity between the amount of specie and notes in circulation. Coin, which it was the object of the regent to depreciate, rose in value on every fresh attempt to diminish it. In February, it was judged advisable that the Royal Bank should be incorporated with the Company of the Indies. An edict to that effect was published and registered by the parliament. The state remained the guarantee for the notes of the bank, and no more were to be issued without an order in council. All the profits of the bank, since the time it had been taken out of Law's hands and made a national institution, were given over by the regent to the Company of the Indies. This measure had the effect of raising for a short time the value of the Louisiana and other shares of the company, but it failed in placing public credit on any permanent basis.

A council of state was held in the beginning of May, at which Law, D'Argenson (his colleague in the administration of the finances), and all the ministers were present. It was then computed that the total amount of notes in circulation was 2600 millions of livres, while the coin in the country was not quite equal to half that amount. It was evident to the majority of the council that some plan must be adopted to equalise the currency. Some proposed that the notes should be reduced to the value of the specie, while others proposed that the nominal value of the specie should be raised till it was on an equality with the paper. Law is said to have opposed both these projects, but failing in suggesting any other, it was agreed that the notes should be depreciated one half. On the 21st of May, an edict was accordingly issued, by which it was decreed that the shares of the Company of the Indies, and the notes of the bank, should gradually diminish in value, till at the end of a year they should only pass current for one-half of their nominal worth. The parliament refused to register the edict — the greatest outcry was excited, and the state of the country became so alarming, that, as the only means of preserving tranquillity, the council of the regency was obliged to stultify its own proceedings, by publishing within seven days another edict, restoring the notes to their original value.

On the same day (the 27th of May) the bank stopped payment in specie. Law and D'Argenson were both dismissed from the ministry. The weak, vacillating, and cowardly regent threw the blame of all the mischief upon Law, who, upon presenting himself at the Palais Royal, was refused admittance. At nightfall, however, he was sent for, and admitted into the palace by a secret door,[12] when the regent endeavoured to console him, and made all manner of excuses for the severity with which in public he had been compelled to treat him. So capricious was his conduct, that, two days afterwards, he took him publicly to the opera, where he sat in the royal box alongside of the regent, who treated him with marked consideration in face of all the people. But such was the hatred against Law that the experiment had well nigh proved fatal to him. The mob assailed his carriage with stones just as he was entering his own door; and if the coachman had not made a sudden jerk into the court-yard, and the domestics closed the gate immediately, he would, in all probability, have been dragged out and torn to pieces. On the following day, his wife and daughter were also assailed by the mob as they were returning in their carriage from the races. When the regent was informed of these occurrences he sent Law a strong detachment of Swiss guards, who were stationed night and day in the court of his residence. The public indignation at last increased so much, that Law, finding his own house, even with this guard, insecure, took refuge in the Palais Royal, in the apartments of the regent.

The Chancellor, D'Aguesseau, who had been dismissed in 1718 for his opposition to the projects of Law, was now recalled to aid in the restoration of credit. The regent acknowledged too late, that he had treated with unjustifiable harshness and mistrust one of the ablest, and perhaps the sole honest public man of that corrupt period. He had retired ever since his disgrace to his country house at Fresnes, where, in the midst of severe but delightful philosophic studies, he had forgotten the intrigues of an unworthy court. Law himself, and the Chevalier de Conflans, a gentleman of the regent's household, were despatched in a post-chaise with orders to bring the ex-chancellor to Paris along with them. D'Aguesseau consented to render what assistance he could, contrary to the advice of his friends, who did not approve that he should accept any recal to office of which Law was the bearer. On his arrival in Paris, five counsellors of the parliament were admitted to confer with the Commissary of Finance; and on the 1st of June an order was published abolishing the law which made it criminal to amass coin to the amount of more than five hundred livres. Every one was permitted to have as much specie as he pleased. In order that the bank-notes might be withdrawn, twenty-five millions of new notes were created, on the security of the revenues of the city of Paris, at two-and-a-half per cent. The bank-notes withdrawn were publicly burned in front of the Hôtel de Ville. The new notes were principally of the value of ten livres each; and on the 10th of June the bank was re-opened, with a sufficiency of silver coin to give in change for them.

D'Aguesseau.

These measures were productive of considerable advantage. All the population of Paris hastened to the bank to get coin for their small notes; and silver becoming scarce, they were paid in copper. Very few complained that this was too heavy, although poor fellows might be continually seen toiling and sweating along the streets, laden with more than they could comfortably carry, in the shape of change for fifty livres. The crowds around the bank were so great, that hardly a day passed that some one was not pressed to death. On the 9th of July, the multitude was so dense and clamorous that the guards stationed at the entrance of the Mazarin Gardens closed the gate and refused to admit any more. The crowd became incensed, and flung stones through the railings upon the soldiers. The latter, incensed in their turn, threatened to fire upon the people. At that instant one of them was hit by a stone, and, taking up his piece, he fired into the crowd. One man fell dead immediately, and another was severely wounded. It was every instant expected that a general attack would have been commenced upon the bank; but the gates of the Mazarin Gardens being opened to the crowd, who saw a whole troop of soldiers, with their bayonets fixed ready to receive them, they contented themselves by giving vent to their indignation in groans and hisses.

Eight days afterwards the concourse of people was so tremendous that fifteen persons were squeezed to death at the doors of the bank. The people were so indignant that they took three of the bodies on stretchers before them, and proceeded, to the number of seven or eight thousand, to the gardens of the Palais Royal, that they might shew the regent the misfortunes that he and Law had brought upon the country. Law's coachman, who was sitting at the box of his master's carriage, in the court-yard of the palace, happened to have more zeal than discretion, and, not liking that the mob should abuse his master, he said, loud enough to be overheard by several persons, that they were all blackguards, and deserved to be hanged. The mob immediately set upon him, and thinking that Law was in the carriage, broke it to pieces. The imprudent coachman narrowly escaped with his life. No further mischief was done; a body of troops making their appearance, the crowd quietly dispersed, after an assurance had been given by the regent that the three bodies they had brought to shew him should be decently buried at his own expense. The parliament was sitting at the time of this uproar, and the president took upon himself to go out and see what was the matter. On his return he informed the councillors that Law's carriage had been broken by the mob. All the members rose simultaneously, and expressed their joy by a loud shout, while one man, more zealous in his hatred than the rest, exclaimed, "*And Law himself, is he torn to pieces?*"[13]

Much, undoubtedly, depended on the credit of the Company of the Indies, which was answerable for so great a sum to the nation. It was therefore suggested in the council of the ministry, that any privileges which could be granted to enable it to fulfil its engagements, would be productive of the best results. With this end in view, it was proposed that the exclusive privilege of all maritime commerce should be secured to it, and an edict to that effect was published. But it was unfortunately forgotten that by such a measure all the merchants of the country would be ruined. The idea of such an immense privilege was generally scouted by the nation, and petition on petition was presented to the parliament that they would refuse to register the decree. They refused accordingly, and the regent, remarking that they did nothing but fan the flame of sedition, exiled them to Blois. At the intercession of D'Aguesseau, the place of banishment was changed to Pontoise, and thither accordingly the councillors repaired, determined to set the regent at defiance. They made every arrangement for rendering their temporary exile as agreeable as possible. The president gave the most elegant suppers, to which he invited all the gayest and wittiest company of Paris. Every night there was a concert and ball for the ladies. The usually grave and solemn judges and councillors joined in cards and other diversions, leading for several weeks a life of the most extravagant pleasure, for no other purpose than to shew the regent of how little consequence they deemed their banishment, and that, when they willed it, they could make Pontoise a pleasanter residence than Paris.

Of all the nations in the world the French are the most renowned for singing over their grievances. Of that country it has been remarked with some truth, that its whole history may be traced in its songs. When Law, by the utter failure of his best-laid plans, rendered himself obnoxious, satire of course seized hold upon him; and while caricatures of his person appeared in all the shops, the streets resounded with songs, in which neither he nor the regent was spared. Many of these songs were far from decent; and one of them in particular counselled the application of all his notes to the most ignoble use to which paper can be applied. But the following, preserved in the letters of the Duchess of Orleans, was the best and the most popular, and was to be heard for months in all the *carrefours* in Paris. The application of the chorus is happy enough:

> *Aussitôt que Lass arriva*
> *Dans notre bonne ville,*
> *Monsieur le Régent publia*
> *Que Lass serait utile*
> *Pour rétablir la nation.*
> *La faridondaine! la faridondon!*

*Mais il nous a tous enrichi,*
*Biribi!*
*A la façon de Barbari,*
*Mon ami!*

*Ce parpaillot, pour attirer*
*Tout l'argent de la France,*
*Songea d'abord à s'assurer*
*De notre confiance.*
*Il fit son abjuration,*
*La faridondaine! la faridondon!*
*Mais le fourbe s'est converti,*
*Biribi!*
*A la façon de Barbari,*
*Mon ami!*

*Lass, le fils aîné de Satan*
*Nous met tous à l'aumône,*
*Il nous a pris tout notre argent*
*Et n'en rend à personne.*
*Mais le Régent, humain et bon,*
*La faridondaine! la faridondon!*
*Nous rendra ce qu'on nous a pris,*
*Biribi!*
*A la façon de Barbari,*
*Mon ami!*

The following epigram is of the same date:
Lundi, j'achetai des actions;
Mardi, je gagnai des millions;
Mercredi, j'arrangeai mon ménage,
Jeudi, je pris un équipage,
Vendredi, je m'en fus au bal,
Et Samedi, à l'hôpital.

Among the caricatures that were abundantly published, and that shewed as plainly as graver matters, that the nation had awakened to a sense of its folly, was one, a fac-simile of which is preserved in the *Mémoires de la Régence*. It was thus described by its author: "The 'Goddess of Shares,' in her triumphal car, driven by the Goddess of Folly. Those who are drawing the car are impersonations of the Mississippi, with his wooden leg, the South Sea, the Bank of England, the Company of the West of Senegal, and of various assurances. Lest the car should not roll fast enough, the agents of these companies, known by their long fox-tails and their cunning looks, turn round the spokes of the wheels, upon which are marked the names of the several stocks and their value, sometimes high and sometimes low, according to the turns of the wheel. Upon the ground are the merchandise, day-books and ledgers of legitimate commerce, crushed under the chariot of Folly. Behind is an immense crowd of persons, of all ages, sexes, and conditions, clamoring after Fortune, and fighting with each other to get a portion of the shares which she distributes so bountifully among them. In the clouds sits a demon, blowing bubbles of soap, which are also the objects of the admiration and cupidity of the crowd, who jump upon one another's backs to reach them ere they burst. Right in the pathway of the car, and blocking up the passage, stands a large building, with three doors, through one of which it must pass, if it proceeds farther, and all the crowd along with it. Over the first door are the words, '*Hôpital des Foux*,' over the second, '*Hôpital des Malades*,' and over the third, '*Hôpital des Gueux*.'" Another caricature represented Law sitting in a large cauldron, boiling over the flames of popular madness, surrounded by an impetuous multitude, who were pouring all their gold and silver into it, and receiving gladly in exchange the bits of paper which he distributed among them by handfuls.

While this excitement lasted, Law took good care not to expose himself unguarded in the streets. Shut up in the apartments of the regent, he was secure from all attack; and whenever he ventured abroad, it was either *incognito*, or in one of the royal carriages, with a powerful escort. An amusing anecdote is recorded of the detestation in which he was held by the people, and the ill-treatment he would have met had he fallen into their hands. A gentleman of the name of Boursel was passing in his carriage down the Rue St. Antoine, when his farther progress was stayed by a hackney-coach that had blocked up the road. M. Boursel's servant called impatiently to the hackney-coachman to get out of the way, and, on his refusal, struck him a blow on the face. A crowd was soon drawn together by the disturbance, and M. Boursel got out of the carriage to restore order. The hackney-coachman, imagining that he had now another assailant, bethought him of an expedient to rid himself of both, and called out as loudly as he was able, "Help! help! murder! murder! Here are Law and his servant going to kill me! Help! help!" At this cry the people came out of their shops, armed with sticks and other weapons, while the mob gathered stones to inflict summary vengeance upon the supposed financier. Happily for M. Boursel and his servant, the door of the church of the Jesuits stood wide open, and, seeing the fearful odds against them, they rushed towards it with all speed. They reached the altar, pursued by the people, and would have been ill-treated even there, if, finding the door open leading to the sacristy, they had not sprang through, and closed it after them. The mob were then persuaded to leave the church by the alarmed and indignant priests, and finding M. Boursel's carriage still in the streets, they vented their ill-will against it, and did it considerable damage.

The twenty-five millions secured on the municipal revenues of the city of Paris, bearing so low an interest as two and a half per cent, were not very popular among the large holders of Mississippi stock. The conversion of the securities was, therefore, a work of considerable difficulty; for many preferred to retain the falling paper of Law's Company, in the hope that a favourable turn might take place. On the 15th of August, with a view to hasten the conversion, an edict was passed, declaring that all notes for sums between one thousand and ten thousand livres, should not pass current, except for the purchase of annuities and bank accounts, or for the payment of instalments still due on the shares of the company.

In October following another edict was passed, depriving these notes of all value whatever after the month of November next ensuing. The management of the mint, the farming of the revenue, and all the other advantages and privileges of the India, or Mississippi Company, were taken from them, and they were reduced to a mere private company. This was the death-blow to the whole system, which had now got into the hands of its enemies. Law had lost all influence in the Council of Finance, and the company, being despoiled of its immunities, could no longer hold out the shadow of a prospect of being able to fulfil its engagements. All those suspected of illegal profits at the time the public delusion was at its height, were sought out and amerced in heavy fines. It was previously ordered that a list of the original proprietors should be made out, and that such persons as still retained their shares should place them in deposit with the company, and that those who had neglected to complete the shares for which they had put down their names, should now purchase them of the company, at the rate of 13,500 livres for each share of 500 livres. Rather than submit to pay this enormous sum for stock which was actually at a discount, the shareholders packed up all their portable effects, and endeavoured to find a refuge in foreign countries. Orders were immediately issued to the authorities at the ports and frontiers, to apprehend all travellers who sought to leave the kingdom, and keep them in custody, until it was ascertained whether they had any plate or jewellery with them, or were concerned in the late stock-jobbing. Against such few as escaped, the punishment of death was recorded, while the most arbitrary proceedings were instituted against those who remained.

Law himself, in a moment of despair, determined to leave a country where his life was no longer secure. He at first only demanded permission to retire from Paris to one of his country-seats—a permission which the regent cheerfully granted. The latter was much affected at the unhappy turn affairs had taken, but his faith continued unmoved in the truth and efficacy of Law's financial system. His eyes were opened to his own errors; and during the few remaining years of his life he constantly longed for an opportunity of again establishing the system upon a securer basis. At Law's last interview with the prince, he is reported to have said,—"I confess that I have committed many faults. I committed them because I am a man, and all men are liable to error; but I declare to you most solemnly that none of them proceeded from wicked or dishonest motives, and that nothing of the kind will be found in the whole course of my conduct."

*Law in a car drawn by cocks.*[14]

Two or three days after his departure the regent sent him a very kind letter, permitting him to leave the kingdom whenever he pleased, and stating that he had ordered his passports to be made ready. He at the same time offered him any sum of money he might require. Law respectfully declined the money, and set out for Brussels in a post-chaise belonging to Madame de Prie, the mistress of the Duke of Bourbon, escorted by six horse-guards. From thence he proceeded to Venice, where he remained for some months, the object of the greatest curiosity to the people, who believed him to be the possessor of enormous wealth. No opinion, however, could be more erroneous. With more generosity than could have been expected from a man who during the greatest part of his life had been a professed gambler, he had refused to enrich himself at the expense of a ruined nation. During the height of the popular frenzy for Mississippi stock, he had never doubted of the final success of his projects in making France the richest and most powerful nation of Europe. He invested all his gains in the purchase of landed property in France—a sure proof of his own belief in the stability of his schemes. He had hoarded no plate or jewellery, and sent no money, like the dishonest jobbers, to foreign countries. His all, with the exception of one diamond, worth about five or six thousand pounds sterling, was invested in the French soil; and when he left that country, he left it almost a beggar. This fact alone ought to rescue his memory from the charge of knavery, so often and so unjustly brought against him.

As soon as his departure was known, all his estates and his valuable library were confiscated. Among the rest, an annuity of 200,000 livres (8000l. sterling) on the lives of his wife and children, which had been purchased for five millions of livres, was forfeited, notwithstanding that a special edict, drawn up for the purpose in the days of his prosperity, had expressly declared that it should never be confiscated for any cause whatever. Great discontent existed among the people that Law had been suffered to escape. The mob and the parliament would have been pleased to have seen him hanged. The few who had not suffered by the commercial revolution rejoiced that the *quack* had left the country; but all those (and they were by far the most numerous class) whose fortunes were implicated regretted that his intimate knowledge of the distress of the country, and of the causes that had led to it, had not been rendered more available in discovering a remedy.

At a meeting of the Council of Finance and the General Council of the Regency, documents were laid upon the table, from which it appeared that the amount of notes in circulation was 2700 millions. The regent was called upon to explain how it happened that there was a discrepancy between the dates at which these issues were made and those of the edicts by which they were authorised. He might have safely taken the whole blame upon himself, but he preferred that an absent man should bear a share of it; and he therefore stated that Law, upon his own authority, had issued 1200 millions of notes at different times, and that he (the regent), seeing that the thing had been irrevocably done, had screened Law by antedating the decrees of the council which authorised the augmentation. It would have been more to his credit if he had told the whole truth while he was about it, and acknowledged that it was mainly through his extravagance and impatience that Law had been induced to overstep the bounds of safe speculation. It was also ascertained that the national debt, on the 1st of January 1721, amounted to upwards of 3100 millions of livres, or more than 124,000,000l. sterling, the interest upon which was 3,196,000l. A commission, or *visa*, was forthwith appointed to examine into all the securities of the state creditors, who were to be divided into five classes; the first four comprising those who had purchased their securities with real effects, and, the latter comprising those who could give no proofs that the transactions they had entered into were real and *bonâ fide*. The securities of the latter were ordered to be destroyed, while those of the first four classes were subjected to a most rigid and jealous scrutiny. The result of the labours of the *visa*, was a report, in which they counselled the reduction of the interest upon these securities to fifty-six millions of livres. They justified, this, advice by a statement of the various acts of peculation and extortion which they had discovered; and an edict to that effect was accordingly published and duly registered by the parliaments of the kingdom.

*D'Argenson.*

Another tribunal was afterwards established, under the title of the *Chambre de l'Arsenal*, which took cognisance of all the malversations committed in the financial departments of the government, during the late unhappy period. A Master of Requests, named Falhonet, together with the Abbé Clement, and two clerks in their employ, had been concerned in divers acts of peculation to the amount of upwards of a million of livres. The first two were sentenced to be beheaded, and the latter to be hanged; but their punishment was afterwards commuted into imprisonment for life in the Bastille. Numerous other acts of dishonesty were discovered, and punished, by fine and imprisonment.

D'Argenson shared with Law and the regent the unpopularity which had alighted upon all those concerned in the Mississippi madness. He was dismissed from his post of Chancellor to make room for D'Aguesseau; but he retained the title of Keeper of the Seals, and was allowed to attend the councils whenever he pleased. He thought it better, however, to withdraw from Paris, and live for a time a life of seclusion at his country-seat. But he was not formed for retirement; and becoming moody and discontented, he aggravated a disease under which he had long laboured, and died in less than a twelve-month. The populace of Paris so detested him, that they carried their hatred even to his grave. As his funeral procession passed to the church of St. Nicholas du Chardonneret, the burying-place of his family, it was beset by a riotous mob, and his two sons, who were following as chief mourners, were obliged to drive as fast as they were able down a by-street to escape personal violence.

As regards Law, he for some time entertained a hope that he should be recalled to France, to aid in establishing its credit upon a firmer basis. The death of the regent in 1723, who expired suddenly as he was sitting by the fireside conversing with his mistress, the Duchess de Phalaris, deprived him of that hope, and he was reduced to lead his former life of gambling. He was more than once obliged to pawn his diamond, the sole remnant of his vast wealth, but successful play generally enabled him to redeem it. Being persecuted by his creditors at Rome, he proceeded to Copenhagen, where he received permission from the English ministry to reside in his native country, his pardon for the murder of Mr. Wilson having been sent over to him in 1719. He was brought over in the admiral's ship—a circumstance which gave occasion for a short debate in the House of Lords. Earl Coningsby complained that a man who had renounced both his country and his religion, should have been treated with such honour, and expressed his belief that his presence in England, at a time when the people were so bewildered by the nefarious practices of the South-Sea directors, would be attended with no little danger. He gave notice of a motion on the subject; but it was allowed to drop, no other member of the House having the slightest participation in his lordship's fears. Law remained for about four years in England, and then proceeded to Venice, where he died in 1729, in very embarrassed circumstances. The following epitaph was written at the time:

> "Ci gît cet Ecossais célébre,
> Ce calculateur sans égal,
> Qui, par les régles de l'algébre,
> A mis la France à l'hôpital."

His brother, William Law, who had been concerned with him in the administration both of the bank and the Louisiana Company, was imprisoned in the Bastille for alleged malversation, but no guilt was ever proved against him. He was liberated after fifteen months, and became the founder of a family, which is still known in France under the title of Marquises of Lauriston.

*Neck or Nothing.*[15]

In the next chapter will be found an account of the madness which infected the people of England at the same time, and under very similar circumstances, but which, thanks to the energies and good sense of a constitutional government, was attended with results far less disastrous than those which were seen in France.

# Chapter 2.

The South-Sea Bubble.

*South-Sea House*

*At length corruption, like a general flood,*
*Did deluge all; and avarice creeping on,*
*Spread, like a low-born mist, and hid the sun.*
*Statesmen and patriots plied alike the stocks,*
*Peeress and butler shared alike the box;*
*And judges jobbed, and bishops bit the town,*
*And mighty dukes packed cards for half-a-crown:*
*Britain was sunk in lucre's sordid charms. – Pope.*

The South-Sea Company was originated by the celebrated Harley Earl of Oxford, in the year 1711, with the view of restoring public credit, which had suffered by the dismissal of the Whig ministry, and of providing for the discharge of the army and navy debentures, and other parts of the floating debt, amounting to nearly ten millions sterling. A company of merchants, at that time without a name, took this debt upon themselves, and the government agreed to secure them for a certain period the interest of six per cent. To provide for this interest, amounting to 600,000l. per annum, the duties upon wines, vinegar, India goods, wrought silks, tobacco, whale-fins, and some other articles, were rendered permanent. The monopoly of the trade to the South Seas was granted, and the company, being incorporated by act of parliament, assumed the title by which it has ever since been known. The minister took great credit to himself for his share in this transaction, and the scheme was always called by his flatterers "the Earl of Oxford's masterpiece."

*Harley Earl Of Oxford*

Even at this early period of its history the most visionary ideas were formed by the company and the public of the immense riches of the eastern coast of South America. Every body had heard of the gold and silver mines of Peru and Mexico; every one believed them to be inexhaustible, and that it was only necessary to send the manufactures of England to the coast to be repaid a hundred fold in gold and silver ingots by the natives. A report, industriously spread, that Spain was willing to concede four ports on the coasts of Chili and Peru for the purposes of traffic, increased the general confidence, and for many years the South-Sea Company's stock was in high favour.

Philip V. of Spain, however, never had any intention of admitting the English to a free trade in the ports of Spanish America. Negotiations were set on foot, but their only result was the *assiento* contract, or the privilege of supplying the colonies with negroes for thirty years, and of sending once a year a vessel, limited both as to tonnage and value of cargo, to trade with Mexico, Peru, or Chili. The latter permission was only granted upon the hard condition, that the King of Spain should enjoy one-fourth of the profits, and a tax of five per cent on the remainder. This was a great disappointment to the Earl of Oxford and his party, who were reminded much oftener than they found agreeable of the

*"Parturiunt montes, nascitur ridiculus mus."*

But the public confidence in the South-Sea Company was not shaken. The Earl of Oxford declared that Spain would permit two ships, in addition to the annual ship, to carry out merchandise during the first year; and a list was published, in which all the ports and harbours of these coasts were pompously set forth as open to the trade of Great Britain. The first voyage of the annual ship was not made till the year 1717, and in the following year the trade was suppressed by the rupture with Spain.

The king's speech, at the opening of the session of 1717, made pointed allusion to the state of public credit, and recommended that proper measures should be taken to reduce the national debt. The two great monetary corporations, the South-Sea Company and the Bank of England, made proposals to parliament on the 20th of May ensuing. The South-Sea Company prayed that their capital stock of ten millions might be increased to twelve, by subscription or otherwise, and offered to accept five per cent instead of six upon the whole amount. The bank made proposals equally advantageous. The house debated for some time, and finally three acts were passed, called the South-Sea Act, the Bank Act, and the General Fund Act. By the first, the proposals of the South-Sea Company were accepted, and that body held itself ready to advance the sum of two millions towards discharging the principal and interest of the debt due by the state for the four lottery funds, of the ninth and tenth years of Queen Anne. By the second act, the bank received a lower rate of interest for the sum of 1,775,027l. 15s. due to it by the state, and agreed to deliver up to be cancelled as many exchequer bills as amounted to two millions sterling, and to accept of an annuity of one hundred thousand pounds, being after the rate of five per cent, the whole redeemable at one year's notice. They were further required to be ready to advance, in case of need, a sum not exceeding 2,500,000l. upon the same terms of five per cent interest, redeemable by parliament. The General Fund Act recited the various deficiencies, which were to be made good by the aids derived from the foregoing sources.

The name of the South-Sea Company was thus continually before the public. Though their trade with the South American States produced little or no augmentation of their revenues, they continued to flourish as a monetary corporation. Their stock was in high request, and the directors, buoyed up with success, began to think of new means for extending their influence. The Mississippi scheme of John Law, which so dazzled and captivated the French people, inspired them with an idea that they could carry on the same game in England. The anticipated failure of his plans did not divert them from their intention. Wise in their own conceit, they imagined they could avoid his faults, carry on their schemes for ever, and stretch the cord of credit to its extremest tension, without causing it to snap asunder.

It was while Law's plan was at its greatest height of popularity, while people were crowding in thousands to the Rue Quincampoix, and ruining themselves with frantic eagerness, that the South-Sea directors laid before parliament their famous plan for paying off the national debt. Visions of boundless wealth floated before the fascinated eyes of the people in the two most celebrated countries of Europe. The English commenced their career of extravagance somewhat later than the French; but as soon as the delirium seized them, they were determined not to be outdone. Upon the 22d of January, 1720, the House of Commons resolved itself into a committee of the whole house, to take into consideration that part of the king's speech at the opening of the session which related to the public debts, and the proposal of the South-Sea Company towards the redemption and sinking of the same. The proposal set forth at great length, and under several heads, the debts of the state, amounting to 30,981,712l., which the company were anxious to take upon themselves, upon consideration of five per cent per annum, secured to them until Midsummer 1727; after which time, the whole was to become redeemable at the pleasure of the legislature, and the interest to be reduced to four per cent. The proposal was received with great favour; but the Bank of England had many friends in the House of Commons, who were desirous that that body should share in the advantages that were likely to accrue. On behalf of this corporation it was represented, that they had performed great and eminent services to the state in the most difficult times, and deserved, at least, that if any advantage was to be made by public bargains of this nature, they should be preferred before a company that had never done any thing for the nation. The further consideration of the matter was accordingly postponed for five days. In the mean time, a plan was drawn up by the governors of the bank. The South-Sea Company, afraid that the bank might offer still more advantageous terms to the government than themselves, reconsidered their former proposal, and made some alterations in it, which they hoped would render it more acceptable. The principal change was a stipulation that the government might redeem these debts at the expiration of four years, instead of seven, as at first suggested. The bank resolved not to be outbidden in this singular auction, and the governors also reconsidered their first proposal, and sent in a new one.

Thus, each corporation having made two proposals, the house began to deliberate. Mr. Robert Walpole was the chief speaker in favour of the bank, and Mr. Aislabie, the Chancellor of the Exchequer, the principal advocate on behalf of the South-Sea Company. It was resolved, on the 2d of February, that the proposals of the latter were most advantageous to the country. They were accordingly received, and leave was given to bring in a bill to that effect.

Exchange Alley was in a fever of excitement. The company's stock, which had been at a hundred and thirty the previous day, gradually rose to three hundred, and continued to rise with the most astonishing rapidity during the whole time that the bill in its several stages was under discussion. Mr. Walpole was almost the only statesman in the House who spoke out boldly against it. He warned them, in eloquent and solemn language, of the evils that would ensue. It countenanced, he said, "the dangerous practice of stock-jobbing, and would divert the genius of the nation from trade and industry. It would hold out a dangerous lure to decoy the unwary to their ruin, by making them part with the earnings of their labour for a prospect of imaginary wealth. The great principle of the project was an evil of first-rate magnitude; it was to raise artificially the value of the stock, by exciting and keeping up a general infatuation, and by promising dividends out of funds which could never be adequate to the purpose." In a prophetic spirit he added, that if the plan succeeded, the directors would become masters of the government, form a new and absolute aristocracy in the kingdom, and control the resolutions of the legislature. If it failed, which he was convinced it would, the result would bring general discontent and ruin upon the country. Such would be the delusion, that when the evil day came, as come it would, the people would start up, as from a dream, and ask themselves if these things could have been true. All his eloquence was in vain. He was looked upon as a false prophet, or compared to the hoarse raven, croaking omens of evil. His friends, however, compared him to Cassandra, predicting evils which would only be believed when they came home to men's hearths, and stared them in the face at their own boards. Although, in former times, the house had listened with the utmost attention to every word that fell from his lips, the benches became deserted when it was known that he would speak on the South-Sea question.

*Sir Robert Walpole*

The bill was two months in its progress through the House of Commons. During this time every exertion was made by the directors and their friends, and more especially by the chairman, the noted Sir John Blunt, to raise the price of the stock. The most extravagant rumours were in circulation. Treaties between England and Spain were spoken of, whereby the latter was to grant a free trade to all her colonies; and the rich produce of the mines of Potosi-la-Paz was to be brought to England until silver should become almost as plentiful as iron. For cotton and woollen goods, with which we could supply them in abundance, the dwellers in Mexico were to empty their golden mines. The company of merchants trading to the South Seas would be the richest the world ever saw, and every hundred pounds invested in it would produce hundreds per annum to the stockholder. At last the stock was raised by these means to near four hundred; but, after fluctuating a good deal, settled at three hundred and thirty, at which price it remained when the bill passed the Commons by a majority of 172 against 55.

In the House of Lords the bill was hurried through all its stages with unexampled rapidity. On the 4th of April it was read a first time; on the 5th, it was read a second time; on the 6th, it was committed; and on the 7th, was read a third time and passed.

Several peers spoke warmly against the scheme; but their warnings fell upon dull, cold ears. A speculating frenzy had seized them as well as the plebeians. Lord North and Grey said the bill was unjust in its nature, and might prove fatal in its consequences, being calculated to enrich the few and impoverish the many. The Duke of Wharton followed; but, as he only retailed at second-hand the arguments so eloquently stated by Walpole in the Lower House, he was not listened to with even the same attention that had been bestowed upon Lord North and Grey. Earl Cowper followed on the same side, and compared the bill to the famous horse of the siege of Troy. Like that, it was ushered in and received with great pomp and acclamations of joy, but bore within it treachery and destruction. The Earl of Sunderland endeavoured to answer all objections; and on the question being put, there appeared only seventeen peers against, and eighty-three in favour of the project. The very same day on which it passed the Lords, it received the royal assent, and became the law of the land.

It seemed at that time as if the whole nation had turned stockjobbers. Exchange Alley was every day blocked up by crowds, and Cornhill was impassable for the number of carriages. Every body came to purchase stock. "Every fool aspired to be a knave." In the words of a ballad published at the time, and sung about the streets,[16]

> "*Then stars and garters did appear*
> *Among the meaner rabble;*
> *To buy and sell, to see and hear*
> *The Jews and Gentiles squabble.*
> *The greatest ladies thither came,*
> *And plied in chariots daily,*
> *Or pawned their jewels for a sum*
> *To venture in the Alley.*"

The inordinate thirst of gain that had afflicted all ranks of society was not to be slaked even in the South Sea. Other schemes, of the most extravagant kind, were started. The share-lists were speedily filled up, and an enormous traffic carried on in shares, while, of course, every means were resorted to to raise them to an artificial value in the market.

*Cornhill, 1720.*

Contrary to all expectation, South-Sea stock fell when the bill received the royal assent. On the 7th of April the shares were quoted at three hundred and ten, and on the following day at two hundred and ninety. Already the directors had tasted the profits of their scheme, and it was not likely that they should quietly allow the stock to find its natural level without an effort to raise it. Immediately their busy emissaries were set to work. Every person interested in the success of the project endeavoured to draw a knot of listeners around him, to whom he expatiated on the treasures of the South American seas. Exchange Alley was crowded with attentive groups. One rumour alone, asserted with the utmost confidence, had an immediate effect upon the stock. It was said that Earl Stanhope had received overtures in France from the Spanish government to exchange Gibraltar and Port Mahon for some places on the coast of Peru, for the security and enlargement of the trade in the South Seas. Instead of one annual ship trading to those ports, and allowing the king of Spain twenty-five per cent out of the profits, the company might build and charter as many ships as they pleased, and pay no per centage whatever to any foreign potentate.

"Visions of ingots danced before their eyes,"

and stock rose rapidly. On the 12th of April, five days after the bill had become law, the directors opened their books for a subscription of a million, at the rate of 300l. for every 100l. capital. Such was the concourse of persons of all ranks, that this first subscription was found to amount to above two millions of original stock. It was to be paid at five payments, of 60l. each for every 100l. In a few days the stock advanced to three hundred and forty, and the subscriptions were sold for double the price of the first payment. To raise the stock still higher, it was declared, in a general court of directors, on the 21st of April, that the midsummer dividend should be ten per cent, and that all subscriptions should be entitled to the same. These resolutions answering the end designed, the directors, to improve the infatuation of the monied men, opened their books for a second subscription of a million, at four hundred per cent. Such was the frantic eagerness of people of every class to speculate in these funds, that in the course of a few hours no less than a million and a half was subscribed at that rate.

In the mean time, innumerable joint-stock companies started up every where. They soon received the name of Bubbles, the most appropriate that imagination could devise. The populace are often most happy in the nicknames they employ. None could be more apt than that of Bubbles. Some of them lasted for a week or a fortnight, and were no more heard of, while others could not even live out that short span of existence. Every evening produced new schemes, and every morning new projects. The highest of the aristocracy were as eager in this hot pursuit of gain as the most plodding jobber in Cornhill. The Prince of Wales became governor of one company, and is said to have cleared 40,000l. by his speculations.[17] The Duke of Bridgewater started a scheme for the improvement of London and Westminster, and the Duke of Chandos another. There were nearly a hundred different projects, each more extravagant and deceptive than the other, To use the words of the *Political State*, they were "set on foot and promoted by crafty knaves, then pursued by multitudes of covetous fools, and at last appeared to be, in effect, what their vulgar appellation denoted them to be—bubbles and mere cheats." It was computed that near one million and a half sterling was won and lost by these unwarrantable practices, to the impoverishment of many a fool, and the enriching of many a rogue.

Some of these schemes were plausible enough, and, had they been undertaken at a time when the public mind was unexcited, might have been pursued with advantage to all concerned. But they were established merely with the view of raising the shares in the market. The projectors took the first opportunity of a rise to sell out, and next morning the scheme was at an end. Maitland, in his *History of London*, gravely informs us, that one of the projects which received great encouragement, was for the establishment of a company "to make deal boards out of sawdust." This is no doubt intended as a joke; but there is abundance of evidence to shew that dozens of schemes, hardly a whit more reasonable, lived their little day, ruining hundreds ere they fell.

One of them was for a wheel for perpetual motion — capital one million; another was "for encouraging the breed of horses in England, and improving of glebe and church lands, and repairing and rebuilding parsonage and vicarage houses." Why the clergy, who were so mainly interested in the latter clause, should have taken so much interest in the first, is only to be explained on the supposition that the scheme was projected by a knot of the fox-hunting parsons, once so common in England. The shares of this company were rapidly subscribed for. But the most absurd and preposterous of all, and which shewed, more completely than any other, the utter madness of the people, was one started by an unknown adventurer, entitled "*A company for carrying on an undertaking of great advantage, but nobody to know what it is*." Were not the fact stated by scores of credible witnesses, it would be impossible to believe that any person could have been duped by such a project. The man of genius who essayed this bold and successful inroad upon public credulity, merely stated in his prospectus that the required capital was half a million, in five thousand shares of 100l. each, deposit 2l. per share. Each subscriber, paying his deposit, would be entitled to 100l. per annum per share. How this immense profit was to be obtained, he did not condescend to inform them at that time, but promised that in a month full particulars should be duly announced, and a call made for the remaining 98l. of the subscription. Next morning, at nine o'clock, this great man opened an office in Cornhill. Crowds of people beset his door, and when he shut up at three o'clock, he found that no less than one thousand shares had been subscribed for, and the deposits paid. He was thus, in five hours, the winner of 2000l. He was philosopher enough to be contented with his venture, and set off the same evening for the Continent. He was never heard of again.

Well might Swift exclaim, comparing Change Alley to a gulf in the South Sea:

*"Subscribers here by thousands float,*
*And jostle one another down,*
*Each paddling in his leaky boat,*
*And here they fish for gold and drown.*

*Now buried in the depths below,*
*Now mounted up to heaven again,*
*They reel and stagger to and fro,*
*At their wit's end, like drunken men.*

*Meantime, secure on Garraway cliffs,*
*A savage race, by shipwrecks fed,*
*Lie waiting for the foundered skiffs,*
*And strip the bodies of the dead."*

Another fraud that was very successful was that of the "Globe *Permits*," as they were called. They were nothing more than square pieces of playing-cards, on which was the impression of a seal, in wax, bearing the sign of the Globe Tavern, in the neighbourhood of Exchange Alley, with the inscription of "Sail-Cloth Permits." The possessors enjoyed no other advantage from them than permission to subscribe at some future time to a new sail-cloth manufactory, projected by one who was then known to be a man of fortune, but who was afterwards involved in the peculation and punishment of the South-Sea directors. These permits sold for as much as sixty guineas in the Alley.

Persons of distinction, of both sexes, were deeply engaged in all these bubbles; those of the male sex going to taverns and coffee-houses to meet their brokers, and the ladies resorting for the same purpose to the shops of milliners and haberdashers. But it did not follow that all these people believed in the feasibility of the schemes to which they subscribed; it was enough for their purpose that their shares would, by stock-jobbing arts, be soon raised to a premium, when they got rid of them with all expedition to the really credulous. So great was the confusion of the crowd in the alley, that shares in the same bubble were known to have been sold at the same instant ten per cent higher at one end of the alley than at the other. Sensible men beheld the extraordinary infatuation of the people with sorrow and alarm. There were some both in and out of parliament who foresaw clearly the ruin that was impending. Mr. Walpole did not cease his gloomy forebodings. His fears were shared by all the thinking few, and impressed most forcibly upon the government. On the 11th of June, the day the parliament rose, the king published a proclamation, declaring that all these unlawful projects should be deemed public nuisances, and prosecuted accordingly, and forbidding any broker, under a penalty of five hundred pounds, from buying or selling any shares in them. Notwithstanding this proclamation, roguish speculators still carried them on, and the deluded people still encouraged them. On the 12th of July, an order of the Lords Justices assembled in privy council was published, dismissing all the petitions that had been presented for patents and charters, and dissolving all the bubble companies. The following copy of their lordships' order, containing a list of all these nefarious projects, will not be deemed uninteresting at the present time, when, at periodic intervals, there is but too much tendency in the public mind to indulge in similar practices:

*"At the Council Chamber, Whitehall, the 12th day of July, 1720. Present, their Excellencies the Lords Justices in Council.*

*"Their Excellencies the Lords Justices, in council, taking into consideration the many inconveniences arising to the public from several projects set on foot for raising of joint-stock for various purposes, and that a great many of his majesty's subjects have been drawn in to part with their money on pretence of assurances that their petitions for patents and charters to enable them to carry on the same would be granted: to prevent such impositions, their excellencies this day ordered the said several petitions, together with such reports from the Board of Trade, and from his majesty's attorney and solicitor-general, as had been obtained thereon, to be laid before them; and after mature consideration thereof, were pleased, by advice of his majesty's privy council, to order that the said petitions be dismissed, which are as follow:*
*"1. Petition of several persons, praying letters patent for carrying on a fishing trade by the name of the Grand Fishery of Great Britain.*
*"2. Petition of the Company of the Royal Fishery of England, praying letters patent for such further powers as will effectually contribute to carry on the said fishery.*

"3. Petition of George James, on behalf of himself and divers persons of distinction concerned in a national fishery, praying letters patent of incorporation, to enable them to carry on the same.

"4. Petition of several merchants, traders, and others, whose names are thereunto subscribed, praying to be incorporated for reviving and carrying on a whale fishery to Greenland and elsewhere.

"5. Petition of Sir John Lambert and others thereto subscribing, on behalf of themselves and a great number of merchants, praying to be incorporated for carrying on a Greenland trade, and particularly a whale fishery in Davis's Straits.

"6. Another petition for a Greenland trade.

"7. Petition of several merchants, gentlemen, and citizens, praying to be incorporated for buying and building of ships to let or freight.

"8. Petition of Samuel Antrim and others, praying for letters patent for sowing hemp and flax.

"9. Petition of several merchants, masters of ships, sail-makers, and manufacturers of sail-cloth, praying a charter of incorporation, to enable them to carry on and promote the said manufactory by a joint-stock.

"10. Petition of Thomas Boyd and several hundred merchants, owners and masters of ships, sail-makers, weavers, and other traders, praying a charter of incorporation, empowering them to borrow money for purchasing lands, in order to the manufacturing sail-cloth and fine holland.

"11. Petition on behalf of several persons interested in a patent granted by the late King William and Queen Mary for the making of linen and sail-cloth, praying that no charter may be granted to any persons whatsoever for making sail-cloth, but that the privilege now enjoyed by them may be confirmed, and likewise an additional power to carry on the cotton and cotton-silk manufactures.

"12. Petition of several citizens, merchants, and traders in London, and others, subscribers to a British stock for a general insurance from fire in any part of England, praying to be incorporated for carrying on the said undertaking.

"13. Petition of several of his majesty's loyal subjects of the city of London and other parts of Great Britain, praying to be incorporated for carrying on a general insurance from losses by fire within the kingdom of England.

"14. Petition of Thomas Surges and others his majesty's subjects thereto subscribing, in behalf of themselves and others, subscribers to a fund of 1,200,000l. for carrying on a trade to his majesty's German dominions, praying to be incorporated by the name of the Harburg Company.

"15. Petition of Edward Jones, a dealer in timber, on behalf of himself and others, praying to be incorporated for the importation of timber from Germany.

"16. Petition of several merchants of London, praying a charter of incorporation for carrying on a salt-work.

"17. Petition of Captain Macphedris of London, merchant, on behalf of himself and several merchants, clothiers, hatters, dyers, and other traders, praying a charter of incorporation empowering them to raise a sufficient sum of money to purchase lands for planting and rearing a wood called madder, for the use of dyers.

"18. Petition of Joseph Galendo of London, snuff-maker, praying a patent for his invention to prepare and cure Virginia tobacco for snuff in Virginia, and making it into the same in all his majesty's dominions."

## List of Bubbles.

The following Bubble-Companies were by the same order declared to be illegal, and abolished accordingly:

1.  For the importation of Swedish iron.
2.  For supplying London with sea-coal. Capital, three millions.
3.  For building and rebuilding houses throughout all England Capital, three millions.
4.  For making of muslin.
5.  For carrying on and improving the British alum-works.
6.  For effectually settling the island of Blanco and Sal Tartagus.
7.  For supplying the town of Deal with fresh water.
8.  For the importation of Flanders lace.
9.  For improvement of lands in Great Britain. Capital, four millions.
10. For encouraging the breed of horses in England, and improving of glebe and church lands, and for repairing and rebuilding parsonage and vicarage houses.
11. For making of iron and steel in Great Britain,

12. For improving the land in the county of Flint. Capital, one million.
13. For purchasing lands to build on. Capital, two millions.
14. For trading in hair.
15. For erecting salt-works in Holy Island. Capital, two millions.
16. For buying and selling estates, and lending money on mortgage.
17. For carrying on an undertaking of great advantage; but nobody to know what it is.
18. For paving the streets of London. Capital, two millions.
19. For furnishing funerals to any part of Great Britain.
20. For buying and selling lands and lending money at interest. Capital, five millions.
21. For carrying on the royal fishery of Great Britain. Capital, ten millions.
22. For assuring of seamen's wages.
23. For erecting loan-offices for the assistance and encouragement of the industrious. Capital, two millions.
24. For purchasing and improving leaseable lands. Capital, four millions.
25. For importing pitch and tar, and other naval stores, from North Britain and America.
26. For the clothing, felt, and pantile trade.
27. For purchasing and improving a manor and royalty in Essex.
28. For insuring of horses. Capital, two millions.
29. For exporting the woollen manufacture, and importing copper, brass, and iron. Capital, four millions.
30. For a grand dispensary. Capital, three millions.
31. For erecting mills and purchasing lead-mines. Capital, two millions.
32. For improving the art of making soap.
33. For a settlement on the island of Santa Cruz.
34. For sinking pits and smelting lead ore in Derbyshire.
35. For making glass bottles and other glass.
36. For a wheel for perpetual motion. Capital, one million.
37. For improving of gardens.
38. For insuring and increasing children's fortunes.

39. For entering and loading goods at the Custom-house, and for negotiating business for merchants.
40. For carrying on a woollen manufacture in the North of England.
41. For importing walnut-trees from Virginia, Capital, two millions.
42. For making Manchester stuffs of thread and cotton.
43. For making Joppa and Castile soap.
44. For improving the wrought-iron and steel manufactures of this kingdom. Capital four millions.
45. For dealing in lace, hollands, cambrics, lawns, &c. Capital, two millions.
46. For trading in and improving certain commodities of the produce of this kingdom, &c. Capital three millions.
47. For supplying the London markets with cattle.
48. For making looking-glasses, coach-glasses, &c. Capital, two millions.
49. For working the tin and lead mines in Cornwall and Derby-shire.
50. For making rape-oil.
51. For importing beaver fur. Capital, two millions.
52. For making pasteboard and packing-paper.
53. For importing of oils and other materials used in the woollen manufacture.
54. For improving and increasing the silk manufactures.
55. For lending money on stock, annuities, tallies, &c.
56. For paying pensions to widows and others, at a small discount. Capital, two millions.
57. For improving malt liquors. Capital, four millions.
58. For a grand American fishery.
59. For purchasing and improving the fenny lands in Lincoln-shire. Capital, two millions.
60. For improving the paper manufacture of Great Britain.
61. The Bottomry Company.
62. For drying malt by hot air.
63. For carrying on a trade in the river Oronooko.

64. For the more effectual making of baize, in Colchester and other parts of Great Britain.
65. For buying of naval stores, supplying the victualling, and paying the wages of the workmen.
66. For employing poor artificers, and furnishing merchants and others with watches.
67. For improvement of tillage and the breed of cattle.
68. Another for the improvement of our breed in horses.
69. Another for a horse-insurance.
70. For carrying on the corn trade of Great Britain.
71. For insuring to all masters and mistresses the losses they may sustain by servants. Capital, three millions.
72. For erecting houses or hospitals for taking in and maintaining illegitimate children. Capital, two millions.
73. For bleaching coarse sugars, without the use of fire or loss of substance.
74. For building turnpikes and wharfs in Great Britain.
75. For insuring from thefts and robberies.
76. For extracting silver from lead.
77. For making china and delft ware. Capital, one million.
78. For importing tobacco, and exporting it again to Sweden and the north of Europe. Capital, four millions.
79. For making iron with pit coal.
80. For furnishing the cities of London and Westminster with hay and straw. Capital, three millions.
81. For a sail and packing-cloth manufactory in Ireland.
82. For taking up ballast.
83. For buying and fitting out ships to suppress pirates.
84. For the importation of timber from Wales. Capital, two millions.
85. For rock-salt.
86. For the transmutation of quicksilver into a malleable fine metal.

*Change-Alley.*[18]

Besides these bubbles, many others sprang up daily, in-spite of the condemnation of the government and the ridicule of the still sane portion of the public. The print-shops teemed with caricatures, and the newspapers with epigrams and satires, upon the prevalent folly. An ingenious cardmaker published a pack of South-Sea playing-cards, which are now extremely rare, each card containing, besides the usual figures, of a very small size, in one corner, a caricature of a bubble-company, with appropriate verses underneath. One of the most famous bubbles was "Puckle's Machine Company," for discharging round and square cannon-balls and bullets, and making a total revolution in the art of war. Its pretensions to public favour were thus summed up on the eight of spades:

"*A rare invention to destroy the crowd*

Of fools at home instead of fools abroad.
Fear not, my friends, this terrible machine,
They're only wounded who have shares therein."

*Tree Caricature*[19]

The nine of hearts was a caricature of the English Copper and Brass Company, with the following epigram:

*"The headlong-fool that wants to be a swopper*
*Of gold and silver coin for English copper,*
*May, in Change Alley, prove himself an ass,*
*And give rich metal for adultrate brass."*

The eight of diamonds celebrated the company for the colonisation of Acadia, with this doggrel:

*"He that is rich and wants to fool away*
*A good round sum in North America,*

*Let him subscribe himself a headlong sharer,*
*And asses' ears shall honour him or bearer."*

And in a similar style every card of the pack exposed some knavish scheme, and ridiculed the persons who were its dupes. It was computed that the total amount of the sums proposed for carrying on these projects was upwards of three hundred millions sterling.

Merchant's Gateway

It is time, however, to return to the great South-Sea gulf, that swallowed the fortunes of so many thousands of the avaricious and the credulous. On the 29th of May, the stock had risen as high as five hundred, and about two-thirds of the government annuitants had exchanged the securities of the state for those of the South-Sea company. During the whole of the month of May the stock continued to rise, and on the 28th it was quoted at five hundred and fifty. In four days after this it took a prodigious leap, rising suddenly from five hundred and fifty to eight hundred and ninety. It was now the general opinion that the stock could rise no higher, and many persons took that opportunity of selling out, with a view of realising their profits.

Many noblemen and persons in the train of the king, and about to accompany him to Hanover, were also anxious to sell out. So many sellers, and so few buyers, appeared in the Alley on the 3d of June, that the stock fell at once from eight hundred and ninety to six hundred and forty. The directors were alarmed, and gave their agents orders to buy. Their efforts succeeded. Towards evening, confidence was restored, and the stock advanced to seven hundred and fifty. It continued at this price, with some slight fluctuation, until the company closed their books on the 22d of June.

It would be needless and uninteresting to detail the various arts employed by the directors to keep up the price of stock. It will be sufficient to state that it finally rose to one thousand per cent. It was quoted at this price in, the commencement of August. The bubble was then full-blown, and began to quiver and shake preparatory to its bursting.

Many of the government annuitants expressed dissatisfaction against the directors. They accused them of partiality in making out the lists for shares in each subscription. Further uneasiness was occasioned by its being generally known that Sir John Blunt the chairman, and some others, had sold out. During the whole of the month of August the stock fell, and on the 2d of September it was quoted at seven hundred only.

The state of things now became alarming. To prevent, if possible, the utter extinction of public confidence in their proceedings, the directors summoned a general court of the whole corporation, to meet in Merchant Tailors' Hall on the 8th of September. By nine o'clock in the morning, the room was filled to suffocation; Cheapside was blocked up by a crowd unable to gain admittance, and the greatest excitement prevailed. The directors and their friends mustered in great numbers. Sir John Fellowes, the sub-governor, was called to the chair. He acquainted the assembly with the cause of their meeting; read to them the several resolutions of the court of directors, and gave them an account of their proceedings; of the taking in the redeemable and unredeemable funds, and of the subscriptions in money. Mr. Secretary Craggs then made a short speech, wherein he commended the conduct of the directors, and urged that nothing could more effectually contribute to the bringing this scheme to perfection than union among themselves. He concluded with a motion for thanking the court of directors for their prudent and skilful management, and for desiring them to proceed in such manner as they should think most proper for the interest and advantage of the corporation. Mr. Hungerford, who had rendered himself very conspicuous in the House of Commons for his zeal in behalf of the South-Sea company, and who was shrewdly suspected to have been a considerable gainer by knowing the right time to sell out, was very magniloquent on this occasion. He said that he had seen the rise and fall, the decay and resurrection of many communities of this nature, but that, in his opinion, none had ever performed such wonderful things in so short a time as the South-Sea company. They had done more than the crown, the pulpit, or the bench could do. They had reconciled all parties in one common interest; they had laid asleep, if not wholly extinguished, all the domestic jars and animosities of the nation. By the rise of their stock, monied men had vastly increased their fortunes; country gentlemen had seen the value of their lands doubled and trebled in their hands. They had at the same time done good to the Church, not a few of the reverend clergy having got great sums by the project. In short, they had enriched the whole nation, and he hoped they had not forgotten themselves. There was some hissing at the latter part of this speech, which for the extravagance of its eulogy was not far removed from satire; but the directors and their friends, and all the winners in the room, applauded vehemently. The Duke of Portland spoke in a similar strain, and expressed his great wonder why any body should be dissatisfied; of course, he was a winner by his speculations, and in a condition similar to that of the fat alderman in *Joe Miller's Jests*, who, whenever he had eaten a good dinner, folded his hands upon his paunch, and expressed his doubts whether there could be a hungry man in the world.

*Mr. Secretary Craggs.*

Several resolutions were passed at this meeting, but they had no effect upon the public. Upon the very same evening the stock fell to six hundred and forty, and on the morrow to five hundred and forty. Day after day it continued to fall, until it was as low as four hundred. In a letter dated September 13th, from Mr. Broderick, M.P., to Lord Chancellor Middleton, and published in Coxe's *Walpole*, the former says: "Various are the conjectures why the South-Sea directors have suffered the cloud to break so early. I made no doubt but they would do so when they found it to their advantage. They have stretched credit so far beyond what it would bear, that specie proves insufficient to support it. Their most considerable men have drawn out, securing themselves by the losses of the deluded, thoughtless numbers, whose understandings have been overruled by avarice and the hope of making mountains out of mole-hills. Thousands of families will be reduced to beggary. The consternation is inexpressible — the rage beyond description, and the case altogether so desperate, that I do not see any plan or scheme so much as thought of for averting the blow, so that I cannot pretend to guess what is next to be done." Ten days afterwards, the stock still falling, he writes: "The company have yet come to no determination, for they are in such a wood that they know not which way to turn. By several gentlemen lately come to town, I perceive the very name of a South-Sea-man grows abominable in every country. A great many goldsmiths are already run off, and more will daily. I question whether one-third, nay, one-fourth of them can stand it.

From the very beginning, I founded my judgment of the whole affair upon the unquestionable maxim, that ten millions (which is more than our running cash) could not circulate two hundred millions, beyond which our paper credit extended. That, therefore, whenever that should become doubtful, be the cause what it would, our noble state machine must inevitably fall to the ground."

On the 12th of September, at the earnest solicitation of Mr. Secretary Craggs, several conferences were held between the directors of the South Sea and the directors of the Bank. A report which was circulated, that the latter had agreed to circulate six millions of the South-Sea company's bonds, caused the stock to rise to six hundred and seventy; but in the afternoon, as soon as the report was known to be groundless, the stock fell again to five hundred and eighty; the next day to five hundred and seventy, and so gradually to four hundred.[20]

The ministry were seriously alarmed at the aspect of affairs. The directors could not appear in the streets without being insulted; dangerous riots were every moment apprehended. Despatches were sent off to the king at Hanover, praying his immediate return. Mr. Walpole, who was staying at his country seat, was sent for, that he might employ his known influence with the directors of the Bank of England to induce them to accept the proposal made by the South-Sea company for circulating a number of their bonds.

The Bank was very unwilling to mix itself up with the affairs of the company; it dreaded being involved in calamities which it could not relieve, and received all overtures with visible reluctance. But the universal voice of the nation called upon it to come to the rescue. Every person of note in commercial politics was called in to advise in the emergency. A rough draft of a contract drawn up by Mr. Walpole was ultimately adopted as the basis of further negotiations, and the public alarm abated a little.

On the following day, the 20th of September, a general court of the South-Sea company was held at Merchant Tailors' Hall, in which resolutions were carried, empowering the directors to agree with the Bank of England, or any other persons, to circulate the company's bonds, or make any other agreement with the Bank which they should think proper. One of the speakers, a Mr. Pulteney, said it was most surprising to see the extraordinary panic which had seized upon the people. Men were running to and fro in alarm and terror, their imaginations filled with some great calamity, the form and dimensions of which nobody knew:

*"Black it stood as night –*
*Fierce as ten furies – terrible as hell."*

At a general court of the Bank of England held two days afterwards, the governor informed them of the several meetings that had been held on the affairs of the South-Sea company, adding that the directors had not yet thought fit to come to any decision upon the matter. A resolution was then proposed, and carried without a dissentient voice, empowering the directors to agree with those of the South Sea to circulate their bonds, to what sum, and upon what terms, and for what time, they might think proper.

Thus both parties were at liberty to act as they might judge best for the public interest. Books were opened at the Bank for a subscription of three millions for the support of public credit, on the usual terms of 15l. per cent deposit, 3l. per cent premium, and 5l. per cent interest. So great was the concourse of people in the early part of the morning, all eagerly bringing their money, that it was thought the subscription would be filled that day; but before noon, the tide turned. In spite of all that could be done to prevent it, the South-Sea company's stock fell rapidly. Their bonds were in such discredit, that a run commenced upon the most eminent goldsmiths and bankers, some of whom, having lent out great sums upon South-Sea stock, were obliged to shut up their shops and abscond. The Sword-blade company, who had hitherto been the chief cashiers of the South-Sea company, stopped payment. This being looked upon as but the beginning of evil, occasioned a great run upon the Bank, who were now obliged to pay out money much faster than they had received it upon the subscription in the morning. The day succeeding was a holiday (the 29th of September), and the Bank had a little breathing time. They bore up against the storm; but their former rivals, the South-Sea company, were wrecked upon it. Their stock fell to one hundred and fifty, and gradually, after various fluctuations, to one hundred and thirty-five.

The Bank, finding they were not able to restore public confidence, and stem the tide of ruin, without running the risk of being swept away with those they intended to save, declined to carry out the agreement into which they had partially entered. They were under no obligation whatever to continue; for the so-called Bank contract was nothing more than the rough draught of an agreement, in which blanks had been left for several important particulars, and which contained no penalty for their secession. "And thus," to use the words of the Parliamentary History, "were seen, in the space of eight months, the rise, progress, and fall of that mighty fabric, which, being wound up by mysterious springs to a wonderful height, had fixed the eyes and expectations of all Europe, but whose foundation, being fraud, illusion, credulity, and infatuation, fell to the ground as soon as the artful management of its directors was discovered."

In the hey-day of its blood, during the progress of this dangerous delusion, the manners of the nation became sensibly corrupted. The parliamentary inquiry, set on foot to discover the delinquents, disclosed scenes of infamy, disgraceful alike to the morals of the offenders and the intellects of the people among whom they had arisen. It is a deeply interesting study to investigate all the evils that were the result. Nations, like individuals, cannot become desperate gamblers with impunity. Punishment is sure to overtake them sooner or later. A celebrated writer[21] is quite wrong when he says, "that such an era as this is the most unfavourable for a historian; that no reader of sentiment and imagination can be entertained or interested by a detail of transactions such as these, which admit of no warmth, no colouring, no embellishment; a detail of which only serves to exhibit an inanimate picture of tasteless vice and mean degeneracy." On the contrary, — and Smollett might have discovered it, if he had been in the humour, — the subject is capable of inspiring as much interest as even a novellist can desire. Is there no warmth in the despair of a plundered people? — no life and animation in the picture which might be drawn of the woes of hundreds of impoverished and ruined families? of the wealthy of yesterday become the beggars of to-day? of the powerful and influential changed into exiles and outcasts, and the voice of self-reproach and imprecation resounding from every corner of the land? Is it a dull or uninstructive picture to see a whole people shaking suddenly off the trammels of reason, and running wild after a golden vision, refusing obstinately to believe that it is not real, till, like a deluded hind running after an *ignis fatuus*, they are plunged into a quagmire? But in this false spirit has history too often been written. The intrigues of unworthy courtiers to gain the favour of still more unworthy kings, or the records of murderous battles and sieges, have been dilated on, and told over and over again, with all the eloquence of style and all the charms of fancy; while the circumstances which have most deeply affected the morals and welfare of the people have been passed over with but slight notice, as dry and dull, and capable of neither warmth nor colouring.

This evil Solomon espid
Among the Rabble rout
That beggers did on Horse back
Whilst Princes walke on foot [ride]
South-Sea has verify dy Same
Tor Mighty Men of late
Are brough to Poverty & shame
Whilst Scoundrels ride in state

Caricature.[22]

During the progress of this famous bubble, England presented a singular spectacle. The public mind was in a state of unwholesome fermentation. Men were no longer satisfied with the slow but sure profits of cautious industry. The hope of boundless wealth for the morrow made them heedless and extravagant for to-day. A luxury, till then unheard-of, was introduced, bringing in its train a corresponding laxity of morals. The over-bearing insolence of ignorant men, who had arisen to sudden wealth by successful gambling, made men of true gentility of mind and manners blush that gold should have power to raise the unworthy in the scale of society. The haughtiness of some of these "cyphering cits," as they were termed by Sir Richard Steele, was remembered against them in the day of their adversity. In the parliamentary inquiry, many of the directors suffered more for their insolence than for their peculation. One of them, who, in the full-blown pride of an ignorant rich man, had said that he would feed his horse upon gold, was reduced almost to bread and water for himself; every haughty look, every overbearing speech, was set down, and repaid them a hundredfold in poverty and humiliation.

The state of matters all over the country was so alarming, that George I. shortened his intended stay in Hanover, and returned in all haste to England. He arrived on the 11th of November, and parliament was summoned to meet on the 8th of December. In the mean time, public meetings were held in every considerable town of the empire, at which petitions were adopted, praying the vengeance of the legislature upon the South-Sea directors, who, by their fraudulent practices, had brought the nation to the brink of ruin. Nobody seemed to imagine that the nation itself was as culpable as the South-Sea company. Nobody blamed the credulity and avarice of the people, — the degrading lust of gain, which had swallowed up every nobler quality in the national character, or the infatuation which had made the multitude run their heads with such frantic eagerness into the net held out for them by scheming projectors. These things were never mentioned. The people were a simple, honest, hard-working people, ruined by a gang of robbers, who were to be hanged, drawn, and quartered without mercy.

This was the almost unanimous feeling of the country. The two Houses of Parliament were not more reasonable. Before the guilt of the South-Sea directors was known, punishment was the only cry. The king, in his speech from the throne, expressed his hope that they would remember that all their prudence, temper, and resolution were necessary to find out and apply the proper remedy for their misfortunes. In the debate on the answer to the address, several speakers indulged in the most violent invectives against the directors of the South-Sea project. The Lord Molesworth was particularly vehement. "It had been said by some, that there was no law to punish the directors of the South-Sea company, who were justly looked upon as the authors of the present misfortunes of the state. In his opinion, they ought upon this occasion to follow the example of the ancient Romans, who, having no law against parricide, because their legislators supposed no son could be so unnaturally wicked as to embrue his hands in his father's blood, made a law to punish this heinous crime as soon as it was committed. They adjudged the guilty wretch to be sown in a sack, and thrown alive into the Tiber. He looked upon the contrivers and executors of the villanous South-Sea scheme as the parricides of their country, and should be satisfied to see them tied in like manner in sacks, and thrown into the Thames." Other members spoke with as much want of temper and discretion. Mr. Walpole was more moderate. He recommended that their first care should be to restore public credit. "If the city of London were on fire, all wise men would aid in extinguishing the flames, and preventing the spread of the conflagration, before they inquired after the incendiaries. Public credit had received a dangerous wound, and lay bleeding, and they ought to apply a speedy remedy to it. It was time enough to punish the assassin afterwards." On the 9th of December an address, in answer to his majesty's speech, was agreed upon, after an amendment, which was carried without a division, that words should be added expressive of the determination of the house not only to seek a remedy for the national distresses, but to punish the authors of them.

*Britannia Stript By A South-Sea Director.*[23]

The inquiry proceeded rapidly. The directors were ordered to lay before the house a full account of all their proceedings. Resolutions were passed to the effect that the calamity was mainly owing to the vile arts of stock-jobbers, and that nothing could tend more to the reestablishment of public credit than a law to prevent this infamous practice. Mr. Walpole then rose, and said, that "as he had previously hinted, he had spent some time upon a scheme for restoring public credit, but that the execution of it depending upon a position which had been laid down as fundamental, he thought it proper, before he opened out his scheme, to be informed whether he might rely upon that foundation. It was, whether the subscription of public debts and encumbrances, money subscriptions, and other contracts, made with the South-Sea company, should remain in the present state?" This question occasioned an animated debate. It was finally agreed, by a majority of 259 against 117, that all these contracts should remain in their present state, unless altered for the relief of the proprietors by a general court of the South-Sea company, or set aside by due course of law. On the following day, Mr. Walpole laid before a committee of the whole house his scheme for the restoration of public credit, which was, in substance, to engraft nine millions of South-Sea stock into the Bank of England, and the same sum into the East India company, upon certain conditions. The plan was favourably received by the house. After some few objections, it was ordered that proposals should be received from the two great corporations. They were both unwilling to lend their aid, and the plan met with a warm but fruitless opposition at the general courts summoned for the purpose of deliberating upon it. They, however, ultimately agreed upon the terms on which they would consent to circulate the South-Sea bonds, and their report being presented to the committee, a bill was brought in under the superintendence of Mr. Walpole, and safely carried through both Houses of Parliament.

A bill was at the same time brought in for restraining the South-Sea directors, governor, sub-governor, treasurer, cashier, and clerks from leaving the kingdom for a twelvemonth, and for discovering their estates and effects, and preventing them from transporting or alienating the same. All the most influential members of the House supported the bill. Mr. Shippen, seeing Mr. Secretary Craggs in his place, and believing the injurious rumours that were afloat of that minister's conduct in the South-Sea business, determined to touch him to the quick. He said, he was glad to see a British House of Commons resuming its pristine vigour and spirit, and acting with so much unanimity for the public good. It was necessary to secure the persons and estates of the South-Sea directors and their officers; "but," he added, looking fixedly at Mr. Craggs as he spoke, "there were other men in high station, whom, in time, he would not be afraid to name, who were no less guilty than the directors." Mr. Craggs arose in great wrath, and said, that if the innuendo were directed against him, he was ready to give satisfaction to any man who questioned him, either in the House or out of it. Loud cries of order immediately arose on every side. In the midst of the uproar, Lord Molesworth got up, and expressed his wonder at the boldness of Mr. Craggs in challenging the whole House of Commons. He, Lord Molesworth, though somewhat old, past sixty, would answer Mr. Craggs whatever he had to say in the House, and he trusted there were plenty of young men beside him, who would not be afraid to look Mr. Craggs in the face out of the House. The cries of order again resounded from every side; the members arose simultaneously; every body seemed to be vociferating at once. The speaker in vain called order. The confusion lasted several minutes, during which Lord Molesworth and Mr. Craggs were almost the only members who kept their seats. At last, the call for Mr. Craggs became so violent, that he thought proper to submit to the universal feeling of the House, and explain his unparliamentary expression. He said, that by giving satisfaction to the impugners of his conduct in that House, he did not mean that he would fight, but that he would explain his conduct. Here the matter ended, and the House proceeded to debate in what manner they should conduct their inquiry into the affairs of the South-Sea company, whether in a grand or a select committee. Ultimately, a secret committee of thirteen was appointed, with power to send for persons, papers, and records.

The Lords were as zealous and as hasty as the Commons. The Bishop of Rochester said the scheme had been like a pestilence. The Duke of Wharton said the House ought to shew no respect of persons; that, for his part, he would give up the dearest friend he had, if he had been engaged in the project. The nation had been plundered in a most shameful and flagrant manner, and he would go as far as any body in the punishment of the offenders. Lord Stanhope said, that every farthing possessed by the criminals, whether directors or not directors, ought to be confiscated, to make good the public losses.

During all this time the public excitement was extreme. We learn from Coxe's *Walpole*, that the very name of a South-Sea director was thought to be synonymous with every species of fraud and villany. Petitions from counties, cities, and boroughs, in all parts of the kingdom, were presented, crying for the justice due to an injured nation and the punishment of the villanous peculators. Those moderate men, who would not go to extreme lengths, even in the punishment of the guilty, were accused of being accomplices, were exposed to repeated insults and virulent invectives, and devoted, both in anonymous letters and public writings, to the speedy vengeance of an injured people. The accusations against Mr. Aislabie, Chancellor of the Exchequer, and Mr. Craggs, another member of the ministry, were so loud, that the House of Lords resolved to proceed at once into the investigation concerning them. It was ordered, on the 21st of January, that all brokers concerned in the South-Sea scheme should lay before the House an account of the stock or subscriptions bought or sold by them for any of the officers of the Treasury or Exchequer, or in trust for any of them, since Michaelmas 1719. When this account was delivered, it appeared that large quantities of stock had been transferred to the use of Mr. Aislabie. Five of the South-Sea directors, including Mr. Edward Gibbon, the grandfather of the celebrated historian, were ordered into the custody of the black rod. Upon a motion made by Earl Stanhope, it was unanimously resolved, that the taking in or giving credit for stock without a valuable consideration actually paid or sufficiently secured; or the purchasing stock by any director or agent of the South-Sea company, for the use or benefit of any member of the administration, or any member of either House of Parliament, during such time as the South-Sea bill was yet pending in parliament, was a notorious and dangerous corruption. Another resolution was passed a few days afterwards, to the effect that several of the directors and officers of the company having, in a clandestine manner, sold their own stock to the company, had been guilty of a notorious fraud and breach of trust, and had thereby mainly caused the unhappy turn of affairs that had so much affected public credit. Mr. Aislabie resigned his office as Chancellor of the Exchequer, and absented himself from parliament, until the formal inquiry into his individual guilt was brought under the consideration of the legislature.

In the mean time, Knight, the treasurer of the company, and who was entrusted with all the dangerous secrets of the dishonest directors, packed up his books and documents, and made his escape from the country. He embarked in disguise, in a small boat on the river, and proceeding to a vessel hired for the purpose, was safely conveyed to Calais. The Committee of Secrecy informed the House of the circumstance, when it was resolved unanimously that two addresses should be presented to the king; the first praying that he would issue a proclamation offering a reward for the apprehension of Knight; and the second, that he would give immediate orders to stop the ports, and to take effectual care of the coasts, to prevent the said Knight, or any other officers of the South-Sea company, from escaping out of the kingdom. The ink was hardly dry upon these addresses before they were carried to the king by Mr. Methuen, deputed by the House for that purpose. The same evening a royal proclamation was issued, offering a reward of two thousand pounds for the apprehension of Knight. The Commons ordered the doors of the House to be locked, and the keys to be placed on the table. General Ross, one of the members of the Committee of Secrecy, acquainted them that they had already discovered a train of the deepest villany and fraud that hell had ever contrived to ruin a nation, which in due time they would lay before the House. In the mean time, in order to a further discovery, the Committee thought it highly necessary to secure the persons of some of the directors and principal South-Sea officers, and to seize their papers. A motion to this effect having been made, was carried unanimously. Sir Robert Chaplin, Sir Theodore Janssen, Mr. Sawbridge, and Mr. F. Eyles, members of the House, and directors of the South-Sea company, were summoned to appear in their places, and answer for their corrupt practices. Sir Theodore Janssen and Mr. Sawbridge answered to their names, and endeavoured to exculpate themselves. The House heard them patiently, and then ordered them to withdraw. A motion was then made, and carried *nemine contradicente*, that they had been guilty of a notorious breach of trust — had occasioned much loss to great numbers of his majesty's subjects, and had highly prejudiced the public credit. It was then ordered that, for their offence, they should be expelled the House, and taken into the custody of the sergeant-at-arms. Sir Robert Chaplin and Mr. Eyles, attending in their places four days afterwards, were also expelled the House. It was resolved at the same time to address the king to give directions to his ministers at foreign courts to make application for Knight, that he might be delivered up to the English authorities, in case he took refuge in any of their dominions. The king at once agreed, and messengers were despatched to all parts of the continent the same night.

Among the directors taken into custody was Sir John Blunt, the man whom popular opinion has generally accused of having been the original author and father of the scheme. This man, we are informed by Pope, in his epistle to Allen Lord Bathurst, was a dissenter, of a most religious deportment, and professed to be a great believer.[24] He constantly declaimed against the luxury and corruption of the age, the partiality of parliaments, and the misery of party spirit. He was particularly eloquent against avarice in great and noble persons. He was originally a scrivener, and afterwards became, not only a director, but the most active manager of the South-Sea company. Whether it was during his career in this capacity that he first began to declaim against the avarice of the great, we are not informed. He certainly must have seen enough of it to justify his severest anathema; but if the preacher had himself been free from the vice he condemned, his declamations would have had a better effect. He was brought up in custody to the bar of the House of Lords, and underwent a long examination. He refused to answer several important questions. He said he had been examined already by a committee of the House of Commons, and as he did not remember his answers, and might contradict himself, he refused to answer before another tribunal. This declaration, in itself an indirect proof of guilt, occasioned some commotion in the House. He was again asked peremptorily whether he had ever sold any portion of the stock to any member of the administration, or any member of either House of Parliament, to facilitate the passing of the bill. He again declined to answer. He was anxious, he said, to treat the House with all possible respect, but he thought it hard to be compelled to accuse himself. After several ineffectual attempts to refresh his memory, he was directed to withdraw. A violent discussion ensued between the friends and opponents of the ministry. It was asserted that the administration were no strangers to the convenient taciturnity of Sir John Blunt. The Duke of Wharton made a reflection upon the Earl Stanhope, which the latter warmly resented. He spoke under great excitement, and with such vehemence as to cause a sudden determination of blood to the head. He felt himself so ill that he was obliged to leave the House and retire to his chamber. He was cupped immediately, and also let blood on the following morning, but with slight relief. The fatal result was not anticipated. Towards evening he became drowsy, and turning himself on his face, expired. The sudden death of this statesman caused great grief to the nation. George I. was exceedingly affected, and shut himself up for some hours in his closet, inconsolable for his loss. Knight, the treasurer of the company, was apprehended at Tirlemont, near Liege, by one of the secretaries of Mr. Leathes, the British resident at Brussels, and lodged in the citadel of Antwerp. Repeated applications were made to the court of Austria to deliver him up, but in vain. Knight threw himself upon the protection of the states of Brabant, and demanded to be tried in that country. It was a privilege granted to the states of Brabant by one of the articles of the *Joyeuse Entrée*, that every criminal apprehended in that country should be tried in that country. The states insisted on their privilege, and refused to deliver Knight to the British authorities. The latter did not cease their solicitations; but in the mean time, Knight escaped from the citadel.

*Brabant Screen.*[25]

On the 16th of February the Committee of Secrecy made their first report to the House. They stated that their inquiry had been attended with numerous difficulties and embarrassments; every one they had examined had endeavoured, as far as in him lay, to defeat the ends of justice. In some of the books produced before them, false and fictitious entries had been made; in others, there were entries of money with blanks for the name of the stockholders. There were frequent erasures and alterations, and in some of the books leaves were torn out. They also found that some books of great importance had been destroyed altogether, and that some had been taken away or secreted. At the very entrance into their inquiry, they had observed that the matters referred to them were of great variety and extent. Many persons had been entrusted with various parts in the execution of the law, and under colour thereof had acted in an unwarrantable manner, in disposing of the properties of many thousands of persons amounting to many millions of money. They discovered that, before the South-Sea Act was passed, there was an entry in the company's books of the sum of 1,259,325l., upon account of stock stated to have been sold to the amount of 574,500l. This stock was all fictitious, and had been disposed of with a view to promote the passing of the bill. It was noted as sold on various days, and at various prices, from 150 to 325 per cent. Being surprised to see so large an account disposed of at a time when the company were not empowered to increase their capital, the Committee determined to investigate most carefully the whole transaction. The governor, sub-governor, and several directors were brought before them, and examined rigidly. They found that, at the time these entries were made, the company was not in possession of such a quantity of stock, having in their own right only a small quantity, not exceeding thirty thousand pounds at the utmost. Pursuing the inquiry, they found that this amount of stock was to be esteemed as taken in or holden by the company for the benefit of the pretended purchasers, although no mutual agreement was made for its delivery or acceptance at any certain time. No money was paid down, nor any deposit or security whatever given to the company by the supposed purchasers; so that if the stock had fallen, as might have been expected had the act not passed, they would have sustained no loss. If, on the contrary, the price of stock advanced (as it actually did by the success of the scheme), the difference by the advanced price was to be made good to them. Accordingly, after the passing of the act, the account of stock was made up and adjusted with Mr. Knight, and the pretended purchasers were paid the difference out of the company's cash. This fictitious stock, which had been chiefly at the disposal of Sir John Blunt, Mr. Gibbon, and Mr. Knight, was distributed among several members of the government and their connexions, by way of bribe, to facilitate the passing of the bill. To the Earl of Sunderland was assigned 50,000l. of this stock; to the Duchess of Kendal, 10,000l.; to the Countess of Platen, 10,000l.; to her two nieces, 10,000l.; to Mr. Secretary Craggs, 30,000l.; to Mr. Charles Stanhope (one of the secretaries of the Treasury), 10,000l.; to the Sword-blade company, 50,000l. It also appeared that Mr. Stanhope had received the enormous sum of 250,000l. as the difference in the price of some stock, through the hands of Turner, Caswall, and Co., but that his name had been partly erased from their books, and altered to Stangape. Aislabie, the Chancellor of the Exchequer, had made profits still more abominable. He had an account with the same firm, who were also South-Sea directors, to the amount of

794,451l. He had, besides, advised the company to make their second subscription one million and a half, instead of a million, by their own authority, and without any warrant. The third subscription had been conducted in a manner as disgraceful. Mr. Aislabie's name was down for 70,000l.; Mr. Craggs, senior, for 659,000l.; the Earl of Sunderland's for 160,000l.; and Mr. Stanhope for 47,000l. This report was succeeded by six others, less important. At the end of the last, the committee declared, that the absence of Knight, who had been principally entrusted, prevented them from carrying on their inquiries.

The first report was ordered to be printed, and taken into consideration on the next day but one succeeding. After a very angry and animated debate, a series of resolutions were agreed to, condemnatory of the conduct of the directors, of the members of the parliament and of the administration concerned with them; and declaring that they ought, each and all, to make satisfaction out of their own estates for the injury they had done the public. Their practices were declared to be corrupt, infamous, and dangerous; and a bill was ordered to be brought in for the relief of the unhappy sufferers.

*Bonfires On Tower Hill*

Mr. Charles Stanhope was the first person brought to account for his share in these transactions. He urged in his defence that, for some years past, he had lodged all the money he was possessed of in Mr. Knight's hands, and whatever stock Mr. Knight had taken in for him, he had paid a valuable consideration for it. As for the stock that had been bought for him by Turner, Caswall, and Co., he knew nothing about it. Whatever had been done in that matter was done without his authority, and he could not be responsible for it. Turner and Co. took the latter charge upon themselves; but it was notorious to every unbiassed and unprejudiced person that Mr. Stanhope was a gainer of the 250,000l. which lay in the hands of that firm to his credit. He was, however, acquitted by a majority of three only. The greatest exertions were made to screen him. Lord Stanhope, the son of the Earl of Chesterfield, went round to the wavering members, using all the eloquence he was possessed of to induce them either to vote for the acquittal, or to absent themselves from the House. Many weak-headed country gentlemen were led astray by his persuasions, and the result was as already stated. The acquittal caused the greatest discontent throughout the country. Mobs of a menacing character assembled in different parts of London; fears of riots were generally entertained, especially as the examination of a still greater delinquent was expected by many to have a similar termination. Mr. Aislabie, whose high office and deep responsibilities should have kept him honest, even had native principle been insufficient, was very justly regarded as perhaps the greatest criminal of all. His case was entered into on the day succeeding the acquittal of Mr. Stanhope. Great excitement prevailed, and the lobbies and avenues of the House were beset by crowds, impatient to know the result. The debate lasted the whole day. Mr. Aislabie found few friends: his guilt was so apparent and so heinous that nobody had courage to stand up in his favour. It was finally resolved, without a dissentient voice, that Mr. Aislabie had encouraged and promoted the destructive execution of the South-Sea scheme with a view to his own exorbitant profit, and had combined with the directors in their pernicious practices, to the ruin of the public trade and credit of the kingdom: that he should for his offences be ignominiously expelled from the House of Commons, and committed a close prisoner to the Tower of London; that he should be restrained from going out of the kingdom for a whole year, or till the end of the next session of Parliament; and that he should make out a correct account of all his estate, in order that it might be applied to the relief of those who had suffered by his mal-practices.

This verdict caused the greatest joy. Though it was delivered at half-past twelve at night, it soon spread over the city. Several persons illuminated their houses in token of their joy. On the following day, when Mr. Aislabie was conveyed to the Tower, the mob assembled on Tower-hill with the intention of hooting and pelting him. Not succeeding in this, they kindled a large bonfire, and danced around it in the exuberance of their delight. Several bonfires were made in other places; London presented the appearance of a holiday, and people congratulated one another as if they had just escaped from some great calamity. The rage upon the acquittal of Mr. Stanhope had grown to such a height that none could tell where it would have ended, had Mr. Aislabie met with the like indulgence.

To increase the public satisfaction, Sir George Caswall, of the firm of Turner, Caswall, and Co., was expelled from the House on the following day, committed to the Tower, and ordered to refund the sum of 250,000l.

*Earl of Sunderland.*

That part of the report of the Committee of Secrecy which related to the Earl of Sunderland was next taken into consideration. Every effort was made to clear his lordship from the imputation. As the case against him rested chiefly on the evidence extorted from Sir John Blunt, great pains were taken to make it appear that Sir John's word was not to be believed, especially in a matter affecting the honour of a peer and privy councillor. All the friends of the ministry rallied around the earl, it being generally reported that a verdict of guilty against him would bring a Tory ministry into power. He was eventually acquitted by a majority of 233 against 172; but the country was convinced of his guilt. The greatest indignation was every where expressed, and menacing mobs again assembled in London. Happily no disturbance took place.

This was the day on which Mr. Craggs the elder expired. The morrow had been appointed for the consideration of his case. It was very generally believed that he had poisoned himself. It appeared, however, that grief for the loss of his son, one of the secretaries of the Treasury, who had died five weeks previously of the small-pox, preyed much on his mind. For this son, dearly beloved, he had been amassing vast heaps of riches: he had been getting money, but not honestly; and he for whose sake he had bartered his honour and sullied his fame was now no more. The dread of further exposure increased his trouble of mind, and ultimately brought on an apoplectic fit, in which he expired. He left a fortune of a million and a half, which was afterwards confiscated for the benefit of the sufferers by the unhappy delusion he had been so mainly instrumental in raising.

One by one the case of every director of the company was taken into consideration. A sum amounting to two millions and fourteen thousand pounds was confiscated from their estates towards repairing the mischief they had done, each man being allowed a certain residue in proportion to his conduct and circumstances, with which he might begin the world anew. Sir John Blunt was only allowed 5,000l. out of his fortune of upwards of 183,000l.; Sir John Fellows was allowed 10,000l. out of 243,000l.; Sir Theodore Janssen, 50,000l. out of 243,000l.; Mr.

Edward Gibbon, 10,000l. out of 106,000l.; Sir John Lambert, 5000l. out of 72,000l. Others, less deeply involved, were treated with greater liberality. Gibbon, the historian, whose grandfather was the Mr. Edward Gibbon so severely mulcted, has given, in the *Memoirs of his Life and Writings*, an interesting account of the proceedings in parliament at this time. He owns that he is not an unprejudiced witness; but, as all the writers from which it is possible to extract any notice of the proceedings of these disastrous years were prejudiced on the other side, the statements of the great historian become of additional value. If only on the principle *audi alteram partem*, his opinion is entitled to consideration. "In the year 1716," he says, "my grandfather was elected one of the directors of the South-Sea company, and his books exhibited the proof that before his acceptance of that fatal office, he had acquired an independent fortune of 60,000l. But his fortune was overwhelmed in the shipwreck of the year 1720, and the labours of thirty years were blasted in a single day. Of the use or abuse of the South-Sea scheme, of the guilt or innocence of my grandfather and his brother directors, I am neither a competent nor a disinterested judge. Yet the equity of modern times must condemn the violent and arbitrary proceedings, which would have disgraced the cause of justice, and rendered injustice still more odious. No sooner had the nation awakened from its golden dream, than a popular and even a parliamentary clamour demanded its victims; but it was acknowledged on all sides, that the directors, however guilty, could not be touched by any known laws of the land. The intemperate notions of Lord Molesworth were not literally acted on; but a bill of pains and penalties was introduced — a retro-active statute, to punish the offences which did not exist at the time they were committed. The legislature restrained the persons of the directors, imposed an exorbitant security for their appearance, and marked their character with a previous note of ignominy. They were compelled to deliver, upon oath, the strict value of their estates, and were disabled from making any transfer or alienation of any part of their property. Against a bill of pains and penalties, it is the common right of every subject to be heard by his counsel at the bar. They prayed to be heard. Their prayer was refused, and their oppressors, who required no evidence, would listen to no defence. It had been at first proposed, that one-eighth of their respective estates should be allowed for the future support of the directors; but it was especially urged that, in the various shades of opulence and guilt, such a proportion would be too light for many, and for some might possibly be too heavy. The character and conduct of each man were separately weighed; but, instead of the calm solemnity of a judicial inquiry, the fortune and honour of thirty-three Englishmen were made the topics of hasty conversation, the sport of a lawless majority; and the basest member of the committee, by a malicious word or a silent vote, might indulge his general spleen or personal animosity. Injury was aggravated by insult, and insult was embittered by pleasantry. Allowances of 20l. or 1s. were facetiously moved. A vague report that a director had formerly been concerned in another project, by which some unknown persons had lost their money, was admitted as a proof of his actual guilt. One man was ruined because he had dropped a foolish speech, that his horses should feed upon gold; another, because he was grown so proud, that one day, at the Treasury, he had refused a civil answer to persons much above him. All were condemned, absent and unheard, in arbitrary fines and forfeitures, which swept away the greatest part of their substance. Such bold oppression can scarcely be shielded by the omnipotence of parliament. My grandfather could not expect to be treated with more lenity than his companions. His Tory principles and connexions rendered him obnoxious to the ruling powers. His name was reported in a suspicious secret. His well-known abilities could not plead the excuse of ignorance or error. In the first proceedings against the South-Sea directors, Mr. Gibbon was one of the first taken into custody, and in the final sentence the measure of his fine proclaimed him eminently guilty. The total estimate, which he delivered on oath to the House of Commons, amounted to 106,543l. 5s. 6d., exclusive of antecedent settlements. Two different allowances of 15,000l. and of 10,000l. were moved for Mr. Gibbon; but on the question being put, it was carried without a division for the smaller sum. On these ruins, with the skill and credit of which parliament had not been able to despoil him, my grandfather, at a mature age, erected the edifice of a new fortune. The labours of sixteen years were amply rewarded; and I have reason to believe that the second structure was not much inferior to the first."

*The South-Sea Bubble. – caricature by hogarth.*[26]

The next consideration of the legislature, after the punishment of the directors, was to restore public credit. The scheme of Walpole had been found insufficient, and had fallen into disrepute. A computation was made of the whole capital stock of the South-Sea company at the end of the year 1720. It was found to amount to thirty-seven millions eight hundred thousand pounds, of which the stock allotted to all the proprietors only amounted to twenty-four millions five hundred thousand pounds. The remainder of thirteen millions three hundred thousand pounds belonged to the company in their corporate capacity, and was the profit they had made by the national delusion. Upwards of eight millions of this were taken from the company, and divided among the proprietors and subscribers generally, making a dividend of about 33l. 6s. 8d. per cent. This was a great relief. It was further ordered, that such persons as had borrowed money from the South-Sea company upon stock actually transferred and pledged at the time of borrowing to or for the use of the company, should be free from all demands, upon payment of ten per cent of the sums so borrowed. They had lent about eleven millions in this manner, at a time when prices were unnaturally raised; and they now received back one million one hundred thousand, when prices had sunk to their ordinary level.

But it was a long time before public credit was thoroughly restored. Enterprise, like Icarus, had soared too high, and melted the wax of her wings; like Icarus, she had fallen into a sea, and learned, while floundering in its waves, that her proper element was the solid ground. She has never since attempted so high a flight.

In times of great commercial prosperity there has been a tendency to over-speculation on several occasions since then. The success of one project generally produces others of a similar kind. Popular imitativeness will always, in a trading nation, seize hold of such successes, and drag a community too anxious for profits into an abyss from which extrication is difficult. Bubble companies, of a kind similar to those engendered by the South-Sea project, lived their little day in the famous year of the panic, 1825. On that occasion, as in 1720, knavery gathered a rich harvest from cupidity, but both suffered when the day of reckoning came. The schemes of the year 1836 threatened, at one time, results as disastrous; but they were happily averted before it was too late.[27]

*Bubblers' arms — despair — from a print in the collection of e. Hawkins, esq.*

# Chapter 3.

The Tulipomania.

*Conrad Gesner.*

Quis furor, ô cives! — *Lucan.*

The tulip, — so named, it is said, from a Turkish word, signifying a turban, — was introduced into western Europe about the middle of the sixteenth century. Conrad Gesner, who claims the merit of having brought it into repute, — little dreaming of the commotion it was shortly afterwards to make in the world, — says that he first saw it in the year 1559, in a garden at Augsburg, belonging to the learned Counsellor Herwart, a man very famous in his day for his collection of rare exotics. The bulbs were sent to this gentleman by a friend at Constantinople, where the flower had long been a favourite. In the course of ten or eleven years after this period, tulips were much sought after by the wealthy, especially in Holland and Germany. Rich people at Amsterdam sent for the bulbs direct to Constantinople, and paid the most extravagant prices for them. The first roots planted in England were brought from Vienna in 1600. Until the year 1634 the tulip annually increased in reputation, until it was deemed a proof of bad taste in any man of fortune to be without a collection of them. Many learned men, including Pompeius de Angelis and the celebrated Lipsius of Leyden, the author of the treatise "De Constantia," were passionately fond of tulips. The rage for possessing them soon caught the middle classes of society, and merchants and shopkeepers, even of moderate means, began to vie with each other in the rarity of these flowers and the preposterous prices they paid for them. A trader at Harlaem was known to pay one-half of his fortune for a single root, not with the design of selling it again at a profit, but to keep in his own conservatory for the admiration of his acquaintance.

One would suppose that there must have been some great virtue in this flower to have made it so valuable in the eyes of so prudent a people as the Dutch; but it has neither the beauty nor the perfume of the rose — hardly the beauty of the "sweet, sweet-pea;" neither is it as enduring as either. Cowley, it is true, is loud in its praise. He says —

> *"The tulip next appeared, all over gay,*
> *But wanton, full of pride, and full of play;*
> *The world can't shew a dye but here has place;*
> *Nay, by new mixtures, she can change her face;*
> *Purple and gold are both beneath her care,*
> *The richest needlework she loves to wear;*
> *Her only study is to please the eye,*
> *And to outshine the rest in finery."*

This, though not very poetical, is the description of a poet. Beckmann, in his *History of Inventions*, paints it with more fidelity, and in prose more pleasing than Cowley's poetry. He says, "There are few plants which acquire, through accident, weakness, or disease, so many variegations as the tulip. When uncultivated, and in its natural state, it is almost of one colour, has large leaves, and an extraordinarily long stem. When it has been weakened by cultivation, it becomes more agreeable in the eyes of the florist. The petals are then paler, smaller, and more diversified in hue; and the leaves acquire a softer green colour. Thus this masterpiece of culture, the more beautiful it turns, grows so much the weaker, so that, with the greatest skill and most careful attention, it can scarcely be transplanted, or even kept alive."

Many persons grow insensibly attached to that which gives them a great deal of trouble, as a mother often loves her sick and ever-ailing child better than her more healthy offspring. Upon the same principle we must account for the unmerited encomia lavished upon these fragile blossoms. In 1634, the rage among the Dutch to possess them was so great that the ordinary industry of the country was neglected, and the population, even to its lowest dregs, embarked in the tulip trade. As the mania increased, prices augmented, until, in the year 1635, many persons were known to invest a fortune of 100,000 florins in the purchase of forty roots. It then became necessary to sell them by their weight in *perits*, a small weight less than a grain. A tulip of the species called *Admiral Liefken*, weighing 400 *perits*, was worth 4400 florins; an *Admiral Van der Eyck*, weighing 446 *perits*, was worth 1260 florins; a *Childer* of 106 *perits* was worth 1615 florins; a *Viceroy* of 400 *perits*, 3000 florins, and, most precious of all, a *Semper Augustus*, weighing 200 *perits*, was thought to be very cheap at 5500 florins. The latter was much sought after, and even an inferior bulb might command a price of 2000 florins. It is related that, at one time, early in 1636, there were only two roots of this description to be had in all Holland, and those not of the best. One was in the possession of a dealer in Amsterdam, and the other in Harlaem. So anxious were the speculators to obtain them, that one person offered the fee-simple of twelve acres of building-ground for the Harlaem tulip. That of Amsterdam was bought for 4600 florins, a new carriage, two grey horses, and a complete suit of harness. Hunting, an industrious author of that day, who wrote a folio volume of one thousand pages upon the tulipomania, has preserved the folio wing list of the various articles, and their value, which were delivered for one single root of the rare species called the *Viceroy*:

|  | florins. |
|---|---|
| Two lasts of wheat | 448 |

| | |
|---|---:|
| Four lasts of rye | 558 |
| Four fat oxen | 480 |
| Eight fat swine | 240 |
| Twelve fat sheep | 120 |
| Two hogsheads of wine | 70 |
| Four tuns of beer | 32 |
| Two tuns of butter | 192 |
| One thousand lbs. of cheese | 120 |
| A complete bed | 100 |
| A suit of clothes | 80 |
| A silver drinking-cup | 60 |
| | 2500 |

People who had been absent from Holland, and whose chance it was to return when this folly was at its maximum, were sometimes led into awkward dilemmas by their ignorance. There is an amusing instance of the kind related in Blainville's *Travels*. A wealthy merchant, who prided himself not a little on his rare tulips, received upon one occasion a very valuable consignment of merchandise from the Levant. Intelligence of its arrival was brought him by a sailor, who presented himself for that purpose at the counting-house, bales of goods of every description. The merchant, to reward him for his news, munificently made him a present of a fine red herring for his breakfast. The sailor had, it appears, a great partiality for onions, and seeing a bulb very like an onion lying upon the counter of this liberal trader, and thinking it, no doubt, very much out of its place among silks and velvets, he slily seized an opportunity and slipped it into his pocket, as a relish for his herring. He got clear off with his prize, and proceeded to the quay to eat his breakfast. Hardly was his back turned when the merchant missed his valuable *Semper Augustus*, worth three thousand florins, or about 280l. sterling. The whole establishment was instantly in an uproar; search was every where made for the precious root, but it was not to be found. Great was the merchant's distress of mind. The search was renewed, but again without success. At last some one thought of the sailor.

The unhappy merchant sprang into the street at the bare suggestion. His alarmed household followed him. The sailor, simple soul! had not thought of concealment. He was found quietly sitting on a coil of ropes, masticating the last morsel of his "*onion*". Little did he dream that he had been eating a breakfast whose cost might have regaled a whole ship's crew for a twelvemonth; or, as the plundered merchant himself expressed it, "might have sumptuously feasted the Prince of Orange and the whole court of the Stadtholder." Anthony caused pearls to be dissolved in wine to drink the health of Cleopatra; Sir Richard Whittington was as foolishly magnificent in an entertainment to King Henry V.; and Sir Thomas Gresham drank a diamond dissolved in wine to the health of Queen Elizabeth, when she opened the Royal Exchange; but the breakfast of this roguish Dutchman was as splendid as either. He had an advantage, too, over his wasteful predecessors: *their* gems did not improve the taste or the wholesomeness of *their* wine, while *his* tulip was quite delicious with his red herring. The most unfortunate part of the business for him was, that he remained in prison for some months on a charge of felony preferred against him by the merchant.

Another story is told of an English traveller, which is scarcely less ludicrous. This gentleman, an amateur botanist, happened to see a tulip-root lying in the conservatory of a wealthy Dutchman. Being ignorant of its quality, he took out his penknife, and peeled off its coats, with the view of making experiments upon it. When it was by this means reduced to half its size, he cut it into two equal sections, making all the time many learned remarks on the singular appearances of the unknown bulb. Suddenly, the owner pounced upon him, and, with fury in his eyes, asked him if he knew what he had been doing? "Peeling a most extraordinary onion," replied the philosopher. "*Hundert tausend duyvel!*" said the Duchman; "it's an *Admiral Van der Eyck*." "Thank you," replied the traveller, taking out his note-book to make a memorandum of the same; "are these admirals common in your country?" "Death and the devil!" said the Dutchman, seizing the astonished man of science by the collar; "come before the syndic, and you shall see." In spite of his remonstrances, the traveller was led through the streets followed by a mob of persons. When brought into the presence of the magistrate, he learned, to his consternation, that the root upon which he had been experimentalising was worth four thousand florins; and, notwithstanding all he could urge in extenuation, he was lodged in prison until he found securities for the payment of this sum.

The demand for tulips of a rare species increased so much in the year 1636, that regular marts for their sale were established on the Stock Exchange of Amsterdam, in Rotterdam, Harlaem, Leyden, Alkmar, Hoorn, and other towns. Symptoms of gambling now became, for the first time, apparent. The stock-jobbers, ever on the alert for a new speculation, dealt largely in tulips, making use of all the means they so well knew how to employ, to cause fluctuations in prices. At first, as in all these gambling mania, confidence was at its height, and every body gained. The tulip-jobbers speculated in the rise and fall of the tulip stocks, and made large profits by buying when prices fell, and selling out when they rose. Many individuals grew suddenly rich. A golden bait hung temptingly out before the people, and one after the other, they rushed to the tulip-marts, like flies around a honey-pot. Every one imagined that the passion for tulips would last for ever, and that the wealthy from every part of the world would send to Holland, and pay whatever prices were asked for them. The riches of Europe would be concentrated on the shores of the Zuyder Zee, and poverty banished from the favoured clime of Holland. Nobles, citizens, farmers, mechanics, sea-men, footmen, maid-servants, even chimney-sweeps and old clothes-women, dabbled in tulips. People of all grades converted their property into cash, and invested it in flowers. Houses and lands were offered for sale at ruinously low prices, or assigned in payment of bargains made at the tulip-mart. Foreigners became smitten with the same frenzy, and money poured into Holland from all directions. The prices of the necessaries of life rose again by degrees: houses and lands, horses and carriages, and luxuries of every sort, rose in value with them, and for some months Holland seemed the very antechamber of Plutus. The operations of the trade became so extensive and so intricate, that it was found necessary to draw up a code of laws for the guidance of the dealers. Notaries and clerks were also appointed, who devoted themselves exclusively to the interests of the trade. The designation of public notary was hardly known in some towns, that of tulip-notary usurping its place. In the smaller towns, where there was no exchange, the principal tavern was usually selected as the "show-place," where high and low traded in tulips, and confirmed their bargains over sumptuous entertainments. These dinners were sometimes attended by two or three hundred persons, and large vases of tulips, in full bloom, were placed at regular intervals upon the tables and sideboards for their gratification during the repast.

At last, however, the more prudent began to see that this folly could not last for ever. Rich people no longer bought the flowers to keep them in their gardens, but to sell them again at cent per cent profit. It was seen that somebody must lose fearfully in the end. As this conviction spread, prices fell, and never rose again. Confidence was destroyed, and a universal panic seized upon the dealers. *A* had agreed to purchase ten *Semper Augustines* from *B*, at four thousand florins each, at six weeks after the signing of the contract. *B* was ready with the flowers at the appointed time; but the price had fallen to three or four hundred florins, and *A* refused either to pay the difference or receive the tulips. Defaulters were announced day after day in all the towns of Holland. Hundreds who, a few months previously, had begun to doubt that there was such a thing as poverty in the land, suddenly found themselves the possessors of a few bulbs, which nobody would buy, even though they offered them at one quarter of the sums they had paid for them. The cry of distress resounded every where, and each man accused his neighbour. The few who had contrived to enrich themselves hid their wealth from the knowledge of their fellow-citizens, and invested it in the English or other funds. Many who, for a brief season, had emerged from the humbler walks of life, were cast back into their original obscurity. Substantial merchants were reduced almost to beggary, and many a representative of a noble line saw the fortunes of his house ruined beyond redemption.

When the first alarm subsided, the tulip-holders in the several towns held public meetings to devise what measures, were best to be taken to restore public credit. It was generally agreed, that deputies should be sent from all parts to Amsterdam, to consult with the government upon some remedy for the evil. The government at first refused to interfere, but advised the tulip-holders to agree to some plan among themselves. Several meetings were held for this purpose; but no measure could be devised likely to give satisfaction to the deluded people, or repair even a slight portion of the mischief that had been done. The language of complaint and reproach was in every body's mouth, and all the meetings were of the most stormy character. At last, however, after much bickering and ill-will, it was agreed, at Amsterdam, by the assembled deputies, that all contracts made in the height of the mania, or prior to the month of November 1636, should be declared null and void, and that, in those made after that date, purchasers should be freed from their engagements, on paying ten per cent to the vendor. This decision gave no satisfaction. The vendors who had their tulips on hand were, of course, discontented, and those who had pledged themselves to purchase, thought themselves hardly treated. Tulips which had, at one time, been worth six thousand florins, were now to be procured for five hundred; so that the composition of ten per cent was one hundred florins more than the actual value. Actions for breach of contract were threatened in all the courts of the country; but the latter refused to take cognisance of gambling transactions.

The matter was finally referred to the Provincial Council at the Hague, and it was confidently expected that the wisdom of this body would invent some measure by which credit should be restored. Expectation was on the stretch for its decision, but it never came. The members continued to deliberate week after week, and at last, after thinking about it for three months, declared that they could offer no final decision until they had more information. They advised, however, that, in the mean time, every vendor should, in the presence of witnesses, offer the tulips *in natura* to the purchaser for the sums agreed upon. If the latter refused to take them, they might be put up for sale by public auction, and the original contractor held responsible for the difference between the actual and the stipulated price. This was exactly the plan recommended by the deputies, and which was already shewn to be of no avail. There was no court in Holland which would enforce payment. The question was raised in Amsterdam, but the judges unanimously refused to interfere, on the ground that debts contracted in gambling were no debts in law.

Thus the matter rested. To find a remedy was beyond the power of the government. Those who were unlucky enough to have had stores of tulips on hand at the time of the sudden reaction were left to bear their ruin as philosophically as they could; those who had made profits were allowed to keep them; but the commerce of the country suffered a severe shock, from which it was many years ere it recovered.

The example of the Dutch was imitated to some extent in England. In the year 1636 tulips were publicly sold in the Exchange of London, and the jobbers exerted themselves to the utmost to raise them to the fictitious value they had acquired in Amsterdam. In Paris also the jobbers strove to create a tulipomania. In both cities they only partially succeeded. However, the force of example brought the flowers into great favour, and amongst a certain class of people tulips have ever since been prized more highly than any other flowers of the field. The Dutch are still notorious for their partiality to them, and continue to pay higher prices for them than any other people. As the rich Englishman boasts of his fine race-horses or his old pictures, so does the wealthy Dutchman vaunt him of his tulips.

In England, in our day, strange as it may appear, a tulip will produce more money than an oak. If one could be found, *rara in terris*, and black as the black swan of Juvenal, its price would equal that of a dozen acres of standing corn. In Scotland, towards the close of the seventeenth century, the highest price for tulips, according to the authority of a writer in the supplement to the third edition of the *Encyclopedia Britannica*, was ten guineas. Their value appears to have diminished from that time till the year 1769, when the two most valuable species in England were the *Don Quevedo* and the *Valentinier*, the former of which was worth two guineas and the latter two guineas and a half. These prices appear to have been the minimum. In the year 1800, a common price was fifteen guineas for a single bulb. In 1835, a bulb of the species called the Miss Fanny Kemble was sold by public auction in London for seventy-five pounds. Still more remarkable was the price of a tulip in the possession of a gardener in the King's Road, Chelsea; — in his catalogues it was labelled at two hundred guineas.

# Chapter 4.

The Alchymists;

or

Searchers for the philosopher's stone and the water of life.

*Mercury (loquitur). The mischief a secret any of them know, above the consuming of coals and drawing of usquebaugh! howsoever they may pretend, under the specious names of Geber, Arnold, Lulli, or bombast of Hohenheim, to commit miracles in art, and treason against nature! As if the title of philosopher, that creature of glory, were to be fetched out of a furnace! I am their crude and their sublimate, their precipitate and their unctions; their male and their female, sometimes their hermaphrodite – what they list to style me! They will calcine you a grave matron, as it might be a mother of the maids, and spring up a young virgin out of her ashes, as fresh as a phœnix; lay you an old courtier on the coals, like a sausage or a bloat-herring, and, after they have broiled him enough, blow a soul into him with a pair of bellows! See, they begin to muster again, and draw their forces out against me! The genius of the place defend me!*

*Ben Jonson's Masque: Mercury vindicated from the Alchymists.*

Dissatisfaction with his lot seems to be the characteristic of man in all ages and climates. So far, however, from being an evil, as at first might be supposed, it has been the great civiliser of our race; and has tended, more than any thing else, to raise us above the condition of the brutes. But the same discontent which has been the source of all improvement, has been the parent of no small progeny of follies and absurdities; to trace these latter is our present object. Vast as the subject appears, it is easily reducible within such limits as will make it comprehensive without being wearisome, and render its study both instructive and amusing. Three causes especially have excited the discontent of mankind; and, by impelling us to seek for remedies for the irremediable, have bewildered us in a maze of madness and error. These are death, toil, and ignorance of the future—the doom of man upon this sphere, and for which he shews his antipathy by his love of life, his longing for abundance, and his craving curiosity to pierce the secrets of the days to come. The first has led many to imagine that they might find means to avoid death, or failing in this, that they might, nevertheless, so prolong existence as to reckon it by centuries instead of units. From this sprang the search, so long continued and still pursued, for the *elixir vitæ*, or *water of life*, which has led thousands to pretend to it and millions to believe in it. From the second sprang the search for the philosopher's stone, which was to create plenty by changing all metals into gold; and from the third, the false sciences of astrology, divination, and their divisions of necromancy, chiromancy, augury, with all their train of signs, portents, and omens. In tracing the career of the erring philosophers, or the wilful cheats, who have encouraged or preyed upon the credulity of mankind, it will simplify and elucidate the subject, if we divide it into three classes: the first comprising alchymists, or those in general who have devoted themselves to the discovering of the philosopher's stone and the water of life; the second comprising astrologers, necromancers, sorcerers, geomancers, and all those who pretended to discover futurity; and the third consisting of the dealers in charms, amulets, philters, universal-panacea mongers, touchers for the evil, seventh sons of a seventh son, sympathetic powder compounders, homœopathists, animal magnetisers, and all the motley tribe of quacks, empirics, and charlatans.

But in narrating the career of such men, it will be found that many of them united several or all of the functions just mentioned; that the alchymist was a fortune-teller, or a necromancer — that he pretended to cure all maladies by touch or charm, and to work miracles of every kind. In the dark and early ages of European history this is more especially the case. Even as we advance to more recent periods, we shall find great difficulty in separating the characters. The alchymist seldom confined himself strictly to his pretended science — the sorcerer and necromancer to theirs, or the medical charlatan to his. Beginning with alchymy, some confusion of these classes is unavoidable; but the ground will clear for us as we advance.

Let us not, in the pride of our superior knowledge, turn with contempt from the follies of our predecessors. The study of the errors into which great minds have fallen in the pursuit of truth can never be uninstructive. As the man looks back to the days of his childhood and his youth, and recalls to his mind the strange notions and false opinions that swayed his actions at that time, that he may wonder at them; so should society, for its edification, look back to the opinions which governed the ages fled. He is but a superficial thinker who would despise and refuse to hear of them merely because they are absurd. No man is so wise but that he may learn some wisdom from his past errors, either of thought or action; and no society has made such advances as to be capable of no improvement from the retrospect of its past folly and credulity. And not only is such a study instructive: he who reads for amusement only will find no chapter in the annals of the human mind more amusing than this. It opens out the whole realm of fiction — the wild, the fantastic, and the wonderful, and all the immense variety of things "that are not, and cannot be; but that have been imagined and believed."

For more than a thousand years the art of alchymy captivated many noble spirits, and was believed in by millions. Its origin is involved in obscurity. Some of its devotees have claimed for it an antiquity coeval with the creation of man himself, others, again, would trace it no further back than the time of Noah. Vincent de Beauvais argues, indeed, that all the antediluvians must have possessed a knowledge of alchymy; and particularly cites Noah as having been acquainted with the *elixir vitæ*, or he could not have lived to so prodigious an age, and have begotten children when upwards of five hundred. Lenglet du Fresnoy, in his *History of the Hermetic Philosophy*, says, "Most of them pretended that Shem, or Chem, the son of Noah, was an adept in the art, and thought it highly probable that the words *chemistry* and *alchymy* are both derived from his name." Others say, the art was derived from the Egyptians, amongst whom it was first founded by Hermes Trismegistus. Moses, who is looked upon as a first-rate alchymist, gained his knowledge in Egypt; but he kept it all to himself, and would not instruct the children of Israel in its mysteries. All the writers upon alchymy triumphantly cite the story of the golden calf, in the 32d chapter of Exodus, to prove that this great lawgiver was an adept, and could make or unmake gold at his pleasure. It is recorded, that Moses was so wrath with the Israelites for their idolatry, "that he took the calf which they had made, and burned it in the fire, and ground it to powder, and strewed it upon the water, and made the children of Israel drink of it." This, say the alchymists, he never could have done had he not been in possession of the philosopher's stone; by no other means could he have made the powder of gold float upon the water. But we must leave this knotty point for the consideration of the adepts in the art, if any such there be, and come to more modern periods of its history. The Jesuit, Father Martini, in his *Historia Sinica*, says, it was practised by the Chinese two thousand five hundred years before the birth of Christ; but his assertion, being unsupported, is worth nothing. It would appear, however, that pretenders to the art of making gold and silver existed in Rome in the first centuries after the Christian era, and that, when discovered, they were liable to punishment as knaves and impostors. At Constantinople, in the fourth century, the transmutation of metals was very generally believed in, and many of the Greek ecclesiastics wrote treatises upon the subject. Their names are preserved, and some notice of their works given, in the third volume of Langlet du Fresnoy's *History of the Hermetic Philosophy*. Their notion appears to have been, that all metals were composed of two substances; the one, metallic earth; and the other, a red inflammable matter, which they called sulphur. The pure union of these substances formed gold; but other metals were mixed with and contaminated by various foreign ingredients. The object of the philosopher's stone was to dissolve or neutralise all these ingredients, by which iron, lead, copper, and all metals would be transmuted into the original gold. Many learned and clever men wasted their time, their health, and their energies, in this vain pursuit; but for several centuries it took no great hold upon the imagination of the people. The history of the delusion appears, in a manner, lost from this time till the eighth century, when it appeared amongst the Arabians. From this period it becomes easier to trace its progress. A master then appeared, who was long looked upon as the father of the science, and whose name is indissolubly connected with it.

## Geber.

Of this philosopher, who devoted his life to the study of alchymy, but few particulars are known. He is thought to have lived in the year 730. His true name was Abou Moussah Djafar, to which was added Al Sofi, or "The Wise," and he was born at Houran, in Mesopotamia.[28] Some have thought he was a Greek, others a Spaniard, and others a prince of Hindostan; but of all the mistakes which have been made respecting him, the most ludicrous was that made by the French translator of Sprenger's *History of Medicine*, who thought, from the sound of his name, that he was a German, and rendered it as the "Donnateur," or Giver. No details of his life are known; but it is asserted, that he wrote more than five hundred works upon the philosopher's stone and the water of life. He was a great enthusiast in his art, and compared the incredulous to little children shut up in a narrow room, without windows or aperture, who, because they saw nothing beyond, denied the existence of the great globe itself. He thought that a preparation of gold would cure all maladies, not only in man, but in the inferior animals and plants. He also imagined that all the metals laboured under disease, with the exception of gold, which was the only one in perfect health. He affirmed, that the secret of the philosopher's stone had been more than once discovered; but that the ancient and wise men who had hit upon it would never, by word or writing, communicate it to men, because of their unworthiness and incredulity.[29] But the life of Geber, though spent in the pursuit of this vain chimera, was not altogether useless. He stumbled upon discoveries which he did not seek; and science is indebted to him for the first mention of corrosive sublimate, the red oxide of mercury, nitric acid, and the nitrate of silver.[30]

For more than two hundred years after the death of Geber, the Arabian philosophers devoted themselves to the study of alchymy, joining with it that of astrology. Of these the most celebrated was

### Alfarabi.

Alfarabi flourished at the commencement of the tenth century, and enjoyed the reputation of being one of the most learned men of his age. He spent his life in travelling from country to country, that he might gather the opinions of philosophers upon the great secrets of nature. No danger dismayed him; no toil wearied him of the pursuit. Many sovereigns endeavoured to retain him at their courts; but he refused to rest until he had discovered the great object of his life — the art of preserving it for centuries, and of making gold as much as he needed. This wandering mode of life at last proved fatal to him. He had been on a visit to Mecca, not so much for religious as for philosophical purposes, when, returning through Syria, he stopped at the court of the Sultan Seifeddoulet, who was renowned as the patron of learning. He presented himself in his travelling attire in the presence of that monarch and his courtiers; and, without invitation, coolly sat himself down on the sofa beside the prince. The courtiers and wise men were indignant; and the sultan, who did not know the intruder, was at first inclined to follow their example. He turned to one of his officers, and ordered him to eject the presumptuous stranger from the room; but Alfarabi, without moving, dared them to lay hands upon him; and, turning himself calmly to the prince, remarked, that he did not know who was his guest, or he would treat him with honour, not with violence. The sultan, instead of being still further incensed, as many potentates would have been, admired his coolness; and, requesting him to sit still closer to him on the sofa, entered into a long conversation with him upon science and divine philosophy. All the court were charmed with the stranger. Questions for discussion were propounded, on all of which he shewed superior knowledge. He convinced every one who ventured to dispute with him; and spoke so eloquently upon the science of alchymy, that he was at once recognised as only second to the great Geber himself. One of the doctors present inquired whether a man who knew so many sciences was acquainted with music? Alfarabi made no reply, but merely requested that a lute should be brought him. The lute was brought; and he played such ravishing and tender melodies, that all the court were melted into tears. He then changed his theme, and played airs so sprightly, that he set the grave philosophers, sultan and all, dancing as fast as their legs could carry them. He then sobered them again by a mournful strain, and made them sob and sigh as if broken-hearted. The sultan, highly delighted with his powers, entreated him to stay, offering him every inducement that wealth, power, and dignity could supply; but the alchymist resolutely refused, it being decreed, he said, that he should never repose till he had discovered the philosopher's stone. He set out accordingly the same evening, and was murdered by some thieves in the deserts of Syria. His biographers give no further particulars of his life beyond mentioning that he wrote several valuable treatises on his art, all of which, however, have been lost. His death happened in the year 954.

## Avicenna.

Avicenna, whose real name was Ebn Cinna, another great alchymist, was born at Bokhara in 980. His reputation as a physician and a man skilled in all sciences was so great, that the Sultan Magdal Douleth resolved to try his powers in the great science of government. He was accordingly made Grand Vizier of that prince, and ruled the state with some advantage; but in a science still more difficult, he failed completely. He could not rule his own passions, but gave himself up to wine and women, and led a life of shameless debauchery. Amid the multifarious pursuits of business and pleasure, he nevertheless found time to write seven treatises upon the philosopher's stone, which were for many ages looked upon as of great value by pretenders to the art. It is rare that an eminent physician as Avicenna appears to have been, abandons himself to sensual gratification; but so completely did he become enthralled in the course of a few years, that he was dismissed from his high office, and died shortly afterwards of premature old age and a complication of maladies, brought on by debauchery. His death took place in the year 1036. After his time few philosophers of any note in Arabia are heard of as devoting themselves to the study of alchymy; but it began shortly afterwards to attract greater attention in Europe. Learned men in France, England, Spain, and Italy, expressed their belief in the science, and many devoted their whole energies to it. In the twelfth and thirteenth centuries especially, it was extensively pursued, and some of the brightest names of that age are connected with it. Among the most eminent of them are

## Albertus Magnus and Thomas Aquinas.

The first of these philosophers was born in the year 1193, of a noble family at Lawingen, in the Duchy of Neuburg, on the Danube. For the first thirty years of his life he appeared remarkably dull and stupid, and it was feared by every one that no good could come of him. He entered a Dominican monastery at an early age; but made so little progress in his studies, that he was more than once upon the point of abandoning them in despair, but he was endowed with extraordinary perseverance. As he advanced to middle age, his mind expanded, and he learned whatever he applied himself to with extreme facility. So remarkable a change was not in that age to be accounted for but by a miracle. It was asserted and believed that the Holy Virgin, touched with his great desire to become learned and famous, took pity upon his incapacity, and appeared to him in the cloister where he sat almost despairing, and asked him whether he wished to excel in philosophy or divinity. He chose philosophy, to the chagrin of the Virgin, who reproached him in mild and sorrowful accents that he had not made a better choice. She, however, granted his request, that he should become the most excellent philosopher of the age; but set this drawback to his pleasure, that he should relapse, when at the height of his fame, into his former incapacity and stupidity. Albertus never took the trouble to contradict the story, but prosecuted his studies with such unremitting zeal, that his reputation speedily spread over all Europe. In the year 1244, the celebrated Thomas Aquinas placed himself under his tuition. Many extraordinary stories are told of the master and his pupil. While they paid all due attention to other branches of science, they never neglected the pursuit of the philosopher's stone and the *elixir vitæ*. Although they discovered neither, it was believed that Albert had seized some portion of the secret of life, and found means to animate a brazen statue, upon the formation of which, under proper conjunctions of the planets, he had been occupied many years of his life. He and Thomas Aquinas completed it together, endowed it with the faculty of speech, and made it perform the functions of a domestic servant. In this capacity it was exceedingly useful; but, through some defect in the machinery, it chattered much more than was agreeable to either philosopher. Various remedies were tried to cure it of its garrulity, but in vain; and one day, Thomas Aquinas was so enraged at the noise it made when he was in the midst of a mathematical problem, that he seized a ponderous hammer and smashed it to pieces.[31] He was sorry afterwards for what he had done, and was reproved by his master for giving way to his anger, so unbecoming in a philosopher. They made no attempt to re-animate the statue.

*Albertus Magnus.*

Such stories as these shew the spirit of the age. Every great man who attempted to study the secrets of nature was thought a magician; and it is not to be wondered at that, when philosophers themselves pretended to discover an elixir for conferring immortality, or a red stone which was to create boundless wealth, that popular opinion should have enhanced upon their pretensions, and have endowed them with powers still more miraculous. It was believed of Albertus Magnus that he could even change the course of the seasons, a feat which the many thought less difficult than the discovery of the grand elixir. Albertus was desirous of obtaining a piece of ground on which to build a monastery in the neighbourhood of Cologne. The ground belonged to William Count of Holland and King of the Romans, who for some reason or other did not wish to part with it. Albertus is reported to have gained it by the following extraordinary method: He invited the prince as he was passing through Cologne to a magnificent entertainment prepared for him and all his court. The prince accepted it, and repaired with a lordly retinue to the residence of the sage. It was in the midst of winter, the Rhine was frozen over, and the cold was so bitter, that the knights could not sit on horseback without running the risk of losing their toes by the frost. Great, therefore, was their surprise, on arriving at Albert's house, to find that the repast was spread in his garden, in which the snow had drifted to the depth of several feet. The earl in high dudgeon remounted his steed, but Albert at last prevailed upon him to take his seat at the table. He had no sooner done so, than the dark clouds rolled away from the sky — a warm sun shone forth — the cold north wind veered suddenly round and blew a mild breeze from the south — the snows melted away — the ice was unbound upon the streams, and the trees put forth their green leaves and their fruit — flowers sprang up beneath their feet, while larks, nightingales, black-birds, cuckoos, thrushes, and every sweet song-bird sang hymns from every tree. The earl and his attendants wondered greatly; but they ate their dinner, and in recompense for it, Albert got his piece of ground to build a convent on. He had not, however, shewn them all his power. Immediately that the repast was over, he gave the word, and dark clouds obscured the sun — the snow fell in large flakes — the singing-birds fell dead — the leaves dropped from the trees, and the winds blew so cold and howled so mournfully, that the guests wrapped themselves up in their thick cloaks, and retreated into the house to warm themselves at the blazing fire in Albert's kitchen.[32]

Thomas Aquinas also could work wonders as well as his master. It is related of him that he lodged in a street at Cologne, where he was much annoyed by the incessant clatter made by the horses' hoofs, as they were led through it daily to exercise by their grooms. He had entreated the latter to select some other spot, where they might not disturb a philosopher; but the grooms turned a deaf ear to all his solicitations. In this emergency he had recourse to the aid of magic. He constructed a small horse of bronze, upon which he inscribed certain cabalistic characters, and buried it at midnight in the midst of the highway. The next morning a troop of grooms came riding along as usual; but the horses, as they arrived at the spot where the magic horse was buried, reared and plunged violently — their nostrils distended with terror — their manes grew erect, and the perspiration ran down their sides in streams. In vain the riders applied the spur — in vain they coaxed or threatened, the animals would not pass the spot. On the following day their success was no better. They were at length compelled to seek another spot for their exercise, and Thomas Aquinas was left in peace.[33]

Albertus Magnus was made Bishop of Ratisbon in 1259; but he occupied the see only four years, when he resigned, on the ground that its duties occupied too much of the time which he was anxious to devote to philosophy. He died in Cologne in 1280, at the advanced age of eighty-seven. The Dominican writers deny that he ever sought the philosopher's stone, but his treatise upon minerals sufficiently proves that he did.

### Artephius.

Artephius, a name noted in the annals of alchymy, was born in the early part of the twelfth century. He wrote two famous treatises; the one upon the philosopher's stone, and the other on the art of prolonging human life. In the latter he vaunts his great qualifications for instructing mankind on such a matter, as he was at that time in the thousand and twenty-fifth year of his age! He had many disciples who believed in his extreme age, and who attempted to prove that he was Apollonius of Tyana, who lived soon after the advent of Jesus Christ, and the particulars of whose life and pretended miracles have been so fully described by Philostratus. He took good care never to contradict a story which so much increased the power he was desirous of wielding over his fellow-mortals. On all convenient occasions, he boasted of it; and having an excellent memory, a fertile imagination, and a thorough knowledge of all existing history, he was never at a loss for an answer when questioned as to the personal appearance, the manners, or the character of the great men of antiquity. He also pretended to have found the philosopher's stone; and said that, in search of it, he had descended to hell, and seen the devil sitting on a throne of gold, with a legion of imps and fiends around him. His works on alchymy have been translated into French, and were published in Paris in 1609 or 1610.

### Alain de Lisle.

Contemporary with Albertus Magnus was Alain de Lisle of Flanders, who was named, from his great learning, the "universal doctor." He was thought to possess a knowledge of all the sciences, and, like Artephius, to have discovered the *elixir vitæ*. He became one of the friars of the abbey of Citeaux, and died in 1298, aged about one hundred and ten years. It was said of him that he was at the point of death when in his fiftieth year, but that the fortunate discovery of the elixir enabled him to add sixty years to his existence. He wrote a commentary on the prophecies of Merlin.

### Arnold de Villeneuve.

This philosopher has left a much greater reputation. He was born in the year 1245, and studied medicine with great success in the university of Paris. He afterwards travelled for twenty years in Italy and Germany, where he made acquaintance with Pietro d'Apone, a man of a character akin to his own, and addicted to the same pursuits. As a physician, he was thought, in his own lifetime, to be the most able the world had ever seen. Like all the learned men of that day, he dabbled in astrology and alchymy, and was thought to have made immense quantities of gold from lead and copper. When Pietro d'Apone was arrested in Italy, and brought to trial as a sorcerer, a similar accusation was made against Arnold; but he managed to leave the country in time, and escape the fate of his unfortunate friend. He lost some credit by predicting the end of the world, but afterwards regained it. The time of his death is not exactly known; but it must have been prior to the year 1311, when Pope Clement V. wrote a circular letter to all the clergy of Europe who lived under his obedience, praying them to use their utmost efforts to discover the famous treatise of Arnold on *The Practice of Medicine*. The author had promised, during his lifetime, to make a present of the work to the Holy See, but died without fulfilling it.

*Arnold de Villeneuve.*

In a very curious work by Monsieur Longeville Harcouet, entitled *The History of the Persons who have lived several centuries and then grown young again*, there is a receipt, said to have been given by Arnold de Villeneuve, by means of which any one might prolong his life for a few hundred years or so. In the first place, say Arnold and Monsieur Harcouet, "the person intending so to prolong his life must rub himself well, two or three times a week, with the juice or marrow of cassia (*moëlle de la casse*). Every night, upon going to bed, he must put upon his heart a plaster, composed of a certain quantity of oriental saffron, red rose-leaves, sandal-wood, aloes, and amber, liquified in oil of roses and the best white wax. In the morning, he must take it off, and enclose it carefully in a leaden box till the next night, when it must be again applied. If he be of a sanguine temperament, he shall take sixteen chickens; if phlegmatic, twenty-five; and if melancholy, thirty, which he shall put into a yard where the air and the water are pure. Upon these he is to feed, eating one a day; but previously the chickens are to be fattened by a peculiar method, which will impregnate their flesh with the qualities that are to produce longevity in the eater. Being deprived of all other nourishment till they are almost dying of hunger, they are to be fed upon broth made of serpents and vinegar, which broth is to be thickened with wheat and bran." Various ceremonies are to be performed in the cooking of this mess, which those may see in the book of M. Harcouet who are at all interested in the matter;

and the chickens are to be fed upon it for two months. They are then fit for table, and are to be washed down with moderate quantities of good white wine or claret. This regimen is to be followed regularly every seven years, and any one may live to be as old as Methuselah! It is right to state that M. Harcouet has but little authority for attributing this precious composition to Arnold of Villeneuve. It is not found in the collected works of that philosopher; but was first brought to light by a M. Poirier, at the commencement of the sixteenth century, who asserted that he had discovered it in MS. in the undoubted writing of Arnold.

## Pietro d'Apone.

This unlucky sage was born at Apone, near Padua, in the year 1250. Like his friend Arnold de Villeneuve, he was an eminent physician, and a pretender to the arts of astrology and alchymy. He practised for many years in Paris, and made great wealth by killing and curing, and telling fortunes. In an evil day for him, he returned to his own country, with the reputation of being a magician of the first order. It was universally believed that he had drawn seven evil spirits from the infernal regions, whom he kept enclosed in seven crystal vases until he required their services, when he sent them forth to the ends of the earth to execute his pleasure. One spirit excelled in philosophy; a second, in alchymy; a third, in astrology; a fourth, in physic; a fifth, in poetry; a sixth, in music; and the seventh, in painting: and whenever Pietro wished for information or instruction in any of these arts, he had only to go to his crystal vase and liberate the presiding spirit. Immediately all the secrets of the art were revealed to him; and he might, if it pleased him, excel Homer in poetry, Apelles in painting, or Pythagoras himself in philosophy. Although he could make gold out of brass, it was said of him that he was very sparing of his powers in that respect, and kept himself constantly supplied with money by other and less creditable means. Whenever he disbursed gold, he muttered a certain charm, known only to himself, and next morning the gold was safe again in his own possession. The trader to whom he gave it might lock it in his strong box and have it guarded by a troop of soldiers, but the charmed metal flew back to its old master. Even if it were buried in the earth, or thrown into the sea, the dawn of the next morning would behold it in the pockets of Pietro. Few people, in consequence, liked to have dealings with such a personage, especially for gold. Some, bolder than the rest, thought that his power did not extend over silver; but, when they made the experiment, they found themselves mistaken. Bolts and bars could not restrain it, and it sometimes became invisible in their very hands, and was whisked through the air to the purse of the magician. He necessarily acquired a very bad character; and, having given utterance to some sentiments regarding religion which were the very reverse of orthodox, he was summoned before the tribunals of the Inquisition to answer for his crimes as a heretic and a sorcerer. He loudly protested his innocence, even upon the rack, where he suffered more torture than nature could support. He died in prison ere his trial was concluded, but was afterwards found guilty. His bones were ordered to be dug up and publicly burned. He was also burned in effigy in the streets of Padua.

*RAYMOND LULLI.*

## Raymond Lulli.

While Arnold de Villeneuve and Pietro d'Apone flourished in France and Italy, a more celebrated adept than either appeared in Spain. This was Raymond Lulli, a name which stands in the first rank among the alchymists. Unlike many of his predecessors, he made no pretensions to astrology or necromancy; but, taking Geber for his model, studied intently the nature and composition of metals, without reference to charms, incantations, or any foolish ceremonies. It was not, however, till late in life that he commenced his study of the art. His early and middle age were spent in a different manner, and his whole history is romantic in the extreme. He was born of an illustrious family, in Majorca, in the year 1235. When that island was taken from the Saracens by James I. king of Aragon, in 1230, the father of Raymond, who was originally of Catalonia, settled there, and received a considerable appointment from the crown. Raymond married at an early age; and, being fond of pleasure, he left the solitudes of his native isle, and passed over with his bride into Spain. He was made Grand Seneschal at the court of King James, and led a gay life for several years. Faithless to his wife, he was always in the pursuit of some new beauty, till his heart was fixed at last by the lovely but unkind Ambrosia de Castello. This lady, like her admirer, was married; but, unlike him, was faithful to her vows, and treated all his solicitations with disdain. Raymond was so enamoured, that repulse only increased his flame; he lingered all night under her windows, wrote passionate verses in her praise, neglected his affairs, and made himself the butt of all the courtiers. One day, while watching under her lattice, he by chance caught sight of her bosom, as her neckerchief was blown aside by the wind. The fit of inspiration came over him, and he sat down and composed some tender stanzas upon the subject, and sent them to the lady. The fair Ambrosia had never before condescended to answer his letters; but she replied to this. She told him that she could never listen to his suit; that it was unbecoming in a wise man to fix his thoughts, as he had done, on any other than his God; and entreated him to devote himself to a religious life, and conquer the unworthy passion which he had suffered to consume him. She, however, offered, if he wished it, to shew him the *fair* bosom which had so captivated him. Raymond was delighted. He thought the latter part of this epistle but ill corresponded with the former, and that Ambrosia, in spite of the good advice she gave him, had at last relented, and would make him as happy as he desired. He followed her about from place to place, entreating her to fulfil her promise: but still Ambrosia was cold, and implored him with tears to importune her no longer; for that she never could be his, and never would, if she were free to-morrow. "What means your letter, then?" said the despairing lover. "I will shew you!" replied Ambrosia, who immediately uncovered her bosom, and exposed to the eyes of her horror-stricken admirer a large cancer which had extended to both breasts. She saw that he was shocked; and, extending her hand to him, she prayed him once more to lead a religious life, and set his heart upon the Creator, and not upon the creature. He went home an altered man. He threw up, on the morrow, his valuable appointment at the court, separated from his wife, and took a farewell of his children, after dividing one-half of his ample fortune among them. The other half he shared among the poor. He then threw himself at the foot of a crucifix, and devoted himself to the service of God, vowing, as the most acceptable atonement for his errors, that he would employ the remainder of his days in the task of converting the Mussulmans to the Christian religion. In his dreams he saw Jesus Christ, who said to him, "Raymond! Raymond! follow me!" The vision was three times repeated, and Raymond was convinced that it was an intimation direct from heaven. Having put his affairs in order, he set out on a pilgrimage to the shrine of St. James of Compostello, and afterwards lived for ten years in solitude amid the mountains of Aranda. Here he learned the Arabic, to qualify himself for his mission of converting the Mahometans. He also studied various sciences, as taught in the works of the learned men of the East, and first made acquaintance with the writings of Geber, which were destined to exercise so much influence over his future life.

At the end of this probation, and when he had entered his fortieth year, he emerged from his solitude into more active life. With some remains of his fortune, which had accumulated during his retirement, he founded a college for the study of Arabic, which was approved of by the pope, with many commendations upon his zeal and piety. At this time he narrowly escaped assassination from an Arabian youth whom he had taken into his service. Raymond had prayed to God, in some of his accesses of fanaticism, that he might suffer martyrdom in his holy cause. His servant had overheard him: and, being as great a fanatic as his master, he resolved to gratify his wish, and punish him, at the same time, for the curses which he incessantly launched against Mahomet and all who believed in him, by stabbing him to the heart. He therefore aimed a blow at his master as he sat one day at table; but the instinct of self-preservation being stronger than the desire of martyrdom, Raymond grappled with his antagonist, and overthrew him. He scorned to take his life himself; but handed him over to the authorities of the town, by whom he was afterwards found dead in his prison.

After this adventure Raymond travelled to Paris, where he resided for some time, and made the acquaintance of Arnold de Villeneuve. From him he probably received some encouragement to search for the philosopher's stone, as he began from that time forth to devote less of his attention to religious matters, and more to the study of alchymy. Still he never lost sight of the great object for which he lived — the conversion of the Mahometans — and proceeded to Rome, to communicate personally with Pope John XXI. on the best measures to be adopted for that end. The Pope gave him encouragement in words, but failed to associate any other persons with him in the enterprise which he meditated. Raymond, therefore, set out for Tunis alone, and was kindly received by many Arabian philosophers, who had heard of his fame as a professor of alchymy. If he had stuck to alchymy while in their country, it would have been well for him; but he began cursing Mahomet, and got himself into trouble. While preaching the doctrines of Christianity in the great bazaar of Tunis, he was arrested and thrown into prison. He was shortly afterwards brought to trial, and sentenced to death. Some of his philosophic friends interceded hard for him, and he was pardoned upon condition that he left Africa immediately and never again set foot in it. If he was found there again, no matter what his object might be, or whatever length of time might intervene, his original sentence would be carried into execution. Raymond was not at all solicitous of martyrdom when it came to the point, whatever he might have been when there was no danger, and he gladly accepted his life upon these conditions, and left Tunis with the intention of proceeding to Rome. He afterwards changed his plan, and established himself at Milan, where, for a length of time, he practised alchymy, and some say astrology, with great success.

Most writers who believed in the secrets of alchymy, and who have noticed the life of Raymond Lulli, assert, that while in Milan, he received letters from Edward King of England, inviting him to settle in his states. They add that Lulli gladly accepted the invitation, and had apartments assigned for his use in the Tower of London, where he refined much gold; superintended the coinage of "rose-nobles," and made gold out of iron, quicksilver, lead, and pewter, to the amount of six millions. The writers in the *Biographie Universelle*, an excellent authority in general, deny that Raymond was ever in England, and say, that in all these stories of his wondrous powers as an alchymist, he has been mistaken for another Raymond, a Jew of Tarragona. Naudé, in his *Apologie*, says, simply, "that six millions were given by Raymond Lulli to King Edward, to make war against the Turks and other infidels:" not that he transmuted so much metal into gold; but, as he afterwards adds, that he advised Edward to lay a tax upon wool, which produced that amount. To shew that Raymond went to England, his admirers quote a work attributed to him, *De Transmutatione Animæ Metallorum*, in which he expressly says that he was in England at the intercession of the king.[34] The hermetic writers are not agreed whether it was Edward I. or Edward II. who invited him over; but, by fixing the date of his journey in 1312, they make it appear that it was

Edward II. Edmond Dickenson, in his work on the *Quintessences of the Philosophers*, says, that Raymond worked in Westminster Abbey, where, a long time after his departure, there was found in the cell which he had occupied a great quantity of golden dust, of which the architects made a great profit. In the biographical sketch of John Cremer, Abbot of Westminster, given by Lenglet, it is said that it was chiefly through his instrumentality that Raymond came to England. Cremer had been himself for thirty years occupied in the vain search for the philosopher's stone, when he accidentally met Raymond in Italy, and endeavoured to induce him to communicate his grand secret. Raymond told him that he must find it for himself, as all great alchymists had done before him. Cremer, on his return to England, spoke to King Edward in high terms of the wonderful attainments of the philosopher, and a letter of invitation was forthwith sent him. Robert Constantinus, in the *Nomenclator Scriptorum Medicorum*, published in 1515, says, that after a great deal of research, he found that Raymond Lulli resided for some time in London, and that he actually made gold, by means of the philosopher's stone, in the Tower; that he had seen the golden pieces of his coinage, which were still named in England the nobles of Raymond, or rose-nobles. Lulli himself appears to have boasted that he made gold; for, in his well-known *Testamentum*, he states that he converted no less than fifty thousand pounds weight of quicksilver, lead, and pewter into that metal.[35] It seems highly probable that the English king, believing in the extraordinary powers of the alchymist, invited him to England to make test of them, and that he was employed in refining gold and in coining. Camden, who is not credulous in matters like these, affords his countenance to the story of his coinage of nobles; and there is nothing at all wonderful in the fact of a man famous for his knowledge of metals being employed in such a capacity. Raymond was, at this time, an old man, in his seventy-seventh year, and somewhat in his dotage. He was willing enough to have it believed that he had discovered the grand secret, and supported the rumour rather than contradicted it. He did not long remain in England, but returned to Rome to carry out the projects which were nearer to his heart than the profession of alchymy. He had proposed them to several successive popes with little or no success. The first was a plan for the introduction of the oriental languages into all the monasteries of Europe; the second, for the reduction into one of all the military orders, that, being united, they might move more efficaciously against the Saracens; and the third, that the sovereign pontiff should forbid the works of Averroes to be read in the schools, as being more favourable to Mahometanism than to Christianity. The pope did not receive the old man with much cordiality; and, after remaining for about two years in Rome, he proceeded once more to Africa, alone and unprotected, to preach the Gospel of Jesus. He landed at Bona in 1314, and so irritated the Mahometans by cursing their prophet, that they stoned him, and left him for dead on the sea-shore. He was found some hours afterwards by a party of Genoese merchants, who conveyed him on board their vessel, and sailed towards Majorca. The unfortunate man still breathed, but could not articulate. He lingered in this state for some days, and expired just as the vessel arrived within sight of his native shores. His body was conveyed with great pomp to the church of St. Eulalia, at Palma, where a public funeral was instituted in his honour. Miracles were afterwards said to have been worked at his tomb. Thus ended the career of Raymond Lulli, one of the most extraordinary men of his age; and, with the exception of his last boast about the six millions of gold, the least inclined to quackery of any of the professors of alchymy. His writings were very numerous, and include nearly five hundred volumes, upon grammar, rhetoric, morals, theology, politics, civil and canon law, physics, metaphysics, astronomy, medicine, and chemistry.

## Roger Bacon.

The powerful delusion of alchymy seized upon a mind still greater than that of Raymond Lulli. Roger Bacon firmly believed in the philosopher's stone, and spent much of his time in search of it. His example helped to render all the learned men of the time more convinced of its practicability, and more eager in the pursuit. He was born at Ilchester, in the county of Somerset, in the year 1214. He studied for some time in the University of Oxford, and afterwards in that of Paris, in which he received the degree of doctor of divinity. Returning to England in 1240, he became a monk of the order of St. Francis. He was by far the most learned man of his age; and his acquirements were so much above the comprehension of his contemporaries, that they could only account for them by supposing that he was indebted for them to the devil. Voltaire has not inaptly designated him "De l'or encrouté de toutes les ordures de son siècle;" but the crust of superstition that enveloped his powerful mind, though it may have dimmed, could not obscure the brightness of his genius. To him, and apparently to him only, among all the inquiring spirits of the time, were known the properties of the concave and convex lens. He also invented the magic lantern; that pretty plaything of modern days, which acquired for him a reputation that embittered his life. In a history of alchymy, the name of this great man cannot be omitted, although unlike many others of whom we shall have occasion to speak, he only made it secondary to other pursuits. The love of universal knowledge that filled his mind, would not allow him to neglect one branch of science, of which neither he nor the world could yet see the absurdity. He made ample amends for his time lost in this pursuit by his knowledge in physics and his acquaintance with astronomy. The telescope, burning-glasses, and gunpowder, are discoveries which may well carry his fame to the remotest time, and make the world blind to the one spot of folly — the diagnosis of the age in which he lived, and the circumstances by which he was surrounded. His treatise on the *Admirable Power of Art and Nature in the Production of the Philosopher's Stone* was translated into French by Girard de Tormes, and published at Lyons in 1557. His *Mirror of Alchymy* was also published in French in the same year, and in Paris in 1612, with some additions from the works of Raymond Lulli. A complete list of all the published treatises upon the subject may be seen in Lenglet du Fresnoy.

**Pope John XXII.**

This prelate is said to have been the friend and pupil of Arnold de Villeneuve, by whom he was instructed in all the secrets of alchymy. Tradition asserts of him, that he made great quantities of gold, and died as rich as Crœsus. He was born at Cahors, in the province of Guienne, in the year 1244. He was a very eloquent preacher, and soon reached high dignity in the Church. He wrote a work on the transmutation of metals, and had a famous laboratory at Avignon. He issued two bulls against the numerous pretenders to the art, who had sprung up in every part of Christendom; from which it might be inferred that he was himself free from the delusion. The alchymists claim him, however, as one of the most distinguished and successful professors of their art, and say that his bulls were not directed against the real adepts, but the false pretenders. They lay particular stress upon these words in his bull, "Spondent, quas non exhibent, divitias, *pauperes* alchymistæ." These, it is clear, they say, relate only to *poor* alchymists, and therefore false ones. He died in the year 1344, leaving in his coffers a sum of eighteen millions of florins. Popular belief alleged that he had made, and not amassed, this treasure; and alchymists complacently cite this as a proof that the philosopher's stone was not such a chimera as the incredulous pretended. They take it for granted that John really left this money, and ask by what possible means he could have accumulated it. Replying to their own question, they say triumphantly, "His book shews it was by alchymy, the secrets of which he learned from Arnold de Villeneuve and Raymond Lulli. But he was as prudent as all other hermetic philosophers. Whoever would read his book to find out his secret, would employ all his labour in vain; the pope took good care not to divulge it." Unluckily for their own credit, all these gold-makers are in the same predicament; their great secret loses its worth most wonderfully in the telling, and therefore they keep it snugly to themselves. Perhaps they thought that, if everybody could transmute metals, gold would be so plentiful that it would be no longer valuable, and that some new art would be requisite to transmute it back again into steel and iron. If so, society is much indebted to them for their forbearance.

## Jean de Meung.

All classes of men dabbled in the art at this time; the last mentioned was a pope, the one of whom we now speak was a poet. Jean de Meung, the celebrated author of the *Roman de la Rose*, was born in the year 1279 or 1280, and was a great personage at the courts of Louis X., Philip the Long, Charles IV., and Philip de Valois. His famous poem of the *Roman de la Rose*, which treats of every subject in vogue at that day, necessarily makes great mention of alchymy. Jean was a firm believer in the art, and wrote, besides his Roman, two shorter poems, the one entitled *The Remonstrance of Nature to the wandering Alchymist* and *The Reply of the Alchymist to Nature*. Poetry and alchymy were his delight, and priests and women were his abomination. A pleasant story is related of him and the ladies of the court of Charles IV. He had written the following libellous couplet upon the fair sex:

> *"Toutes êtes, serez, ou fûtes,*
> *De fait ou de volonté, putains;*
> *Et qui très bien vous chercherait,*
> *Toutes putains vous trouverait."*[36]

This naturally gave great offence; and being perceived one day in the king's antechamber, by some ladies who were waiting for an audience, they resolved to punish him. To the number of ten or twelve, they armed themselves with canes and rods, and surrounding the unlucky poet, called upon the gentlemen present to strip him naked, that they might wreak just vengeance upon him, and lash him through the streets of the town. Some of the lords present were in no wise loath, and promised themselves great sport from his punishment. But Jean de Meung was unmoved by their threats, and stood up calmly in the midst of them, begging them to hear him first, and then, if not satisfied, they might do as they liked with him. Silence being restored, he stood upon a chair, and entered on his defence. He acknowledged that he was the author of the obnoxious verses, but denied that they bore reference to all womankind. He only meant to speak of the vicious and abandoned, whereas those whom he saw around him were patterns of virtue, loveliness, and modesty. If, however, any lady present thought herself aggrieved, he would consent to be stripped, and she might lash him till her arms were wearied. It is added, that by this means Jean escaped his flogging, and that the wrath of the fair ones immediately subsided. The gentlemen present were, however, of opinion, that if every lady in the room whose character corresponded with the verses had taken him at his word; the poet would in all probability have been beaten to death. All his life long he evinced a great animosity towards the priesthood, and his famous poem abounds with passages reflecting upon their avarice, cruelty, and immorality. At his death he left a large box, filled with some weighty material, which he bequeathed to the Cordeliers, as a peace-offering, for the abuse he had lavished upon them. As his practice of alchymy was well known, it was thought the box was filled with gold and silver, and the Cordeliers congratulated each other on their rich acquisition. When it came to be opened, they found to their horror that it was filled only with *slates*, scratched with hieroglyphic and cabalistic characters. Indignant at the insult, they determined to refuse him Christian burial, on pretence that he was a sorcerer. He was, however, honourably buried in Paris, the whole court attending his funeral.

**Nicholas Flamel.**

The story of this alchymist, as handed down by tradition, and enshrined in the pages of Lenglet da Fresnoy, is not a little marvellous. He was born at Pontoise, of a poor but respectable family, at the end of the thirteenth, or beginning of the fourteenth century. Having no patrimony, he set out for Paris at an early age, to try his fortune as a public scribe. He had received a good education, was well skilled in the learned languages, and was an excellent penman. He soon procured occupation as a letter-writer and copyist, and used to sit at the corner of the Rue de Marivaux, and practise his calling; but he hardly made profit enough to keep body and soul together. To mend his fortunes he tried poetry; but this was a more wretched occupation still. As a transcriber he had at least gained bread and cheese; but his rhymes were not worth a crust. He then tried painting with as little success; and as a last resource, began to search for the philosopher's stone and tell fortunes. This was a happier idea; he soon increased in substance, and had wherewithal to live comfortably. He therefore took unto himself his wife Petronella, and began to save money; but continued to all outward appearance as poor and miserable as before. In the course of a few years, he became desperately addicted to the study of alchymy, and thought of nothing but the philosopher's stone, the elixir of life, and the universal alkahest. In the year 1257, he bought by chance an old book for two florins, which soon became his sole study. It was written with a steel instrument upon the bark of trees, and contained twenty-one, or as he himself always expressed it, three times seven, leaves. The writing was very elegant and in the Latin language. Each seventh leaf contained a picture and no writing. On the first of these was a serpent swallowing rods; on the second, a cross with a serpent crucified; and on the third, the representation of a desert, in the midst of which was a fountain, with serpents crawling from side to side. It purported to be written by no less a personage than "Abraham, patriarch, Jew, prince, philosopher, priest, Levite, and astrologer;" and invoked curses upon any one who should cast eyes upon it, without being "a sacrificer or a scribe." Nicholas Flamel never thought it extraordinary that Abraham should have known Latin, and was convinced that the characters on his book had been traced by the hands of that great patriarch himself. He was at first afraid to read it, after he became aware of the curse it contained; but he got over that difficulty by recollecting that, although he was not a sacrificer, he had practised as a scribe. As he read he was filled with admiration, and found that it was a perfect treatise upon the transmutation of metals. All the processes were clearly explained; the vessels, the retorts, the mixtures, and the proper times and seasons for experiment. But as ill-luck would have it, the possession of the philosopher's stone, or prime agent in the work, was presupposed. This was a difficulty which was not to be got over. It was like telling a starving man how to cook a beef-steak, instead of giving him the money to buy one. But Nicholas did not despair, and set about studying the hieroglyphics and allegorical representations with which the book abounded. He soon convinced himself that it had been one of the sacred books of the Jews, and that it was taken from the temple of Jerusalem on its destruction by Titus. The process of reasoning by which he arrived at this conclusion is not stated.

From some expression in the treatise, he learned that the allegorical drawings on the fourth and fifth leaves enshrined the secret of the philosopher's stone, without which all the fine Latin of the directions was utterly unavailing. He invited all the alchymists and learned men of Paris to come and examine them, but they all departed as wise as they came. Nobody could make any thing either of Nicholas or his pictures; and some even went so far as to say that his invaluable book was not worth a farthing. This was not to be borne; and Nicholas resolved to discover the great secret by himself, without troubling the philosophers. He found on the first page of the fourth leaf, the picture of Mercury attacked by an old man resembling Saturn or Time. The latter had an hour-glass on his head, and in his hand a scythe, with which he aimed a blow at Mercury's feet. The reverse of the leaf represented a flower growing on a mountain top, shaken rudely by the wind, with a blue stalk, red and white blossoms, and leaves of pure gold. Around it were a great number of dragons and griffins. On the first page of the fifth leaf was a fine garden, in the midst of which was a rose-tree in full bloom, supported against the trunk of a gigantic oak. At the foot of this there bubbled up a fountain of milk-white water, which, forming a small stream, flowed through the garden, and was afterwards lost in the sands. On the second page was a king, with a sword in his hand, superintending a number of soldiers, who, in execution of his orders, were killing a great multitude of young children, spurning the prayers and tears of their mothers, who tried to save them from destruction. The blood of the children was carefully collected by another party of soldiers, and put into a large vessel, in which two allegorical figures of the sun and moon were bathing themselves.

For twenty-one years poor Nicholas wearied himself with the study of these pictures, but still he could make nothing of them. His wife Petronella at last persuaded him to find out some learned rabbi; but there was no rabbi in Paris learned enough to be of any service to him. The Jews met but small encouragement to fix their abode in France, and all the chiefs of that people were located in Spain. To Spain accordingly Nicholas Flamel repaired. He left his book in Paris, for fear, perhaps, that he might be robbed of it on the road; and telling his neighbours that he was going on a pilgrimage to the shrine of St. James of Compostello, he trudged on foot towards Madrid in search of a rabbi. He was absent two years in that country, and made himself known to a great number of Jews, descendants of those who had been expelled from France in the reign of Philip Augustus. The believers in the philosopher's stone give the following account of his adventures: They say that at Leon he made the acquaintance of a converted Jew, named Cauches, a very learned physician, to whom he explained the title and nature of his little book. The doctor was transported with joy as soon as he heard it named, and immediately resolved to accompany Nicholas to Paris, that he might have a sight of it. The two set out together; the doctor on the way entertaining his companion with the history of his book, which, if the genuine book he thought it to be, from the description he had heard of it, was in the handwriting of Abraham himself, and had been in the possession of personages no less distinguished than Moses, Joshua, Solomon, and Esdras. It contained all the secrets of alchymy and of many other sciences, and was the most valuable book that had ever existed in this world. The doctor was himself no mean adept, and Nicholas profited greatly by his discourse, as in the garb of poor pilgrims they wended their way to Paris, convinced of their power to turn every old shovel in that capital into pure gold. But, unfortunately, when they reached Orleans, the doctor was taken dangerously ill. Nicholas watched by his bedside, and acted the double part of a physician and nurse to him; but he died after a few days, lamenting with his last breath that he had not lived long enough to see the precious volume. Nicholas rendered the last honours to his body; and with a sorrowful heart, and not one *sou* in his pocket, proceeded home to his wife Petronella. He immediately recommenced the study of his pictures; but for two whole years he was as far from understanding them as ever. At last, in the third year, a glimmer of light stole over his understanding. He recalled some expression of his friend the doctor, which had hitherto escaped his memory, and he found that all his previous experiments had been conducted on a wrong basis. He recommenced them now with renewed energy, and at the end of the year had the satisfaction to see all his toils rewarded. On the 13th January 1382, says Lenglet, he made a projection on mercury, and had some very excellent silver. On the 25th April following, he converted a large quantity of mercury into gold, and the great secret was his.

Nicholas was now about eighty years of age, and still a hale and stout old man. His friends say that by a simultaneous discovery of the elixir of life, he found means to keep death at a distance for another quarter of a century; and that he died in 1415, at the age of 116. In this interval he made immense quantities of gold, though to all outward appearance he was as poor as a mouse. At an early period of his changed fortune, he had, like a worthy man, taken counsel with his old wife Petronella, as to the best use he could make of his wealth. Petronella replied, that as unfortunately they had no children, the best thing he could do, was to build hospitals and endow churches. Nicholas thought so too, especially when he began to find that his elixir could not keep off death, and that the grim foe was making rapid advances upon him. He richly endowed the church of St. Jacques de la Boucherie, near the Rue de Marivaux, where he had all his life resided, besides seven others in different parts of the kingdom. He also endowed fourteen hospitals, and built three chapels.

The fame of his great wealth and his munificent benefactions soon spread over all the country, and he was visited, among others, by the celebrated doctors of that day, Jean Gerson, Jean de Courtecuisse, and Pierre d'Ailli. They found him in his humble apartment, meanly clad, and eating porridge out of an earthen vessel; and with regard to his secret, as impenetrable as all his predecessors in alchymy. His fame reached the ears of the king, Charles VI., who sent M. de Cramoisi, the Master of Requests, to find out whether Nicholas had indeed discovered the philosopher's stone. But M. de Cramoisi took nothing by his visit; all his attempts to sound the alchymist were unavailing, and he returned to his royal master no wiser than he came. It was in this year, 1414, that he lost his faithful Petronella. He did not long survive her, but died in the following year, and was buried with great pomp by the grateful priests of St. Jacques de la Boucherie. The great wealth of Nicholas Flamel is undoubted, as the records of several churches and hospitals in France can testify. That he practised alchymy is equally certain, as he left behind several works upon the subject. Those who knew him well, and who were incredulous about the philosopher's stone, give a satisfactory solution of the secret of his wealth. They say that he was always a miser and a usurer; that his journey to Spain was undertaken with very different motives from those pretended by the alchymists; that, in fact, he went to collect debts due from Jews in that country to their brethren in Paris, and that he charged a commission of fully cent per cent in consideration of the difficulty of collecting and the dangers of the road; that when he possessed thousands, he lived upon almost nothing; and was the general money-lender, at enormous profits, to all the dissipated young men at the French court.

Among the works written by Nicholas Flamel on the subject of alchymy is *The Philosophic Summary*, a poem, reprinted in 1735, as an appendix to the third volume of the *Roman de la Rose*. He also wrote three treatises upon natural philosophy, and an alchymic allegory, entitled *Le Désir désiré*. Specimens of his writing, and a fac-simile of the drawings in his book of Abraham, may be seen in Salmon's *Bibliothèque des Philosophes Chimiques*. The writer of the article *Flamel* in the *Biographie Universelle* says, that for a hundred years after the death of Flamel, many of the adepts believed that he was still alive, and that he would live for upwards of six hundred years. The house he formerly occupied, at the corner of the Rue de Marivaux, has been often taken by credulous speculators, and ransacked from top to bottom, in the hopes that gold might be found. A report was current in Paris, not long previous to the year 1816, that some lodgers had found in the cellars several jars filled with a dark-coloured ponderous matter. Upon the strength of the rumour, a believer in all the wondrous tales told of Nicholas Flamel bought the house, and nearly pulled it to pieces in ransacking the walls and wainscoting for hidden gold. He got nothing for his pains, however, and had a heavy bill to pay to restore his dilapidations.

**George Ripley.**

While alchymy was thus cultivated on the continent of Europe, it was not neglected in the isles of Britain. Since the time of Roger Bacon, it had fascinated the imagination of many ardent men in England. In the year 1404 an act of parliament was passed declaring the making of gold and silver to be felony. Great alarm was felt at that time lest any alchymist should succeed in his projects, and perhaps bring ruin upon the state by furnishing boundless wealth to some designing tyrant, who would make use of it to enslave his country. This alarm appears to have soon subsided; for, in the year 1455, King Henry VI., by advice of his council and parliament, granted four successive patents and commissions to several knights, citizens of London, chemists, monks, mass-priests, and others, to find out the philosopher's stone and elixir, "to the great benefit," said the patent, "of the realm, and the enabling of the king to pay all the debts of the crown in real gold and silver." Prinn, in his *Aurum Reginæ*, observes, as a note to this passage, that the king's reason for granting this patent to ecclesiastics was, that "they were such good artists in transubstantiating bread and wine in the eucharist, and therefore the more likely to be able to effect the transmutation of baser metals into better." No gold, of course, was ever made; and next year the king, doubting very much of the practicability of the thing, took further advice, and appointed a commission of ten learned men and persons of eminence to judge and certify to him whether the transmutation of metals were a thing practicable or no. It does not appear whether the commission ever made any report upon the subject.

In the succeeding reign an alchymist appeared who pretended to have discovered the secret. This was George Ripley, the canon of Bridlington, in Yorkshire. He studied for twenty years in the universities of Italy, and was a great favourite with Pope Innocent VIII., who made him one of his domestic chaplains, and master of the ceremonies in his household. Returning to England in 1477, he dedicated to King Edward IV. his famous work, *The Compound of Alchymy*; or, *the Twelve Gates leading to the Discovery of the Philosopher's Stone*. These gates he described to be calcination, solution, separation, conjunction, putrefaction, congelation, cibation, sublimation, fermentation, exaltation, multiplication, and projection; to which he might have added botheration, the most important process of all. He was very rich, and allowed it to be believed that he could make gold out of iron. Fuller, in his *Worthies of England*, says that an English gentleman of good credit reported, that in his travels abroad he saw a record in the island of Malta which declared that Ripley gave yearly to the knights of that island, and of Rhodes, the enormous sum of one hundred thousand pounds sterling to enable them to carry on the war against the Turks. In his old age he became an anchorite near Boston, and wrote twenty-five volumes upon the subject of alchymy, the most important of which is the *Duodecim Portarum* already mentioned. Before he died, he seems to have acknowledged that he had mis-spent his life in this vain study, and requested that all men, when they met with any of his books, would burn them, or afford them no credit, as they had been written merely from his opinion, and not from proof; and that subsequent trial had made manifest to him that they were false and vain.[37]

### Basil Valentine.

Germany also produced many famous alchymists in the fifteenth century, the chief of whom are Basil Valentine, Bernard of

Trèves, and the Abbot Trithemius. Basil Valentine was born at Mayence, and was made prior of St. Peter's, at Erfurt, about the year 1414. It was known, during his life, that he diligently sought the philosopher's stone, and that he had written some works upon the process of transmutation. They were thought for many years to be lost, but were, after his death, discovered enclosed in the stone-work of one of the pillars in the Abbey. They were twenty-one in number, and are fully set forth in the third volume of Lenglet's *History of the Hermetic Philosophy*. The alchymists asserted that heaven itself conspired to bring to light these extraordinary works; and that the pillar in which they were enclosed was miraculously shattered by a thunderbolt; and that as soon as the manuscripts were liberated, the pillar closed up again of its own accord!

**Bernard of Treves.**

The life of this philosopher is a remarkable instance of talent and perseverance misapplied. In the search of his chimera nothing could daunt him. Repeated disappointment never diminished his hopes; and from the age of fourteen to that of eighty-five he was incessantly employed among the drugs and furnaces of his laboratory, wasting his life with the view of prolonging it, and reducing himself to beggary in the hopes of growing rich.

He was born at either Trèves or Padua in the year 1406. His father is said by some to have been a physician in the latter city, and by others to have been Count of the Marches of Trèves, and one of the most wealthy nobles of his country. At all events, whether noble or physician, he was a rich man, and left his son a magnificent estate. At the age of fourteen he first became enamoured of the science of alchymy, and read the Arabian authors in their own language. He himself has left a most interesting record of his labours and wanderings, from which the following particulars are chiefly extracted. The first book which fell into his hands was that of the Arabian philosopher Rhazes, from the reading of which he imagined that he had discovered the means of augmenting gold a hundredfold. For four years he worked in his laboratory, with the book of Rhazes continually before him. At the end of that time, he found that he had spent no less than eight hundred crowns upon his experiment, and had got nothing but fire and smoke for his pains. He now began to lose confidence in Rhazes, and turned to the works of Geber. He studied him assiduously for two years; and being young, rich, and credulous, was beset by all the alchymists of the town, who kindly assisted him in spending his money. He did not lose his faith in Geber, or patience with his hungry assistants, until he had lost two thousand crowns — a very considerable sum in those days.

Among all the crowd of pretended men of science who surrounded him, there was but one as enthusiastic and as disinterested as himself. With this man, who was a monk of the order of St. Francis, he contracted an intimate friendship, and spent nearly all his time. Some obscure treatises of Rupecissa and Sacrobosco having fallen into their hands, they were persuaded, from reading them, that highly rectified spirits of wine was the universal alkahest, or dissolvent, which would aid them greatly in the process of transmutation. They rectified the alcohol thirty times, till they made it so strong as to burst the vessels which contained it. After they had worked three years, and spent three hundred crowns in the liquor, they discovered that they were on the wrong track. They next tried alum and copperas; but the great secret still escaped them. They afterwards imagined that there was a marvellous virtue in all excrement, especially the human, and actually employed more than two years in experimentalising upon it with mercury, salt, and molten lead! Again the adepts flocked around him from far and near to aid him with their counsels. He received them all hospitably, and divided his wealth among them so generously and unhesitatingly, that they gave him the name of the "Good Trevisan," by which he is still often mentioned in works that treat on alchymy. For twelve years he led this life, making experiments every day upon some new substance, and praying to God night and morning that he might discover the secret of transmutation.

In this interval he lost his friend the monk, and was joined by a magistrate of the city of Trèves, as ardent as himself in the search. His new acquaintance imagined that the ocean was the mother of gold, and that sea-salt would change lead or iron into the precious metals. Bernard resolved to try; and, transporting his laboratory to a house on the shores of the Baltic, he worked upon salt for more than a year, melting it, sublimating it, crystallising it, and occasionally drinking it, for the sake of other experiments. Still the strange enthusiast was not wholly discouraged, and his failure in one trial only made him the more anxious to attempt another.

He was now approaching the age of fifty, and had as yet seen nothing of the world. He therefore determined to travel through Germany, Italy, France, and Spain. Wherever he stopped he made inquiries whether there were any alchymists in the neighbourhood. He invariably sought them out; and if they were poor, relieved, and if affluent, encouraged them. At Citeaux he became acquainted with one Geoffrey Leuvier, a monk of that place, who persuaded him that the essence of egg-shells was a valuable ingredient. He tried, therefore, what could be done; and was only prevented from wasting a year or two on the experiment by the opinions of an attorney, at Berghem, in Flanders, who said that the great secret resided in vinegar and copperas. He was not convinced of the absurdity of this idea until he had nearly poisoned himself. He resided in France for about five years, when, hearing accidentally that one Master Henry, confessor to the Emperor Frederic III., had discovered the philosopher's stone, he set out for Germany to pay him a visit. He had, as usual, surrounded himself with a set of hungry dependants, several of whom determined to accompany him. He had not heart to refuse them, and he arrived at Vienna with five of them. Bernard sent a polite invitation to the confessor, and gave him a sumptuous entertainment, at which were present nearly all the alchymists of Vienna. Master Henry frankly confessed that he had not discovered the philosopher's stone, but that he had all his life been employed in searching for it, and would so continue till he found it, or died. This was a man after

Bernard's own heart, and they vowed with each other an eternal friendship. It was resolved, at supper, that each alchymist present should contribute a certain sum towards raising forty-two marks of gold, which, in five days, it was confidently asserted by Master Henry, would increase, in his furnace, fivefold. Bernard, being the richest man, contributed the lion's share, ten marks of gold, Master Henry five, and the others one or two a-piece, except the dependants of Bernard, who were obliged to borrow their quota from their patron. The grand experiment was duly made; the golden marks were put into a crucible, with a quantity of salt, copperas, aquafortis, egg-shells, mercury, lead, and dung. The alchymists watched this precious mess with intense interest, expecting that it would agglomerate into one lump of pure gold. At the end of three weeks they gave up the trial, upon some excuse that the crucible was not strong enough, or that some necessary ingredient was wanting. Whether any thief had put his hands into the crucible is not known, but it is alleged that the gold found therein at the close of the experiment was worth only sixteen marks, instead of the forty-two, which were put there at the beginning.

Bernard, though he made no gold at Vienna, made away with a very considerable quantity. He felt the loss so acutely, that he vowed to think no more of the philosopher's stone. This wise resolution he kept for two months; but he was miserable. He was in the condition of the gambler, who cannot resist the fascination of the game while he has a coin remaining, but plays on with the hope of retrieving former losses, till hope forsakes him, and he can live no longer. He returned once more to his beloved crucibles, and resolved to prosecute his journey in search of a philosopher who had discovered the secret, and would communicate it to so zealous and persevering an adept as himself. From Vienna he travelled to Rome, and from Rome to Madrid. Taking ship at Gibraltar, he proceeded to Messina; from Messina to Cyprus; from Cyprus to Greece; from Greece to Constantinople; and thence into Egypt, Palestine, and Persia. These wanderings occupied him about eight years. From Persia he made his way back to Messina, and from thence into France. He afterwards passed over into England, still in search of his great chimera; and this occupied four years more of his life. He was now growing both old and poor; for he was sixty-two years of age, and had been obliged to sell a great portion of his patrimony to provide for his expenses. His journey to Persia had cost upwards of thirteen thousand crowns, about one-half of which had been fairly melted in his all-devouring furnaces; the other half was lavished upon the sycophants that he made it his business to search out in every town he stopped at.

On his return to Trèves he found, to his sorrow, that, if not an actual beggar, he was not much better. His relatives looked upon him as a madman, and refused even to see him. Too proud to ask for favours from any one, and still confident that, some day or other, he would be the possessor of unbounded wealth, he made up his mind to retire to the island of Rhodes, where he might, in the mean time, hide his poverty from the eyes of the world. Here he might have lived unknown and happy; but, as ill luck would have it, he fell in with a monk as mad as himself upon the subject of transmutation. They were, however, both so poor that they could not afford to buy the proper materials to work with. They kept up each other's spirits by learned discourses on the hermetic philosophy, and in the reading of all the great authors who had written upon the subject. Thus did they nurse their folly, as the good wife of Tam O'Shanter did her wrath, "to keep it warm." After Bernard had resided about a year in Rhodes, a merchant, who knew his family, advanced him the sum of eight thousand florins, upon the security of the last-remaining acres of his formerly large estate. Once more provided with funds, he recommenced his labours with all the zeal and enthusiasm of a young man. For three years he hardly stepped out of his laboratory: he ate there, and slept there, and did not even give himself time to wash his hands and clean his beard, so intense was his application. It is melancholy to think that such wonderful perseverance should have been wasted in so vain a pursuit, and that energies so unconquerable should have had no worthier field to strive in. Even when he had fumed away his last coin, and had nothing left in prospective to keep his old age from starvation, hope never forsook him. He still dreamed of ultimate success, and sat down a grey-headed man of eighty, to read over all the authors on the hermetic mysteries, from Geber to his own day, lest he should have misunderstood some process, which it was not yet too late to recommence. The alchymists say, that he succeeded at last, and discovered the secret of transmutation in his eighty-second year. They add that he lived three years afterwards to enjoy his wealth. He lived, it is true, to this great age, and made a valuable discovery — more valuable than gold or gems. He learned, as he himself informs us, just before he had attained his eighty-third year, that the great secret of philosophy was contentment with our lot. Happy would it have been for him if he had discovered it sooner, and before he became decrepit, a beggar, and an exile!

He died at Rhodes, in the year 1490, and all the alchymists of Europe sang elegies over him, and sounded his praise as the "good Trevisan." He wrote several treatises upon his chimera, the chief of which are, the *Book of Chemistry*, the *Verbum dimissum*, and an essay *De Natura Ovi*.

## Trithemius.

The name of this eminent man has become famous in the annals of alchymy, although he did but little to gain so questionable an honour. He was born in the year 1462, at the village of Trittheim, in the electorate of Trèves. His father was John Heidenberg, a vine-grower, in easy circumstances, who, dying when his son was but seven years old, left him to the care of his mother. The latter married again very shortly afterwards, and neglected the poor boy, the offspring of her first marriage. At the age of fifteen he did not even know his letters, and was, besides, half starved, and otherwise ill-treated by his step-father; but the love of knowledge germinated in the breast of the unfortunate youth, and he learned to read at the house of a neighbour. His father-in-law set him to work in the vineyards, and thus occupied all his days; but the nights were his own. He often stole out unheeded, when all the household were fast asleep, poring over his studies in the fields, by the light of the moon; and thus taught himself Latin and the rudiments of Greek. He was subjected to so much ill-usage at home, in consequence of this love of study, that he determined to leave it. Demanding the patrimony which his father had left him, he proceeded to Trèves; and assuming the name of Trithemius, from that of his native village of Trittheim, lived there for some months under the tuition of eminent masters, by whom he was prepared for the university. At the age of twenty, he took it into his head that he should like to see his mother once more; and he set out on foot from the distant university for that purpose. On his arrival near Spannheim, late in the evening of a gloomy winter's day, it came on to snow so thickly, that he could not proceed onwards to the town. He therefore took refuge for the night in a neighbouring monastery; but the storm continued several days, the roads became impassable, and the hospitable monks would not hear of his departure. He was so pleased with them and their manner of life, that he suddenly resolved to fix his abode among them, and renounce the world. They were no less pleased with him, and gladly received him as a brother. In the course of two years, although still so young, he was unanimously elected their abbot. The financial affairs of the establishment had been greatly neglected, the walls of the building were falling into ruin, and every thing was in disorder. Trithemius, by his good management and regularity, introduced a reform in every branch of expenditure. The monastery was repaired, and a yearly surplus, instead of a deficiency, rewarded him for his pains. He did not like to see the monks idle, or occupied solely between prayers for their business, and chess for their relaxation. He, therefore, set them to work to copy the writings of eminent authors. They laboured so assiduously, that, in the course of a few years, their library, which had contained only about forty volumes, was enriched with several hundred valuable manuscripts, comprising many of the classical Latin authors, besides the works of the early fathers, and the principal historians, and philosophers of more modern date. He retained the dignity of Abbot of Spannheim for twenty-one years, when the monks, tired of the severe discipline he maintained, revolted against him, and chose another abbot in his place. He was afterwards made Abbot of St. James, in Wurzburg, where he died in 1516.

During his learned leisure at Spannheim, he wrote several works upon the occult sciences, the chief of which are an essay on geomancy, or divination by means of lines and circles on the ground; another upon sorcery; a third upon alchymy; and a fourth upon the government of the world by its presiding angels, which was translated into English, and published by the famous William Lilly in 1647.

It has been alleged by the believers in the possibility of transmutation, that the prosperity of the abbey of Spannheim, while under his superintendence, was owing more to the philosopher's stone than to wise economy. Trithemius, in common with many other learned men, has been accused of magic; and a marvellous story is told of his having raised from the grave the form of Mary of Burgundy, at the intercession of her widowed husband, the Emperor Maximilian. His work on steganographia, or cabalistic writing, was denounced to the Count Palatine, Frederic II., as magical and devilish; and it was by him taken from the shelves of his library and thrown into the fire. Trithemius is said to be the first writer who makes mention of the wonderful story of the devil and Dr. Faustus, the truth of which he firmly believed. He also recounts the freaks of a spirit named *Hudekin*, by whom he was at times tormented.[38]

### The Marechal de Rays.

One of the greatest encouragers of alchymy in the fifteenth century was Gilles de Laval, Lord of Rays and a Marshal of France. His name and deeds are little known; but in the annals of crime and folly, they might claim the highest and worst preeminence. Fiction has never invented any thing wilder or more horrible than his career; and were not the details but too well authenticated by legal and other documents which admit no doubt, the lover of romance might easily imagine they were drawn to please him from the stores of the prolific brain, and not from the page of history.

He was born about the year 1420, of one of the noblest families of Brittany. His father dying when Gilles had attained his twentieth year, he came into uncontrolled possession, at that early age, of a fortune which the monarchs of France might have envied him. He was a near kinsman of the Montmorencys, the Roncys, and the Craons; possessed fifteen princely domains, and had an annual revenue of about three hundred thousand livres. Besides this, he was handsome, learned, and brave. He distinguished himself greatly in the wars of Charles VII., and was rewarded by that monarch with the dignity of a marshal of France. But he was extravagant and magnificent in his style of living, and accustomed from his earliest years to the gratification of every wish and passion; and this, at last, led him from vice to vice and from crime to crime, till a blacker name than his is not to be found in any record of human iniquity.

In his castle of Champtocé he lived with all the splendour of an eastern caliph. He kept up a troop of two hundred horsemen to accompany him wherever he went; and his excursions for the purposes of hawking and hunting were the wonder of all the country around, so magnificent were the caparisons of his steeds and the dresses of his retainers. Day and night his castle was open all the year round to comers of every degree. He made it a rule to regale even the poorest beggar with wine and hippocrass. Every day an ox was roasted whole in his spacious kitchens, besides sheep, pigs, and poultry sufficient to feed five hundred persons. He was equally magnificent in his devotions. His private chapel at Champtocé was the most beautiful in France, and far surpassed any of those in the richly-endowed cathedrals of Notre Dame in Paris, of Amiens, of Beauvais, or of Rouen. It was hung with cloth of gold and rich velvet. All the chandeliers were of pure gold curiously inlaid with silver. The great crucifix over the altar was of solid silver, and the chalices and incense-burners were of pure gold. He had besides a fine organ, which he caused to be carried from one castle to another on the shoulders of six men, whenever he changed his residence. He kept up a choir of twenty-five young children of both sexes, who were instructed in singing by the first musicians of the day. The master of his chapel he called a bishop, who had under him his deans, arch-deacons, and vicars, each receiving great salaries; the bishop four hundred crowns a year, and the rest in proportion. He also maintained a whole troop of players, including ten dancing girls and as many ballad-singers, besides morris-dancers, jugglers, and mountebanks of every description. The theatre on which they performed was fitted up without any regard to expense, and they played mysteries or danced the morris-dance every evening for the amusement of himself and household, and such strangers as were sharing his prodigal hospitality.

At the age of twenty-three he married Catherine, the wealthy heiress of the house of Touars, for whom he refurnished his castle at an expense of a hundred thousand crowns. His marriage was the signal for new extravagance, and he launched out more madly than ever he had done before; sending for fine singers or celebrated dancers from foreign countries to amuse him and his spouse; and instituting tilts and tournaments in his great court-yard almost every week for all the knights and nobles of the province of Brittany. The Duke of Brittany's court was not half so splendid as that of the Maréchal de Rays. His utter disregard for wealth was so well known, that he was made to pay three times its value for every thing he purchased. His castle was filled with needy parasites and panderers to his pleasures, amongst whom he lavished rewards with an unsparing hand. But the ordinary round of sensual gratification ceased at last to afford him delight; he was observed to be more abstemious in the pleasures of the table, and to neglect the beauteous dancing girls who used formerly to occupy so much of his attention. He was sometimes gloomy and reserved, and there was an unnatural wildness in his eye which gave indications of incipient madness. Still his discourse was as reasonable as ever, his urbanity to the guests that flocked from far and near to Champtocé suffered no diminution; and learned priests, when they conversed with him, thought to themselves that few of the nobles of France were so well informed as Gilles de Laval. But dark rumours spread gradually over the country; murder, and, if possible, still more atrocious deeds were hinted at; and it was remarked that many young children of both sexes suddenly disappeared, and were never afterwards heard of. One or two had been traced to the castle of Champtocé, and had never been seen to leave it; but no one dared to accuse openly so powerful a man as the Maréchal de Rays. Whenever the subject of the lost children was mentioned in his presence, he manifested the greatest astonishment at the mystery which involved their fate, and indignation against those who might be guilty of kidnapping them. Still the world was not wholly deceived; his name became as formidable to young children as that of the devouring ogre in fairy tales, and they were taught to go miles round, rather than pass under the turrets of Champtocé.

In the course of a few years, the reckless extravagance of the marshal drained him of all his funds, and he was obliged to put up some of his estates for sale. The Duke of Brittany entered into a treaty with him for the valuable seignory of Ingrande; but the heirs of Gilles implored the interference of Charles VII. to stay the sale. Charles immediately issued an edict, which was confirmed by the provincial Parliament of Brittany, forbidding him to alienate his paternal estates. Gilles had no alternative but to submit. He had nothing to support his extravagance but his allowance as a marshal of France, which did not cover the one-tenth of his expenses. A man of his habits and character could not retrench his wasteful expenditure, and live reasonably; he could not dismiss without a pang his horsemen, his jesters, his morris-dancers, his choristers, and his parasites, or confine his hospitality to those who really needed it. Notwithstanding his diminished resources, he resolved to live as he had lived before, and turn alchymist, that he might make gold out of iron, and be still the wealthiest and most magnificent among the nobles of Brittany.

In pursuance of this determination, he sent to Paris, Italy, Germany, and Spain, inviting all the adepts in the science to visit him at Champtocé. The messengers he despatched on this

mission were two of his most needy and unprincipled dependants, Gilles de Sillé and Roger de Bricqueville. The latter, the
obsequious panderer to his most secret and abominable pleasures, he had entrusted with the education of his motherless
daughter, a child but five years of age, with permission that he
might marry her at the proper time to any person he chose, or to
himself if he liked it better. This man entered into the new plans
of his master with great zeal, and introduced to him one Prelati,
an alchymist of Padua, and a physician of Poitou, who was
addicted to the same pursuits.

The marshal caused a splendid laboratory to be fitted up for
them, and the three commenced the search for the philosopher's
stone. They were soon afterwards joined by another pretended
philosopher, named Anthony Palermo, who aided in their
operations for upwards of a year. They all fared sumptuously at
the marshal's expense, draining him of the ready money he
possessed, and leading him on from day to day with the hope
that they would succeed in the object of their search. From time
to time new aspirants from the remotest parts of Europe arrived
at his castle, and for months he had upwards of twenty alchymists at work, trying to transmute copper into gold; and wasting
the gold which was still his own in drugs and elixirs.

But the Lord of Rays was not a man to abide patiently their
lingering processes. Pleased with their comfortable quarters, they
jogged on from day to day, and would have done so for years,
had they been permitted. But he suddenly dismissed them all,
with the exception of the Italian Prelati, and the physician of
Poitou. These he retained to aid him to discover the secret of the
philosopher's stone by a bolder method. The Poitousan had
persuaded him that the devil was the great depository of that
and all other secrets, and that he would raise him before Gilles,
who might enter into any contract he pleased with him. Gilles
expressed his readiness, and promised to give the devil any thing
but his soul, or do any deed that the arch-enemy might impose
upon him. Attended solely by the physician, he proceeded at
midnight to a wild-looking place in a neighbouring forest; the
physician drew a magic circle around them on the sward, and

muttered for half an hour an invocation to the evil spirit to arise at his bidding, and disclose the secrets of alchymy. Gilles looked on with intense interest, and expected every moment to see the earth open, and deliver to his gaze the great enemy of mankind. At last the eyes of the physician became fixed, his hair stood on end, and he spoke, as if addressing the fiend. But Gilles saw nothing except his companion. At last the physician fell down on the sward as if insensible. Gilles looked calmly on to see the end. After a few minutes the physician arose, and asked him if he had not seen how angry the devil looked? Gilles replied that he had seen nothing; upon which his companion informed him that Beelzebub had appeared in the form of a wild leopard, growled at him savagely, and said nothing; and that the reason why the marshal had neither seen nor heard him was, that he hesitated in his own mind as to devoting himself entirely to the service. De Rays owned that he had indeed misgivings, and inquired what was to be done to make the devil speak out, and unfold his secret? The physician replied, that some person must go to Spain and Africa to collect certain herbs which only grew in those countries, and offered to go himself, if De Rays would provide the necessary funds. De Rays at once consented; and the physician set out on the following day with all the gold that his dupe could spare him. The marshal never saw his face again.

But the eager Lord of Champtocé could not rest. Gold was necessary for his pleasures; and unless by supernatural aid, he had no means of procuring any further supplies. The physician was hardly twenty leagues on his journey, before Gilles resolved to make another effort to force the devil to divulge the art of gold-making. He went out alone for that purpose; but all his conjurations were of no effect. Beelzebub was obstinate, and would not appear. Determined to conquer him if he could, he unbosomed himself to the Italian alchymist, Prelati. The latter offered to undertake the business, upon condition that De Rays did not interfere in the conjurations, and consented besides to furnish him with all the charms and talismans that might be required. He was further to open a vein in his arm, and sign with his blood a contract that "he would work the devil's will in all things," and offer up to him a sacrifice of the heart, lungs, hands, eyes, and blood of a young child. The grasping monomaniac made no hesitation, but agreed at once to the disgusting terms proposed to him. On the following night, Prelati went out alone, and after having been absent for three or four hours, returned to Gilles, who sat anxiously awaiting him. Prelati then informed him that he had seen the devil in the shape of a handsome youth of twenty. He further said, that the devil desired to be called *Barron* in all future invocations; and had shewn him a great number of ingots of pure gold, buried under a large oak in the neighbouring forest, all of which, and as many more as he desired, should become the property of the Maréchal de Rays if he remained firm, and broke no condition of the contract. Prelati further shewed him a small casket of black dust, which would turn iron into gold; but as the process was very troublesome, he advised that they should be contented with the ingots they found under the oak tree, and which would more than supply all the wants that the most extravagant imagination could desire. They were not, however, to attempt to look for the gold till a period of seven times seven weeks, or they would find nothing but slates and stones for their pains. Gilles expressed the utmost chagrin and disappointment, and at once said that he could not wait for so long a period; if the devil were not more, prompt Prelati might tell him that the Maréchal de Rays was not to be trifled with, and would decline all further communication with him. Prelati at last persuaded him to wait seven times seven days. They then went at midnight with picks and shovels to dig up the ground under the oak, where they found nothing to reward them but a great quantity of slates, marked with hieroglyphics. It was now Prelati's turn to be angry; and he loudly swore that the devil was nothing but a liar and a cheat. The marshal joined cordially in the opinion, but was easily persuaded by the cunning Italian to make one more trial. He promised at the same time that he would endeavour on the following night to discover the reason why the devil had broken his word. He went out alone accordingly, and on his return informed his patron that he had seen Barron, who was exceedingly angry that they had not waited the proper time ere they looked for the ingots. Barron had also said, that the Maréchal de Rays could hardly expect any favours from him, at a time when he must know that he had been meditating a pilgrimage to the Holy Land to make atonement for his sins. The Italian had doubtless surmised this from some incautious expression of his patron, for de Rays frankly confessed that there were times when, sick of the world and all its pomps and vanities, he thought of devoting himself to the service of God.

In this manner the Italian lured on from month to month his credulous and guilty patron, extracting from him all the valuables he possessed, and only waiting a favourable opportunity to decamp with his plunder. But the day of retribution was at hand for both. Young girls and boys continued to disappear in the most mysterious manner; and the rumours against the owner of Champtocé grew so loud and distinct, that the Church was compelled to interfere. Representations were made by the Bishop of Nantes to the Duke of Brittany, that it would be a public scandal if the accusations against the Maréchal de Rays were not inquired into. He was arrested accordingly in his own castle, along with his accomplice Prelati, and thrown into a dungeon at Nantes to await his trial.

The judges appointed to try him were the Bishop of Nantes Chancellor of Brittany, the Vicar of the Inquisition in France, and the celebrated Pierre l'Hôpital, the President of the provincial Parliament. The offences laid to his charge were, sorcery, sodomy, and murder. Gilles, on the first day of his trial, conducted himself with the utmost insolence. He braved the judges on the judgment-seat, calling them simoniacs and persons of impure life, and said he would rather be hanged by the neck like a dog without trial, than plead either guilty or not guilty before such contemptible miscreants. But his confidence forsook him as the trial proceeded, and he was found guilty on the clearest evidence of all the crimes laid to his charge. It was proved that he took insane pleasure in stabbing the victims of his lust and in observing the quivering of their flesh, and the fading lustre of their eyes as they expired. The confession of Prelati first made the judges acquainted with this horrid madness, and Gilles himself confirmed it before his death. Nearly a hundred children of the villagers around his two castles of Champtocé and Machecoue, had been missed within three years, the greater part, if not all, of whom were immolated to the lust or the cupidity of this monster. He imagined that he thus made the devil his friend, and that his recompense would be the secret of the philosopher's stone.

Gilles and Prelati were both condemned to be burned alive. At the place of execution they assumed the air of penitence and religion. Gilles tenderly embraced Prelati, saying, "*Farewell, friend Francis! In this world we shall never meet again; but let us place our hopes in God; we shall see each other in Paradise.*" Out of consideration for his high rank and connexions, the punishment of the marshal was so far mitigated, that he was not burned alive like Prelati. He was first strangled, and then thrown into the flames: his body, when half consumed, was given over to his relatives for interment, while that of the Italian was burned to ashes, and then scattered to the winds.[39]

## Jacques Cœur.

This remarkable pretender to the secret of the philosopher's stone was contemporary with the last mentioned. He was a great personage at the court of Charles VII., and in the events of his reign played a prominent part. From a very humble origin he rose to the highest honours of the state, and amassed enormous wealth by peculation and plunder of the country which he should have served. It was to hide his delinquencies in this respect, and to divert attention from the real source of his riches, that he boasted of having discovered the art of transmuting the inferior metals into gold and silver.

His father was a goldsmith in the city of Bourges; but so reduced in circumstances towards the latter years of his life, that he was unable to pay the necessary fees to procure his son's admission into the guild. Young Jacques became, however, a workman in the Royal Mint of Bourges, in 1428, and behaved himself so well, and shewed so much knowledge of metallurgy, that he attained rapid promotion in that establishment. He had also the good fortune to make the acquaintance of the fair Agnes Sorel, by whom he was patronised and much esteemed. Jacques had now three things in his favour — ability, perseverance, and the countenance of the king's mistress. Many a man succeeds with but one of these to help him forward; and it would have been strange indeed if Jacques Cœur, who had them all, should have languished in obscurity. While still a young man, he was made master of the mint, in which he had been a journeyman, and installed at the same time into the vacant office of grand treasurer of the royal household.

He possessed an extensive knowledge of finance, and turned it wonderfully to his own advantage, as soon as he became entrusted with extensive funds. He speculated in articles of the first necessity, and made himself popular by buying up grain, honey, wines, and other produce, till there was a scarcity, when he sold it again at enormous profit. Strong in the royal favour, he did not hesitate to oppress the poor by continual acts of forestalling and monopoly. As there is no enemy so bitter as the estranged friend, so of all the tyrants and tramplers upon the poor, there is none so fierce and reckless as the upstart that sprang from their ranks. The offensive pride of Jacques Cœur to his inferiors was the theme of indignant reproach in his own city, and his cringing humility to those above him was as much an object of contempt to the aristocrats into whose society he thrust himself. But Jacques did not care for the former, and to the latter he was blind. He continued his career till he became the richest man in France, and so useful to the king that no important enterprise was set on foot until he had been consulted. He was sent, in 1446, on an embassy to Genoa, and in the following year to Pope Nicholas V. In both these missions he acquitted himself to the satisfaction of his sovereign, and was rewarded with a lucrative appointment, in addition to those which he already held.

In the year 1449, the English in Normandy, deprived of their great general, the Duke of Bedford, broke the truce with the French king, and took possession of a small town belonging to the Duke of Brittany. This was the signal for the recommence-ment of a war, in which the French regained possession of nearly the whole province. The money for this war was advanced, for the most part, by Jacques Cœur. When Rouen yielded to the French, and Charles made his triumphal entry into that city, accompanied by Dunois and his most famous generals, Jacques was among the most brilliant of his *cortège*. His chariot and horses vied with those of the king in the magnificence of their trappings; and his enemies said of him that he publicly boasted that he alone had driven out the English, and that the valour of the troops would have been nothing without his gold.

Dunois appears, also, to have been partly of the same opinion. Without disparaging the courage of the army, he acknowledged the utility of the able financier, by whose means they had been fed and paid, and constantly afforded him his powerful protection.

When peace returned, Jacques again devoted himself to commerce, and fitted up several galleys to trade with the Genoese. He also bought large estates in various parts of France; the chief of which were the baronies of St. Fargeau, Meneton, Salone, Maubranche, Meaune, St. Gerant de Vaux, and St. Aon de Boissy; the earldoms or counties of La Palisse, Champignelle, Beaumont, and Villeneuve la Genêt, and the marquisate of Toucy. He also procured for his son, Jean Cœur, who had chosen the Church for his profession, a post no less distinguished than that of Archbishop of Bourges.

Every body said that so much wealth could not have been honestly acquired; and both rich and poor longed for the day that should humble the pride of the man, whom the one class regarded as an upstart and the other as an oppressor. Jacques was somewhat alarmed at the rumours that were afloat respecting him, and of dark hints that he had debased the coin of the realm and forged the king's seal to an important document, by which he had defrauded the state of very considerable sums. To silence these rumours, he invited many alchymists from foreign countries to reside with him, and circulated a counter rumour, that he had discovered the secret of the philosopher's stone. He also built a magnificent house in his native city, over the entrance of which he caused to be sculptured the emblems of that science. Some time afterwards he built another, no less splendid, at Montpellier, which he inscribed in a similar manner. He also wrote a treatise upon the hermetic philosophy, in which he pretended that he knew the secret of transmuting metals.

*House of Jacques Cœur, Bourges.*

But all these attempts to disguise his numerous acts of peculation proved unavailing; and he was arrested in 1452, and brought to trial on several charges. Upon one only, which the malice of his enemies invented to ruin him, was he acquitted; which was, that he had been accessory to the death, by poison, of his kind patroness, Agnes Sorel. Upon the others he was found guilty, and sentenced to be banished the kingdom, and to pay the enormous fine of four hundred thousand crowns. It was proved that he had forged the king's seal; that in his capacity of master of the mint of Bourges, he had debased, to a very great extent, the gold and silver coin of the realm; and that he had not hesitated to supply the Turks with arms and money to enable them to carry on war against their Christian neighbours, for which service he had received the most munificent recompenses.

Charles VII. was deeply grieved at his condemnation, and believed to the last that he was innocent. By his means the fine was reduced within a sum which Jacques Cœur could pay. After remaining for some time in prison, he was liberated, and left France with a large sum of money, part of which, it was alleged, was secretly paid him by Charles out of the produce of his confiscated estates. He retired to Cyprus, where he died about 1460, the richest and most conspicuous personage of the island. The writers upon alchymy all claim Jacques Cœur as a member of their fraternity, and treat as false and libellous the more rational explanation of his wealth which the records of his trial afford. Pierre Borel, in his *Antiquités Gauloises*, maintains the opinion that Jacques was an honest man, and that he made his gold out of lead and copper by means of the philosopher's stone. The alchymic adepts in general were of the same opinion; but they found it difficult to persuade even his contemporaries of the fact. Posterity is still less likely to believe it.

### Inferior Adepts of the Fourteenth and Fifteenth Centuries.

Many other pretenders to the secrets of the philosopher's stone appeared in every country in Europe, during the fourteenth and fifteenth centuries. The possibility of transmutation was so generally admitted, that every chemist was more or less an alchymist. Germany, Holland, Italy, Spain, Poland, France, and England produced thousands of obscure adepts, who supported themselves, in the pursuit of their chimera, by the more profitable resources of astrology and divination. The monarchs of Europe were no less persuaded than their subjects of the possibility of discovering the philosopher's stone. Henry VI. and Edward IV. of England encouraged alchymy. In Germany, the Emperors Maximilian, Rudolph, and Frederic II. devoted much of their attention to it; and every inferior potentate within their dominions imitated their example. It was a common practice in Germany, among the nobles and petty sovereigns, to invite an alchymist to take up his residence among them, that they might confine him in a dungeon till he made gold enough to pay millions for his ransom. Many poor wretches suffered perpetual imprisonment in consequence. A similar fate appears to have been intended by Edward II. for Raymond Lulli, who, upon the pretence that he was thereby honoured, was accommodated with apartments in the Tower of London. He found out in time the trick that was about to be played him, and managed to make his escape; some of his biographers say, by jumping into the Thames, and swimming to a vessel that lay waiting to receive him. In the sixteenth century, the same system was pursued, as will be shewn more fully in the life of Seton the Cosmopolite.

The following is a catalogue of the chief authors upon alchymy, who flourished during this epoch, and whose lives and adventures are either unknown or are unworthy of more detailed notice. John Dowston, an Englishman, lived in 1315, and wrote two treatises on the philosopher's stone. Richard, or, as some call him, Robert, also an Englishman, lived in 1330, and wrote a work entitled *Correctorium Alchymiæ*, which was much esteemed till the time of Paracelsus. In the same year lived Peter of Lombardy, who wrote what he called a *Complete Treatise upon the Hermetic Science*, an abridgment of which was afterwards published by Lacini, a monk of Calabria. In 1330 the most famous alchymist of Paris was one Odomare, whose work, *De Practica Magistri*, was for a long time a hand-book among the brethren of the science. John de Rupecissa, a French monk of the order of St. Francis, flourished in 1357, and pretended to be a prophet as well as an alchymist. Some of his prophecies were so disagreeable to Pope Innocent VI., that the pontiff determined to put a stop to them, by locking up the prophet in the dungeons of the Vatican. It is generally believed that he died there, though there is no evidence of the fact. His chief works are, the *Book of Light*, the *Five Essences*, the *Heaven of Philosophers*, and his grand work, *De Confectione Lapidis*. He was not thought a shining light among the adepts. Ortholani was another pretender, of whom nothing is known, but that he exercised the arts of alchymy and astrology at Paris, shortly before the time of Nicholas Flamel. His work on the practice of alchymy was written in that city in 1358. Isaac of Holland wrote, it is supposed, about this time; and his son also devoted himself to the science. Nothing worth repeating is known of their lives. Boerhaave speaks with commendation of many passages in their works, and Paracelsus esteemed them highly: the chief are, *De Triplici Ordine Elixiris et Lapidis Theoria*, printed at Berne in 1608; and *Mineralia Opera, seu de Lapide Philosophico*, printed at Middleburg in 1600. They also wrote eight other works upon the same subject. Koffstky, a Pole, wrote an alchymical treatise, entitled *The Tincture of Minerals*, about the year 1488. In this list of authors a royal name must not be forgotten. Charles VI. of France, one of the most credulous princes of the day, whose court absolutely swarmed with alchymists, conjurers, astrologers, and quacks of every description, made several attempts to discover the philosopher's stone, and thought he knew so much about it, that he determined to enlighten the world with a treatise; it is called the *Royal Work of Charles VI. of France, and the Treasure of Philosophy*. It is said to be the original from which Nicholas Flamel took the idea of his *Désir désiré*. Lenglet du Fresnoy says it is very allegorical, and utterly incomprehensible. For a more complete list of the hermetic philosophers of the fourteenth and fifteenth centuries, the reader is referred to the third volume of Lenglet's History, already quoted.

---

**Progress of the infatuation during the sixteenth and seventeenth centuries. — present state of the science.**

During the sixteenth and seventeenth centuries, the search for the philosopher's stone was continued by thousands of the enthusiastic and the credulous; but a great change was introduced during this period. The eminent men who devoted themselves to the study totally changed its aspect, and referred to the possession of their wondrous stone and elixir, not only the conversion of the base into the precious metals, but the solution of all the difficulties of other sciences. They pretended that by its means man would be brought into closer communion with his Maker; that disease and sorrow would be banished from the world; and that "the millions of spiritual beings who walk the earth unseen" would be rendered visible, and become the friends, companions, and instructors of mankind. In the seventeenth century more especially, these poetical and fantastic doctrines excited the notice of Europe; and from Germany, where they had been first disseminated by Rosencreutz, spread into France and England, and ran away with the sound judgment of many clever but too enthusiastic searchers for the truth. Paracelsus, Dee, and many others of less note, were captivated by the grace and beauty of the new mythology, which was arising to adorn the literature of Europe. Most of the alchymists of the sixteenth century, although ignorant of the Rosicrucians as a sect, were, in some degree, tinctured with their fanciful tenets: but before we speak more fully of these poetical visionaries, it will be necessary to resume the history of the hermetic folly, and trace the gradual change that stole over the dreams of the adepts. It will be seen that the infatuation increased rather than diminished as the world grew older.

**Augurello.**

Among the alchymists who were born in the fifteenth, and distinguished themselves in the sixteenth century, the first in point of date is John Aurelio Augurello. He was born at Rimini in 1441, and became professor of the *belles lettres* at Venice and Trevisa. He was early convinced of the truth of the hermetic science, and used to pray to God that he might be happy enough to discover the philosopher's stone. He was continually surrounded by the paraphernalia of chemistry, and expended all his wealth in the purchase of drugs and metals. He was also a poet, but of less merit than pretensions. His *Chrysopeia*, in which he pretended to teach the art of making gold, he dedicated to Pope Leo X., in the hope that the pontiff would reward him handsomely for the compliment; but the pope was too good a judge of poetry to be pleased with the worse than mediocrity of his poem, and too good a philosopher to approve of the strange doctrines which it inculcated; he was, therefore, far from gratified at the dedication. It is said, that when Augurello applied to him for a reward, the pope, with great ceremony and much apparent kindness and cordiality, drew an empty purse from his pocket, and presented it to the alchymist, saying, that since he was able to make gold, the most appropriate present that could be made him, was a purse to put it in. This scurvy reward was all that the poor alchymist ever got either for his poetry or his alchymy. He died in a state of extreme poverty, in the eighty-third year of his age.

## Cornelius Agrippa.

This alchymist has left a distinguished reputation. The most extraordinary tales were told and believed of his powers. He could turn iron into gold by his mere word. All the spirits of the air and demons of the earth were under his command, and bound to obey him in everything. He could raise from the dead the forms of the great men of other days, and make them appear, "in their habit as they lived," to the gaze of the curious who had courage enough to abide their presence.

*Cornelius Agrippa.*

He was born at Cologne in 1486, and began at an early age the study of chemistry and philosophy. By some means or other, which have never been very clearly explained, he managed to impress his contemporaries with a great idea of his wonderful attainments. At the early age of twenty, so great was his reputation as an alchymist, that the principal adepts of Paris wrote to

Cologne, inviting him to settle in France, and aid them with his experience in discovering the philosopher's stone. Honours poured upon him in thick succession; and he was highly esteemed by all the learned men of his time. Melancthon speaks of him with respect and commendation. Erasmus also bears testimony in his favour; and the general voice of his age proclaimed him a light of literature and an ornament to philosophy. Some men, by dint of excessive egotism, manage to persuade their contemporaries that they are very great men indeed: they publish their acquirements so loudly in people's ears, and keep up their own praises so incessantly, that the world's applause is actually taken by storm. Such seems to have been the case with Agrippa. He called himself a sublime theologian, an excellent jurisconsult, an able physician, a great philosopher, and a successful alchymist. The world at last took him at his word; and thought that a man who talked so big, must have some merit to recommend him, — that it was, indeed, a great trumpet which sounded so obstreperous a blast. He was made secretary to the Emperor Maximilian, who conferred upon him the title of chevalier, and gave him the honorary command of a regiment. He afterwards became professor of Hebrew and the *belles lettres* at the University of Dôle, in France; but quarrelling with the Franciscan monks upon some knotty points of divinity, he was obliged to quit the town. He took refuge in London, where he taught Hebrew and cast nativities, for about a year. From London he proceeded to Pavia, and gave lectures upon the writings, real or supposed, of Hermes Trismegistus; and might have lived there in peace and honour, had he not again quarrelled with the clergy. By their means his position became so disagreeable that he was glad to accept an offer made him by the magistracy of Metz, to become their syndic and advocate-general. Here, again, his love of disputation made him enemies: the theological wiseacres of that city asserted that St. Ann had three husbands, in which opinion they were confirmed by the popular belief of the day. Agrippa needlessly ran foul of this opinion, or prejudice as he called it, and thereby lost much of his influence. Another dispute, more creditable to his character, occurred soon after, and sank him for ever in the estimation of the Metzians. Humanely taking the part of a young girl who was accused of witchcraft, his enemies asserted that he was himself a sorcerer, and raised such a storm over his head, that he was forced to fly the city. After this he became physician to Louisa de Savoy, mother of King Francis I. This lady was curious to know the future, and required her physician to cast her nativity. Agrippa replied that he would not encourage such idle curiosity. The result was, he lost her confidence, and was forthwith dismissed. If it had been through his belief in the worthlessness of astrology, that he had made his answer, we might admire his honest and fearless independence; but when it is known that, at the very same time, he was in the constant habit of divination and fortune-telling, and that he was predicting splendid success, in all his undertakings, to the Constable of Bourbon, we can only wonder at his thus estranging a powerful friend through mere petulance and perversity.

He was about this time invited, both by Henry VIII. of England, and Margaret of Austria, governess of the Low Countries, to fix his residence in their dominions. He chose the service of the latter, by whose influence he was made historiographer to the Emperor Charles V. Unfortunately for Agrippa, he never had stability enough to remain long in one position, and offended his patrons by his restlessness and presumption. After the death of Margaret he was imprisoned at Brussels, on a charge of sorcery. He was released after a year; and quitting the country, experienced many vicissitudes. He died in great poverty in 1534, aged forty-eight years.

While in the service of Margaret of Austria, he resided principally at Louvain, in which city he wrote his famous work on the *Vanity and Nothingness of Human Knowledge*. He also wrote to please his royal mistress, a treatise upon the *Superiority of the Female Sex*, which he dedicated to her in token of his gratitude for the favours she had heaped upon him. The reputation he left behind him in these provinces was any thing but favourable. A great number of the marvellous tales that are told of him relate to this period of his life. It was said, that the gold which he paid to the traders with whom he dealt, always looked remarkably bright, but invariably turned into pieces of slate and stone in the course of four-and-twenty hours. Of this spurious gold he was believed to have made large quantities by the aid of the devil, who, it would appear from this, had but a very superficial knowledge of alchymy, and much less than the Maréchal de Rays gave him credit for. The Jesuit Delrio, in his book on magic and sorcery, relates a still more extraordinary story of him. One day, Agrippa left his house at Louvain, and intending to be absent for some time, gave the key of his study to his wife, with strict orders that no one should enter it during his absence. The lady herself, strange as it may appear, had no curiosity to pry into her husband's secrets, and never once thought of entering the forbidden room; but a young student, who had been accommodated with an attic in the philosopher's house, burned with a fierce desire to examine the study; hoping, perchance, that he might purloin some book or implement which would instruct him in the art of transmuting metals. The youth, being handsome, eloquent, and, above all, highly complimentary to the charms of the lady, she was persuaded without much difficulty to lend him the key, but gave him strict orders not to remove any thing. The student promised implicit obedience, and entered Agrippa's study. The first object that caught his attention was a large *grimoire*, or book of spells, which lay open on the philosopher's desk. He sat himself down immediately and began to read. At the first word he uttered, he fancied he heard a knock at the door. He listened, but all was silent. Thinking that his imagination had deceived him, he read on, when immediately a louder knock was heard, which so terrified him, that he started to his feet. He tried to say "Come in," but his tongue refused its office, and he could not articulate a sound. He fixed his eyes upon the door, which, slowly opening, disclosed a stranger of majestic form, but scowling features, who demanded sternly, why he was summoned? "I did not summon you," said the trembling student. "You did!" said the stranger, advancing angrily; "and the demons are not to be invoked in vain." The student could make no reply; and the demon, enraged that one of the uninitiated should have summoned him out of mere presumption, seized him by the throat and strangled him. When Agrippa returned, a few days afterwards, he found his house beset with devils. Some of them were sitting on the chimney-pots, kicking up their legs in the air; while others were playing at leapfrog on the very edge of the parapet. His study was so filled with them, that he found it difficult to make his way to his desk. When, at last, he had elbowed his way through them, he found his book open, and the student lying dead upon the floor. He saw immediately how the mischief had been done; and dismissing all the inferior imps, asked the principal demon how he could have been so rash as to kill the young man. The demon replied, that he had been needlessly invoked by an insulting youth, and could do no less than kill him for his presumption. Agrippa reprimanded him severely, and ordered him immediately to reanimate the dead body, and walk about with it in the market-place for the whole of the afternoon. The demon did so; the student revived, and putting his arm through that of his unearthly murderer, walked very lovingly with him in sight of all the people. At sunset, the body fell down again, cold and lifeless as before, and was carried by the crowd to the hospital, it being the general opinion that he had expired in a fit of apoplexy. His conductor immediately disappeared. When the body was examined, marks of strangulation were found on the neck, and prints of the long claws of the demon on various parts of it. These appearances, together with a story, which soon obtained currency, that the companion of the young man had vanished in a cloud of flame and smoke, opened people's eyes to the truth. The magistrates of Louvain instituted inquiries, and the result was, that Agrippa was obliged to quit the town.

Other authors besides Delrio relate similar stories of this philosopher. The world in those days was always willing enough to believe in tales of magic and sorcery; and when, as in Agrippa's case, the alleged magician gave himself out for such, and claimed credit for the wonders he worked, it is not surprising that the age should have allowed his pretensions. It was dangerous boasting, which sometimes led to the stake or the gallows, and therefore was thought to be not without foundation. Paulus Jovius, in his *Eulogia Doctorum Virorum*, says, that the devil, in the shape of a large black dog, attended Agrippa wherever he went. Thomas Nash, in his *Adventures of Jack Wilton*, relates, that, at the request of Lord Surrey, Erasmus, and some other learned men, Agrippa called up from the grave many of the great philosophers of antiquity; among others, Tully, whom he caused to re-deliver his celebrated oration for Roscius. He also shewed Lord Surrey, when in Germany, an exact resemblance in a glass of his mistress, the fair Geraldine. She was represented on a couch weeping for the absence of her lover. Lord Surrey made a note of the exact time at which he saw this vision, and ascertained afterwards that his mistress was actually so employed at the very minute. To Thomas Lord Cromwell, Agrippa represented King Henry VIII. hunting in Windsor Park, with the principal lords of his court; and to please the Emperor Charles V. he summoned King David and King Solomon from the tomb.

Naudé, in his *"Apology for the great Men who have been falsely suspected of Magic,"* takes a great deal of pains to clear Agrippa from the imputations cast upon him by Delrio, Paulus Jovius, and other such ignorant and prejudiced scribblers. Such stories demanded refutation in the days of Naudé, but they may now be safely left to decay in their own absurdity. That they should have attached, however, to the memory of a man who claimed the power of making iron obey him when he told it to become gold, and who wrote such a work as that upon magic, which goes by his name, is not at all surprising.

### Paracelsus.

This philosopher, called by Naudé "the zenith and rising sun of all the alchymists," was born at Einsiedeln, near Zurich, in the year 1493. His true name was Hohenheim; to which, as he himself informs us, were prefixed the baptismal names of Aureolus Theophrastus Bombastes Paracelsus. The last of these he chose for his common designation while he was yet a boy; and rendered it, before he died, one of the most famous in the annals of his time. His father, who was a physician, educated his son for the same pursuit. The latter was an apt scholar, and made great progress. By chance the work of Isaac Hollandus fell into his hands, and from that time he became smitten with the mania of the philosopher's stone. All his thoughts henceforth were devoted to metallurgy; and he travelled into Sweden that he might visit the mines of that country, and examine the ores while they yet lay in the bowels of the earth. He also visited Trithemius at the monastery of Spannheim, and obtained instructions from him in the science of alchymy. Continuing his travels, he proceeded through Prussia and Austria into Turkey, Egypt, and Tartary, and thence returning to Constantinople, learned, as he boasted, the art of transmutation, and became possessed of the *elixir vitæ*. He then established himself as a physician in his native Switzerland at Zurich, and commenced writing works upon alchymy and medicine, which immediately fixed the attention of Europe. Their great obscurity was no impediment to their fame; for the less the author was understood, the more the demonologists, fanatics, and philosopher's-stone hunters seemed to appreciate him. His fame as a physician kept pace with that which he enjoyed as an alchymist, owing to his having effected some happy cures by means of mercury and opium, — drugs unceremoniously condemned by his professional brethren. In the year 1526, he was chosen professor of physics and natural philosophy in the University of Basle, where his lectures attracted vast numbers of students. He denounced the writings of all former physicians as tending to mislead; and publicly burned the works of Galen and Avicenna, as quacks and impostors. He exclaimed, in presence of the admiring and half-bewildered crowd, who assembled to witness the ceremony, that there was more knowledge in his shoe-strings than in the writings of these physicians. Continuing in the same strain, he said, all the Universities in the world were full of ignorant quacks; but that he, Paracelsus, overflowed with wisdom. "You will all follow my new system," said he, with furious gesticulations, "Avicenna, Galen, Rhazis, Montagnana, Memé, — you will all follow me, ye professors of Paris, Montpellier, Germany, Cologne, and Vienna!

and all ye that dwell on the Rhine and the Danube, — ye that inhabit the isles of the sea; and ye also, Italians, Dalmatians, Athenians, Arabians, Jews, — ye will all follow my doctrines, for I am the monarch of medicine!"

*Paracelsus.*

But he did not long enjoy the esteem of the good citizens of Basle. It is said that he indulged in wine so freely, as not unfrequently to be seen in the streets in a state of intoxication. This was ruinous for a physician, and his good fame decreased rapidly. His ill fame increased in still greater proportion, especially when he assumed the airs of a sorcerer. He boasted of the legions of spirits at his command; and of one especially, which he kept imprisoned in the hilt of his sword. Wetteras, who lived twenty-seven months in his service, relates that he often threatened to invoke a whole army of demons, and shew him the great authority which he could exercise over them. He let it be believed that the spirit in his sword had custody of the elixir of life, by means of which he could make any one live to be as old as the antediluvians. He also boasted that he had a spirit at his command, called "Azoth," whom he kept imprisoned in a jewel; and in many of the old portraits he is represented with a jewel, inscribed with the word "Azoth, in his hand."

If a sober prophet has little honour in his own country, a drunken one has still less. Paracelsus found it at last convenient to quit Basle, and establish himself at Strasbourg. The immediate cause of this change of residence was as follows. A citizen lay at the point of death, and was given over by all the physicians of the town. As a last resource Paracelsus was called in, to whom the sick man promised a magnificent recompense, if, by his means, he were cured. Paracelsus gave him two small pills, which the man took, and rapidly recovered. When he was quite well, Paracelsus sent for his fee; but the citizen had no great opinion of the value of a cure which had been so speedily effected. He had no notion of paying a handful of gold for two pills, although they had saved his life, and he refused to pay more than the usual fee for a single visit. Paracelsus brought an action against him, and lost it. This result so exasperated him, that he left Basle in high dudgeon. He resumed his wandering life, and travelled in Germany and Hungary, supporting himself as he went on the credulity and infatuation of all classes of society. He cast nativities — told fortunes — aided those who had money to throw away upon the experiment, to find the philosopher's stone — prescribed remedies for cows and pigs, and aided in the recovery of stolen goods. After residing successively at Nuremburg, Augsburg, Vienna, and Mindelheim, he retired in the year 1541 to Saltzbourg, and died in a state of abject poverty in the hospital of that town.

If this strange charlatan found hundreds of admirers during his life, he found thousands after his death. A sect of Paracelsists sprang up in France and Germany, to perpetuate the extravagant doctrines of their founder upon all the sciences, and upon alchymy in particular. The chief leaders were Bodenstein and Dorneus. The following is a summary of his doctrine, founded upon the supposed existence of the philosopher's stone; it is worth preserving from its very absurdity, and is altogether unparalleled in the history of philosophy. First of all, he maintained that the contemplation of the perfection of the Deity sufficed to procure all wisdom and knowledge; that the Bible was the key to the theory of all diseases, and that it was necessary to search into the Apocalypse to know the signification of magic medicine. The man who blindly obeyed the will of God, and who succeeded in identifying himself with the celestial intelligences, possessed the philosopher's stone — he could cure all diseases, and prolong life to as many centuries as he pleased;

it being by the very same means that Adam and the antediluvian patriarchs prolonged theirs. Life was an emanation from the stars—the sun governed the heart, and the moon the brain. Jupiter governed the liver, Saturn the gall, Mercury the lungs, Mars the bile, and Venus the loins. In the stomach of every human being there dwelt a demon, or intelligence, that was a sort of alchymist in his way, and mixed, in their due proportions, in his crucible, the various aliments that were sent into that grand laboratory, the belly.[40] He was proud of the title of magician, and boasted that he kept up a regular correspondence with Galen from hell; and that he often summoned Avicenna from the same regions to dispute with him on the false notions he had promulgated respecting alchymy, and especially regarding potable gold and the elixir of life. He imagined that gold could cure ossification of the heart, and, in fact, all diseases, if it were gold which had been transmuted from an inferior metal by means of the philosopher's stone, and if it were applied under certain conjunctions of the planets. The mere list of the works in which he advances these frantic imaginings, which he called a doctrine, would occupy several pages.

### George Agricola.

This alchymist was born in the province of Misnia, in 1494. His real name was *Bauer*, meaning a husbandman, which, in accordance with the common fashion of his age, he latinised into Agricola. From his early youth, he delighted in the visions of the hermetic science. Ere he was sixteen, he longed for the great elixir which was to make him live for seven hundred years, and for the stone which was to procure him wealth to cheer him in his multiplicity of days. He published a small treatise upon the subject at Cologne, in 1531, which obtained him the patronage of the celebrated Maurice duke of Saxony. After practising for some years as a physician at Joachimsthal, in Bohemia, he was employed by Maurice as superintendent of the silver mines of Chemnitz. He led a happy life among the miners, making various experiments in alchymy while deep in the bowels of the earth. He acquired a great knowledge of metals, and gradually got rid of his extravagant notions about the philosopher's stone. The miners had no faith in alchymy; and they converted him to their way of thinking, not only in that but in other respects. From their legends, he became firmly convinced that the bowels of the earth were inhabited by good and evil spirits, and that firedamp and other explosions sprang from no other causes than the mischievous propensities of the latter. He died in the year 1555, leaving behind him the reputation of a very able and intelligent man.

## Denis Zachaire.

Autobiography, written by a wise man who was once a fool, is not only the most instructive, but the most delightful of reading. Denis Zachaire, an alchymist of the sixteenth century, has performed this task, and left a record of his folly and infatuation in pursuit of the philosopher's stone, which well repays perusal. He was born in the year 1510, of an ancient family in Guienne, and was early sent to the university of Bordeaux, under the care of a tutor to direct his studies. Unfortunately his tutor was a searcher for the grand elixir, and soon rendered his pupil as mad as himself upon the subject. With this introduction, we will allow Denis Zachaire to speak for himself, and continue his narrative in his own words: "I received from home," says he, "the sum of two hundred crowns for the expenses of myself and master; but before the end of the year, all our money went away in the smoke of our furnaces. My master, at the same time, died of a fever, brought on by the parching heat of our laboratory, from which he seldom or never stirred, and which was scarcely less hot than the arsenal of Venice. His death was the more unfortunate for me, as my parents took the opportunity of reducing my allowance, and sending me only sufficient for my board and lodging, instead of the sum I required to continue my operations in alchymy.

"To meet this difficulty and get out of leading-strings, I returned home at the age of twenty-five, and mortgaged part of my property for four hundred crowns. This sum was necessary to perform an operation of the science, which had been communicated to me by an Italian at Toulouse, and who, as he said, had proved its efficacy. I retained this man in my service, that we might see the end of the experiment. I then, by means of strong distillations, tried to calcinate gold and silver; but all my labour was in vain. The weight of the gold I drew out of my furnace was diminished by one-half since I put it in, and my four hundred crowns were very soon reduced to two hundred and thirty. I gave twenty of these to my Italian, in order that he might travel to Milan, where the author of the receipt resided, and ask him the explanation of some passages which we thought obscure. I remained at Toulouse all the winter, in the hope of his return; but I might have remained there till this day if I had waited for him, for I never saw his face again.

"In the succeeding summer there was a great plague, which forced me to quit the town. I did not, however, lose sight of my work. I went to Cahors, where I remained six months, and made the acquaintance of an old man, who was commonly known to the people as 'the Philosopher;' a name which, in country places, is often bestowed upon people whose only merit is, that they are less ignorant than their neighbours. I shewed him my collection of alchymical receipts, and asked his opinion upon them. He picked out ten or twelve of them, merely saying that they were better than the others. When the plague ceased, I returned to Toulouse, and recommenced my experiments in search of the stone. I worked to such effect that my four hundred crowns were reduced to one hundred and seventy.

"That I might continue my work on a safer method, I made acquaintance, in 1537, with a certain abbé who resided in the neighbourhood. He was smitten with the same mania as myself, and told me that one of his friends, who had followed to Rome in the retinue of the Cardinal d'Armagnac, had sent him from that city a new receipt which could not fail to transmute iron and copper, but which would cost two hundred crowns. I provided half this money, and the abbé the rest; and we began to operate at our joint expense. As we required spirits of wine for our experiment, I bought a tun of excellent vin de Gaillac. I extracted the spirit, and rectified it several times. We took a quantity of this, into which we put four marks of silver and one of gold that had been undergoing the process of calcination for a month. We put this mixture cleverly into a sort of horn-shaped vessel, with another to serve as a retort; and placed the whole apparatus upon our furnace to produce congelation. This experiment lasted a year; but, not to remain idle, we amused ourselves with many other less important operations. We drew quite as much profit from these as from our great work.

"The whole of the year 1537 passed over without producing any change whatever; in fact we might have waited till doomsday for the congelation of our spirits of wine. However, we made a projection with it upon some heated quicksilver; but all was in vain. Judge of our chagrin, especially of that of the abbé, who had already boasted to all the monks of his monastery, that they had only to bring the large pump which stood in a corner of the cloister, and he would convert it into gold: but this ill luck did not prevent us from persevering. I once more mortgaged my paternal lands for four hundred crowns, the whole of which I determined to devote to a renewal of my search for the great secret. The abbé contributed the same sum; and with these eight hundred crowns I proceeded to Paris, a city more abounding with alchymists than any other in the world, resolved never to leave it until I had either found the philosopher's stone or spent all my money. This journey gave the greatest offence to all my relations and friends, who, imagining that I was fitted to be a great lawyer, were anxious that I should establish myself in that profession. For the sake of quietness, I pretended, at last, that such was my object.

"After travelling for fifteen days, I arrived in Paris on the 9th of January 1539. I remained for a month almost unknown; but I had no sooner begun to frequent the amateurs of the science, and visited the shops of the furnace-makers, than I had the acquaintance of more than a hundred operative alchymists, each of whom had a different theory and a different mode of working. Some of them preferred cementation; others sought the universal alkahest or dissolvent; and some of them boasted the great efficacy of the essence of emery. Some of them endeavoured to extract mercury from other metals, to fix it afterwards; and, in order that each of us should be thoroughly acquainted with the proceedings of the others, we agreed to meet somewhere every night and report progress. We met sometimes at the house of one, and sometimes in the garret of another; not only on week days, but on Sundays and the great festivals of the Church. 'Ah!' one used to say, 'if I had the means of recommencing this experiment, I should do something.' 'Yes,' said another, 'if my crucible had not cracked, I should have succeeded before now;' while a third exclaimed, with a sigh, 'If I had but had a round copper vessel of sufficient strength, I would have fixed mercury with silver.' There was not one among them who had not some excuse for his failure; but I was deaf to all their speeches. I did not want to part with my money to any of them, remembering how often I had been the dupe of such promises.

"A Greek at last presented himself; and with him I worked a long time uselessly upon nails made of cinnabar or vermilion. I was also acquainted with a foreign gentleman newly arrived in Paris, and often accompanied him to the shops of the goldsmiths to sell pieces of gold and silver, the produce, as he said, of his experiments. I stuck closely to him for a long time, in the hope that he would impart his secret. He refused for a long time, but acceded at last on my earnest entreaty, and I found that it was nothing more than an ingenious trick. I did not fail to inform my friend the abbé, whom I had left at Toulouse, of all my adventures; and sent him, among other matters, a relation of the trick by which this gentleman pretended to turn lead into gold. The abbé still imagined that I should succeed at last, and advised me to remain another year in Paris, where I had made so good a beginning. I remained there three years; but, notwithstanding all my efforts, I had no more success than I had had elsewhere.

"I had just got to the end of my money, when I received a letter from the abbé, telling me to leave every thing, and join him immediately at Toulouse. I went accordingly, and found that he had received letters from the king of Navarre (grandfather of Henry IV.). This prince was a great lover of philosophy, full of curiosity, and had written to the abbé that I should visit him at Pau; and that he would give me three or four thousand crowns if I would communicate the secret I had learned from the foreign gentleman. The abbé's ears were so tickled with the four thousand crowns, that he let me have no peace night or day until he had fairly seen me on the road to Pau. I arrived at that place in the month of May 1542. I worked away, and succeeded, according to the receipt I had obtained. When I had finished to the satisfaction of the king, he gave me the reward that I expected. Although he was willing enough to do me further service, he was dissuaded from it by the lords of his court; even by many of those who had been most anxious that I should come. He sent me then about my business, with many thanks; saying, that if there was any thing in his kingdom which he could give me — such as the *produce of confiscations or the like – he should be most happy. I thought I might stay long enough for these prospective confiscations, and never get them at last; and I therefore determined to go back to my friend the abbé.*

*"I learned that, on the road between Pau and Toulouse, there resided a monk who was very skilful in all matters of natural philosophy. On my return, I paid him a visit. He pitied me very much, and advised me, with much warmth and kindness of expression, not to amuse myself any longer with such experiments as these, which were all false and sophistical; but that I should read the good books of the old philosophers, where I might not only find the true matter of the science of alchymy, but learn also the exact order of operations which ought to be followed. I very much approved of this wise advice; but before I acted upon it, I went back to my abbé of Toulouse, to give him an account of the eight hundred crowns which we had had in common, and, at the same time, share with him such reward as I had received from the king of Navarre. If he was little satisfied with the relation of my adventures since our first separation, he appeared still less satisfied when I told him I had formed a resolution to renounce the search for the philosopher's stone. The reason was that he thought me a good artist. Of our eight hundred crowns, there remained but one hundred and seventy-six. When I quitted the abbé, I went to my own house with the intention of remaining there, till I had read all the old philosophers, and of then proceeding to Paris.*

*"I arrived in Paris on the day after All Saints, of the year 1546, and devoted another year to the assiduous study of great authors. Among others, the Turba Philosophorum of the Good Trevisan, the Remonstrance of Nature to the Wandering Alchymist, by Jean de Meung, and several others of the best books; but, as I had no right principles, I did not well know what course to follow.*

*"At last I left my solitude, not to see my former acquaintances, the adepts and operators, but to frequent the society of true philosophers. Among them I fell into still greater uncertainties; being, in fact, completely bewildered by the variety of operations which they shewed me. Spurred on, nevertheless, by a sort of frenzy or inspiration, I threw myself into the works of Raymond Lulli and of Arnold de Villeneuve. The reading of these, and the reflections I made upon them, occupied me for another year, when I finally determined on the course I should*

adopt. I was obliged to wait, however, until I had mortgaged another very considerable portion of my patrimony. This business was not settled until the beginning of Lent, 1549, when I commenced my operations. I laid in a stock of all that was necessary, and began to work the day after Easter. It was not, however, without some disquietude and opposition from my friends who came about me; one asking me what I was going to do, and whether I had not already spent money enough upon such follies? Another assured me that, if I bought so much charcoal, I should strengthen the suspicion already existing, that I was a coiner of base money. Another advised me to purchase some place in the magistracy, as I was already a Doctor of Laws. My relations spoke in terms still more annoying to me, and even threatened that, if I continued to make such a fool of myself, they would send a posse of police-officers into my house, and break all my furnaces and crucibles into atoms. I was wearied almost to death by this continued persecution; but I found comfort in my work and in the progress of my experiment, to which I was very attentive, and which went on bravely from day to day. About this time, there was a dreadful plague in Paris, which interrupted all intercourse between man and man, and left me as much to myself as I could desire. I soon had the satisfaction to remark the progress and succession of the three colours which, according to the philosophers, always prognosticate the approaching perfection of the work. I observed them distinctly, one after the other; and next year, being Easter Sunday, 1550, I made the great trial. Some common quicksilver, which I put into a small crucible on the fire, was, in less than an hour, converted into very good gold. You may judge how great was my joy, but I took care not to boast of it. I returned thanks to God for the favour he had shewn me, and prayed that I might only be permitted to make such use of it as would redound to his glory.

"On the following day, I went towards Toulouse to find, the abbé, in accordance with a mutual promise, that we should communicate our discoveries to each other. On my way, I called in to see the sage monk who had assisted me with his counsels; but I had the sorrow to learn that they were both dead. After this, I would not return to my own home, but retired to another place, to await one of my relations whom I had left in charge of my estate. I gave him orders to sell all that belonged to me, as well movable as immovable — to pay my debts with the proceeds, and divide all the rest among those in any way related to me *who might stand in need of it, in order that they might enjoy some share of the good fortune which had befallen me. There was a great deal of talk in the neighbourhood about my precipitate retreat; the wisest of my acquaintance imagining that, broken down and ruined by my mad expenses, I sold my little remaining property, that I might go and hide my shame in distant countries.*

*"My relative already spoken of rejoined me on the 1st of July, after having performed all the business I had entrusted him with. We took our departure together, to seek a land of liberty. We first retired to Lausanne, in Switzerland, when, after remaining there for some time, we resolved to pass the remainder of our days in some of the most celebrated cities of Germany, living quietly and without splendour."*

Thus ends the story of Denis Zachaire, as written by himself. He has not been so candid at its conclusion as at its commencement, and has left the world in doubt as to his real motives for pretending that he had discovered the philosopher's stone. It seems probable that the sentence he puts into the mouths of his wisest acquaintances was the true reason of his retreat; that he was, in fact, reduced to poverty, and hid his shame in foreign countries. Nothing further is known of his life, and his real name has never yet been discovered. He wrote a work on alchymy, entitled *The true Natural Philosophy of Metals.*

## Dr. Dee and Edward Kelly.

John Dee and Edward Kelly claim to be mentioned together, having been so long associated in the same pursuits, and undergone so many strange vicissitudes in each other's society. Dee was altogether a wonderful man, and had he lived in an age when folly and superstition were less rife, he would, with the same powers which he enjoyed, have left behind him a bright and enduring reputation. He was born in London in the year 1527, and very early manifested a love for study. At the age of fifteen he was sent to Cambridge, and delighted so much in his books, that he passed regularly eighteen hours every day among them. Of the other six, he devoted four to sleep and two for refreshment. Such intense application did not injure his health, and could not fail to make him one of the first scholars of his time. Unfortunately, however, he quitted the mathematics and the pursuits of true philosophy, to indulge in the unprofitable reveries of the occult sciences. He studied alchymy, astrology, and magic, and thereby rendered himself obnoxious to the authorities at Cambridge. To avoid persecution, he was at last obliged to retire to the university of Louvain; the rumours of sorcery that were current respecting him rendering his longer stay in England not altogether without danger. He found at Louvain many kindred spirits who had known Cornelius Agrippa while he resided among them, and by whom he was constantly entertained with the wondrous deeds of that great master of the hermetic mysteries. From their conversation he received much encouragement to continue the search for the philosopher's stone, which soon began to occupy nearly all his thoughts.

*Dr. Dee.*

He did not long remain on the Continent, but returned to England in 1551, being at that time in the twenty-fourth year of his age. By the influence of his friend Sir John Cheek, he was kindly received at the court of King Edward VI., and rewarded (it is difficult to say for what) with a pension of one hundred crowns. He continued for several years to practise in London as an astrologer; casting nativities, telling fortunes, and pointing out lucky and unlucky days. During the reign of Queen Mary he got into trouble, being suspected of heresy, and charged with attempting Mary's life by means of enchantments. He was tried for the latter offence, and acquitted; but was retained in prison on the former charge, and left to the tender mercies of Bishop

Bonner. He had a very narrow escape from being burned in Smithfield, but he somehow or other contrived to persuade that fierce bigot that his orthodoxy was unimpeachable, and was set at liberty in 1555.

On the accession of Elizabeth, a brighter day dawned upon him. During her retirement at Woodstock, her servants appear to have consulted him as to the time of Mary's death, which circumstance no doubt first gave rise to the serious charge for which he was brought to trial. They now came to consult him more openly as to the fortunes of their mistress; and Robert Dudley, the celebrated Earl of Leicester, was sent by command of the Queen herself to know the most auspicious day for her coronation. So great was the favour he enjoyed, that, some years afterwards, Elizabeth condescended to pay him a visit at his house in Mortlake, to view his museum of curiosities, and when he was ill, sent her own physician to attend upon him.

Astrology was the means whereby he lived, and he continued to practise it with great assiduity; but his heart was in alchymy. The philosopher's stone and the elixir of life haunted his daily thoughts and his nightly dreams. The Talmudic mysteries, which he had also deeply studied, impressed him with the belief, that he might hold converse with spirits and angels, and learn from them all the mysteries of the universe. Holding the same idea as the then obscure sect of the Rosicrucians, some of whom he had perhaps encountered in his travels in Germany, he imagined that, by means of the philosopher's stone, he could summon these kindly spirits at his will. By dint of continually brooding upon the subject, his imagination became so diseased, that he at last persuaded himself that an angel appeared to him, and promised to be his friend and companion as long as he lived. He relates that, one day, in November 1582, while he was engaged in fervent prayer, the window of his museum looking towards the west suddenly glowed with a dazzling light, in the midst of which, in all his glory, stood the great angel Uriel. Awe and wonder rendered him speechless; but the angel smiling graciously upon him, gave him a crystal, of a convex form, and told him that whenever he wished to hold converse with the beings of another sphere, he had only to gaze intently upon it, and they would appear in the crystal, and unveil to him all the secrets of futurity.[41] Thus saying, the angel disappeared. Dee found from experience of the crystal that it was necessary that all the faculties of the soul should be concentrated upon it, otherwise the spirits did not appear. He also found that he could never recollect the conversations he had with the angels. He therefore determined to communicate the secret to another person, who might converse with the spirit while he (Dee) sat in another part of the room, and took down in writing the revelations which they made.

*Shew-stone of Dr. Dee, in the British Museum.*

He had at this time in his service, as his assistant, one Edward Kelly, who, like himself, was crazy upon the subject of the philosopher's stone. There was this difference, however, between them, that, while Dee was more of an enthusiast than an impostor, Kelly was more of an impostor than an enthusiast. In early life he was a notary, and had the misfortune to lose both his ears for forgery. This mutilation, degrading enough in any man, was destructive to a philosopher; Kelly, therefore, lest his wisdom should suffer in the world's opinion, wore a black skull-cap, which, fitting close to his head, and descending over both his cheeks, not only concealed his loss, but gave him a very solemn and oracular appearance. So well did he keep his secret, that even Dee, with whom he lived so many years, appears never to have discovered it. Kelly, with this character, was just the man to carry on any piece of roguery for his own advantage, or to nurture the delusions of his master for the same purpose. No sooner did Dee inform him of the visit he had received from the glorious Uriel, than Kelly expressed such a fervour of belief, that

Dee's heart glowed with delight. He set about consulting his crystal forthwith, and on the 2d of December, 1581, the spirits appeared, and held a very extraordinary discourse with Kelly, which Dee took down in writing. The curious reader may see this farrago of nonsense among the Harleian Mss. in the British Museum. The later consultations were published in a folio volume, in 1659, by Dr. Meric Casaubon, under the title of *A true and faithful Relation of what passed between Dr. John Dee and some Spirits; tending, had it succeeded, to a general Alteration of most States and Kingdoms in the World.*[42]

The fame of these wondrous colloquies soon spread over the country, and even reached the Continent. Dee at the same time pretended to be in possession of the *elixir vitæ*, which he stated he had found among the ruins of Glastonbury Abbey, in Somersetshire. People flocked from far and near to his house at Mortlake to have their nativities cast, in preference to visiting astrologers of less renown. They also longed to see a man who, according to his own account, would never die. Altogether, he carried on a very profitable trade, but spent so much in drugs and metals to work out some peculiar process of transmutation, that he never became rich.

About this time there came into England a wealthy polish nobleman, named Albert Laski, Count Palatine of Siradz. His object was principally, he said, to visit the court of Queen Elizabeth, the fame of whose glory and magnificence had reached him in distant Poland. Elizabeth received this flattering stranger with the most splendid hospitality, and appointed her favourite Leicester to shew him all that was worth seeing in England. He visited all the curiosities of London and Westminster, and from thence proceeded to Oxford and Cambridge, that he might converse with some of the great scholars whose writings shed lustre upon the land of their birth. He was very much disappointed at not finding Dr. Dee among them, and told the Earl of Leicester that he would not have gone to Oxford if he had known that Dee was not there. The earl promised to introduce him to the great alchymist on their return to London, and the Pole was satisfied. A few days afterwards, the earl and Laski being in the antechamber of the Queen, awaiting an audience of her majesty, Dr. Dee arrived on the same errand, and was introduced to the Pole.[43] An interesting conversation ensued, which ended by the stranger inviting himself to dine with the astrologer at his house at Mortlake. Dee returned home in some tribulation, for he found he had not money enough, without pawning his plate, to entertain Count Laski and his retinue in a manner becoming their dignity. In this emergency he sent off an express to the Earl of Leicester, stating frankly the embarrassment he laboured under, and praying his good offices in representing the matter to her majesty. Elizabeth immediately sent him a present of twenty pounds.

On the appointed day Count Laski came, attended by a numerous retinue, and expressed such open and warm admiration of the wonderful attainments of his host, that Dee turned over in his own mind how he could bind irretrievably to his interests a man who seemed so well inclined to become his friend. Long acquaintance with Kelly had imbued him with all the roguery of that personage, and he resolved to make the Pole pay dearly for his dinner. He found out before many days that he possessed great estates in his own country, as well as great influence, but that an extravagant disposition had reduced him to temporary embarrassment. He also discovered that he was a firm believer in the philosopher's stone and the water of life. He was therefore just the man upon whom an adventurer might fasten himself. Kelly thought so too; and both of them set to work to weave a web, in the meshes of which they might firmly entangle the rich and credulous stranger. They went very cautiously about it; first throwing out obscure hints of the stone and the elixir, and finally of the spirits, by means of whom they could turn over the pages of the book of futurity, and read the awful secrets inscribed therein. Laski eagerly implored that he might be admitted to one of their mysterious interviews with Uriel and the angels; but they knew human nature too well to accede at once to the request. To the count's entreaties they only replied by hints of the difficulty or impropriety of summoning the spirits in the presence of a stranger, or of one who might perchance have no other motive than the gratification of a vain curiosity; but they only meant to whet the edge of his appetite by this delay, and would have been sorry indeed if the count had been discouraged. To shew how exclusively the thoughts both of Dee and Kelly were fixed upon their dupe at this time, it is only necessary to read the introduction to their first interview with the spirits, related in the volume of Dr. Casaubon. The entry made by Dee, under the date of the 25th of May, 1583, says, that when the spirit appeared to them, "I [John Dee] and E. K. [Edward Kelly] sat together, conversing of that noble Polonian Albertus Laski, his great honour here with us obtained, and of his great liking among all sorts of the people." No doubt they were discussing how they might make the most of the "noble Polonian," and concocting the fine story with which they afterwards excited his curiosity, and drew him firmly within their toils. "Suddenly," says Dee, as they were thus employed, "there seemed to come out of the oratory a spiritual creature, like a pretty girl of seven or nine years of age, attired on her head, with her hair rolled up before and hanging down behind, with a gown of silk, of changeable red and green, and with a train. She seemed to play up and down, and seemed to go in and out behind the books; and as she seemed to go between them, the books displaced themselves, and made way for her." With such tales as these they lured on the Pole from day to day, and at last persuaded him to be a witness of their mysteries. Whether they played off any optical delusions upon him, or whether, by the force of a strong imagination, he deluded himself, does not appear, but certain it is that he became a complete tool in their hands, and consented to do whatever they wished him. Kelly, at these interviews, placed himself at a certain distance from the wondrous crystal, and gazed intently upon it, while Dee took his place in a corner, ready to set down the prophecies as they were uttered by the spirits. In this manner they prophesied to the Pole that he should become the fortunate possessor of the philosopher's stone; that he should live for centuries, and be chosen King of Poland, in which capacity he should gain many great victories over the Saracens, and make his name illustrious over all the earth. For this purpose it was necessary, however, that Laski should leave England, and take them with him, together with their wives and families; that he should treat them all sumptuously, and allow them to want for nothing. Laski at once consented; and very shortly afterwards they were all on the road to Poland.

It took them upwards of four months to reach the count's estates in the neighbourhood of Cracow. In the mean time, they led a pleasant life, and spent money with an unsparing hand. When once established in the count's palace, they commenced the great hermetic operation of transmuting iron into gold. Laski provided them with all necessary materials, and aided them himself with his knowledge of alchymy; but, somehow or other, the experiment always failed at the very moment it ought to have succeeded, and they were obliged to recommence operations on a grander scale. But the hopes of Laski were not easily extinguished. Already, in idea, the possessor of countless millions, he was not to be cast down for fear of present expenses. He thus continued from day to day, and from month to month, till he was at last obliged to sell a portion of his deeply-mortgaged estates to find aliment for the hungry crucibles of Dee and Kelly, and the no less hungry stomachs of their wives and families. It was not till ruin stared him in the face that he awoke from his dream of infatuation, too happy, even then, to find that he had escaped utter beggary. Thus restored to his senses, his first thought was how to rid himself of his expensive visitors. Not wishing to quarrel with them, he proposed that they should proceed to Prague, well furnished with letters of recommendation to the Emperor Rudolph. Our alchymists too plainly saw that nothing more was to be made of the almost destitute Count Laski. Without hesitation, therefore, they accepted the proposal, and set out forthwith to the imperial residence. They had no difficulty, on their arrival at Prague, in obtaining an audience of the emperor. They found him willing enough to believe that such a thing as the philosopher's stone existed, and flattered themselves that they had made a favourable impression upon him; but, from some cause or other—perhaps the look of low cunning and quackery upon the face of Kelly—the emperor conceived no very high opinion of their abilities. He allowed them, however, to remain for some months at Prague, feeding themselves upon the hope that he would employ them; but the more he saw of them, the less he liked them; and, when the pope's nuncio represented to him that he ought not to countenance such heretic magicians, he gave orders that they should quit his dominions within four-and-twenty hours. It was fortunate for them that so little time was given them; for, had they remained six hours longer, the nuncio had received orders to procure a perpetual dungeon or the stake for them.

Not knowing well whither to direct their steps, they resolved to return to Cracow, where they had still a few friends; but, by this time, the funds they had drawn from Laski were almost exhausted, and they were many days obliged to go dinnerless and supperless. They had great difficulty to keep their poverty a secret from the world; but they managed to bear privation without murmuring, from a conviction that if the fact were known, it would militate very much against their pretensions. Nobody would believe that they were possessors of the philosopher's stone, if it were once suspected that they did not know how to procure bread for their subsistence. They still gained a little by casting nativities, and kept starvation at arm's length, till a new dupe, rich enough for their purposes, dropped into their toils, in the shape of a royal personage. Having procured an introduction to Stephen king of Poland, they predicted to him that the Emperor Rudolph would shortly be assassinated, and that the Germans would look to Poland for his successor. As this prediction was not precise enough to satisfy the king, they tried their crystal again, and a spirit appeared who told them that the new sovereign of Germany would be Stephen of Poland. Stephen was credulous enough to believe them, and was once present when Kelly held his mystic conversations with the shadows of his crystal. He also appears to have furnished them with money to carry on their experiments in alchymy; but he grew tired, at last, of their broken promises and their constant drains upon his pocket, and was on the point of discarding them with disgrace, when they met with another dupe, to whom they eagerly transferred their services. This was Count Rosenberg, a noble-man of large estates at Trebona in Bohemia. So comfortable did they find themselves in the palace of this munificent patron, that they remained nearly four years with him, faring sumptuously, and having an almost unlimited command of his money. The count was more ambitious than avaricious: he had wealth enough, and did not care for the philosopher's stone on account of the gold, but of the length of days it would bring him. They had their predictions, accordingly, all ready framed to suit his character. They prophesied that he should be chosen king of Poland; and promised, moreover, that he should live for five hundred years to enjoy his dignity, provided always that he found them sufficient money to carry on their experiments.

But now, while fortune smiled upon them, while they revelled in the rewards of successful villany, retributive justice came upon them in a shape they had not anticipated. Jealousy and mistrust sprang up between the two confederates, and led to such violent and frequent quarrels, that Dee was in constant fear of exposure. Kelly imagined himself a much greater personage than Dee; measuring, most likely, by the standard of impudent roguery; and was displeased that on all occasions, and from all persons, Dee received the greater share of honour and consideration. He often threatened to leave Dee to shift for himself; and the latter, who had degenerated into the mere tool of his more daring associate, was distressed beyond measure at the prospect of his desertion. His mind was so deeply imbued with superstition, that he believed the rhapsodies of Kelly to be, in a great measure, derived from his intercourse with angels; and he knew not where, in the whole world, to look for a man of depth and wisdom enough to succeed him. As their quarrels every day became more and more frequent, Dee wrote letters to Queen Elizabeth to secure a favourable reception on his return to England, whither he intended to proceed if Kelly forsook him. He also sent her a round piece of silver, which he pretended he had made of a portion of brass cut out of a warming-pan. He afterwards sent her the warming-pan also, that she might convince herself that the piece of silver corresponded exactly with the hole which was cut into the brass. While thus preparing for the worst, his chief desire was to remain in Bohemia with Count Rosenberg, who treated him well, and reposed much confidence in him. Neither had Kelly any great objection to remain; but a new passion had taken possession of his breast, and he was laying deep schemes to gratify it. His own wife was ill-favoured and ill-natured; Dee's was comely and agreeable; and he longed to make an exchange of partners without exciting the jealousy or shocking the morality of Dee. This was a difficult matter; but to a man like Kelly, who was as deficient in rectitude and right feeling as he was full of impudence and ingenuity, the difficulty was not insurmountable. He had also deeply studied the character and the foibles of Dee; and he took his measures accordingly. The next time they consulted the spirits, Kelly pretended to be shocked at their language, and refused to tell Dee what they had said. Dee insisted, and was informed that they were henceforth to have their wives in common. Dee, a little startled, inquired whether the spirits might not mean that they were to live in common harmony and good-will? Kelly tried again, with apparent reluctance, and said the spirits insisted upon the literal interpretation. The poor fanatic Dee resigned himself to their will; but it suited Kelly's purpose to appear coy a little longer. He declared that the spirits must be spirits not of good, but of evil; and refused to consult them any more. He thereupon took his departure, saying that he would never return. Dee, thus left to himself, was in sore trouble and distress of mind. He knew not on whom to fix as the successor to Kelly for consulting the spirits; but at last chose his son Arthur, a boy of eight years of age. He consecrated him to this service with great ceremony, and impressed upon the child's mind the dignified and awful nature of the duties he was called upon to perform; but the poor boy had neither the imagination, the faith, nor the artifice of Kelly. He looked intently upon the crystal as he was told; but could see nothing and hear nothing. At last, when his eyes ached, he said he could see a vague indistinct shadow, but nothing more. Dee was in despair. The deception had been carried on so long, that he was never so happy as when he fancied he was holding converse with superior beings; and he cursed the day that had put estrangement between him and his dear friend Kelly. This was exactly what Kelly had foreseen; and, when he thought the doctor had grieved sufficiently for his absence, he returned unexpectedly, and entered the room where the little Arthur was in vain endeavouring to distinguish something in the crystal. Dee, in entering this circumstance in his journal, ascribes this sudden return to a "miraculous fortune" and a "divine fate;" and goes on to record that Kelly immediately saw the spirits which had remained invisible to little Arthur. One of these spirits reiterated the previous command, that they should have their wives in common. Kelly bowed his head and submitted; and Dee, in all humility, consented to the arrangement.

This was the extreme depth of the wretched man's degradation. In this manner they continued to live for three or four months, when, new quarrels breaking out, they separated once more. This time their separation was final. Kelly, taking the *elixir* which he had found in Glastonbury Abbey, proceeded to Prague, forgetful of the abrupt mode in which he had previously been expelled from that city. Almost immediately after his arrival, he was seized by order of the Emperor Rudolph, and thrown into prison. He was released after some months' confinement, and continued for five years to lead a vagabond life in Germany, telling fortunes at one place, and pretending to make gold at another. He was a second time thrown into prison, on a charge of heresy and sorcery; and he then resolved, if ever he obtained his liberty, to return to England. He soon discovered that there was no prospect of this, and that his imprisonment was likely to be for life. He twisted his bed-clothes into a rope, one stormy night in February 1595, and let himself down from the window of his dungeon, situated at the top of a very high tower. Being a corpulent man, the rope gave way, and he was precipitated to the ground. He broke two of his ribs and both his legs; and was otherwise so much injured, that he expired a few days afterwards.

Dee, for a while, had more prosperous fortune. The warming-pan he had sent to Queen Elizabeth was not without effect. He was rewarded soon after Kelly had left him with an invitation to return to England. His pride, which had been sorely humbled, sprang up again to its pristine dimensions, and he set out from Bohemia with a train of attendants becoming an ambassador. How he procured the money does not appear, unless from the liberality of the rich Bohemian Rosenberg, or perhaps from his plunder. He travelled with three coaches for himself and family, and three wagons to carry his baggage. Each coach had four horses, and the whole train was protected by a guard of four and twenty soldiers. This statement may be doubted; but it is on the authority of Dee himself, who made it on oath before the commissioners appointed by Elizabeth to inquire into his circumstances. On his arrival in England he had an audience of the queen, who received him kindly as far as words went, and gave orders that he should not be molested in his pursuits of chemistry and philosophy. A man who boasted of the power to turn baser metals into gold, could not, thought Elizabeth, be in want of money; and she therefore gave him no more substantial marks of her approbation than her countenance and protection.

Thrown thus unexpectedly upon his own resources, Dee began in earnest the search for the philosopher's stone. He worked incessantly among his furnaces, retorts, and crucibles, and almost poisoned himself with deleterious fumes. He also consulted his miraculous crystal; but the spirits appeared not to him. He tried one Bartholomew to supply the place of the invaluable Kelly; but he being a man of some little probity, and of no imagination at all, the spirits would not hold any communication with him. Dee then tried another pretender to philosophy, of the name of Hickman, but had no better fortune. The crystal had lost its power since the departure of its great high priest. From this quarter, then, Dee could get no information on the stone or elixir of the alchymists, and all his efforts to discover them by other means were not only fruitless but expensive. He was soon reduced to great distress, and wrote piteous letters to the queen praying relief. He represented that, after he left England with

Count Laski, the mob had pillaged his house at Mortlake, accusing him of being a necromancer and a wizard; and had broken all his furniture, burned his library, consisting of four thousand rare volumes, and destroyed all the philosophical instruments and curiosities in his museum. For this damage he claimed compensation; and furthermore stated, that, as he had come to England by the queen's command, she ought to pay the expenses of his journey. Elizabeth sent him small sums of money at various times; but Dee still continuing his complaints, a commission was appointed to inquire into his circumstances. He finally obtained a small appointment as Chancellor of St. Paul's cathedral, which he exchanged, in 1595, for the wardenship of the college at Manchester. He remained in this capacity till 1602 or 1603, when, his strength and intellect beginning to fail him, he was compelled to resign. He retired to his old dwelling at Mortlake, in a state not far removed from actual want, supporting himself as a common fortune-teller, and being often obliged to sell or pawn his books to procure a dinner. James I. was often applied to on his behalf, but he refused to do any thing for him. It may be said to the discredit of this king, that the only reward he would grant the indefatigable Stowe, in his days of old age and want, was the royal permission to beg; but no one will blame him for neglecting such a quack as John Dee. He died in 1608, in the eighty-first year of his age, and was buried at Mortlake.

**The Cosmopolite.**

Many disputes have arisen as to the real name of the alchymist who wrote several works under the above designation. The general opinion is that he was a Scotsman named Seton, and that by a fate very common to alchymists who boasted too loudly of their powers of transmutation, he ended his days miserably in a dungeon, into which he was thrown by a German potentate until he made a million of gold to pay his ransom. By some he has been confounded with Michael Sendivog, or Sendivogius, a Pole, a professor of the same art, who made a great noise in Europe at the commencement of the seventeenth century. Lenglet du

Fresnoy, who is in general well informed with respect to the alchymists, inclines to the belief that these personages were distinct; and gives the following particulars of the Cosmopolite, extracted from George Morhoff, in his *Epistola ad Langelottum*, and other writers.

About the year 1600, one Jacob Haussen, a Dutch pilot, was shipwrecked on the coast of Scotland. A gentleman, named Alexander Seton, put off in a boat, and saved him from drowning, and afterwards entertained him hospitably for many weeks at his house on the shore. Haussen saw that he was addicted to the pursuits of chemistry, but no conversation on the subject passed between them at the time. About a year and a half afterwards, Haussen being then at home at Enkhuysen, in Holland, received a visit from his former host. He endeavoured to repay the kindness that had been shewn him; and so great a friendship arose between them that Seton, on his departure, offered to make him acquainted with the great secret of the philosopher's stone. In his presence the Scotsman transmuted a great quantity of base metal into pure gold, and gave it him as a mark of his esteem. Seton then took leave of his friend, and travelled into Germany. At Dresden he made no secret of his wonderful powers, having, it is said, performed transmutation successfully before a great assemblage of the learned men of that city. The circumstance coming to the ears of the Duke or Elector of Saxony, he gave orders for the arrest of the alchymist. He caused him to be imprisoned in a high tower, and set a guard of forty men to watch that he did not escape, and that no strangers were admitted to his presence. The unfortunate Seton received several visits from the elector, who used every art of persuasion to make him divulge his secret. Seton obstinately refused either to communicate his secret, or to make any gold for the tyrant; on which he was stretched upon the rack, to see if the argument of torture would render him more tractable. The result was still the same; neither hope of reward nor fear of anguish could shake him. For several months he remained in prison, subjected alternately to a sedative and a violent regimen, till his health broke, and he wasted away almost to a skeleton.

There happened at that time to be in Dresden a learned Pole, named Michael Sendivogius, who had wasted a good deal of his time and substance in the unprofitable pursuits of alchymy. He was touched with pity for the hard fate, and admiration for the intrepidity of Seton; and determined, if possible, to aid him in escaping from the clutch of his oppressor. He requested the elector's permission to see the alchymist, and obtained it with some difficulty. He found him in a state of great wretchedness, shut up from the light of day in a noisome dungeon, and with no better couch or fare than those allotted to the worst of criminals. Seton listened eagerly to the proposal of escape, and promised the generous Pole that he would make him richer than an eastern monarch if by his means he were liberated. Sendivogius immediately commenced operations; he sold some property which he possessed near Cracow, and with the proceeds led a merry life at Dresden. He gave the most elegant suppers, to which he regularly invited the officers of the guard, and especially those who did duty at the prison of the alchymist. He insinuated himself at last into their confidence, and obtained free ingress to his friend as often as he pleased; pretending that he was using his utmost endeavours to conquer his obstinacy and worm his secret out of him. When their project was ripe, a day was fixed upon for the grand attempt; and Sendivogius was ready with a post-chariot to convey him with all speed into Poland. By drugging some wine which he presented to the guards of the prison, he rendered them so drowsy that he easily found means to scale a wall unobserved, with Seton, and effect his escape. Seton's wife was in the chariot awaiting him, having safely in her possession a small packet of a black powder, which was, in fact, the philosopher's stone, or ingredient for the transmutation of iron and copper into gold. They all arrived in safety at Cracow; but the frame of Seton was so wasted by torture of body and starvation, to say nothing of the anguish of mind he had endured, that he did not long survive. He died in Cracow, in 1603 or 1604, and was buried under the cathedral church of that city. Such is the story related of the author of the various works which bear the name of the Cosmopolite. A list of them may be found in the third volume of the *History of the Hermetic Philosophy*.

## Sendivogius.

On the death of Seton, Sendivogius married his widow, hoping to learn from her some of the secrets of her deceased lord in the art of transmutation. The ounce of black powder stood him, however, in better service; for the alchymists say, that by its means he converted great quantities of quicksilver into the purest gold. It is also said that he performed this experiment successfully before the Emperor Rudolph II., at Prague; and that the emperor, to commemorate the circumstance, caused a marble tablet to be affixed to the wall of the room in which it was performed, bearing this inscription, "Faciat hoc quispiam alius, quod fecit Sendivogius Polonus." M. Desnoyers, secretary to the Princess Mary of Gonzaga, Queen of Poland, writing from Warsaw in 1651, says that he saw this tablet, which existed at that time, and was often visited by the curious.

The after-life of Sendivogius is related in a Latin memoir of him by one Brodowski, his steward; and is inserted by Pierre Borel in his *Treasure of Gaulish Antiquities*. The Emperor Rudolph, according to this authority, was so well pleased with his success, that he made him one of his councillors of state, and invited him to fill a station in the royal household and inhabit the palace. But Sendivogius loved his liberty, and refused to become a courtier. He preferred to reside on his own patrimonial estate of Gravarna, where, for many years, he exercised a princely hospitality. His philosophic powder, which, his steward says, was red, and not black, he kept in a little box of gold; and with one grain of it he could make five hundred ducats, or a thousand rix-dollars. He generally made his projection upon quicksilver. When he travelled, he gave this box to his steward, who hung it round his neck by a gold chain next his skin. But the greatest part of the powder he used to hide in a secret place cut into the step of his chariot. He thought that, if attacked at any time by robbers, they would not search such a place as that. When he anticipated any danger, he would dress himself in his valet's clothes, and, mounting the coach-box, put the valet inside. He was induced to take these precautions, because it was no secret that he possessed the philosopher's stone; and many unprincipled adventurers were on the watch for an opportunity to plunder him. A German prince, whose name Brodowski has not thought fit to chronicle, served him a scurvy trick, which ever afterwards put him on his guard. This prince went on his knees to Sendivogius, and entreated him in the most pressing terms to satisfy his curiosity, by converting some quicksilver into gold before him. Sendivogius, wearied by his importunity, consented, upon a promise of inviolable secrecy. After his departure, the prince called a German alchymist, named Muhlenfels, who resided in his house, and told him all that had been done. Muhlenfels entreated that he might have a dozen mounted horsemen at his command, that he might instantly ride after the philosopher, and either rob him of all his powder, or force from him the secret of making it. The prince desired nothing better; Muhlenfels, being provided with twelve men well mounted and armed, pursued Sendivogius in hot haste. He came up with him at a lonely inn by the road-side, just as he was sitting down to dinner. He at first endeavoured to persuade him to divulge the secret; but finding this of no avail, he caused his accomplices to strip the unfortunate Sendivogius and tie him naked to one of the pillars of the house. He then took from him his golden box, containing a small quantity of the powder; a manuscript book on the philosopher's stone; a golden medal, with its chain, presented to him by the Emperor Rudolph; and a rich cap, ornamented with diamonds, of the value of one hundred thousand rix-dollars. With this booty he decamped, leaving Sendivogius still naked and firmly bound to the pillar. His servants had been treated in a similar manner; but the people of the inn released them all as soon as the robbers were out of sight.

Sendivogius proceeded to Prague, and made his complaint to the emperor. An express was instantly sent off to the prince, with orders that he should deliver up Muhlenfels and all his plunder. The prince, fearful of the emperor's wrath, caused three large gallows to be erected in his court-yard; on the highest of which he hanged Muhlenfels, with another thief on each side of him. He thus propitiated the emperor, and got rid of an ugly witness against himself. He sent back, at the same time, the bejewelled hat, the medal and chain, and the treatise upon the philosopher's stone, which had been stolen from Sendivogius. As regarded the powder, he said he had not seen it, and knew nothing about it.

This adventure made Sendivogius more prudent; he would no longer perform the process of transmutation before any strangers, however highly recommended. He pretended also to be very poor; and sometimes lay in bed for weeks together, that people might believe he was suffering from some dangerous malady, and could not therefore, by any possibility, be the owner of the philosopher's stone. He would occasionally coin false money, and pass it off as gold; preferring to be esteemed a cheat rather than a successful alchymist.

Many other extraordinary tales are told of this personage by his steward Brodowski, but they are not worth repeating. He died in 1636, aged upwards of eighty, and was buried in his own chapel at Gravarna. Several works upon alchymy have been published under his name.

### The Rosicrucians.

It was during the time of the last-mentioned author that the sect of the Rosicrucians first began to create a sensation in Europe. The influence which they exercised upon opinion during their brief career, and the permanent impression which they have left upon European literature, claim for them especial notice. Before their time, alchymy was but a grovelling delusion; and theirs is the merit of having spiritualised and refined it. They also enlarged its sphere, and supposed the possession of the philosopher's stone to be, not only the means of wealth, but of health and happiness, and the instrument by which man could command the services of superior beings, control the elements to his will, defy the obstructions of time and space, and acquire the most intimate knowledge of all the secrets of the universe. Wild and visionary as they were, they were not without their uses; if it were only for having purged the superstitions of Europe of the dark and disgusting forms with which the monks had peopled it, and substituted, in their stead, a race of mild, graceful, and beneficent beings.

They are said to have derived their name from Christian Rosencreutz, or "Rose-cross," a German philosopher, who travelled in the Holy Land towards the close of the fourteenth century. While dangerously ill at a place called Damcar, he was visited by some learned Arabs, who claimed him as their brother in science, and unfolded to him, by inspiration, all the secrets of his past life, both of thought and of action. They restored him to health by means of the philosopher's stone, and afterwards instructed him in all their mysteries. He returned to Europe in 1401, being then only twenty-three years of age; and drew a chosen number of his friends around him, whom he initiated into the new science, and bound by solemn oaths to keep it secret for a century. He is said to have lived eighty-three years after this period, and to have died in 1484.

Many have denied the existence of such a personage as Rosencreutz, and have fixed the origin of this sect at a much later epoch. The first dawning of it, they say, is to be found in the theories of Paracelsus and the dreams of Dr. Dee, who, without intending it, became the actual, though never the recognised founders of the Rosicrucian philosophy. It is now difficult, and indeed impossible, to determine whether Dee and Paracelsus obtained their ideas from the then obscure and unknown Rosicrucians, or whether the Rosicrucians did but follow and improve upon them. Certain it is, that their existence was never suspected till the year 1605, when they began to excite attention in Germany. No sooner were their doctrines promulgated, than all the visionaries, Paracelsists, and alchymists, flocked around their standard, and vaunted Rosencreutz as the new regenerator of the human race. Michael Mayer, a celebrated physician of that day, and who had impaired his health and wasted his fortune in searching for the philosopher's stone, drew up a report of the tenets and ordinances of the new fraternity, which was published at Cologne, in the year 1615. They asserted, in the first place, "that the meditations of their founders surpassed every thing that had ever been imagined since the creation of the world, without even excepting the revelations of the Deity; that they were destined to accomplish the general peace and regeneration of man before the end of the world arrived; that they possessed all wisdom and piety in a supreme degree; that they possessed all the graces of nature, and could distribute them among the rest of mankind according to their pleasure; that they were subject to neither hunger, nor thirst, nor disease, nor old age, nor to any other inconvenience of nature; that they knew by inspiration, and at the first glance, every one who was worthy to be admitted into their society; that they had the same knowledge then which they would have possessed if they had lived from the beginning of the world, and had been always acquiring it; that they had a volume in which they could read all that ever was or ever would be written in other books till the end of time; that they could force to, and retain in their service the most powerful spirits and demons; that, by the virtue of their songs, they could attract pearls and precious stones from the depths of the sea or the bowels of the earth; that God had covered them with a thick cloud, by means of which they could shelter themselves from the malignity of their enemies, and that they could thus render themselves invisible from all eyes; that the first eight brethren of the 'Rose-cross' had power to cure all maladies; that, by means of the fraternity, the triple diadem of the pope would be reduced into dust; that they only admitted two sacraments, with the ceremonies of the primitive Church, renewed by them; that they recognised the Fourth Monarchy and the Emperor of the Romans as their chief and the chief of all Christians; that they would provide him with more gold, their treasures being inexhaustible, than the King of Spain had ever drawn from the golden regions of Eastern and Western Ind." This was their confession of faith. Their rules of conduct were six in number, and as follow:

First. That, in their travels, they should gratuitously cure all diseases.

Secondly. That they should always dress in conformity to the fashion of the country in which they resided.

Thirdly. That they should, once every year, meet together in the place appointed by the fraternity, or send in writing an available excuse.

Fourthly. That every brother, whenever he felt inclined to die, should choose a person worthy to succeed him.

Fifthly. That the words "Rose-cross" should be the marks by which they should recognise each other.

Sixthly. That their fraternity should be kept secret for six times twenty years.

They asserted that these laws had been found inscribed in a golden book in the tomb of Rosencreutz, and that the six times twenty years from his death expired in 1604. They were consequently called upon from that time forth to promulgate their doctrine for the welfare of mankind[44].

For eight years these enthusiasts made converts in Germany, but they excited little or no attention in other parts of Europe. At last they made their appearance in Paris, and threw all the learned, all the credulous, and all the lovers of the marvellous into commotion. In the beginning of March 1623, the good folks of that city, when they arose one morning, were surprised to find all their walls placarded with the following singular manifesto: *"We, the deputies of the principal College of the Brethren of the Rose-cross, have taken up our abode, visible and invisible, in this city, by the grace of the Most High, towards whom are turned the hearts of the just. We shew and teach without books or signs, and speak all sorts of languages in the countries where we dwell, to draw mankind, our fellows, from error and from death."*

For a long time this strange placard was the sole topic of conversation in all public places. Some few wondered, but the greater number only laughed at it. In the course of a few weeks two books were published, which raised the first alarm respecting this mysterious society, whose dwelling-place no one knew, and no members of which had ever been seen. The first was called a history of *The frightful Compacts entered into between the Devil and the pretended 'Invisibles;' with their damnable Instructions, the deplorable Ruin of their Disciples, and their miserable end*. The other was called an *Examination of the new and unknown Cabala of the Brethren of the Rose-cross, who have lately inhabited the City of Paris; with the History of their Manners, the Wonders worked by them, and many other particulars*.

These books sold rapidly. Every one was anxious to know something of this dreadful and secret brotherhood. The *badauds* of Paris were so alarmed that they daily expected to see the arch-enemy walking *in propria persona* among them. It was said in these volumes that the Rosicrucian society consisted of six-and-thirty persons in all, who had renounced their baptism and hope of resurrection. That it was not by means of good angels, as they pretended, that they worked their prodigies; but that it was the devil who gave them power to transport themselves from one end of the world to the other with the rapidity of thought; to speak all languages; to have their purses always full of money, however much they might spend; to be invisible, and penetrate into the most secret places, in spite of fastenings of bolts and bars; and to be able to tell the past and future. These thirty-six brethren were divided into bands or companies: six of them only had been sent on the mission to Paris, six to Italy, six to Spain, six to Germany, four to Sweden, and two into Switzerland, two into Flanders, two into Lorraine, and two into Franche Comté. It was generally believed that the missionaries to France resided somewhere in the Marais du Temple. That quarter of Paris soon acquired a bad name, and people were afraid to take houses in it, lest they should be turned out by the six invisibles of the Rose-cross. It was believed by the populace, and by many others whose education should have taught them better, that persons of a mysterious aspect used to visit the inns and hotels of Paris, and eat of the best meats and drink of the best wines, and then suddenly melt away into thin air when the landlord came with the reckoning. That gentle maidens, who went to bed alone, often awoke in the night and found men in bed with them, of shape more beautiful than the Grecian Apollo, who immediately became invisible when an alarm was raised. It was also said that many persons found large heaps of gold in their houses without knowing from whence they came. All Paris was in alarm. No man thought himself secure of his goods, no maiden of her virginity, or wife of her chastity, while these Rosicrucians were abroad. In the midst of the commotion, a second placard was issued to the following effect:

*"If any one desires to see the brethren of the Rose-cross from curiosity only, he will never communicate with us. But if his* will *really induces him to inscribe his name in the register of our brotherhood, we, who can judge of the thoughts of all men, will convince him of the truth of our promises. For this reason we do not publish to the world the place of our abode. Thought alone, in unison with the sincere* will *of those who desire to know us, is sufficient to make us known to them, and them to us."*

Though the existence of such a society as that of the Rose-cross was problematical, it was quite evident that somebody or other was concerned in the promulgation of these placards, which were stuck up on every wall in Paris. The police endeavoured in vain to find out the offenders, and their want of success only served to increase the perplexity of the public. The Church very soon took up the question; and the Abbé Gaultier, a Jesuit, wrote a book to prove that, by their enmity to the pope, they could be no other than disciples of Luther, sent to promulgate his heresy. Their very name, he added, proved that they were heretics; a *cross* surmounted by a *rose* being the heraldic device of the arch-heretic Luther. One Garasse said they were a confraternity of drunken impostors; and that their name was derived from the garland of roses, in the form of a cross, hung over the tables of taverns in Germany as the emblem of secrecy, and from whence was derived the common saying, when one man communicated a secret to another, that it was said "under the rose." Others interpreted the letters F. R. C. to mean, not Brethren of the Rose-cross, but *Fratres Roris Cocti*, or Brothers of Boiled Dew; and explained this appellation by alleging that they collected large quantities of morning dew, and boiled it, in order to extract a very valuable ingredient in the composition of the philosopher's stone and the water of life.

The fraternity thus attacked defended themselves as well as they were able. They denied that they used magic of any kind, or that they consulted the devil. They said they were all happy; that they had lived more than a century, and expected to live many centuries more; and that the intimate knowledge which they possessed of all nature was communicated to them by God himself as a reward for their piety and utter devotion to his service. Those were in error who derived their name from a cross of roses, or called them drunkards. To set the world right on the first point, they reiterated that they derived their name from Christian Rosencreutz, their founder; and to answer the latter charge, they repeated that they knew not what thirst was, and had higher pleasures than those of the palate. They did not desire to meddle with the politics or religion of any man or set of men, although they could not help denying the supremacy of the pope, and looking upon him as a tyrant. Many slanders, they said, had been repeated respecting them, the most unjust of which was, that they indulged in carnal appetites, and, under the cloak of their invisibility, crept into the chambers of beautiful maidens. They asserted, on the contrary, that the first vow they took on entering the society was a vow of chastity, and that any one among them who transgressed in that particular would immediately lose all the advantages he enjoyed, and be exposed once more to hunger, woe, disease, and death, like other men. So strongly did they feel on the subject of chastity, that they attributed the fall of Adam solely to his want of this virtue. Besides defending themselves in this manner, they entered into a further confession of their faith. They discarded for ever all the old tales of sorcery and witchcraft, and communion with the devil. They said there were no such horrid, unnatural, and disgusting beings as the incubi and succubi, and the innumerable grotesque imps that men had believed in for so many ages. Man was not surrounded with enemies like these, but with myriads of beautiful and beneficent beings, all anxious to do him service. The air was peopled with sylphs, the water with undines or naiads, the bowels of the earth with gnomes, and the fire with salamanders. All these beings were the friends of man, and desired nothing so much as that men should purge themselves of all uncleanness, and thus be enabled to see and converse with them. They possessed great power, and were unrestrained by the barriers of space or the obstructions of matter. But man was in one particular their superior. He had an immortal soul, and they had not. They might, however, become sharers in man's immortality if they could inspire one of that race with the passion of love towards them. Hence it was the constant endeavour of the female spirits to captivate the admiration of men, and of the male gnomes, sylphs, salamanders, and undines to be beloved by a woman. The object of this passion, in returning their love, imparted a portion of that celestial fire, the soul; and from that time forth the beloved became equal to the lover, and both, when their allotted course was run, entered together into the mansions of felicity. These spirits, they said, watched constantly over mankind by night and day. Dreams, omens, and presentiments were all their works, and the means by which they gave warning of the approach of danger. But though so well inclined to befriend man for their own sakes, the want of a soul rendered them at times capricious and revengeful; they took offence on slight causes, and heaped injuries instead of benefits on the heads of those who extinguished the light of reason that was in them by gluttony, debauchery, and other appetites of the body. The excitement produced in Paris by the placards of the brotherhood and the attacks of the clergy wore itself away after a few months. The stories circulated about them became at last too absurd even for that age of absurdity, and men began to laugh once more at those invisible gentlemen and their fantastic doctrines. Gabriel Naudé at that conjuncture brought out his *Avis à la France sur les Frères de la Rose-croix*, in which he very successfully exposed the folly of the new sect. This work, though not well written, was well timed. It quite extinguished the Rosicrucians of France; and after that year little more was heard of them. Swindlers in different parts of the country assumed the name at times to cloak their depredations; and now and then one of them was caught and hanged for his too great ingenuity in enticing pearls and precious stones from the pockets of other people into his own, or for passing off lumps of gilded brass for pure gold, made by the agency of the philosopher's stone. With these exceptions, oblivion shrouded them.

The doctrine was not confined to a sphere so narrow as France alone; it still nourished in Germany, and drew many converts in England. The latter countries produced two great masters in the persons of Jacob Böhmen and Robert Fludd — pretended philosophers, of whom it is difficult to say which was the more absurd and extravagant. It would appear that the sect was divided into two classes — the brothers *Roseæ Crucis*, who devoted themselves to the wonders of this sublunary sphere, and the brothers *Aureæ Crucis*, who were wholly occupied in the contemplation of things divine. Fludd belonged to the first class, and Böhmen to the second. Fludd may be called the father of the English Rosicrucians, and as such merits a conspicuous niche in the temple of Folly.

He was born in the year 1574 at Milgate, in Kent, and was the son of Sir Thomas Fludd, Treasurer of War to Queen Elizabeth. He was originally intended for the army; but he was too fond of study, and of a disposition too quiet and retiring, to shine in that sphere. His father would not therefore press him to adopt a course of life for which he was unsuited, and encouraged him in the study of medicine, for which he early manifested a partiality. At the age of twenty-five he proceeded to the continent; and being fond of the abstruse, the marvellous, and the incomprehensible, he became an ardent disciple of the school of Paracelsus, whom he looked upon as the regenerator not only of medicine, but of philosophy. He remained six years in Italy, France, and Germany, storing his mind with fantastic notions, and seeking the society of enthusiasts and visionaries. On his return to England in 1605, he received the degree of Doctor of Medicine from the University of Oxford, and began to practise as a physician in London.

He soon made himself conspicuous. He latinised his name from Robert Fludd into Robertus à Fluctibus, and began the promulgation of many strange doctrines. He avowed his belief in the philosopher's stone, the water of life, and the universal alkahest;

and maintained that there were but two principles of all things,—which were, condensation, the boreal or northern virtue; and rarefaction, the southern or austral virtue. A number of demons, he said, ruled over the human frame, whom he arranged in their places in a rhomboid. Every disease had its peculiar demon who produced it, which demon could only be combated by the aid of the demon whose place was directly opposite to his in the rhomboidal figure. Of his medical notions we shall have further occasion to speak in another part of this book, when we consider him in his character as one of the first founders of the magnetic delusion, and its offshoot, animal magnetism, which has created so much sensation in our own day.

As if the doctrines already mentioned were not wild enough, he joined the Rosicrucians as soon as they began to make a sensation in Europe, and succeeded in raising himself to high consideration among them. The fraternity having been violently attacked by several German authors, and among others by Libavius, Fludd volunteered a reply, and published, in 1616, his defence of the Rosicrucian philosophy, under the title of the *Apologia compendiaria Fraternitatem de Rosea-cruce suspicionis et infamiæ maculis aspersam abluens*. This work immediately procured him great renown upon the Continent, and he was henceforth looked upon as one of the high-priests of the sect. Of so much importance was he considered, that Keppler and Gassendi thought it necessary to refute him; and the latter wrote a complete examination of his doctrine. Mersenne also, the friend of Descartes, and who had defended that philosopher when accused of having joined the Rosicrucians, attacked Dr. à Fluctibus, as he preferred to be called, and shewed the absurdity of the brothers of the Rose-cross in general, and of Dr. à Fluctibus in particular. Fluctibus wrote a long reply, in which he called Mersenne an ignorant calumniator, and reiterated that alchymy was a profitable science, and the Rosicrucians worthy to be the regenerators of the world. This book was published at Frankfort, and was entitled *Summum Bonum, quod est Magiæ, Cabalæ, Alchimiæ, Fratrum, Roseæ-Crucis verorum, et adversus Mersenium*

*Calumniatorem.* Besides this, he wrote several other works upon alchymy, a second answer to Libavius upon the Rosicrucians, and many medical works. He died in London in 1637.

After his time there was some diminution of the sect in England. They excited but little attention, and made no effort to bring themselves into notice. Occasionally some obscure and almost incomprehensible work made its appearance, to shew the world that the folly was not extinguished. Eugenius Philalethes, a noted alchymist, who has veiled his real name under this assumed one, translated *The Fame and Confession of the Brethren of the Rosie Cross*, which was published in London in 1652. A few years afterwards, another enthusiast, named John Heydon, wrote two works on the subject: the one entitled *The Wise Man's Crown, or the Glory of the Rosie Cross*; and the other, *The Holy Guide, leading the way to unite Art and Nature with the Rosie Crosse uncovered.* Neither of these attracted much notice. A third book was somewhat more successful; it was called *A new Method of Rosicrucian Physic; by John Heydon, the servant of God and the Secretary of Nature.* A few extracts will shew the ideas of the English Rosicrucians about this period. Its author was an attorney, "practising (to use his own words) at Westminster Hall all term times as long as he lived, and in the vacations devoting himself to alchymical and Rosicrucian meditation." In his preface, called by him an Apologue for an Epilogue, he enlightens the public upon the true history and tenets of his sect. Moses, Elias, and Ezekiel were, he says, the most ancient masters of the Rosicrucian philosophy. Those few then existing in England and the rest of Europe, were as the eyes and ears of the great king of the universe, seeing and hearing all things; seraphically illuminated; companions of the holy company of unbodied souls and immortal angels; turning themselves, Proteus-like, into any shape, and having the power of working miracles. The most pious and abstracted brethren could slack the plague in cities, silence the violent winds and tempests, calm the rage of the sea and rivers, walk in the air, frustrate the malicious aspect of witches, cure all diseases, and turn all metals into gold. He had known in his time two famous brethren of the Rosie Cross, named Walfourd and Williams, who had worked miracles in his sight, and taught him many excellent predictions of astrology and earthquakes. "I desired one of these to tell me," says he, "whether my complexion were capable of the society of my good genius. 'When I see you again,' said he (which was when he pleased to come to me, for I knew not where to go to him), 'I will tell you.' When I saw him afterwards, he said, 'You should pray to God; for a good and holy man can offer no greater or more acceptable service to God than the oblation of himself — his soul.' He said also, that the good genii were the benign eyes of God, running to and fro in the world, and with love and pity beholding the innocent endeavours of harmless and single-hearted men, ever ready to do them good and to help them."

Heydon held devoutly true that dogma of the Rosicrucians which said that neither eating nor drinking was necessary to men. He maintained that any one might exist in the same manner as that singular people dwelling near the source of the Ganges, of whom mention was made in the travels of his namesake, Sir Christopher Heydon, who had no mouths, and therefore could not eat, but lived by the breath of their nostrils; except when they took a far journey, and then they mended their diet with the smell of flowers. He said that in really pure air "there was a fine foreign fatness," with which it was sprinkled by the sunbeams, and which was quite sufficient for the nourishment of the generality of mankind. Those who had enormous appetites, he had no objection to see take animal food, since they could not do without it; but he obstinately insisted that there was no necessity why they should *eat* it. If they put a plaster of nicely-cooked meat upon their epigastrium, it would be sufficient for the wants of the most robust and voracious! They would by that means let in no diseases, as they did at the broad and common gate, the mouth, as any one might see by example of drink; for all the while a man sat in water, he was never athirst. He had known, he said, many Rosicrucians, who by applying wine in this manner, had fasted for years together. In fact, quoth Heydon, we may easily fast all our life, though it be three hundred years, without any kind of meat, and so cut off all danger of disease.

This "sage philosopher" further informed his wondering contemporaries that the chiefs of the doctrine always carried about with them to their place of meeting their symbol, called the R. C. which was an ebony cross, flourished and decked with roses of gold; the cross typifying Christ's sufferings upon the cross for our sins, and the roses of gold the glory and beauty of his Resurrection. This symbol was carried alternately to Mecca, Mount Calvary, Mount Sinai, Haran, and to three other places, which must have been in mid-air, called *Cascle*, *Apamia* and *Chaulateau Virissa Caunuch*, where the Rosicrucian brethren met when they pleased, and made resolution of all their actions. They always took their pleasures in one of these places, where they resolved all questions of whatsoever had been done, was done, or should be done in the world, from the beginning to the end thereof. "And these," he concludes, "are the men called Rosicrucians!"

Towards the end of the seventeenth century, more rational ideas took possession of the sect, which still continued to boast of a few members. They appear to have considered that contentment was the true philosopher's stone, and to have abandoned the insane search for a mere phantom of the imagination. Addison, in *The Spectator*,[45] gives an account of his conversation with a Rosicrucian; from which it may be inferred that the sect had grown wiser in their deeds, though in their talk they were as foolish as ever. "I was once," says he, "engaged in discourse with a Rosicrucian about the great secret. He talked of the secret as of a spirit which lived within an emerald, and converted every thing that was near it to the highest perfection that it was capable of. 'It gives a lustre,' says he, 'to the sun, and water to the diamond. It irradiates every metal, and enriches lead with all the properties of gold. It heightens smoke into flame, flame into light, and light into glory.' He further added, 'that a single ray of it dissipates pain and care and melancholy from the person on whom it falls. In short,' says he, 'its presence naturally changes every place into a kind of heaven.' After he had gone on for some time in this unintelligible cant, I found that he jumbled natural and moral ideas together into the same discourse, and that his great secret was nothing else but content."

## Jacob Böhmen.

It is now time to speak of Jacob Böhmen, who thought he could discover the secret of the transmutation of metals in the Bible, and who invented a strange heterogeneous doctrine of mingled alchymy and religion, and founded upon it the sect of the Aurea-crucians. He was born at Görlitz, in Upper Lusatia, in 1575, and followed till his thirtieth year the occupation of a shoemaker. In this obscurity he remained, with the character of a visionary and a man of unsettled mind, until the promulgation of the Rosicrucian philosophy in his part of Germany, toward the year 1607 or 1608. From that time he began to neglect his leather, and buried his brain under the rubbish of metaphysics. The works of Paracelsus fell into his hands; and these, with the reveries of the Rosicrucians, so completely engrossed his attention, that he abandoned his trade altogether, sinking, at the same time, from a state of comparative independence into poverty and destitution. But he was nothing daunted by the miseries and privations of the flesh; his mind was fixed upon the beings of another sphere, and in thought he was already the new apostle of the human race. In the year 1612, after a meditation of four years, he published his first work, entitled *Aurora, or the Rising of the Sun*; embodying the ridiculous notions of Paracelsus, and worse confounding the confusion of that writer. The philosopher's stone might, he contended, be discovered by a diligent search of the Old and New Testaments, and more especially of the Apocalypse, which alone contained all the secrets of alchymy. He contended that the divine grace operated by the same rules, and followed the same methods, that the divine providence observed in the natural world; and that the minds of men were purged from their vices and corruptions in the very same manner that metals were purified from their dross, namely, by fire.
Besides the sylphs, gnomes, undines, and salamanders, he acknowledged various ranks and orders of demons. He pretend-

ed to invisibility and absolute chastity. He also said that, if it pleased him, he could abstain for years from meat and drink, and all the necessities of the body. It is needless, however, to pursue his follies any further. He was reprimanded for writing this work by the magistrates of Görlitz, and commanded to leave the pen alone and stick to his wax, that his family might not become chargeable to the parish. He neglected this good advice, and continued his studies; burning minerals and purifying metals one day, and mystifying the Word of God on the next. He afterwards wrote three other works, as sublimely ridiculous as the first. The one was entitled *Metallurgia*, and has the slight merit of being the least obscure of his compositions. Another was called *The Temporal Mirror of Eternity*; and the last his *Theosophy revealed*, full of allegories and metaphors,

> *"All strange and geason,*
> *Devoid of sense and ordinary reason."*

Böhmen died in 1624, leaving behind him a considerable number of admiring disciples. Many of them became, during the seventeenth century, as distinguished for absurdity as their master; amongst whom may be mentioned Gifftheil, Wendenhagen, John Jacob Zimmermann, and Abraham Frankenberg. Their heresy rendered them obnoxious to the Church of Rome; and many of them suffered long imprisonment and torture for their faith. One, named Kuhlmann, was burned alive at Moscow, in 1684, on a charge of sorcery. Böhmen's works were translated into English, and published, many years afterwards, by an enthusiast named William Law.

## Mormius.

Peter Mormius, a notorious alchymist and contemporary of Böhmen, endeavoured, in 1630, to introduce the Rosicrucian philosophy into Holland. He applied to the States-General to grant him a public audience, that he might explain the tenets of the sect, and disclose a plan for rendering Holland the happiest and richest country on the earth, by means of the philosopher's stone and the service of the elementary spirits. The States-

General wisely resolved to have nothing to do with him. He thereupon determined to shame them by printing his book, which he did at Leyden the same year. It was entitled *The Book of the most Hidden Secrets of Nature*, and was divided into three parts; the first treating of "perpetual motion;" the second of the "transmutation of metals;" and the third of the "universal medicine." He also published some German works upon the Rosicrucian philosophy, at Frankfort, in 1617.

Poetry and romance are deeply indebted to the Rosicrucians for many a graceful creation. The literature of England, France, and Germany contains hundreds of sweet fictions, whose machinery has been borrowed from their day-dreams. The "delicate Ariel" of Shakspeare stands pre-eminent among the number. From the same source Pope drew the airy tenants of Belinda's dressing-room, in his charming *Rape of the Lock*; and La Motte Fouqué, the beautiful and capricious water-nymph Undine, around whom he has thrown more grace and loveliness, and for whose imaginary woes he has excited more sympathy, than ever were bestowed on a supernatural being. Sir Walter Scott also endowed the White Lady of Avenel with many of the attributes of the undines or water-sprites. German romance and lyrical poetry teem with allusions to sylphs, gnomes, undines, and salamanders; and the French have not been behind in substituting them, in works of fiction, for the more cumbrous mythology of Greece and Rome. The sylphs, more especially, have been the favourites of the bards, and have become so familiar to the popular mind as to be, in a manner, confounded with that other race of ideal beings, the fairies, who can boast of an antiquity much more venerable in the annals of superstition. Having these obligations to the Rosicrucians, no lover of poetry can wish, however absurd they were, that such a sect of philosophers had never existed.

### Borri.

Just at the time that Michael Mayer was making known to the world the existence of such a body as the Rosicrucians, there was born in Italy a man who was afterwards destined to become the most conspicuous member of the fraternity. The alchymic mania never called forth the ingenuity of a more consummate or more successful impostor than Joseph Francis Borri. He was born in 1616, according to some authorities, and in 1627 according to others, at Milan; where his father, the Signor Branda Borri, practised as a physician. At the age of sixteen Joseph was sent to finish his education at the Jesuits' college in Rome, where he distinguished himself by his extraordinary memory. He learned every thing to which he applied himself with the utmost ease. In the most voluminous works no fact was too minute for his retention, and no study was so abstruse but that he could master it; but any advantages he might have derived from this facility were neutralised by his ungovernable passions and his love of turmoil and debauchery. He was involved in continual difficulty, as well with the heads of the college as with the police of Rome, and acquired so bad a character that years could not remove it. By the aid of his friends he established himself as a physician in Rome, and also obtained some situation in the pope's household. In one of his fits of studiousness he grew enamoured of alchymy, and determined to devote his energies to the discovery of the philosopher's stone. Of unfortunate propensities he had quite sufficient, besides this, to bring him to poverty. His pleasures were as expensive as his studies, and both were of a nature to destroy his health and ruin his fair fame. At the age of thirty-seven he found that he could not live by the practice of medicine, and began to look about for some other employment. He became, in 1653, private secretary to the Marquis di Mirogli, the minister of the Archduke of Innsprück at the court of Rome. He continued in this capacity for two years; leading, however, the same abandoned life as heretofore, frequenting the society of game-sters, debauchees, and loose women, involving himself in disgraceful street quarrels, and alienating the patrons who were desirous to befriend him.

All at once a sudden change was observed in his conduct. The abandoned rake put on the outward sedateness of a philosopher; the scoffing sinner proclaimed that he had forsaken his evil ways, and would live thenceforth a model of virtue. To his friends this reformation was as pleasing as it was unexpected; and Borri gave obscure hints that it had been brought about by some miraculous manifestation of a superior power. He pretended that he held converse with beneficent spirits; that the secrets of God and nature were revealed to him; and that he had obtained possession of the philosopher's stone. Like his predecessor, Jacob Böhmen, he mixed up religious questions with his philosophical jargon, and took measures for declaring himself the founder of a new sect. This, at Rome itself, and in the very palace of the pope, was a hazardous proceeding; and Borri just awoke to a sense of it in time to save himself from the dungeons of the Castle of St. Angelo. He fled to Innsprück, where he remained about a year, and then returned to his native city of Milan.

*Innspruck.*

The reputation of his great sanctity had gone before him; and he found many persons ready to attach themselves to his fortunes. All who were desirous of entering into the new communion took an oath of poverty, and relinquished their possessions for the general good of the fraternity. Borri told them that he had received from the archangel Michael a heavenly sword, upon the hilt of which were engraven the names of the seven celestial intelligences. "Whoever shall refuse," said he, "to enter into my new sheepfold shall be destroyed by the papal armies, of whom God has predestined me to be the chief. To those who follow me all joy shall be granted. I shall soon bring my chemical studies to a happy conclusion, by the discovery of the philosopher's stone, and by this means we shall all have as much gold as we desire. I am assured of the aid of the angelic hosts, and more especially of the archangel Michael's. When I began to walk in the way of the spirit, I had a vision of the night, and was assured by an angelic voice that I should become a prophet. In sign of it I saw a palm-tree, surrounded with all the glory of paradise. The angels come to me whenever I call, and reveal to me all the secrets of the universe. The sylphs and elementary spirits obey me, and fly to the uttermost ends of the world to serve me, and those whom I delight to honour." By force of continually repeating such stories as these, Borri soon found himself at the head of a very considerable number of adherents. As he figures in these pages as an alchymist, and not as a religious sectarian, it will be unnecessary to repeat the doctrines which he taught with regard to some of the dogmas of the Church of Rome, and which exposed him to the fierce resentment of the papal authority. They were to the full as ridiculous as his philosophical pretensions. As the number of his followers increased, he appears to have cherished the idea of becoming one day a new Mahomet, and of founding, in his native city of Milan, a monarchy and religion of which he should be the king and the prophet. He had taken measures, in the year 1658, for seizing the guards at all the gates of that city, and formally declaring himself the monarch of the Milanese. Just as he thought the plan ripe for execution, it was discovered. Twenty of his followers were arrested, and he himself managed, with the utmost difficulty, to escape to the neutral territory of Switzerland, where the papal displeasure could not reach him.

The trial of his followers commenced forthwith, and the whole of them were sentenced to various terms of imprisonment. Borri's trial proceeded in his absence, and lasted for upwards of two years. He was condemned to death as a heretic and sorcerer in 1661, and was burned in effigy in Rome by the common hangman.

Borri, in the mean time, lived quietly in Switzerland, indulging himself in railing at the Inquisition and its proceedings. He afterwards went to Strasbourg, intending to fix his residence in that town. He was received with great cordiality, as a man persecuted for his religious opinions, and withal a great alchymist. He found that sphere too narrow for his aspiring genius, and retired in the same year to the more wealthy city of Amsterdam. He there hired a magnificent house, established an equipage which eclipsed in brilliancy those of the richest merchants, and assumed the title of Excellency. Where he got the money to live in this expensive style was long a secret: the adepts in alchymy easily explained it, after their fashion. Sensible people were of opinion that he had come by it in a less wonderful manner; for it was remembered that among his unfortunate disciples in Milan, there were many rich men, who, in conformity with one of the fundamental rules of the sect, had given up all their earthly wealth into the hands of their founder. In whatever manner the money was obtained, Borri spent it in Holland with an unsparing hand, and was looked up to by the people with no little respect and veneration. He performed several able cures, and increased his reputation so much that he was vaunted as a prodigy. He continued diligently the operations of alchymy, and was in daily expectation that he should succeed in turning the inferior metals into gold. This hope never abandoned him, even in the worst extremity of his fortunes; and in his prosperity it led him into the most foolish expenses: but he could not long continue to live so magnificently upon the funds he had brought from Italy; and the philosopher's stone, though it promised all for the wants of the morrow, never brought any thing for the necessities of to-day. He was obliged in a few months to retrench, by giving up his large house, his gilded coach and valuable blood-horses, his liveried domestics, and his luxurious entertainments. With this diminution of splendour came a diminution of renown. His cures did not appear so miraculous, when he went out on foot to perform them, as they had seemed when "his Excellency" had driven to a poor man's door in his carriage with six horses. He sank from a prodigy into an ordinary man. His great friends shewed him the cold shoulder, and his humble flatterers carried their incense to some other shrine. Borri now thought it high time to change his quarters. With this view he borrowed money wherever he could get it, and succeeded in obtaining two hundred thousand florins from a merchant named De Meer, to aid, as he said, in discovering the water of life. He also obtained six diamonds of great value, on pretence that he could remove the flaws from them without diminishing their weight. With this booty he stole away secretly by night, and proceeded to Hamburgh.

On his arrival in that city, he found the celebrated Christina, the ex-queen of Sweden. He procured an introduction to her, and requested her patronage in his endeavour to discover the philosopher's stone. She gave him some encouragement; but Borri, fearing that the merchants of Amsterdam, who had connexions in Hamburgh, might expose his delinquencies if he remained in the latter city, passed over to Copenhagen, and sought the protection of Frederick III., the king of Denmark.

This prince was a firm believer in the transmutation of metals. Being in want of money, he readily listened to the plans of an adventurer who had both eloquence and ability to recommend him. He provided Borri with the means to make experiments, and took a great interest in the progress of his operations. He expected every month to possess riches that would buy Peru; and, when he was disappointed, accepted patiently the excuses of Borri, who, upon every failure, was always ready with some plausible explanation. He became in time much attached to him; and defended him from the jealous attacks of his courtiers, and the indignation of those who were grieved to see their monarch the easy dupe of a charlatan. Borri endeavoured, by every means in his power, to find aliment for this good opinion. His knowledge of medicine was useful to him in this respect, and often stood between him and disgrace. He lived six years in this manner at the court of Frederick; but that monarch dying in 1670 he was left without a protector.

As he had made more enemies than friends in Copenhagen, and had nothing to hope from the succeeding sovereign, he sought an asylum in another country. He went first to Saxony; but met so little encouragement, and encountered so much danger from the emissaries of the Inquisition, that he did not remain there many months. Anticipating nothing but persecution in every country that acknowledged the spiritual authority of the pope, he appears to have taken the resolution to dwell in Turkey, and turn Mussulman. On his arrival at the Hungarian frontier, on his way to Constantinople, he was arrested on suspicion of being concerned in the conspiracy of the Counts Nadasdi and Frangipani, which had just been discovered. In vain he protested his innocence, and divulged his real name and profession. He was detained in prison, and a letter despatched to the Emperor Leopold, to know what should be done with him. The star of his fortunes was on the decline. The letter reached Leopold at an unlucky moment. The pope's nuncio was closeted with his majesty; and he no sooner heard the name of Joseph Francis Borri, than he demanded him as a prisoner of the Holy See. The request was complied with; and Borri, closely manacled, was sent under an escort of soldiers to the prison of the Inquisition at Rome. He was too much of an impostor to be deeply tinged with fanaticism, and was not unwilling to make a public recantation of his heresies, if he could thereby save his life. When the proposition was made to him, he accepted it with eagerness. His punishment was to be commuted into the hardly less severe one of perpetual imprisonment; but he was too happy to escape the clutch of the executioner at any price, and he made the *amende honorable* in face of the assembled multitudes of Rome on the 27th of October 1672. He was then transferred to the prisons of the Castle of St. Angelo, where he remained till his death, twenty-three years afterwards. It is said that, towards the close of his life, considerable indulgence was granted him; that he was allowed to have a laboratory, and to cheer the solitude of his dungeon by searching for the philosopher's stone. Queen Christina, during her residence at Rome, frequently visited the old man, to converse with him upon chemistry and the doctrines of the Rosicrucians. She even obtained permission that he should leave his prison occasionally for a day or two, and reside in her palace, she being responsible for his return to captivity. She encouraged him to search for the great secret of the alchymists, and provided him with money for the purpose. It may well be supposed that Borri benefited most by this acquaintance, and that Christina got nothing but experience. It is not sure that she gained even that; for until her dying day she was convinced of the possibility of finding the philosopher's stone, and ready to assist any adventurer either zealous or impudent enough to pretend to it.

After Borri had been about eleven years in confinement, a small volume was published at Cologne, entitled *The Key of the Cabinet of the Chevalier Joseph Francis Borri, in which are contained many curious Letters upon Chemistry and other Sciences, written by him, together with a Memoir of his Life.* This book contained a complete exposition of the Rosicrucian philosophy, and afforded materials to the Abbé de Villars for his interesting *Count de Gabalis*, which excited so much attention at the close of the seventeenth century. Borri lingered in the prison of St. Angelo till 1695, when he died, in his eightieth year. Besides *The Key of the Cabinet*, written originally in Copenhagen, in 1666, for the edification of King Frederick III., he published a work upon alchymy and the secret sciences, under the title of *The Mission of Romulus to the Romans*.

**Inferior Alchymists of the Seventeenth Century.**

Besides the pretenders to the philosopher's stone whose lives have been already narrated, this and the preceding century produced a great number of writers, who inundated literature with their books upon the subject. In fact, most of the learned men of that age had some faith in it. Van Helmont, Borrichius, Kircher, Boerhaave, and a score of others, though not professed alchymists, were fond of the science, and countenanced its professors. Helvetius, the grandfather of the celebrated philosopher of the same name, asserts that he saw an inferior metal turned into gold by a stranger, at the Hague, in 1666. He says, that, sitting one day in his study, a man, who was dressed as a respectable burgher of North Holland, and very modest and simple in his appearance, called upon him, with the intention of dispelling his doubts relative to the philosopher's stone. He asked Helvetius if he thought he should know that rare gem if he saw it. To which Helvetius replied, that he certainly should not. The burgher immediately drew from his pocket a small ivory box, containing three pieces of metal, of the colour of brimstone, and extremely heavy; and assured Helvetius, that of them he could make as much as twenty tons of gold. Helvetius informs us, that he examined them very attentively; and seeing that they were very brittle, he took the opportunity to scrape off a small portion with his thumb-nail. He then returned them to the stranger, with an entreaty that he would perform the process of transmutation before him. The stranger replied, that he was not allowed to do so, and went away. After his departure, Helvetius procured a crucible and a portion of lead, into which, when in a state of fusion, he threw the stolen grain from the philosopher's stone. He was disappointed to find that the grain evaporated altogether, leaving the lead in its original state.

Some weeks afterwards, when he had almost forgotten the subject, he received another visit from the stranger. He again entreated him to explain the processes by which he pretended to transmute lead. The stranger at last consented, and informed him, that one grain was sufficient; but that it was necessary to envelope it in a ball of wax before throwing it on the molten metal; otherwise its extreme volatility would cause it to go off in vapour. They tried the experiment, and succeeded to their heart's content. Helvetius repeated the experiment alone, and converted six ounces of lead into very pure gold.

The fame of this event spread all over the Hague, and all the notable persons of the town flocked to the study of Helvetius to convince themselves of the fact. Helvetius performed the experiment again, in the presence of the Prince of Orange, and several times afterwards, until he exhausted the whole of the powder he had received from the stranger, from whom it is necessary to state, he never received another visit; nor did he ever discover his name or condition. In the following year, Helvetius published his *Golden Calf*,[46] in which he detailed the above circumstances.

About the same time, the celebrated Father Kircher published his *Subterranean World*, in which he called the alchymists a congregation of knaves and impostors, and their science a delusion. He admitted that he had himself been a diligent labourer in the field, and had only come to this conclusion after mature consideration and repeated fruitless experiments. All the alchymists were in arms immediately, to refute this formidable antagonist. One Solomon de Blauenstein was the first to grapple with him, and attempted to convict him of wilful misrepresentation, by recalling to his memory the transmutations by Sendivogius, before the Emperor Frederick III. and the Elector of Mayence, all performed within a recent period. Zwelfer and Glauber also entered into the dispute, and attributed the enmity of Father Kircher to spite and jealousy against adepts who had been more successful than himself.

It was also pretended that Gustavus Adolphus transmuted a quantity of quicksilver into pure gold. The learned Borrichius relates, that he saw coins which had been struck of this gold; and Lenglet du Fresnoy deposes to the same circumstance. In the *Travels of Monconis* the story is told in the following manner: "A merchant of Lubeck, who carried on but little trade, but who knew how to change lead into very good gold, gave the King of Sweden a lingot which he had made, weighing at least one hundred pounds. The king immediately caused it to be coined into ducats; and because he knew positively that its origin was such as had been stated to him, he had his own arms graven upon the one side, and emblematical figures of Mercury and Venus on the other. I (continued Monconis) have one of these ducats in my possession; and was credibly informed that, after the death of the Lubeck merchant, who had never appeared very rich, a sum of no less than one million seven hundred thousand crowns was found in his coffers."[47]

Such stories as these, confidently related by men high in station, tended to keep up the infatuation of the alchymists in every country of Europe. It is astonishing to see the number of works which were written upon the subject during the seventeenth century alone, and the number of clever men who sacrificed themselves to the delusion. Gabriel de Castaigne, a monk of the order of St. Francis, attracted so much notice in the reign of Louis XIII., that that monarch secured him in his household, and made him his Grand Almoner. He pretended to find the elixir of life, and Louis expected by his means to have enjoyed the crown for a century. Van Helmont also pretended to have once performed with success the process of transmuting quicksilver, and was in consequence invited by the Emperor Rudolph II. to fix his residence at the court of Vienna. Glauber, the inventor of the salts which still bear his name, and who practised as a physician at Amsterdam about the middle of the seventeenth century, established a public school in that city for the study of alchymy, and gave lectures himself upon the science. John Joachim Becher of Spire acquired great reputation at the same period, and was convinced that much gold might be made out of flint-stones by a peculiar process, and the aid of that grand and incomprehensible substance the philosopher's stone. He made a proposition to the Emperor Leopold of Austria to aid him in these experiments; but the hope of success was too remote, and the present expense too great, to tempt that monarch, and he therefore gave Becher much of his praise, but none of his money. Becher afterwards tried the States-General of Holland with no better success.

With regard to the innumerable tricks by which impostors persuaded the world that they had succeeded in making gold, and of which so many stories were current about this period, a very satisfactory report was read by M. Geoffroy the elder, at the sitting of the Royal Academy of Sciences at Paris, on the 15th of April, 1722. As it relates principally to the alchymic cheats of the sixteenth and seventeenth centuries, the following abridgment of it may not be out of place in this portion of our history. The instances of successful transmutation were so numerous, and apparently so well authenticated, that nothing short of so able an exposure as that of M. Geoffroy could disabuse the public mind. The trick to which they oftenest had recourse was to use a double-bottomed crucible, the under surface being of iron or copper, and the upper one of wax, painted to resemble the same metal. Between the two they placed as much gold or silver dust as was necessary for their purpose. They then put in their lead, quicksilver, or other ingredients, and placed their pot upon the fire. Of course, when the experiment was concluded, they never failed to find a lump of gold at the bottom. The same result was produced in many other ways. Some of them used a hollow wand, filled with gold or silver dust, and stopped at the ends with wax or butter. With this they stirred the boiling metal in their crucibles, taking care to accompany the operation with many ceremonies, to divert attention from the real purpose of the manœuvre. They also drilled holes in lumps of lead, into which they poured molten gold, and carefully closed the aperture with the original metal. Sometimes they washed a piece of gold with quicksilver. When in this state, they found no difficulty in palming it off upon the uninitiated as an inferior metal, and very easily transmuted it into fine sonorous gold again with the aid of a little aquafortis.

Others imposed by means of nails, half iron and half gold or silver. They pretended that they really transmuted the precious half from iron, by dipping it in a strong alcohol. M. Geoffroy produced several of these nails to the Academy of Sciences, and shewed how nicely the two parts were soldered together. The golden or silver half was painted black to resemble iron, and the colour immediately disappeared when the nail was dipped into aquafortis. A nail of this description was, for a long time, in the cabinet of the Grand Duke of Tuscany. Such also, said M. Geoffroy, was the knife presented by a monk to Queen Elizabeth of England; the blade of which was half gold and half steel. Nothing at one time was more common than to see coins, half gold and half silver, which had been operated upon by alchymists, for the same purposes of trickery. In fact, says M. Geoffroy, in concluding his long report, there is every reason to believe that all the famous histories which have been handed down to us about the transmutation of metals into gold or silver, by means of the powder of projection or philosophical elixirs, are founded upon some successful deception of the kind above narrated. These pretended philosophers invariably disappeared after the first or second experiment, or their powders or elixirs have failed to produce their effect, either because attention being excited they have found no opportunity to renew the trick without being discovered, or because they have not had sufficient gold dust for more than one trial.

The disinterestedness of these would-be philosophers looked, at first sight, extremely imposing. Instances were not rare in which they generously abandoned all the profits of their transmutations—even the honour of the discovery. But this apparent disinterestedness was one of the most cunning of their manœuvres. It served to keep up the popular expectation; it seemed to shew the possibility of discovering the philosopher's stone, and provided the means of future advantages, which they were never slow to lay hold of—such as entrances into royal households, maintenance at the public expense, and gifts from ambitious potentates, too greedy after the gold they so easily promised.

It now only remains to trace the progress of the delusion from the commencement of the eighteenth century until the present day. It will be seen that, until a very recent period, there were but slight signs of a return to reason.

### Jean Delisle.

In the year 1705, there was much talk in France of a blacksmith, named Delisle, who had discovered the philosopher's stone, and who went about the country turning lead into gold. He was a native of Provence, from which place his fame soon spread to the capital. His early life is involved in obscurity; but Lenglet du Fresnoy has industriously collected some particulars of his later career, which possess considerable interest. He was a man without any education, and had been servant in his youth to an alchymist, from whom he learned many of the tricks of the fraternity. The name of his master has never been discovered; but it is pretended that he rendered himself in some manner obnoxious to the government of Louis XIV., and was obliged, in consequence, to take refuge in Switzerland. Delisle accompanied him as far as Savoy, and there, it is said, set upon him in a solitary mountain-pass, and murdered and robbed him. He then disguised himself as a pilgrim, and returned to France. At a lonely inn, by the road-side, where he stopped for the night, he became acquainted with a woman, named Aluys; and so sudden a passion was enkindled betwixt them, that she consented to leave all, follow him, and share his good or evil fortune wherever he went. They lived together for five or six years in Provence, without exciting any attention, apparently possessed of a decent independence. At last, in 1706, it was given out that he was the possessor of the philosopher's stone; and people from far and near came flocking to his residence, at the Château de la Palu, at Sylanez, near Barjaumont, to witness the wealth he could make out of pumps and fire-shovels. The following account of his operations is given in a letter addressed by M. de Cerisy, the Prior of Châteauneuf, in the Diocese of Riez, in Provence, to the Vicar of St. Jacques du Hautpas, at Paris, and dated the 18th of November, 1706:

"I have something to relate to you, my dear cousin, which will be interesting to you and your friends. The philosopher's stone, which so many persons have looked upon as a chimera, is at last found. It is a man named Delisle, of the parish of Sylanez, and residing within a quarter of a league of me, that has discovered this great secret. He turns lead into gold, and iron into silver, by merely heating these metals red hot, and pouring upon them in that state some oil and powder he is possessed of; so that it would not be impossible for any man to make a million a day, if he had sufficient of this wondrous mixture. Some of the pale gold which he had made in this manner, he sent to the jewellers of Lyons, to have their opinion on its quality. He also sold twenty pounds weight of it to a merchant of Digne, named Taxis. All the jewellers say they never saw such fine gold in their lives. He makes nails, part gold, part iron, and part silver. He promised to give me one of them, in a long conversation which I had with him the other day, by order of the Bishop of Senés, who saw his operations with his own eyes, and detailed all the circumstances to me.

*"The Baron and Baroness de Rheinwald shewed me a lingot of gold made out of pewter before their eyes by M. Delisle. My brother-in-law Sauveur, who has wasted fifty years of his life in this great study, brought me the other day a nail which he had seen changed into gold by Delisle, and fully convinced me that all his previous experiments were founded on an erroneous principle. This excellent workman received, a short time ago, a very kind letter from the superintendent of the royal household, which I read. He offered to use all his influence with the ministers to prevent any attempts upon his liberty, which has twice been attacked by the agents of government. It is believed that the oil he makes use of, is gold or silver reduced to that state. He leaves it for a long time exposed to the rays of the sun. He told me that it generally took him six months to make all his preparations. I told him that, apparently, the king wanted to see him. He replied that he could not exercise his art in every place, as a certain climate and temperature were absolutely necessary to his success. The truth is, that this man appears to have no ambition. He only keeps two horses and two men-servants. Besides, he loves his liberty, has no politeness, and speaks very bad French; but his judgment seems to be solid. He was formerly no more than a blacksmith, but excelled in that trade without having been taught it. All the great lords and seigneurs from far and near come to visit him, and pay such court to him, that it seems more like idolatry than any thing else. Happy would France be if this man would discover his secret to the king, to whom the superintendent has already sent some lingots! But the happiness is too great to be hoped for; for I fear that the workman and his secret will expire together. There is no doubt that this discovery will make a great noise in the kingdom, unless the character of the man, which I have just depicted to you, prevent it. At all events, posterity will hear of him."*

In another letter to the same person, dated the 27th of January 1707, M. de Cerisy says, "My dear cousin, I spoke to you in my last letter of the famous alchymist of Provence, M. Delisle. A good deal of that was only hearsay, but now I am enabled to speak from my own experience. I have in my possession a nail, half iron and half silver, which I made myself. That great and admirable workman also bestowed a still greater privilege upon me—he allowed me turn a piece of lead which I had brought with me into pure gold, by means of his wonderful oil and powder. All the country have their eyes upon this gentleman; some deny loudly, others are incredulous; but those who have seen acknowledge the truth. I have read the passport that has been sent to him from court, with orders that he should present himself at Paris early in the spring. He told me that he would go willingly, and that it was himself who fixed the spring for his departure; as he wanted to collect his materials, in order that, immediately on his introduction to the king, he might make an experiment worthy of his majesty, by converting a large quantity of lead into the finest gold. I sincerely hope that he will not allow his secret to die with him, but that he will communicate it to the king. As I had the honour to dine with him on Thursday last, the 20th of this month, being seated at his side, I told him in a whisper that he could, if he liked, humble all the enemies of France. He did not deny it, but began to smile. In fact, this man is the miracle of art. Sometimes he employs the oil and powder mixed, sometimes the powder only; but in so small a quantity that, when the lingot which I made was rubbed all over with it, it did not shew at all."

This soft-headed priest was by no means the only person in the neighbourhood who lost his wits in hopes of the boundless wealth held out by this clever impostor. Another priest, named De Lions, a chanter in the cathedral of Grenoble, writing on the 30th January 1707, says: "M. Mesnard, the curate of Montier, has written to me, stating that there is a man, about thirty-five years of age, named Delisle, who turns lead and iron into gold and silver; and that this transmutation is so veritable and so true, that the goldsmiths affirm that his gold and silver are the purest and finest they ever saw. For five years this man was looked upon as a madman or a cheat; but the public mind is now disabused with respect to him. He now resides with M. de la Palu, at the château of the same name. M. de la Palu is not very easy in his circumstances, and wants money to portion his daughters, who have remained single till middle age, no man being willing to take them without a dowry. M. Delisle has promised to make them the richest girls in the province before he goes to court, having been sent for by the king. He has asked for a little time before his departure, in order that he may collect powder enough to make several quintals of gold before the eyes of his majesty, to whom he intends to present them. The principal matter of his wonderful powder is composed of simples, principally the herbs *Lunaria major* and *minor*. There is a good deal of the first planted by him in the gardens of La Palu; and he gets the other from the mountains that stretch about two leagues from Montier. What I tell you now is not a mere story invented for your diversion: M. Mesnard can bring forward many witnesses to its truth; among others, the Bishop of Senés, who saw these surprising operations performed; and M. de Cerisy, whom you know well. Delisle transmutes his metals in public. He rubs the lead or iron with his powder, and puts it over burning charcoal. In a short time it changes colour; the lead becomes yellow, and is found to be converted into excellent gold; the iron becomes white, and is found to be pure silver. Delisle is altogether an illiterate person. M. de St. Auban endeavoured to teach him to read and write, but he profited very little by his lessons. He is unpolite, fantastic, and a dreamer, and acts by fits and starts."

Delisle, it would appear, was afraid of venturing to Paris. He knew that his sleight of hand would be too narrowly watched in the royal presence; and upon some pretence or other he delayed the journey for more than two years. Desmarets, the Minister of Finance to Louis XIV., thinking the "philosopher" dreaded foul play, twice sent him a safe conduct under the king's seal; but Delisle still refused. Upon this, Desmarets wrote to the Bishop of Senés for his real opinion as to these famous transmutations. The following was the answer of that prelate:

> "Copy of a report addressed to M. Desmarets, Comptroller-General of the Finances to His Majesty Louis XIV., by the Bishop of Senés, dated March 1709.

*"Sir, – A twelvemonth ago, or a little more, I expressed to you my joy at hearing of your elevation to the ministry; I have now the honour to write you my opinion of the Sieur Delisle, who has been working at the transmutation of metals in my diocese. I have, during the last two years, spoken of him several times to the Count de Pontchartrain, because he asked me; but I have not written to you, sir, or to M. de*

Chamillart, because you neither of you requested my opinion upon the subject. Now, however, that you have given me to understand that you wish to know my sentiments on the matter, I will unfold myself to you in all sincerity, for the interests of the king and the glory of your ministry.

"There are two things about the Sieur Delisle which, in my opinion, should be examined without prejudice: the one relates to his secret; the other, to his person; that is to say, whether his transmutations are real, and whether his conduct has been regular. As regards the secret of the philosopher's stone, I deemed it impossible, for a long time; and for more than three years I was more mistrustful of the pretensions of this Sieur Delisle than of any other person. During this period I afforded him no countenance; I even aided a person, who was highly recommended to me by an influential family of this province, to prosecute Delisle for some offence or other which it was alleged he had committed. But this person, in his anger against him, having told me that he had himself been several times the bearer of gold and silver to the goldsmiths of Nice, Aix, and Avignon, which had been transmuted by Delisle from lead and iron, I began to waver a little in my opinions respecting him. I afterwards met Delisle at the house of one of my friends. To please me, the family asked Delisle to operate before me, to which he immediately consented. I offered him some iron nails, which he changed into silver in the chimney-place before six or seven credible witnesses. I took the nails thus transmuted, and sent them by my almoner to Imbert, the jeweller of Aix, who, having subjected them to the necessary trial, returned them to me, saying they were very good silver. Still, however, I was not quite satisfied. M. de Pontchartrain having hinted to me, two years previously, that I should do a thing agreeable to his majesty if I examined into this business of Delisle, I resolved to do so now. I therefore summoned the alchymist to come to me at Castellane. He came; and I had him escorted by eight or ten vigilant men, to whom I had given notice to watch his hands strictly. Before all of us he changed two pieces of lead into gold and silver. I sent them both to M. de Pontchartrain; and he afterwards informed me by a letter, now lying before me, that he had shewn them to the most experienced goldsmiths of Paris, who unanimously pronounced them to be gold and silver of the very purest quality, and without alloy. My former bad opinion of Delisle was now indeed shaken. It was much more so when he performed transmutation five or six times before me at Senés, and made me perform it myself before him without his putting his hand to any thing. You have seen, sir, the letter of my nephew, the Père Berard, of the Oratoire at Paris, on the experiment that he performed at Castellane, and the truth of which I hereby attest. Another nephew of mine, the Sieur Bourget, who was here three weeks ago, performed the same experiment in my presence, and will detail all the circumstances to you personally at Paris. A hundred persons in my diocese have been witnesses of these things. I confess to you, sir, that, after the testimony of so many spectators and so many goldsmiths, and after the repeatedly successful experiments that I saw performed, all my prejudices vanished. My reason was convinced by my eyes; and the phantoms of impossibility which I had conjured up were dissipated by the work of my own hands.

"It now only remains for me to speak to you on the subject of his person and conduct. Three suspicions have been excited against him: the first, that he was implicated in some criminal proceeding at Cisteron, and that he falsified the coin of the realm; the second, that the king sent him two safe-conducts without effect; and the third, that he still delays going to court to operate before the king. You may see, sir, that I do not hide or avoid any thing. As regards the business at Cisteron, the Sieur Delisle has repeatedly assured me that there was nothing against him which could reasonably draw him within the pale of justice, and that he had never carried on any calling injurious to the king's service. It was true that, six or seven years ago, he had been to Cisteron to gather herbs necessary for his powder, and that he had lodged at the house of one Pelouse, whom he thought an honest man. Pelouse was accused of clipping Louis-d'ors; and as he had lodged with him, he was suspected of being his accomplice. This mere suspicion, without any proof whatever, had caused him to be condemned for contumacy; a common case enough with judges, who always proceed with much rigour against those who are absent. During my own sojourn at Aix, it was well known that a man, named André Aluys, had spread about reports injurious to the character of Delisle, because he hoped thereby to avoid paying him a sum of forty Louis that he owed him. But permit me, sir, to go further, and to add that, even if there were well-founded suspicions against Delisle, we should look with some little indulgence on the faults of a man who possesses a secret so useful to the state. As regards the two safe-conducts sent him by the king, I think I can answer certainly that it was through no fault of his that he paid so little attention to them. His year, strictly speaking, consists only of the four summer months; and when by any means he is prevented from making the proper use of them, he loses a whole year. Thus the first safe-conduct became useless by the irruption of the Duke of Savoy in 1707 and the second had hardly been obtained, at the end of June 1708, when the said Delisle was insulted by a party of armed men, pretending to act under the authority of the Count de Grignan, to whom he wrote several letters of complaint, without receiving any answer, or promise that his safety would be attended to. What I have now told you, sir, removes the third objection, and is the reason why, at the present time, he cannot go to Paris to the king, in fulfilment of his promises made two years ago. Two, or even three, summers have been lost to him, owing to the continual inquietude he has laboured under. He has, in consequence, been unable to work, and has not collected a sufficient quantity of his oil and powder, or brought what he has got to the necessary degree of perfection. For this reason also he could not give the Sieur de Bourget the portion he promised him for your inspection. If the other day he changed some lead into gold with a few grains of his powder, they were assuredly all he had; for he told me that such was the fact long before he knew my nephew was coming. Even if he had preserved this small quantity to operate before the king, I am sure that, on second thoughts, he would never have adventured with so little; because the slightest obstacles in the metals (their being too hard or too soft, which is only discovered in operating,) would have caused him to be looked upon as an impostor, if, in case his first powder had proved ineffectual, he had not been possessed of more to renew the experiment and surmount the difficulty.

"Permit me, sir, in conclusion, to repeat, that such an artist as this should not be driven to the last extremity, nor forced to seek an asylum offered to him in other countries, but which he has despised, as much from his own inclinations as from the advice I have given him. You risk nothing in giving him a little time, and in hurrying him you may lose a great deal. The genuineness of his gold can no longer be doubted, after the testimony of so many jewellers of Aix, Lyons, and Paris in its favour. As it is not his fault that the previous safe-conducts sent to him have been of no service, it will be necessary to send him another; for the success of which I will be answerable, if you will confide the matter to *me, and trust to my zeal for the service of his majesty, to whom I pray you to communicate this letter, that I may be spared the just reproaches he might one day heap upon me if he remained ignorant of the facts I have now written to you. Assure him, if you please, that, if you send me such a safe-conduct, I will oblige the Sieur Delisle to depose with me such precious pledges of his fidelity as shall enable me to be responsible myself to the king. These are my sentiments, and I submit them to your superior knowledge; and have the honour to remain, with much respect, &c.*

*"? John Bishop of Senes.*
*"To M. Desmarets, Minister of State, and Comptroller-General of the Finances, at Paris."*

That Delisle was no ordinary impostor, but a man of consummate cunning and address, is very evident from this letter. The bishop was fairly taken in by his clever legerdemain, and when once his first distrust was conquered, appeared as anxious to deceive himself as even Delisle could have wished. His faith was so abundant that he made the case of his *protégé* his own, and would not suffer the breath of suspicion to be directed against him. Both Louis and his minister appear to have been dazzled by the brilliant hopes he had excited, and a third pass, or safe-conduct, was immediately sent to the alchymist, with a command from the king that he should forthwith present himself at Versailles, and make public trial of his oil and powder. But this did not suit the plans of Delisle. In the provinces he was regarded as a man of no small importance; the servile flattery that awaited him wherever he went was so grateful to his mind that he could not willingly relinquish it, and run upon certain detection at the court of the monarch. Upon one pretext or another he delayed his journey, notwithstanding the earnest solicitations of his good friend the bishop. The latter had given his word to the minister, and pledged his honour that he would induce Delisle to go, and he began to be alarmed when he found he could not subdue the obstinacy of that individual. For more than two years he continued to remonstrate with him, and was always met by some excuse, that there was not sufficient powder, or that it had not been long enough exposed to the rays of the sun. At last his patience was exhausted; and fearful that he might suffer in the royal estimation by longer delay, he wrote to the king for a *lettre de cachet*, in virtue of which the alchymist was seized at the castle of La Palu, in the month of June 1711, and carried off to be imprisoned in the Bastille.

The gendarmes were aware that their prisoner was supposed to be the lucky possessor of the philosopher's stone, and on the road they conspired to rob and murder him. One of them pretended to be touched with pity for the misfortunes of the philosopher, and offered to give him an opportunity of escape whenever he could divert the attention of his companions. Delisle was profuse in his thanks, little dreaming of the snare that was laid for him. His treacherous friend gave notice of the success of the stratagem so far; and it was agreed that Delisle should be allowed to struggle with and overthrow one of them while the rest were at some distance. They were then to pursue him and shoot him through the heart; and after robbing the corpse of the philosopher's stone, convey it to Paris on a cart, and tell M. Desmarets that the prisoner had attempted to escape, and would have succeeded if they had not fired after him and shot him through the body. At a convenient place the scheme was executed. On a given signal from the friendly gendarme, Delisle fled, while another gendarme took aim and shot him through the thigh. Some peasants arriving at the instant, they were prevented from killing him as they intended, and he was transported to Paris, maimed and bleeding. He was thrown into a dungeon in the Bastille, and obstinately tore away the bandages which the surgeons applied to his wound. He never afterwards rose from his bed.

The Bishop of Senés visited him in prison, and promised him his liberty if he would transmute a certain quantity of lead into gold before the king. The unhappy man had no longer the means of carrying on the deception; he had no gold, and no double-bottomed crucible or hollow wand to conceal it in, even if he had. He would not, however, confess that he was an impostor; but merely said he did not know how to make the powder of projection, but had received a quantity from an Italian philosopher, and had used it all in his various transmutations in Provence. He lingered for seven or eight months in the Bastille, and died from the effects of his wound, in the forty-first year of his age.

## Albert Aluys.

This pretender to the philosopher's stone was the son, by a former husband, of the woman Aluys, with whom Delisle became acquainted at the commencement of his career, in the cabaret by the road-side, and whom he afterwards married. Delisle performed the part of a father towards him, and thought he could shew no stronger proof of his regard, than by giving him the necessary instructions to carry on the deception which had raised himself to such a pitch of greatness. The young Aluys was an apt scholar, and soon mastered all the jargon of the alchymists. He discoursed learnedly upon projections, cimentations, sublimations, the elixir of life, and the universal alkahest; and on the death of Delisle gave out that the secret of that great adept had been communicated to him, and to him only. His mother aided in the fraud, with the hope they might both fasten themselves, in the true alchymical fashion, upon some rich dupe, who would entertain them magnificently while the operation was in progress. The fate of Delisle was no inducement for them to stop in France. The Provençals, it is true, entertained as high an opinion as ever of his skill, and were well inclined to believe the tales of the young adept on whom his mantle had fallen; but the dungeons of the Bastille were yawning for their prey, and Aluys and his mother decamped with all convenient expedition. They travelled about the Continent for several years, sponging upon credulous rich men, and now and then performing successful transmutations by the aid of double-bottomed crucibles and the like. In the year 1726, Aluys, without his mother, who appears to have died in the interval, was at Vienna, where he introduced himself to the Duke de Richelieu, at that time ambassador from the court of France. He completely deceived this nobleman; he turned lead into gold (apparently) on several occasions, and even made the ambassador himself turn an iron nail into a silver one. The duke afterwards boasted to Lenglet du Fresnoy of his achievements as an alchymist, and regretted that he had not been able to discover the secret of the precious powder by which he performed them.

Aluys soon found that, although he might make a dupe of the Duke de Richelieu, he could not get any money from him. On the contrary, the duke expected all his pokers and fire-shovels to be made silver, and all his pewter utensils gold; and thought the honour of his acquaintance was reward sufficient for a *roturier*, who could not want wealth since he possessed so invaluable a secret. Aluys, seeing that so much was expected of him, bade adieu to his excellency, and proceeded to Bohemia accompanied by a pupil, and by a young girl who had fallen in love with him in Vienna. Some noblemen in Bohemia received him kindly, and entertained him at their houses for months at a time. It was his usual practice to pretend that he possessed only a few grains of his powder, with which he would operate in any house where he intended to fix his quarters for the season. He would make the proprietor the present of a piece of gold thus transmuted, and promise him millions, if he could only be provided with leisure to gather his *lunaria major* and *minor* on their mountain-tops, and board, lodging, and loose cash for himself, his wife, and his pupil, in the interval.

He exhausted in this manner the patience of some dozen of people, when, thinking that there was less danger for him in France under the young king Louis XV. than under his old and morose predecessor, he returned to Provence. On his arrival at Aix, he presented himself before M. le Bret, the president of the province, a gentleman who was much attached to the pursuits of alchymy, and had great hopes of being himself able to find the philosopher's stone. M. le Bret, contrary to his expectation, received him very coolly, in consequence of some rumours that were spread abroad respecting him; and told him to call upon him on the morrow. Aluys did not like the tone of the voice, or the expression of the eye of the learned president, as that functionary looked down upon him. Suspecting that all was not right, he left Aix secretly the same evening, and proceeded to Marseilles. But the police were on the watch for him; and he had not been there four-and-twenty hours, before he was arrested on a charge of coining, and thrown into prison.

As the proofs against him were too convincing to leave him much hope of an acquittal, he planned an escape from durance. It so happened that the gaoler had a pretty daughter, and Aluys soon discovered that she was tender-hearted. He endeavoured to gain her in his favour, and succeeded. The damsel, unaware that he was a married man, conceived and encouraged a passion for him, and generously provided him with the means of escape. After he had been nearly a year in prison he succeeded in getting free, leaving the poor girl behind to learn that he was already married, and to lament in solitude that she had given her heart to an ungrateful vagabond.

When he left Marseilles, he had not a shoe to his foot or a decent garment to his back, but was provided with some money and clothes by his wife in a neighbouring town. They then found their way to Brussels, and by dint of excessive impudence, brought themselves into notice. He took a house, fitted up a splendid laboratory, and gave out that he knew the secret of transmutation. In vain did M. Percel, the brother-in-law of Lenglet du Fresnoy, who resided in that city, expose his pretensions, and hold him up to contempt as an ignorant impostor: the world believed him not. They took the alchymist at his word, and besieged his doors to see and wonder at the clever legerdemain by which he turned iron nails into gold and silver. A rich *greffier* paid him a large sum of money that he might be instructed in the art, and Aluys gave him several lessons on the most common principles of chemistry. The greffier studied hard for a twelvemonth, and then discovered that his master was a quack. He demanded his money back again; but Aluys was not inclined to give it him, and the affair was brought before the civil tribunal of the province. In the mean time, however, the greffier died suddenly; poisoned, according to the popular rumour, by his debtor, to avoid repayment. So great an outcry arose in the city, that Aluys, who may have been innocent of the crime, was nevertheless afraid to remain and brave it. He withdrew secretly in the night, and retired to Paris. Here all trace of him is lost. He was never heard of again; but Lenglet du Fresnoy conjectures that he ended his days in some obscure dungeon, into which he was cast for coining or other malpractices.

## The Count de St. Germain.

This adventurer was of a higher grade than the last, and played a distinguished part at the court of Louis XV. He pretended to have discovered the elixir of life, by means of which he could make any one live for centuries; and allowed it to believed that his own age was upwards of two thousand years. He entertained many of the opinions of the Rosicrucians; boasted of his inter-course with sylphs and salamanders; and of his power of drawing diamonds from the earth, and pearls from the sea, by the force of his incantations. He did not lay claim to the merit of having discovered the philosopher's stone; but devoted so much of his time to the operations of alchymy, that it was very general-ly believed, that if such a thing as the philosopher's stone had ever existed, or could be called into existence, he was the man to succeed in finding it.

It has never yet been discovered what was his real name, or in what country he was born. Some believed, from the Jewish cast of his handsome countenance, that he was the "wandering Jew;" others asserted that he was the issue of an Arabian princess, and that his father was a salamander; while others, more reasonable, affirmed him to be the son of a Portuguese Jew established at Bourdeaux. He first carried on his imposture in Germany, where he made considerable sums by selling an elixir to arrest the progress of old age. The Maréchal de Belle-Isle purchased a dose of it; and was so captivated with the wit, learning, and good manners of the charlatan, and so convinced of the justice of his most preposterous pretensions, that he induced him to fix his residence in Paris. Under the marshal's patronage, he first appeared in the gay circles of that capital. Every one was de-lighted with the mysterious stranger; who, at this period of his life, appears to have been about seventy years of age, but did not look more than forty-five. His easy assurance imposed upon most people. His reading was extensive, and his memory extraordinarily tenacious of the slightest circumstances. His pretension to have lived for so many centuries naturally exposed him to some puzzling questions, as to the appearance, life, and conversation of the great men of former days; but he was never at a loss for an answer. Many who questioned him for the purpose of scoffing at him, refrained in perplexity, quite bewildered by his presence of mind, his ready replies, and his astonishing accuracy on every point mentioned in history. To increase the mystery by which he was surrounded, he permitted no person to know how he lived. He dressed in a style of the greatest magnificence; sported valuable diamonds in his hat, on his fingers, and in his shoe-buckles; and sometimes made the most costly presents to the ladies of the court. It was suspected by many that he was a spy, in the pay of the English ministry; but there never was a tittle of evidence to support the charge. The king looked upon him with marked favour, was often closeted with him for hours together, and would not suffer any body to speak disparagingly of him. Voltaire constantly turned him into ridicule; and, in one of his letters to the King of Prussia, mentions him as "un comte pour rire;" and states that he pretended to have dined with the holy fathers at the Council of Trent!

In the *Memoirs of Madame du Hausset*, chamber-woman to Madame du Pompadour, there are some amusing anecdotes of this personage. Very soon after his arrival in Paris, he had the *entrée* of her dressing-room; a favour only granted to the most powerful lords at the court of her royal lover. Madame was fond of conversing with him; and, in her presence, he thought fit to lower his pretensions very considerably; but he often allowed her to believe that he had lived two or three hundred years at least. "One day," says Madame du Hausset, "madame said to him, in my presence, 'What was the personal appearance of Francis I.? He was a king I should have liked.' 'He was, indeed, very captivating,' replied St. Germain; and he proceeded to describe his face and person, as that of a man whom he had accurately observed. 'It is a pity he was too ardent. I could have given him some good advice, which would have saved him from all his misfortunes: but he would not have followed it; for it seems as if a fatality attended princes, forcing them to shut their ears to the wisest counsel.' 'Was his court very brilliant?' inquired Madame du Pompadour. 'Very,' replied the count; 'but those of his grandsons surpassed it. In the time of Mary Stuart and Margaret of Valois, it was a land of enchantment—a temple sacred to pleasures of every kind.' Madame said, laughing, 'You seem to have seen all this.' 'I have an excellent memory,' said he, 'and have read the history of France with great care. I sometimes amuse myself, not by making, but by letting, it be believed that I lived in old times.'

"'But you do not tell us your age,' said Madame du Pompadour to him on another occasion; 'and yet you pretend you are very old. The Countess de Gergy, who was, I believe, ambassadress at Vienna some fifty years ago, says she saw you there, exactly the same as you now appear.'

"'It is true, madame,' replied St. Germain; 'I knew Madame de Gergy many years ago.'

"'But, according to her account, you must be more than a hundred years old?'

"'That is not impossible,' said he, laughing; 'but it is much more possible that the good lady is in her dotage.'

"'You gave her an elixir, surprising for the effects it produced; for she says, that during a length of time, she only appeared to be eighty-four; the age at which she took it. Why don't you give it to the king?'

"'Oh, madam,' he exclaimed, 'the physicians would have me broken on the wheel, were I to think of drugging his majesty.'"

When the world begins to believe extraordinary things of an individual, there is no telling where its extravagance will stop. People, when once they have taken the start, vie with each other who shall believe most. At this period all Paris resounded with the wonderful adventures of the Count de St. Germain; and a company of waggish young men tried the following experiment upon its credulity: A clever mimic, who, on account of the amusement he afforded, was admitted into good society, was taken by them, dressed as the Count de St. Germain, into several houses in the Rue du Marais. He imitated the count's peculiarities admirably, and found his auditors open-mouthed to believe any absurdity he chose to utter. No fiction was too monstrous for their all-devouring credulity. He spoke of the Saviour of the world in terms of the greatest familiarity; said he had supped with him at the marriage in Canaan of Galilee, where the water was miraculously turned into wine. In fact, he said he was an intimate friend of his, and had often warned him to be less romantic and imprudent, or he would finish his career miserably. This infamous blasphemy, strange to say, found believers; and ere three days had elapsed, it was currently reported that St. Germain was born soon after the deluge, and that he would never die!

St. Germain himself was too much a man of the world to assert any thing so monstrous; but he took no pains to contradict the story. In all his conversations with persons of rank and education, he advanced his claims modestly, and as if by mere inadvertency, and seldom pretended to a longevity beyond three hundred years, except when he found he was in company with persons who would believe any thing. He often spoke of Henry VIII. as if he had known him intimately, and of the Emperor Charles V. as if that monarch had delighted in his society. He would describe conversations which took place with such an apparent truthfulness, and be so exceedingly minute and particular as to the dress and appearance of the individuals, and even the weather at the time and the furniture of the room, that three persons out of four were generally inclined to credit him. He had constant applications from rich old women for an elixir to make them young again, and it would appear gained large sums in this manner. To those whom he was pleased to call his friends he said his mode of living and plan of diet were far superior to any elixir, and that any body might attain a patriarchal age by refraining from drinking at meals, and very sparingly at any other time. The Baron de Gleichen followed this system, and took great quantities of senna leaves, expecting to live for two hundred years. He died, however, at seventy-three. The Duchess de Choiseul was desirous of following the same system, but the duke her husband in much wrath forbade her to follow any system prescribed by a man who had so equivocal a reputation as M. de St. Germain.

Madame du Hausset says she saw St. Germain and conversed with him several times. He appeared to her to be about fifty years of age, was of the middle size, and had fine expressive features. His dress was always simple, but displayed much taste. He usually wore diamond rings of great value, and his watch and snuff-box were ornamented with a profusion of precious stones. One day, at Madame du Pompadour's apartments, where the principal courtiers were assembled, St. Germain made his appearance in diamond knee and shoe buckles of so fine a water, that madame said she did not think the king had any equal to them. He was entreated to pass into the antechamber and undo them, which he did, and brought them to madame for closer inspection. M. de Gontant, who was present, said their value could not be less than two hundred thousand livres, or upwards of eight thousand pounds sterling. The Baron de Gleichen, in his *Memoirs*, relates that the count one day shewed him so many diamonds, that he thought he saw before him all the treasures of Aladdin's lamp; and adds, that he had had great experience in precious stones, and was convinced that all those possessed by the count were genuine. On another occasion St. Germain shewed Madame du Pompadour a small box, containing topazes, emeralds, and diamonds worth half a million of livres. He affected to despise all this wealth, to make the world more easily believe that he could, like the Rosicrucians, draw precious stones out of the earth by the magic of his song. He gave away a great number of these jewels to the ladies of the court; and Madame du Pompadour was so charmed with his generosity, that she gave him a richly enamelled snuff-box as a token of her regard, on the lid of which was beautifully painted a portrait of Socrates, or some other Greek sage, to whom she compared him. He was not only lavish to the mistresses, but to the maids. Madame du Hausset says: "The count came to see Madame du Pompadour, who was very ill, and lay on the sofa. He shewed her diamonds enough to furnish a king's treasury. Madame sent for me to see all those beautiful things. I looked at them with an air of the utmost astonishment; but I made signs to her that I thought them all false. The count felt for something in a pocket-book about twice as large as a spectacle-case, and at length drew out two or three little paper packets, which he unfolded, and exhibited a superb ruby. He threw on the table, with a contemptuous air, a little cross of green and white stones. I looked at it, and said it was not to be despised. I then put it on, and admired it greatly. The count begged me to accept it; I refused. He urged me to take it. At length he pressed so warmly, that madame, seeing it could not be worth more than a thousand livres, made me a sign to accept it. I took the cross, much pleased with the count's politeness."

How the adventurer obtained his wealth remains a secret. He could not have made it all by the sale of his *elixir vitæ* in Germany, though no doubt some portion of it was derived from that source. Voltaire positively says he was in the pay of foreign governments; and in his letter to the King of Prussia, dated the 5th of April 1758, says that he was initiated in all the secrets of Choiseul, Kaunitz, and Pitt. Of what use he could be to any of those ministers, and to Choiseul especially, is a mystery of mysteries.

There appears no doubt that he possessed the secret of removing spots from diamonds; and in all probability he gained considerable sums by buying at inferior prices such as had flaws in them, and afterwards disposing of them at a profit of cent per cent. Madame du Hausset relates the following anecdote on this particular: "The king," says she, "ordered a middling-sized diamond, which had a flaw in it, to be brought to him. After having it weighed, his majesty said to the count, 'The value of this diamond as it is, and with the flaw in it, is six thousand livres; without the flaw, it would be worth at least ten thousand. Will you undertake to make me a gainer of four thousand livres?' St. Germain examined it very attentively, and said, 'It is possible; it may be done. I will bring it you again in a month.' At the time appointed the count brought back the diamond without a spot, and gave it to the king. It was wrapped in a cloth of amianthos, which he took off. The king had it weighed immediately, and found it very little diminished. His majesty then sent it to his jeweller by M. de Gontant, without telling him of any thing that had passed. The jeweller gave nine thousand six hundred livres for it. The king, however, sent for the diamond back again, and said he would keep it as a curiosity. He could not overcome his surprise, and said M. de St. Germain must be worth millions, especially if he possessed the secret of making large diamonds out of small ones. The count neither said that he could or could not, but positively asserted that he knew how to make pearls grow, and give them the finest water. The king paid him great attention, and so did Madame du Pompadour. M. du Quesnoy once said that St. Germain was a quack, but the king reprimanded him. In fact, his majesty appears infatuated by him, and sometimes talks of him as if his descent were illustrious."

St. Germain had a most amusing vagabond for a servant, to whom he would often appeal for corroboration, when relating some wonderful event that happened centuries before. The fellow, who was not without ability, generally corroborated him in a most satisfactory manner. Upon one occasion, his master was telling a party of ladies and gentlemen, at dinner, some conversation he had had in Palestine with King Richard I. of England, whom he described as a very particular friend of his. Signs of astonishment and incredulity were visible on the faces of the company; upon which St. Germain very coolly turned to his servant, who stood behind his chair, and asked him if he had not spoken truth? "I really cannot say," replied the man, without moving a muscle; "you forget, sir, I have only been five hundred years in your service!" "Ah! true," said his master; "I remember now; it was a little before your time!"

Occasionally, when with men whom he could not so easily dupe, he gave utterance to the contempt with which he could scarcely avoid regarding such gaping credulity. "These fools of Parisians," said he to the Baron de Gleichen, "believe me to be more than five hundred years old; and, since they will have it so, I confirm them in their idea. Not but that I really am much older than I appear."

Many other stories are related of this strange impostor; but enough have been quoted to shew his character and pretensions. It appears that he endeavoured to find the philosopher's stone; but never boasted of possessing it. The Prince of Hesse Cassel, whom he had known years before, in Germany, wrote urgent letters to him, entreating him to quit Paris, and reside with him. St. Germain at last consented. Nothing further is known of his career. There were no gossipping memoir-writers at the court of Hesse Cassel to chronicle his sayings and doings. He died at Sleswig, under the roof of his friend the prince, in the year 1784.

## Cagliostro.

This famous charlatan, the friend and successor of St. Germain, ran a career still more extraordinary. He was the arch-quack of his age, the last of the great pretenders to the philosopher's stone and the water of life, and during his brief season of prosperity, one of the most conspicuous characters of Europe.

His real name was Joseph Balsamo. He was born at Palermo, about the year 1743, of humble parentage. He had the misfortune to lose his father during his infancy, and his education was left in consequence to some relatives of his mother, the latter being too poor to afford him any instruction beyond mere reading and writing. He was sent in his fifteenth year to a monastery, to be taught the elements of chemistry and physic; but his temper was so impetuous, his indolence so invincible, and his vicious habits so deeply rooted, that he made no progress. After remaining some years, he left it with the character of an uninformed and dissipated young man, with good natural talents but a bad disposition. When he became of age, he abandoned himself to a life of riot and debauchery, and entered himself, in fact, into that celebrated fraternity, known in France and Italy as the "Knights of Industry," and in England as the "Swell Mob." He was far from being an idle or unwilling member of the corps. The first way in which he distinguished himself was by forging orders of admission to the theatres. He afterwards robbed his uncle, and counterfeited a will. For acts like these, he paid frequent compulsory visits to the prisons of Palermo. Somehow or other he acquired the character of a sorcerer — of a man who had failed in discovering the secrets of alchymy, and had sold his soul to the devil for the gold which he was not able to make by means of transmutation. He took no pains to disabuse the popular mind on this particular, but rather encouraged the belief than otherwise. He at last made use of it to cheat a silversmith named Marano, of about sixty ounces of gold, and was in consequence obliged to leave Palermo. He persuaded this man that he could shew him a treasure hidden in a cave, for which service he was to receive the sixty ounces of gold, while the silversmith was to have all the treasure for the mere trouble of digging it up. They went together at midnight to an excavation in the vicinity of Palermo, where Balsamo drew a magic circle, and invoked the devil to shew his treasures. Suddenly there appeared half a dozen fellows, the accomplices of the swindler, dressed to represent devils, with horns on their heads, claws to their fingers, and vomiting apparently red and blue flame. They were armed with pitchforks, with which they belaboured poor Marano till he was almost dead, and robbed him of his sixty ounces of gold and all the valuables he carried about his person. They then made off, accompanied by Balsamo, leaving the unlucky silversmith to recover or die at his leisure. Nature chose the former course; and soon after daylight he was restored to his senses, smarting in body from his blows and in spirit for the deception of which he had been the victim. His first impulse was to denounce Balsamo to the magistrates of the town; but on further reflection he was afraid of the ridicule that a full exposure of all the circumstances would draw upon him; he therefore took the truly Italian resolution of being revenged on Balsamo, by murdering him at the first convenient opportunity. Having given utterance to this threat in the hearing of a friend of Balsamo, it was reported to the latter, who immediately packed up his valuables and quitted Europe.

He chose Medina, in Arabia, for his future dwelling-place, and there became acquainted with a Greek named Altotas, a man exceedingly well versed in all the languages of the East, and an indefatigable student of alchymy. He possessed an invaluable collection of Arabian manuscripts on his favourite science, and studied them with such unremitting industry that he found he had not sufficient time to attend to his crucibles and furnaces without neglecting his books. He was looking about for an assistant when Balsamo opportunely presented himself, and made so favourable an impression that he was at once engaged in that capacity. But the relation of master and servant did not long subsist between them; Balsamo was too ambitious and too clever to play a secondary part, and within fifteen days of their first acquaintance they were bound together as friends and partners. Altotas, in the course of a long life devoted to alchymy, had stumbled upon some valuable discoveries in chemistry, one of which was an ingredient for improving the manufacture of flax, and imparting to goods of that material a gloss and softness almost equal to silk. Balsamo gave him the good advice to leave the philosopher's stone for the present undiscovered, and make gold out of their flax. The advice was taken, and they proceeded together to Alexandria to trade, with a large stock of that article. They stayed forty days in Alexandria, and gained a considerable sum by their venture. They afterwards visited other cities in Egypt, and were equally successful. They also visited Turkey, where they sold drugs and amulets. On their return to Europe, they were driven by stress of weather into Malta, and were hospitably received by Pinto, the Grand Master of the Knights, and a famous alchymist. They worked in his laboratory for some months, and tried hard to change a pewter platter into a silver one. Balsamo, having less faith than his companions, was sooner wearied; and obtaining from his host many letters of introduction to Rome and Naples, he left him and Altotas to find the philosopher's stone and transmute the pewter platter without him.

He had long since dropped the name of Balsamo on account of the many ugly associations that clung to it; and during his travels had assumed at least half a score others, with titles annexed to them. He called himself sometimes the Chevalier de Fischio, the Marquis de Melissa, the Baron de Belmonte, de Pelligrini, d'Anna, de Fenix, de Harat, but most commonly the Count de Cagliostro. Under the latter title he entered Rome, and never afterwards changed it. In this city he gave himself out as the restorer of the Rosicrucian philosophy; said he could transmute all metals into gold; that he could render himself invisible, cure all diseases, and administer an elixir against old age and decay. His letters from the Grand Master Pinto procured him an introduction into the best families. He made money rapidly by the sale of his *elixir vitæ*; and, like other quacks, performed many remarkable cures by inspiring his patients with the most complete faith and reliance upon his powers; an advantage which the most impudent charlatans often possess over the regular practitioner.

While thus in a fair way of making his fortune he became acquainted with the beautiful Lorenza Feliciana, a young lady of noble birth, but without fortune. Cagliostro soon discovered that she possessed accomplishments that were invaluable. Besides her ravishing beauty, she had the readiest wit, the most engaging manners, the most fertile imagination, and the least principle of any of the maidens of Rome. She was just the wife for Cagliostro, who proposed himself to her, and was accepted. After their marriage, he instructed his fair Lorenza in all the secrets of his calling—taught her pretty lips to invoke angels, and genii, sylphs, salamanders, and undines, and, when need required, devils and evil spirits. Lorenza was an apt scholar; she soon learned all the jargon of the alchymists and all the spells of the enchanters; and thus accomplished the hopeful pair set out on their travels, to levy contributions on the superstitious and the credulous.

They first went to Sleswig on a visit to the Count de St. Germain, their great predecessor in the art of making dupes, and were received by him in the most magnificent manner. They no doubt fortified their minds for the career they had chosen by the sage discourse of that worshipful gentleman; for immediately after they left him, they began their operations. They travelled for three or four years in Russia, Poland, and Germany, transmuting metals, telling fortunes, raising spirits, and selling the *elixir vitæ* wherever they went; but there is no record of their doings from whence to draw a more particular detail. It was not until they made their appearance in England in 1776, that the names of the Count and Countess di Cagliostro began to acquire a European reputation. They arrived in London in the July of that year, possessed of property, in plate, jewels, and specie, to the amount of about three thousand pounds. They hired apartments in Whitcombe Street, and lived for some months quietly. In the same house there lodged a Portuguese woman, named Blavary, who, being in necessitous circumstances, was engaged by the count as interpreter. She was constantly admitted into his laboratory, where he spent much of his time in search of the philosopher's stone. She spread abroad the fame of her entertainer in return for his hospitality, and laboured hard to impress every body with as full a belief in his extraordinary powers as she felt herself; but as a female interpreter of the rank and appearance of Madame Blavary did not exactly correspond with the count's notions either of dignity or decorum, he hired a person named Vitellini, a teacher of languages, to act in that capacity. Vitellini was a desperate gambler, a man who had tried almost every resource to repair his ruined fortunes, including among the rest the search for the philosopher's stone. Immediately that he saw the count's operations, he was convinced that the great secret was his, and that the golden gates of the palace of fortune were open to let him in. With still more enthusiasm than Madame Blavary, he held forth to his acquaintance, and in all public places, that the count was an extraordinary man, a true adept, whose fortune was immense, and who could transmute into pure and solid gold as much lead, iron, and copper as he pleased. The consequence was, that the house of Cagliostro was besieged by crowds of the idle, the credulous, and the avaricious, all eager to obtain a sight of the "philosopher," or to share in the boundless wealth which he could call into existence.

Unfortunately for Cagliostro, he had fallen into evil hands. Instead of duping the people of England, as he might have done, he became himself the victim of a gang of swindlers, who, with the fullest reliance on his occult powers, only sought to make money of him. Vitellini introduced to him a ruined gambler like himself, named Scot, whom he represented as a Scottish nobleman, attracted to London solely by his desire to see and converse with the extraordinary man whose fame had spread to the distant mountains of the north. Cagliostro received him with great kindness and cordiality; and "Lord" Scot thereupon introduced a woman named Fry as Lady Scot, who was to act as chaperone to the Countess di Cagliostro, and make her acquainted with all the noble families of Britain. Thus things went swimmingly. "His lordship," whose effects had not arrived from Scotland, and who had no banker in London, borrowed two hundred pounds of the count. They were lent without scruple, so flattered was Cagliostro by the attentions they paid him, the respect, nay veneration they pretended to feel for him, and the complete deference with which they listened to every word that fell from his lips.

Superstitious like all desperate gamesters, Scot had often tried magical and cabalistic numbers, in the hope of discovering lucky numbers in the lottery or at the roulette-tables. He had in his possession a cabalistic manuscript, containing various arithmetical combinations of the kind, which he submitted to Cagliostro, with an urgent request that he would select a number. Cagliostro took the manuscript and studied it, but, as he himself informs us, with no confidence in its truth. He, however, predicted twenty as the successful number for the 6th of November following. Scot ventured a small sum upon this number out of the two hundred pounds he had borrowed, and won. Cagliostro, incited by this success, prognosticated number twenty-five for the next drawing. Scot tried again, and won a hundred guineas. The numbers fifty-five and fifty-seven were announced with equal success for the 18th of the same month, to the no small astonishment and delight of Cagliostro, who thereupon resolved to try fortune for himself, and not for others. To all the entreaties of Scot and his lady that he would predict more numbers for them, he turned a deaf ear, even while he still thought him a lord and a man of honour; but when he discovered that he was a mere swindler, and the pretended Lady Scot an artful woman of the town, he closed his door upon them and on all their gang.

Having complete faith in the supernatural powers of the count, they were in the deepest distress at having lost his countenance. They tried by every means their ingenuity could suggest to propitiate him again. They implored, they threatened, and endeavoured to bribe him; but all was vain. Cagliostro would neither see nor correspond with them. In the mean time they lived extravagantly, and in the hope of future, exhausted all their present gains. They were reduced to the last extremity, when Miss Fry obtained access to the countess, and received a guinea from her on the representation that she was starving. Miss Fry, not contented with this, begged her to intercede with her husband, that for the last time he would point out a lucky number in the lottery. The countess promised to exert her influence; and Cagliostro, thus entreated, named the number eight, at the same time reiterating his determination to have no more to do with any of them. By an extraordinary hazard, which filled Cagliostro with surprise and pleasure, number eight was the greatest prize in the lottery. Miss Fry and her associates cleared fifteen hundred guineas by the adventure, and became more than ever convinced of the occult powers of Cagliostro, and strengthened in their determination never to quit him until they had made their fortunes. Out of the proceeds Miss Fry bought a handsome necklace at a pawnbroker's for ninety guineas. She then ordered a richly-chased gold box, having two compartments, to be made at a jeweller's, and putting the necklace in the one, filled the other with a fine aromatic snuff. She then sought another interview with Madame di Cagliostro, and urged her to accept the box as a small token of her esteem and gratitude, without mentioning the valuable necklace that was concealed in it. Madame di Cagliostro accepted the present, and was from that hour exposed to the most incessant persecution from all the confederates — Blavary, Vitellini, and the pretended Lord and

Lady Scot. They flattered themselves they had regained their lost footing in the house, and came day after day to know lucky numbers in the lottery, sometimes forcing themselves up the stairs, and into the count's laboratory, in spite of the efforts of the servants to prevent them. Cagliostro, exasperated at their pertinacity, threatened to call in the assistance of the magistrates, and taking Miss Fry by the shoulders, pushed her into the street. From that time may be dated the misfortunes of Cagliostro. Miss Fry, at the instigation of her paramour, determined on vengeance. Her first act was to swear a debt of two hundred pounds against Cagliostro, and to cause him to be arrested for that sum. While he was in custody in a sponging-house, Scot, accompanied by a low attorney, broke into his laboratory, and carried off a small box, containing, as they believed, the powder of transmutation, and a number of cabalistic manuscripts and treatises upon alchymy. They also brought an action against him for the recovery of the necklace; and Miss Fry accused both him and his countess of sorcery and witchcraft, and of foretelling numbers in the lottery by the aid of the Devil. This latter charge was actually heard before Mr. Justice Miller. The action of trover for the necklace was tried before the Lord Chief Justice of the Common Pleas, who recommended the parties to submit to arbitration. In the mean time Cagliostro remained in prison for several weeks, till having procured bail, he was liberated. He was soon after waited upon by an attorney named Reynolds, also deep in the plot, who offered to compromise all the actions upon certain conditions. Scot, who had accompanied him, concealed himself behind the door, and suddenly rushing out, presented a pistol at the heart of Cagliostro, swearing he would shoot him instantly, if he would not tell him truly the art of predicting lucky numbers and of transmuting metals. Reynolds pretending to be very angry, disarmed his accomplice, and entreated the count to satisfy them by fair means, and disclose his secrets, promising that if he would do so, they would discharge all the actions, and offer him no further molestation. Cagliostro replied, that threats and entreaties were alike useless; that he knew no secrets; and that the powder of transmutation of which they had robbed him, was of no value to any body but himself. He offered, however, if they would discharge the actions, and return the powder and the manuscripts, to forgive them all the money they had swindled him out of. These conditions were refused; and Scot and Reynolds departed, swearing vengeance against him.

Cagliostro appears to have been quite ignorant of the forms of law in England, and to have been without a friend to advise him as to the best course he should pursue. While he was conversing with his countess on the difficulties that beset them, one of his bail called, and invited him to ride in a hackney coach to the house of a person who would see him righted. Cagliostro consented, and was driven to the King's Bench prison, where his friend left him. He did not discover for several hours that he was a prisoner, or, in fact, understand the process of being surrendered by one's bail.

He regained his liberty in a few weeks; and the arbitrators between him and Miss Fry made their award against him. He was ordered to pay the two hundred pounds she had sworn against him, and to restore the necklace and gold box which had been presented to the countess. Cagliostro was so disgusted, that he determined to quit England. His pretensions, besides, had been unmercifully exposed by a Frenchman, named Morande, the editor of the *Courrier de l'Europe*, published in London. To add to his distress, he was recognised in Westminster Hall as Joseph Balsamo, the swindler of Palermo. Such a complication of disgrace was not to be borne. He and his countess packed up their small effects, and left England with no more than fifty pounds, out of the three thousand they had brought with them. They first proceeded to Brussels, where fortune was more auspicious. They sold considerable quantities of the elixir of life, performed many cures, and recruited their finances. They then took their course through Germany to Russia, and always with the same success. Gold flowed into their coffers faster than they could count it. They quite forgot all the woes they had endured in England, and learned to be more circumspect in the choice of their acquaintance.

In the year 1780, they made their appearance in Strasbourg. Their fame had reached that city before them. They took a magnificent hotel, and invited all the principal persons of the place to their table. Their wealth appeared to be boundless, and their hospitality equal to it. Both the count and countess acted as physicians, and gave money, advice, and medicine to all the necessitous and suffering of the town. Many of the cures they performed astonished those regular practitioners who did not make sufficient allowance for the wonderful influence of imagination in certain cases. The countess, who at this time was not more than five-and-twenty, and all radiant with grace, beauty, and cheerfulness, spoke openly of her eldest son as a fine young man of eight-and-twenty, who had been for some years a captain in the Dutch service. The trick succeeded to admiration. All the ugly old women in Strasbourg, and for miles around, thronged the saloon of the countess to purchase the liquid which was to make them as blooming as their daughters; the young women came in equal abundance, that they might preserve their charms, and when twice as old as Ninon de l'Enclos, be more captivating than she; while men were not wanting who were fools enough to imagine that they might keep off the inevitable stroke of the grim foe by a few drops of the same incomparable elixir. The countess, sooth to say, looked like an incarnation of immortal loveliness, a very goddess of youth and beauty; and it is possible that the crowds of young men and old, who at all convenient seasons haunted the perfumed chambers of this enchantress, were attracted less by their belief in her occult powers than from admiration of her languishing bright eyes and sparkling conversation. But amid all the incense that was offered at her shrine, Madame di Cagliostro was ever faithful to her spouse. She encouraged hopes, it is true, but she never realised them; she excited admiration, yet kept it within bounds; and made men her slaves, without ever granting a favour of which the vainest might boast.

In this city they made the acquaintance of many eminent persons, and, among others, of the Cardinal Prince de Rohan, who was destined afterwards to exercise so untoward an influence over their fate. The cardinal, who seems to have had great faith in him as a philosopher, persuaded him to visit Paris in his company, which he did, but remained only thirteen days. He preferred the society of Strasbourg, and returned thither with the intention of fixing his residence far from the capital. But he soon found that the first excitement of his arrival had passed away. People began to reason with themselves, and to be ashamed of their own admiration. The populace, among whom he had lavished his charity with a bountiful hand, accused him of being the Antichrist, the Wandering Jew, the man of fourteen hundred years of age, a demon in human shape, sent to lure the ignorant to their destruction; while the more opulent and better informed called him a spy in the pay of foreign governments, an agent of the police, a swindler, and a man of evil life. The outcry grew at last so strong, that he deemed it prudent to try his fortune elsewhere.

He went first to Naples, but that city was too near Palermo; he dreaded recognition from some of his early friends, and, after a short stay, returned to France. He chose Bourdeaux as his next dwelling-place, and created as great a sensation there as he had done in Strasbourg. He announced himself as the founder of a new school of medicine and philosophy, boasted of his ability to cure all diseases, and invited the poor and suffering to visit him, and he would relieve the distress of the one class, and cure the ailings of the other. All day long the street opposite his magnificent hotel was crowded by the populace; the halt and the blind, women with sick babes in their arms, and persons suffering under every species of human infirmity, flocked to this wonderful doctor. The relief he afforded in money more than counterbalanced the failure of his nostrums; and the affluence of people from all the surrounding country became so great, that the *jurats* of the city granted him a military guard, to be stationed day and night before his door, to keep order. The anticipations of Cagliostro were realised. The rich were struck with admiration of his charity and benevolence, and impressed with a full conviction of his marvellous powers. The sale of the elixir went on admirably. His saloons were thronged with wealthy dupes who came to purchase immortality. Beauty, that would endure for centuries, was the attraction for the fair sex; health and strength for the same period were the baits held out to the other. His charming countess, in the meantime, brought grist to the mill by telling fortunes and casting nativities, or granting attendant sylphs to any ladies who would pay sufficiently for their services. What was still better, as tending to keep up the credit of her husband, she gave the most magnificent parties in Bourdeaux.

But as at Strasbourg, the popular delusion lasted for a few months only, and burned itself out; Cagliostro forgot, in the intoxication of success, that there was a limit to quackery which once passed inspired distrust. When he pretended to call spirits from the tomb, people became incredulous. He was accused of being an enemy to religion, of denying Christ, and of being the Wandering Jew. He despised these rumours as long as they were confined to a few; but when they spread over the town, when he received no more fees, when his parties were abandoned, and his acquaintance turned away when they met him in the street, he thought it high time to shift his quarters.

*House of Cagliostro, Paris.*

He was by this time wearied of the provinces, and turned his thoughts to the capital. On his arrival he announced himself as the restorer of Egyptian Freemasonry, and the founder of a new philosophy. He immediately made his way into the best society by means of his friend the Cardinal de Rohan. His success as a magician was quite extraordinary: the most considerable persons of the time visited him. He boasted of being able, like the Rosicrucians, to converse with the elementary spirits; to invoke the mighty dead from the grave, to transmute metals, and to discover occult things by means of the special protection of God towards him. Like Dr. Dee, he summoned the angels to reveal the future; and they appeared and conversed with him in crystals and under glass bells.[48] "There was hardly," says the *Biographie des Contemporains*, "a fine lady in Paris who would not sup with the shade of Lucretius in the apartments of Cagliostro; a military officer who would not discuss the art of war with Cæsar, Hannibal, or Alexander; or an advocate or counsellor who would not argue legal points with the ghost of Cicero." These interviews with the departed were very expensive; for, as Cagliostro said, the dead would not rise for nothing. The countess, as usual, exercised all her ingenuity to support her husband's credit. She was a great favourite with her own sex, to many a delighted and wondering auditory of whom she detailed the marvellous powers of Cagliostro. She said he could render himself invisible, traverse the world with the rapidity of thought, and be in several places at the same time.[49]

He had not been long at Paris before he became involved in the celebrated affair of the queen's necklace. His friend the Cardinal de Rohan, enamoured of the charms of Marie Antoinette, was in sore distress at her coldness, and the displeasure she had so often manifested against him. There was at that time a lady named La Motte in the service of the queen, of whom the cardinal was foolish enough to make a confidant. Madame de la Motte, in return, endeavoured to make a tool of the cardinal, and succeeded but too well in her projects. In her capacity of chamber-woman, or lady of honour to the queen, she was present at an interview between her majesty and M. Boehmer, a wealthy jeweller of Paris, when the latter offered for sale a magnificent diamond necklace, valued at 1,600,000 francs, or about 64,000l. sterling. The queen admired it greatly, but dismissed the jeweller, with the expression of her regret that she was too poor to purchase it. Madame de la Motte formed a plan to get this costly ornament into her own possession, and determined to make the Cardinal de Rohan the instrument by which to effect it. She therefore sought an interview with him, and pretending to sympathise in his grief for the queen's displeasure, told him she knew a way by which he might be restored to favour. She then mentioned the necklace, and the sorrow of the queen that she could not afford to buy it. The cardinal, who was as wealthy as he was foolish, immediately offered to purchase the necklace, and make a present of it to the queen. Madame de la Motte told him by no means to do so, as he would thereby offend her majesty. His plan would be to induce the jeweller to give her majesty credit, and accept her promissory note for the amount at a certain date, to be hereafter agreed upon. The cardinal readily agreed to the proposal, and instructed the jeweller to draw up an agreement, and he would procure the queen's signature. He placed this in the hands of Madame de la Motte, who returned it shortly afterwards, with the words, "Bon, bon—approuvé—Marie Antoinette," written in the margin. She told him at the same time that the queen was highly pleased with his conduct in the matter, and would appoint a meeting with him in the gardens of Versailles, when she would present him with a flower, as a token of her regard. The cardinal shewed the forged document to the jeweller, obtained the necklace, and delivered it into the hands of Madame de la Motte. So far all was well. Her next object was to satisfy the cardinal, who awaited impatiently the promised interview with his royal mistress. There was at that time in Paris a young woman named D'Oliva, noted for her resemblance to the queen; and Madame de la Motte, on the promise of a handsome reward, found no difficulty in persuading her to personate Marie Antoinette, and meet the Cardinal de Rohan at the evening twilight in the gardens of Versailles. The meeting took place accordingly. The cardinal was deceived by the uncertain light, the great resemblance of the counterfeit, and his own hopes; and having received the flower from Mademoiselle D'Oliva, went home with a lighter heart than had beat in his bosom for many a day.[50]

In the course of time the forgery of the queen's signature was discovered. Boehmer the jeweller immediately named the Cardinal de Rohan and Madame de la Motte as the persons with whom he had negotiated, and they were both arrested and thrown into the Bastille. La Motte was subjected to a rigorous examination, and the disclosures she made implicating Cagliostro, he was seized, along with his wife, and also sent to the Bastille. A story involving so much scandal necessarily excited great curiosity. Nothing was to be heard of in Paris but the queen's necklace, with surmises of the guilt or innocence of the several parties implicated. The husband of Madame de la Motte escaped to England, and in the opinion of many took the necklace with him, and there disposed of it to different jewellers in small quantities at a time. But Madame de la Motte insisted that she had entrusted it to Cagliostro, who had seized and taken it to pieces, to "swell the treasures of his immense unequalled fortune." She spoke of him as "an empiric, a mean alchymist, a dreamer on the philosopher's stone, a false prophet, a profaner of the true worship, the self-dubbed Count Cagliostro!" She further said that he originally conceived the project of ruining the Cardinal de Rohan; that he persuaded her, by the exercise of some magic influence over her mind, to aid and abet the scheme; and that he was a robber, a swindler, and a sorcerer!

After all the accused parties had remained for upwards of six months in the Bastille, the trial commenced. The depositions of the witnesses having been heard, Cagliostro, as the principal culprit, was first called upon for his defence. He was listened to with the most breathless attention. He put himself into a theatrical attitude, and thus began: — "I am oppressed! — I am accused! — I am calumniated! Have I deserved this fate? I descend into my conscience, and I there find the peace that men refuse me! I have travelled a great deal — I am known over all Europe, and a great part of Asia and Africa. I have every where shewn myself the friend of my fellow-creatures. My knowledge, my time, my fortune have ever been employed in the relief of distress. I have studied and practised medicine; but I have never degraded that most noble and most consoling of arts by mercenary speculations of any kind. Though always giving, and never receiving, I have preserved my independence. I have even carried my delicacy so far as to refuse the favours of kings. I have given gratuitously my remedies and my advice to the rich; the poor have received from me both remedies and money. I have never contracted any debts, and my manners are pure and uncorrupted." After much more self-laudation of the same kind, he went on to complain of the great hardships he had endured in being separated for so many months from his innocent and loving wife, who, as he was given to understand, had been detained in the Bastille, and perhaps chained in an unwholesome dungeon. He denied unequivocally that he had the necklace, or that he had ever seen it; and to silence the rumours and accusations against him, which his own secrecy with regard to the events of his life had perhaps originated, he expressed himself ready to satisfy the curiosity of the public, and to give a plain and full account of his career. He then told a romantic and incredible tale, which imposed upon no one. He said he neither knew the place of his birth nor the name of his parents, but that he spent his infancy in Medina, in Arabia, and was brought up under the name of Acharat. He lived in the palace of the Great Muphti in that city, and always had three servants to wait upon him, besides his preceptor, named Althotas. This Althotas was very fond of him, and told him that his father and mother, who were Christians and nobles, died when he was three months old, and left him in the care of the Muphti. He could never, he said, ascertain their names, for whenever he asked Althotas the question, he was told that it would be dangerous for him to know. Some incautious expressions dropped by his preceptor gave him reason to think they were from Malta. At the age of twelve he began his travels, and learned the various languages of the East. He remained three years in Mecca, where the cherif, or governor, shewed him so much kindness, and spoke to him so tenderly and affectionately, that he sometimes thought that personage was his father. He quitted this good man with tears in his eyes, and never saw him afterwards; but he was convinced that he was, even at that moment, indebted to his care for all the advantages he enjoyed. Whenever he arrived in any city, either of Europe or Asia, he found an account opened for him at the principal bankers' or merchants'. He could draw upon them to the amount of thousands and hundreds of thousands; and no questions were ever asked beyond his name. He had only to mention the word 'Acharat,' and all his wants were supplied. He firmly believed that the Cherif of Mecca was the friend to whom all was owing. This was the secret of his wealth, and he had no occasion to resort to swindling for a livelihood. It was not worth his while to steal a diamond necklace when he had wealth enough to purchase as many as he pleased, and more magnificent ones than had ever been worn by a queen of France. As to the other charges brought against him by Madame de la Motte, he had but a short answer to give. She had called him an empiric. He was not unfamiliar with the word. If it meant a man who, without being a physician, had some knowledge of medicine, and took no fees — who cured both rich and poor, and took no money from either, he confessed that he was such a man, that he was an empiric. She had also called him a mean alchymist. Whether he were an alchymist or not, the epithet *mean* could only be applied to those who begged and cringed, and he had never done either. As regarded his being a dreamer about the philosopher's stone, whatever his opinions upon that subject might be, he had been silent, and had never troubled the public with his dreams. Then, as to his being a false prophet, he had not always been so; for he had prophesied to the Cardinal de Rohan, that Madame de la Motte would prove a dangerous woman, and the result had verified the prediction. He denied that he was a profaner of the true worship, or that he had ever striven to bring religion into contempt; on the contrary, he respected every man's religion, and never meddled with it. He also denied that he was a Rosicrucian, or that he had ever pretended to be three hundred years of age, or to have had one man in his service for a hundred and fifty years. In conclusion, he said every statement that Madame de la Motte had made regarding him was false, and that she was *mentiris impudentissime*, which two words he begged her counsel to translate for her, as it was not polite to tell her so in French.

Such was the substance of his extraordinary answer to the charges against him; an answer which convinced those who were before doubtful that he was one of the most impudent impostors that had ever run the career of deception. Counsel were then heard on behalf of the Cardinal de Rohan and Madame de la Motte. It appearing clearly that the cardinal was himself the dupe of a vile conspiracy, and there being no evidence against Cagliostro, they were both acquitted. Madame de la Motte was found guilty, and sentenced to be publicly whipped, and branded with a hot iron on the back.

Cagliostro and his wife were then discharged from custody. On applying to the officers of the Bastille for the papers and effects which had been seized at his lodgings, he found that many of them had been abstracted. He thereupon brought an action against them for the recovery of his Mss. and a small portion of the powder of transmutation. Before the affair could be decided, he received orders to quit Paris within four-and-twenty hours. Fearing that if he were once more enclosed in the dungeons of the Bastille he should never see daylight again, he took his departure immediately and proceeded to England. On his arrival in London he made the acquaintance of the notorious Lord George Gordon, who espoused his cause warmly, and inserted a letter in the public papers, animadverting upon the conduct of the Queen of France in the affair of the necklace, and asserting that she was really the guilty party. For this letter Lord George was exposed to a prosecution at the instance of the French ambassador, found guilty of libel, and sentenced to fine and a long imprisonment.

Cagliostro and the countess afterwards travelled in Italy, where they were arrested by the Papal government in 1789, and condemned to death. The charges against him were, that he was a freemason, a heretic, and a sorcerer. This unjustifiable sentence was afterwards commuted into one of perpetual imprisonment in the Castle of St. Angelo. His wife was allowed to escape severer punishment by immuring herself in a nunnery. Cagliostro did not long survive. The loss of liberty preyed upon his mind—accumulated misfortunes had injured his health and broken his spirit, and he died early in 1790. His fate may have been no better than he deserved, but it is impossible not to feel that his sentence for the crimes assigned was utterly disgraceful to the government that pronounced it.

## Present State of Alchymy.

We have now finished the list of the persons who have most distinguished themselves in this unprofitable pursuit. Among them are men of all ranks, characters, and conditions: the truth-seeking but erring philosopher; the ambitious prince and the needy noble, who have believed in it; as well as the designing charlatan, who has not believed in it, but has merely made the pretension to it the means of cheating his fellows, and living upon their credulity. One or more of all these classes will be found in the foregoing pages. It will be seen, from the record of their lives, that the delusion was not altogether without its uses. Men, in striving to gain too much, do not always overreach themselves; if they cannot arrive at the inaccessible mountain-top, they may perhaps get half way towards it, and pick up some scraps of wisdom and knowledge on the road. The useful science of chemistry is not a little indebted to its spurious brother of alchymy. Many valuable discoveries have been made in that search for the impossible, which might otherwise have been hidden for centuries yet to come. Roger Bacon, in searching for the philosopher's stone, discovered gunpowder, a still more extraordinary substance. Van Helmont, in the same pursuit, discovered the properties of gas; Geber made discoveries in chemistry which were equally important; and Paracelsus, amidst his perpetual visions of the transmutation of metals, found that mercury was a remedy for one of the most odious and excruciating of all the diseases that afflict humanity.

In our day little mention is made in Europe of any new devotees of the science, though it is affirmed that one or two of our most illustrious men of science do not admit the pursuit to be so absurd and vain as it has been commonly considered in recent times. The belief in witchcraft, which is scarcely more absurd, still lingers in the popular mind; but few are so credulous as to believe that any elixir could make man live for centuries, or turn all our iron and pewter into gold. Alchymy, in Europe, may be said to be almost wholly exploded; but in the East it still flourishes in as great repute as ever. Recent travellers make constant mention of it, especially in China, Hindostan, Persia, Tartary, Egypt, and Arabia.

# Chapter 5.

Modern Prophecies.

An epidemic terror of the end of the world has several times spread over the nations. The most remarkable was that which seized Christendom about the middle of the tenth century. Numbers of fanatics appeared in France, Germany, and Italy at that time, preaching that the thousand years prophesied in the Apocalypse as the term of the world's duration were about to expire, and that the Son of Man would appear in the clouds to judge the godly and the ungodly. The delusion appears to have been discouraged by the Church, but it nevertheless spread rapidly among the people.[51]

The scene of the last judgment was expected to be at Jerusalem. In the year 999, the number of pilgrims proceeding eastward, to await the coming of the Lord in that city, was so great that they were compared to a desolating army. Most of them sold their goods and possessions before they quitted Europe, and lived upon the proceeds in the Holy Land. Buildings of every sort were suffered to fall into ruins. It was thought useless to repair them, when the end of the world was so near. Many noble edifices were deliberately pulled down. Even churches, usually so well maintained, shared the general neglect. Knights, citizens, and serfs, travelled eastwards in company, taking with them their wives and children, singing psalms as they went, and looking with fearful eyes upon the sky, which they expected each minute to open, to let the Son of God descend in his glory.

During the thousandth year the number of pilgrims increased. Most of them were smitten with terror as with a plague. Every phenomenon of nature filled them with alarm. A thunder-storm sent them all upon their knees in mid-march. It was the opinion that thunder was the voice of God, announcing the day of judgment. Numbers expected the earth to open, and give up its dead at the sound. Every meteor in the sky seen at Jerusalem brought the whole Christian population into the streets to weep and pray. The pilgrims on the road were in the same alarm:

> "Lorsque, pendant la nuit, un globe de lumière
> S'échappa quelquefois de la voûte de cieux,
> Et traça dans sa chûte un long sillon de feux,
> La troupe suspendit sa marche solitaire."[52]

Fanatic preachers kept up the flame of terror. Every shooting star furnished occasion for a sermon, in which the sublimity of the approaching judgment was the principal topic.

The appearance of comets has been often thought to foretell the speedy dissolution of this world. Part of this belief still exists; but the comet is no longer looked upon as the sign, but the agent of destruction. So lately as in the year 1832 the greatest alarm spread over the continent of Europe, especially in Germany, lest the comet, whose appearance was then foretold by astronomers, should destroy the earth. The danger of our globe was gravely discussed. Many persons refrained from undertaking or concluding any business during that year, in consequence solely of their apprehension that this terrible comet would dash us and our world to atoms.

During seasons of great pestilence, men have often believed the prophecies of crazed fanatics, that the end of the world was come. Credulity is always greatest in times of calamity. During the great plague, which ravaged all Europe between the years 1345 and 1350, it was generally considered that the end of the world was at hand. Pretended prophets were to be found in all the principal cities of Germany, France, and Italy, predicting that within ten years the trump of the archangel would sound, and the Saviour appear in the clouds to call the earth to judgment.

No little consternation was created in London in 1736 by the prophecy of the famous Whiston, that the world would be destroyed in that year, on the 13th of October. Crowds of people went out on the appointed day to Islington, Hampstead, and the fields intervening, to see the destruction of London, which was to be the "beginning of the end." A satirical account of this folly is given in Swift's *Miscellanies*, vol. iii., entitled *A true and faithful Narrative of what passed in London on a Rumour of the Day of Judgment*. An authentic narrative of this delusion would be interesting; but this solemn witticism of Pope and Gay is not to be depended upon.

In the year 1761 the citizens of London were alarmed by two shocks of an earthquake, and the prophecy of a third, which was to destroy them altogether. The first shock was felt on the 8th of

February, and threw down several chimneys in the neighbour-hood of Limehouse and Poplar; the second happened on the 8th of March, and was chiefly felt in the north of London, and towards Hampstead and Highgate. It soon became the subject of general remark, that there was exactly an interval of a month between the shocks; and a crack-brained fellow, named Bell, a soldier in the Life Guards, was so impressed with the idea that there would be a third in another month, that he lost his senses altogether, and ran about the streets predicting the destruction of London on the 5th of April. Most people thought that the *first* would have been a more appropriate day; but there were not wanting thousands who confidently believed the prediction, and took measures to transport themselves and families from the scene of the impending calamity. As the awful day approached, the excitement became intense, and great numbers of credulous people resorted to all the villages within a circuit of twenty miles, awaiting the doom of London. Islington, Highgate, Hampstead, Harrow, and Blackheath, were crowded with panic-stricken fugitives, who paid exorbitant prices for accommodation to the housekeepers of these secure retreats. Such as could not afford to pay for lodgings at any of those places, remained in London until two or three days before the time, and then encamped in the surrounding fields, awaiting the tremendous shock which was to lay their high city all level with the dust. As happened during a similar panic in the time of Henry VIII., the fear became conta-gious, and hundreds who had laughed at the prediction a week before, packed up their goods, when they saw others doing so, and hastened away. The river was thought to be a place of great security, and all the merchant-vessels in the port were filled with people, who passed the night between the 4th and 5th on board, expecting every instant to see St. Paul's totter, and the towers of Westminster Abbey rock in the wind and fall amid a cloud of dust. The greater part of the fugitives returned on the following day, convinced that the prophet was a false one; but many judged it more prudent to allow a week to elapse before they trusted their dear limbs in London. Bell lost all credit in a short time, and was looked upon even by the most credulous as a mere madman. He tried some other prophecies, but nobody was deceived by them; and, in a few months afterwards, he was confined in a lunatic asylum.

A panic terror of the end of the world seized the good people of Leeds and its neighbourhood in the year 1806. It arose from the following circumstances. A hen, in a village close by, laid eggs, on which were inscribed the words, *Christ is coming.* Great numbers visited the spot, and examined these wondrous eggs, convinced that the day of judgment was near at hand. Like sailors in a storm, expecting every instant to go to the bottom, the believers suddenly became religious, prayed violently, and flattered themselves that they repented them of their evil courses. But a plain tale soon put them down, and quenched their religion entirely. Some gentlemen, hearing of the matter, went one fine morning, and caught the poor hen in the act of laying one of her miraculous eggs. They soon ascertained beyond doubt that the egg had been inscribed with some corrosive ink, and cruelly forced up again into the bird's body. At this explanation, those who had prayed, now laughed, and the world wagged as merrily as of yore.

At the time of the plague in Milan, in 1630, of which so affecting a description has been left us by Ripamonte, in his interesting work, *De Peste Mediolani*, the people, in their distress, listened with avidity to the predictions of astrologers and other impostors. It is singular enough that the plague was foretold a year before it broke out. A large comet appearing in 1628, the opinions of astrologers were divided with regard to it. Some insisted that it was a forerunner of a bloody war; others maintained that it predicted a great famine; but the greater number, founding their judgment upon its pale colour, thought it portended a pestilence. The fulfilment of their prediction brought them into great repute while the plague was raging.

Other prophecies were current, which were asserted to have been delivered hundreds of years previously. They had a most pernicious effect upon the mind of the vulgar, as they induced a belief in fatalism. By taking away the hope of recovery — that greatest balm in every malady — they increased threefold the ravages of the disease. One singular prediction almost drove the unhappy people mad. An ancient couplet, preserved for ages by tradition, foretold, that in the year 1630 the devil would poison all Milan. Early one morning in April, and before the pestilence had reached its height, the passengers were surprised to see that all the doors in the principal streets of the city were marked with a curious daub, or spot, as if a sponge, filled with the purulent matter of the plague-sores, had been pressed against them. The whole population were speedily in movement to remark the strange appearance, and the greatest alarm spread rapidly. Every means was taken to discover the perpetrators, but in vain. At last the ancient prophecy was remembered, and prayers were offered up in all the churches, that the machinations of the Evil One might be defeated. Many persons were of opinion that the emissaries of foreign powers were employed to spread infectious poison over the city; but by far the greater number were convinced that the powers of hell had conspired against them, and that the infection was spread by supernatural agencies. In the mean time the plague increased fearfully. Distrust and alarm took possession of every mind. Every thing was believed to have been poisoned by the Devil; the waters of the wells, the standing corn in the fields, and the fruit upon the trees. It was believed that all objects of touch were poisoned; the walls of the houses, the pavements of the streets, and the very handles of the doors. The populace were raised to a pitch of ungovernable fury. A strict watch was kept for the Devil's emissaries, and any man who wanted to be rid of an enemy, had only to say that he had seen him besmearing a door with ointment; his fate was certain death at the hands of the mob. An old man, upwards of eighty years of age, a daily frequenter of the church of St. Antonio, was seen, on rising from his knees, to wipe with the skirt of his cloak the stool on which he was about to sit down. A cry was raised immediately that he was besmearing the seat with poison. A mob of women, by whom the church was crowded, seized hold of the feeble old man, and dragged him out by the hair of his head, with horrid oaths and imprecations. He was trailed in this manner through the mire to the house of the municipal judge, that he might be put to the rack, and forced to discover his accomplices; but he expired on the way. Many other victims were sacrificed to the popular fury. One Mora, who appears to have been half a chemist and half a barber, was accused of being in league with the Devil to poison Milan. His house was surrounded, and a number of chemical preparations were found. The poor man asserted, that they were intended as preservatives against infection; but some physicians, to whom they were submitted, declared they were poison, Mora was put to the rack, where he for a long time asserted his innocence. He confessed at last, when his courage was worn down by torture, that he was in league with the Devil and foreign powers to poison the whole city; that he had anointed the doors, and infected the fountains of water. He named several persons as his accomplices, who were apprehended and put to a similar torture. They were all found guilty, and executed. Mora's house was rased to the ground, and a column erected on the spot, with an inscription to commemorate his guilt.

While the public mind was filled with these marvellous occurrences, the plague continued to increase. The crowds that were brought together to witness the executions spread the infection among one another. But the fury of their passions, and the extent of their credulity, kept pace with the violence of the plague; every wonderful and preposterous story was believed. One, in particular, occupied them to the exclusion, for a long time, of every other. The Devil himself had been seen. He had taken a house in Milan, in which he prepared his poisonous unguents, and furnished them to his emissaries for distribution. One man had brooded over such tales till he became firmly convinced that the wild nights of his own fancy were realities. He stationed himself in the market-place of Milan, and related the following story to the crowds that gathered round him. He was standing, he said, at the door of the cathedral, late in the evening; and when there was nobody nigh, he saw a dark-coloured chariot, drawn by six milk-white horses, stop close beside him. The chariot was followed by a numerous train of domestics in dark liveries, mounted on dark-coloured steeds. In the chariot there sat a tall stranger of a majestic aspect; his long black hair floated in the wind — fire flashed from his large black eyes, and a curl of ineffable scorn dwelt upon his lips. The look of the stranger was so sublime that he was awed, and trembled with fear when he gazed upon him. His complexion was much darker than that of any man he had ever seen, and the atmosphere around him was hot and suffocating. He perceived immediately that he was a being of another world. The stranger, seeing his trepidation, asked him blandly, yet majestically, to mount beside him. He had no power to refuse, and before he was well aware that he had moved, he found himself in the chariot. Onwards they went, with the rapidity of the wind, the stranger speaking no word, until they stopped before a door in the high-street of Milan. There was a crowd of people in the street, but, to his great surprise, no one seemed to notice the extraordinary equipage and its numerous train. From this he concluded that they were invisible. The house at which they stopped appeared to be a shop, but the interior was like a vast half-ruined palace. He went with his mysterious guide through several large and dimly-lighted rooms. In one of them, surrounded by huge pillars of marble, a senate of ghosts was assembled, debating on the progress of the plague. Other parts of the building were enveloped in the thickest darkness, illumined at intervals by flashes of lightning, which allowed him to distinguish a number of gibing and chattering skeletons, running about and pursuing each other, or playing at leap-frog over one another's backs. At the rear of the mansion was a wild, uncultivated plot of ground, in the midst of which arose a black rock. Down its sides rushed with fearful noise a torrent of poisonous water, which, insinuating itself through the soil, penetrated to all the springs of the city, and rendered them unfit for use. After he had been shewn all this, the stranger led him into another large chamber, filled with gold and precious stones, all of which he offered him if he would kneel down and worship him, and consent to smear the doors and houses of Milan with a pestiferous salve which he held out to him. He now knew him to be the Devil, and in that moment of temptation, prayed to God to give him strength to resist. His prayer was heard—he refused the bribe. The stranger scowled horribly upon him—a loud clap of thunder burst over his head—the vivid lightning flashed in his eyes, and the next moment he found himself standing alone at the porch of the cathedral. He repeated this strange tale day after day, without any variation, and all the populace were firm believers in its truth. Repeated search was made to discover the mysterious house, but all in vain. The man pointed out several as resembling it, which were searched by the police; but the Demon of the Pestilence was not to be found, nor the hall of ghosts, nor the poisonous fountain. But the minds of the people were so impressed with the idea, that scores of witnesses, half crazed by disease, came forward to swear that they also had seen the diabolical stranger, and had heard his chariot, drawn by the milk-white steeds, rumbling over the streets at midnight with a sound louder than thunder.

The number of persons who confessed that they were employed by the Devil to distribute poison is almost incredible. An epidemic frenzy was abroad, which seemed to be as contagious as the plague. Imagination was as disordered as the body, and day after day persons came voluntarily forward to accuse themselves. They generally had the marks of disease upon them, and some died in the act of confession.

During the great plague of London, in 1665, the people listened with similar avidity to the predictions of quacks and fanatics. Defoe says, that at that time the people were more addicted to prophecies and astronomical conjurations, dreams, and old wives' tales than ever they were before or since. Almanacs, and their predictions, frightened them terribly. Even the year before the plague broke out, they were greatly alarmed by the comet which then appeared, and anticipated that famine, pestilence, or fire would follow. Enthusiasts, while yet the disease had made but little progress, ran about the streets, predicting that in a few days London would be destroyed.

A still more singular instance of the faith in predictions occurred in London in the year 1524. The city swarmed at that time with fortune-tellers and astrologers, who were consulted daily by people of every class in society on the secrets of futurity. As early as the month of June 1523, several of them concurred in predicting that, on the 1st day of February 1524, the waters of the Thames would swell to such a height as to overflow the whole city of London, and wash away ten thousand houses. The prophecy met implicit belief. It was reiterated with the utmost confidence month after month, until so much alarm was excited that many families packed up their goods, and removed into Kent and Essex. As the time drew nigh, the number of these emigrants increased. In January, droves of workmen might be seen, followed by their wives and children, trudging on foot to the villages within fifteen or twenty miles, to await the catastrophe. People of a higher class were also to be seen in wagons and other vehicles bound on a similar errand. By the middle of January, at least twenty thousand persons had quitted the doomed city, leaving nothing but the bare walls of their homes to be swept away by the impending floods. Many of the richer sort took up their abode on the heights of Highgate, Hampstead, and Blackheath; and some erected tents as far away as Waltham Abbey on the north, and Croydon on the south of the Thames. Bolton, the prior of St. Bartholomew's, was so alarmed, that he erected, at a very great expense, a sort of fortress at Harrow-on-the-Hill, which he stocked with provisions for two months. On the 24th of January, a week before the awful day which was to see the destruction of London, he removed thither, with the brethren and officers of the priory and all his household. A number of boats were conveyed in wagons to his fortress, furnished abundantly with expert rowers, in case the flood, reaching so high as Harrow, should force them to go farther for a resting-place. Many wealthy citizens prayed to share his retreat; but the prior, with a prudent forethought, admitted only his personal friends, and those who brought stores of eatables for the blockade.

At last the morn, big with the fate of London, appeared in the east. The wondering crowds were astir at an early hour to watch the rising of the waters. The inundation, it was predicted, would be gradual, not sudden; so that they expected to have plenty of time to escape as soon as they saw the bosom of old Thames heave beyond the usual mark. But the majority were too much alarmed to trust to this, and thought themselves safer ten or twenty miles off. The Thames, unmindful of the foolish crowds upon its banks, flowed on quietly as of yore. The tide ebbed at its usual hour, flowed to its usual height, and then ebbed again, just as if twenty astrologers had not pledged their words to the contrary. Blank were their faces as evening approached, and as blank grew the faces of the citizens to think that they had made such fools of themselves. At last night set in, and the obstinate river would not lift its waters to sweep away even one house out of the ten thousand. Still, however, the people were afraid to go to sleep. Many hundreds remained up till dawn of the next day, lest the deluge should come upon them like a thief in the night. On the morrow, it was seriously discussed whether it would not be advisable to duck the false prophets in the river. Luckily for them, they thought of an expedient which allayed the popular fury. They asserted that, by an error (a very slight one,) of a little figure, they had fixed the date of this awful inundation a whole century too early. The stars were right after all, and they, erring mortals, were wrong. The present generation of cockneys was safe, and London would be washed away, not in 1524, but in 1624. At this announcement, Bolton the prior dismantled his fortress, and the weary emigrants came back.

An eye-witness of the great fire of London, in an account preserved among the Harleian Mss. in the British Museum, and published in the transactions of the Royal Society of Antiquaries, relates another instance of the credulity of the Londoners. The writer, who accompanied the Duke of York day by day through the district included between the Fleet-bridge and the Thames, states that, in their efforts to check the progress of the flames, they were much impeded by the superstition of the people. Mother Shipton, in one of her prophecies, had said that London would be reduced to ashes, and they refused to make any efforts to prevent it.[53] A son of the noted Sir Kenelm Digby, who was also a pretender to the gifts of prophecy, persuaded them that no power on earth could prevent the fulfilment of the prediction; for it was written in the great book of fate that London was to be destroyed. Hundreds of persons, who might have rendered valuable assistance, and saved whole parishes from devastation, folded their arms and looked on. As many more gave themselves up, with the less compunction, to plunder a city which they could not save.[54]

The prophecies of Mother Shipton are still believed in many of the rural districts of England. In cottages and servants' halls her reputation is great; and she rules, the most popular of British prophets, among all the uneducated, or half-educated, portions of the community. She is generally supposed to have been born at Knaresborough, in the reign of Henry VII., and to have sold her soul to the Devil for the power of foretelling future events. Though during her lifetime she was looked upon as a witch, she yet escaped the witch's fate, and died peaceably in her bed at an extreme old age, near Clifton in Yorkshire. A stone is said to have been erected to her memory in the churchyard of that place, with the following epitaph:

> *"Here lies she who never lied,*
> *Whose skill often has been tried:*
> *Her prophecies shall still survive,*
> *And ever keep her name alive."*

"Never a day passed," says her traditionary biography, "wherein, she did not relate something remarkable, and that required the most serious consideration. People flocked to her from far and near, her fame was so great. They went to her of all sorts, both old and young, rich and poor, especially young maidens, to be resolved of their doubts relating to things to come; and all returned wonderfully satisfied in the explanations she gave to their questions." Among the rest, went the Abbot of Beverley, to whom she foretold the suppression of the monasteries by Henry VIII., his marriage with Anne Boleyn, the fires for heretics in Smithfield, and the execution of Mary Queen of Scots. She also foretold the accession of James I., adding that, with him,

> *"From the cold North*
> *Every evil should come forth."*

On a subsequent visit she uttered another prophecy, which, in the opinion of her believers, still remains unfulfilled, but may be expected to be realised during the present century:

> *"The time shall come when seas of blood*
> *Shall mingle with a greater flood.*
> *Great noise there shall be heard — great shouts and cries,*
> *And seas shall thunder louder than the skies;*
> *Then shall three lions fight with three and bring*
> *Joy to a people, honour to a king.*
> *That fiery year as soon as o'er,*
> *Peace shall then be as before;*
> *Plenty shall every where be found,*
> *And men with swords shall plough the ground."*

But the most famous of all her prophecies is one relating to London. Thousands of persons still shudder to think of the woes that are to burst over this unhappy realm, when London and Highgate are joined by one continuous line of houses. This junction, which, if the rage for building lasts much longer, in the same proportion as heretofore, bids fair to be soon accomplished, was predicted by her shortly before her death. Revolutions — the fall of mighty monarchs, and the shedding of much blood are to signalise that event. The very angels, afflicted by our woes, are to turn aside their heads, and weep for hapless Britain.

But great as is the fame of Mother Shipton, she ranks but second in the list of British prophets. Merlin, the mighty Merlin, stands alone in his high pre-eminence — the first and greatest. As old Drayton sings, in his *Poly-olbion*:

> *"Of Merlin and his skill what region doth not hear?*
> *The world shall still be full of Merlin every year.*
> *A thousand lingering years his prophecies have run,*
> *And scarcely shall have end till time itself be done."*

Spenser, in his divine poem, has given us a powerful description of this renowned seer —

> *"who had in magic more insight*
> *Than ever him before, or after, living wight.*
> *For he by words could call out of the sky*
> *Both sun and moon, and make them him obey;*
> *The land to sea, and sea to mainland dry,*

> *And darksome night he eke could turn to day —*
> *Huge hosts of men he could, alone, dismay.*
> *And hosts of men and meanest things could frame,*
> *Whenso him list his enemies to fray,*
> *That to this day, for terror of his name,*
> *The fiends do quake, when any him to them does name.*
> *And soothe men say that he was not the sonne*
> *Of mortal sire or other living wighte,*
> *But wondrously begotten and begoune*
> *By false illusion of a guileful sprite*
> *On a faire ladye nun."*

In these verses the poet has preserved the popular belief with regard to Merlin, who is generally supposed to have been a contemporary of Vortigern. Opinion is divided as to whether he were a real personage, or a mere impersonation, formed by the poetic fancy of a credulous people. It seems most probable that such a man did exist, and that, possessing knowledge as much above the comprehension of his age, as that possessed by Friar Bacon was beyond the reach of his, he was endowed by the wondering crowd with the supernatural attributes that Spenser has enumerated.

Geoffrey of Monmouth translated Merlin's poetical odes, or prophecies, into Latin prose; and he was much reverenced not only by Geoffrey, but by most of the old annalists. In a *Life of Merlin, with his Prophecies and Predictions interpreted and made good by our English Annals*, by Thomas Heywood, published in the reign of Charles I., we find several of these pretended prophecies. They seem, however, to have been all written by Heywood himself. They are in terms too plain and positive to allow any one to doubt for a moment of their having been composed *ex post facto*. Speaking of Richard I., he says:

> *"The Lion's heart will 'gainst the Saracen rise,*
> *And purchase from him many a glorious prize;*
> *The rose and lily shall at first unite,*
> *But, parting of the prey prove opposite.* * * *
> *But while abroad these great acts shall be done,*
> *All things at home shall to disorder run.*
> *Cooped up and caged then shall the Lion be,*

> *But, after sufferance, ransomed and set free."*

The simple-minded Thomas Heywood gravely goes on to inform us, that all these things actually came to pass. Upon Richard III. he is equally luminous. He says:

> *"A hunch-backed monster, who with teeth is born,*
> *The mockery of art and nature's scorn;*
> *Who from the womb preposterously is hurled,*
> *And with feet forward thrust into the world,*
> *Shall, from the lower earth on which he stood,*
> *Wade, every step he mounts, knee-deep in blood.*
> *He shall to th' height of all his hopes aspire,*
> *And, clothed in state, his ugly shape admire;*
> *But, when he thinks himself most safe to stand,*
> *From foreign parts a native whelp shall land."*

Another of these prophecies after the event tells us that Henry VIII. should take the power from Rome, "and bring it home unto his British bower;" that he should "root out from the land all the razored skulls;" and that he should neither spare "man in his rage nor woman in his lust;" and that, in the time of his next successor but one, "there should come in the fagot and the stake." Master Heywood closes Merlin's prophecies at his own day, and does not give even a glimpse of what was to befall England after his decease. Many other prophecies, besides those quoted by him, were, he says, dispersed abroad, in his day, under the name of Merlin; but he gives his readers a taste of one only, and that is the following:

> *"When hempe is ripe and ready to pull,*
> *Then, Englishman, beware thy skull."*

This prophecy, which, one would think, ought to have put him in mind of the gallows, at that time the not unusual fate of false prophets, he explains thus: "In this word HEMPE be five letters. Now, by reckoning the five successive princes from Henry VIII., this prophecy is easily explained: H signifieth King Henry before-named; E, Edward, his son, the sixth of that name; M, Mary, who succeeded him; P, Philip of Spain, who, by marrying Queen Mary, participated with her in the English diadem; and, lastly, E signifieth Queen Elizabeth, after whose death there was a great feare that some troubles might have arisen about the crown." As this did not happen, Heywood, who was a sly rogue in a small way, gets out of the scrape by saying, "Yet proved this augury true, though not according to the former expectation; for, after the peaceful inauguration of King James, there was great mortality, not in London only, but through the whole kingdom, and from which the nation was not quite clean in seven years after."

This is not unlike the subterfuge of Peter of Pontefract, who had prophesied the death and deposition of King John, and who was hanged by that monarch for his pains. A very graphic and amusing account of this pretended prophet is given by Grafton, in his *Chronicles of England*.[55] "In the meanwhile," says he, "the priestes within England had provided them a false and counterfeated prophet, called Peter Wakefielde, a Yorkshire man, who was an hermite, an idle gadder about, and a pratlyng marchant. Now, to bring this Peter in credite, and the kyng out of all credite with his people, diverse vaine persons bruted dayly among the commons of the realme, that Christe had twice appered unto him in the shape of a childe, betwene the prieste's handes, once at Yorke, another tyme at Pomfret; and that he had breathed upon him thrice, saying, '*Peace, peace, peace,*' and teachyng many things, which he anon declared to the bishops, and bid the people amend their naughtie living. Being rapt also in spirite, they sayde he behelde the joyes of heaven and sorrowes of hell; for scant were there three in the realme, sayde he, that lived christianly.

"*This counterfeated soothsayer prophesied of King John, that he should reigne no longer than the Ascension-day next followyng, which was in the yere of our Lord 1211, and was the thirteenth yere from his coronation; and this, he said, he had by revelation. Then it was of him demanded, whether he should be slaine or be deposed, or should voluntarily give over the crowne? He aunswered, that he could not tell; but of this he was sure (he sayd), that neither he nor any of his stock or lineage should reigne after that day.*

"*The king, hering of this, laughed much at it, and made but a scoff thereat. 'Tush!' saith he, 'it is but an ideot knave, and such an one as lacketh his right wittes.' But when this foolish prophet had so escaped the daunger of the kinge's displeasure, and that he made no more of it,* he gate him abroad, and prated thereof at large, as he was a very idle vagabond, and used to trattle and talke more than ynough; so that they which loved the king caused him anon after to be apprehended as a malefactor, and to be throwen in prison, the king not yet knowing thereof.

"Anone after the fame of this phantasticall prophet went all the realme over, and his name was knowen every where, as foolishnesse is much regarded of the people, where wisdome is not in place; specially because he was then imprisoned for the matter, the rumour was the larger, their wonderynges were the wantoner, their practises the foolisher, their busye talkes and other idle doinges the greater. Continually from thence, as the rude manner of people is, old gossyps tales went abroad, new tales were invented, fables were added to fables, and lyes grew upon lyes. So that every daye newe slanders were laide upon the king, and not one of them true. Rumors arose, blasphemyes were sprede, the enemyes rejoyced, and treasons by the priestes were mainteyned; and what lykewise was surmised, or other subtiltye practised, all was then fathered upon this foolish prophet, as 'thus saith Peter Wakefield;' 'thus hath he prophesied;' 'and thus it shall come to pass;' yea, many times, when he thought nothing lesse. And when the Ascension-day was come, which was prophecyed of before, King John commanded his royal tent to be spread in the open fielde, passing that day with his noble counseyle and men of honour in the greatest solemnitie that ever he did before; solacing himself with musickale instrumentes and songs, most in sight among his trustie friendes. When that day was paste in all prosperitie and myrth, his enemyes being confused, turned all into an allegorical understanding to make the prophecie good, and sayde, 'He is no longer king, for the pope reigneth, and not he.' [King John was labouring under a sentence of excommunication at the time.]

"Then was the king by his council perswaded that this false prophet had troubled the realme, perverted the heartes of the people, and raysed the Commons against him; for his wordes went over the sea, by the help of his prelates, and came to the French king's eare, and gave to him a great encouragement to invade the lande. He had not else done it so sodeinely. But he was most fowly deceived, as all they are and shall be that put their trust in such dark drowsye dreames of hipocrites. The king therefore commended that he should be hanged up, and his sonne also with him, lest any more false prophets should arise of that race."

Heywood, who was a great stickler for the truth of all sorts of prophecies, gives a much more favourable account of this Peter of Pomfret, or Pontefract, whose fate he would, in all probability, have shared, if he had had the misfortune to have flourished in the same age. He says, that Peter, who was not only a prophet, but a bard, predicted divers of King John's disasters, which fell out accordingly. On being taxed for a lying prophet in having predicted that the king would be deposed before he entered into the fifteenth year of his reign, he answered him boldly, that all he had said was justifiable and true; for that, having given up his crown to the pope, and paying him an annual tribute, the pope reigned, and not he. Heywood thought this explanation to be perfectly satisfactory, and the prophet's faith for ever established.

But to return to Merlin. Of him even to this day it may be said, in the words which Burns has applied to another notorious personage,

> "Great was his power and great his fame;
> Far kenned and noted is his name."

His reputation is by no means confined to the land of his birth, but extends through most of the nations of Europe. A very curious volume of his *Life, Prophecies, and Miracles*, written, it is supposed, by Robert de Bosron, was printed at Paris in 1498, which states, that the devil himself was his father, and that he spoke the instant he was born, and assured his mother, a very virtuous young woman, that she should not die in childbed with him, as her ill-natured neighbours had predicted. The judge of the district, hearing of so marvellous an occurrence, summoned both mother and child to appear before him; and they went accordingly the same day. To put the wisdom of the young prophet most effectually to the test, the judge asked him if he knew his own father? To which the infant Merlin replied, in a clear, sonorous voice, "Yes, my father is the Devil; and I have his power, and know all things, past, present, and to come." His worship clapped his hands in astonishment, and took the prudent resolution of not molesting so awful a child or its mother either.

Early tradition attributes the building of Stonehenge to the power of Merlin. It was believed that those mighty stones were whirled through the air, at his command, from Ireland to Salisbury Plain; and that he arranged them in the form in which they now stand, to commemorate for ever the unhappy fate of three hundred British chiefs, who were massacred on that spot by the Saxons.

At Abergwylly, near Carmarthen, is still shewn the cave of the prophet and the scene of his incantations. How beautiful is the description of it given by Spenser in his *Faerie Queene*! The lines need no apology for their repetition here, and any sketch of the great prophet of Britain would be incomplete without them:

> "There the wise Merlin, whilom wont (they say,)
> To make his wonne low underneath the ground,
> In a deep delve far from the view of day,
> That of no living wight he mote be found,
> Whenso he counselled with his sprites encompassed round.
> And if thou ever happen that same way
> To travel, go to see that dreadful place;
> It is a hideous, hollow cave, they say,
> Under a rock that lies, a little space
> From the swift Barry, tumbling down apace
> Amongst the woody hills of Dynevoure;
> But dare thou not, I charge, in any case,
> To enter into that same baleful bower,
> For fear the cruel fiendes should thee unwares devour!
> But, standing high aloft, low lay thine eare,
> And there such ghastly noise of iron chaines
> And brazen caudrons thou shalt rombling heare,
> Which thousand sprites with long-enduring paines
> Doe tosse, that it will stun thy feeble braines;
> And often times great groans and grievous stownds,
> When too huge toile and labour them constraines;
> And often times loud strokes and ringing sounds
> From under that deep rock most horribly rebounds.
> The cause, they say, is this. A little while
> Before that Merlin died, he did intend
> A brazen wall in compass, to compile

> *About Cayr Merdin, and did it commend*
> *Unto these sprites to bring to perfect end;*
> *During which work the Lady of the Lake,*
> *Whom long he loved, for him in haste did send,*
> *Who thereby forced his workmen to forsake,*
> *Them bound till his return their labour not to slake.*
> *In the mean time, through that false ladie's traine,*
> *He was surprised, and buried under biere,*
> *Ne ever to his work returned again;*
> *Natheless these fiendes may not their work forbeare,*
> *So greatly his commandement they fear,*
> *But there doe toile and travaile day and night,*
> *Until that brazen wall they up doe reare."*[56]

Amongst other English prophets, a belief in whose power has not been entirely effaced by the light of advancing knowledge, is Robert Nixon, the Cheshire idiot, a contemporary of Mother Shipton. The popular accounts of this man say, that he was born of poor parents, not far from Vale Royal, on the edge of the forest of Delamere. He was brought up to the plough, but was so ignorant and stupid, that nothing could be made of him. Every body thought him irretrievably insane, and paid no attention to the strange, unconnected discourses which he held. Many of his prophecies are believed to have been lost in this manner. But they were not always destined to be wasted upon dull and inattentive ears. An incident occurred which brought him into notice, and established his fame as a prophet of the first calibre. He was ploughing in a field when he suddenly stopped from his labour, and with a wild look and strange gesture, exclaimed, *"Now, Dick! now, Harry! O, ill done, Dick! O, well done, Harry! Harry has gained the day!"* His fellow-labourers in the field did not know what to make of this rhapsody; but the next day cleared up the mystery. News was brought by a messenger, in hot haste, that at the very instant when Nixon had thus ejaculated, Richard III. had been slain at the battle of Bosworth, and Henry VII. proclaimed king of England.

It was not long before the fame of the new prophet reached the ears of the king, who expressed a wish to see and converse with him. A messenger was accordingly despatched to bring him to court; but long before he reached Cheshire, Nixon knew and dreaded the honours that awaited him. Indeed it was said, that at the very instant the king expressed the wish, Nixon was, by supernatural means, made acquainted with it, and that he ran about the town of Over in great distress of mind, calling out, like a madman, that Henry had sent for him, and that he must go to court, and be *clammed*, that is, starved to death. These expressions excited no little wonder; but, on the third day, the messenger arrived, and carried him to court, leaving on the minds of the good people of Cheshire an impression that their prophet was one of the greatest ever born. On his arrival King Henry appeared to be troubled exceedingly at the loss of a valuable diamond, and asked Nixon if he could inform him where it was to be found. Henry had hidden the diamond himself, with a view to test the prophet's skill. Great, therefore, was his surprise when Nixon answered him in the words of the old proverb, "Those who hide can find." From that time forth the king implicitly believed that he had the gift of prophecy, and ordered all his words to be taken down.

During all the time of his residence at court he was in constant fear of being starved to death, and repeatedly told the king that such would be his fate, if he were not allowed to depart, and return into his own country. Henry would not suffer it, but gave strict orders to all his officers and cooks to give him as much to eat as he wanted. He lived so well, that for some time he seemed to be thriving like a nobleman's steward, and growing as fat as an alderman. One day the king went out hunting, when Nixon ran to the palace gate, and entreated on his knees that he might not be left behind to be starved. The king laughed, and calling an officer, told him to take especial care of the prophet during his absence, and rode away to the forest. After his departure, the servants of the palace began to jeer at and insult Nixon, whom they imagined to be much better treated than he deserved. Nixon complained to the officer, who, to prevent him from being further molested, locked him up in the king's own closet, and brought him regularly his four meals a day. But it so happened that a messenger arrived from the king to this officer, requiring his immediate presence at Winchester, on a matter of life and death. So great was his haste to obey the king's command, that he mounted on the horse behind the messenger, and rode off, without bestowing a thought upon poor Nixon. He did not return till three days afterwards, when, remembering the prophet for the first time, he went to the king's closet, and found him lying upon the floor, starved to death, as he had predicted. Among the prophecies of his which are believed to have been fulfilled are the following, which relate to the times of the Pretender:

> *"A great man shall come into England,*
> *But the son of a king*
> *Shall take from him the victory."*
> *"Crows shall drink the blood of many nobles,*
> *And the North shall rise against the South."*
> *"The coek of the North shall be made to flee,*
> *And his feather be plucked for his pride,*
> *That he shall almost curse the day that he was born."*

All these, say his admirers, are as clear as the sun at noon-day. The first denotes the defeat of Prince Charles Edward, at the battle of Culloden, by the Duke of Cumberland; the second, the execution of Lords Derwentwater, Balmerino, and Lovat; and the third, the retreat of the Pretender from the shores of Britain. Among the prophecies that still remain to be accomplished are the following:

> *"Between seven, eight, and nine,*
> *In England wonders shall be seen;*
> *Between nine and thirteen*
> *All sorrow shall be done."*
> *"Through our own money and our men*
> *Shall a dreadful war begin.*
> *Between the sickle and the suck*
> *All England shall have a pluck."*
> *"Foreign nations shall invade England with snow on their helmets,*
> *and shall bring plague, famine, and murder in the skirts of their*
> *garments."*
> *"The town of Nantwich shall be swept away by a flood."*

Of the two first of these no explanation has yet been attempted; but some event or other will doubtless be twisted into such a shape as will fit them. The third, relative to the invasion of England by a nation with snow on their helmets, is supposed by the old women to foretell most clearly a coming war with Russia. As to the last, there are not a few in the town mentioned who devoutly believe that such will be its fate. Happily for their peace of mind, the prophet said nothing of the year that was to witness the awful calamity; so that they think it as likely to be two centuries hence as now.

The popular biographers of Nixon conclude their account of him by saying, that "his prophecies are by some persons thought fables; yet by what has come to pass, it is now thought, and very plainly appears, that most of them have proved, or will prove, true; for which we, on all occasions, ought not only to exert our utmost might to repel by force our enemies, but to refrain from our abandoned and wicked course of life, and to make our continual prayer to God for protection and safety." To this, though a *non sequitur*, every one will cry, Amen!

Besides the prophets, there have been the almanac-makers Lilly, Poor Robin, Partridge, and Francis Moore physician, in England and Matthew Laensbergh, in France and Belgium. But great as were their pretensions, they were modesty itself in comparison with Merlin, Shipton, and Nixon, who fixed their minds upon higher things than the weather, and were not so restrained as to prophesy for only one year at a time. After such prophets the almanac-makers hardly deserve to be mentioned; not even the renowned Partridge, whose prognostications set all England agog in 1708, and whose death while still alive was so pleasantly and satisfactorily proved by Isaac Bickerstaff. The anti-climax would be too palpable, and they and their doings must be left uncommemorated.

*Mother Shipton's House.*[57]

# Chapter 6.

Fortune-Telling.

*And men still grope t' anticipate*
*The cabinet designs of Fate;*
*Apply to wizards to foresee*
*What shall and what shall never be.*

*Hudibras, part iii. canto 3.*

In accordance with the plan laid down, we proceed to the consideration of the follies into which men have been led by their eager desire to pierce the thick darkness of futurity. God himself, for his own wise purposes, has more than once undrawn the impenetrable veil which shrouds those awful secrets; and, for purposes just as wise, he has decreed that, except in these instances, ignorance shall be our lot for ever. It is happy for man that he does not know what the morrow is to bring forth; but, unaware of this great blessing, he has, in all ages of the world, presumptuously endeavoured to trace the events of unborn centuries, and anticipate the march of time. He has reduced this presumption into a study. He has divided it into sciences and systems without number, employing his whole life in the vain pursuit. Upon no subject has it been so easy to deceive the world as upon this. In every breast the curiosity exists in a greater or less degree, and can only be conquered by a long course of self-examination, and a firm reliance that the future would not be hidden from our sight, if it were right that we should be acquainted with it.

An undue opinion of our own importance in the scale of creation is at the bottom of all our unwarrantable notions in this respect. How flattering to the pride of man to think that the stars in their courses watch over him, and typify, by their movements and aspects, the joys or the sorrows that await him! He, less in proportion to the universe than the all-but invisible insects that feed in myriads on a summer's leaf are to this great globe itself, fondly imagines that eternal worlds were chiefly created to prognosticate his fate. How we should pity the arrogance of the worm that crawls at our feet, if we knew that it also desired to know the secrets of futurity, and imagined that meteors shot athwart the sky to warn it that a tom-tit was hovering near to gobble it up; that storms and earthquakes, the revolutions of empires, or the fall of mighty monarchs, only happened to predict its birth, its progress, and its decay! Not a whit less presuming has man shewn himself; not a whit less arrogant are the sciences, so called, of astrology, augury, necromancy, geomancy, palmistry, and divination of every kind.

Leaving out of view the oracles of pagan antiquity and religious predictions in general, and confining ourselves solely to the persons who, in modern times, have made themselves most conspicuous in foretelling the future, we shall find that the sixteenth and seventeenth centuries were the golden age of these impostors. Many of them have been already mentioned in their character of alchymists. The union of the two pretensions is not at all surprising. It was to be expected that those who assumed a power so preposterous as that of prolonging the life of man for several centuries, should pretend, at the same time, to foretell the events which were to mark that preternatural span of existence. The world would as readily believe that they had discovered all secrets, as that they had only discovered one. The most celebrated astrologers of Europe, three centuries ago, were alchymists. Agrippa, Paracelsus, Dr. Dee, and the Rosicrucians, all laid as much stress upon their knowledge of the days to come, as upon their pretended possession of the philosopher's stone and the elixir of life. In their time, ideas of the wonderful, the diabolical, and the supernatural, were rifer than ever they were before. The devil or the stars were universally believed to meddle constantly in the affairs of men; and both were to be consulted with proper ceremonies. Those who were of a melancholy and gloomy temperament betook themselves to necromancy and sorcery; those more cheerful and aspiring devoted themselves to astrology. The latter science was encouraged by all the monarchs and governments of that age. In England, from the time of Elizabeth to that of William and Mary, judicial astrology was in high repute. During that period flourished Drs. Dee, Lamb, and Forman; with Lilly, Booker, Gadbury, Evans, and scores of nameless impostors in every considerable town and village in the country, who made it their business to cast nativities, aid in the recovery of stolen goods, prognosticate happy or unhappy marriages, predict whether journeys would be prosperous, and note lucky moments for the commencement of any enterprise, from the setting up of a cobbler's shop to the marching of an army. Men who, to use the words of Butler, did

"Deal in Destiny's dark counsel,
And sage opinion of the moon sell;
To whom all people far and near
On deep importance did repair,
When brass and pewter pots did stray,
And linen slunk out of the way."

Henry Andrews, the original "Francis Moore."

In Lilly's *Memoirs of his Life and Times*, there are many notices of the inferior quacks who then abounded, and upon whom he pretended to look down with supreme contempt; not because they were astrologers, but because they debased that noble art by taking fees for the recovery of stolen property. From Butler's *Hudibras*, and its curious notes, we may learn what immense numbers of these fellows lived upon the credulity of mankind in that age of witchcraft and diablerie. Even in our day, how great is the reputation enjoyed by the almanac-makers, who assume the name of Francis Moore! But in the time of Charles I. and the Commonwealth the most learned, the most noble, and the most conspicuous characters did not hesitate to consult astrologers in the most open manner. Lilly, whom Butler has immortalised under the name of Sydrophel, relates, that he proposed to write a work called *An Introduction to Astrology*, in which he would satisfy the whole kingdom of the lawfulness of that art. Many of the soldiers were for it, he says, and many of the Independent party, and abundance of worthy men in the House of Commons, his assured friends, and able to take his part against the Presbyterians, who would have silenced his predictions if they could. He afterwards carried his plan into execution, and when his book was published, went with another astrologer named Booker to the headquarters of the parliamentary army at Windsor, where they were welcomed and feasted in the garden where General Fairfax lodged. They were afterwards introduced to the general, who received them very kindly, and made allusion to some of their predictions. He hoped their art was lawful and agreeable to God's word; but he did not understand it himself. He did not doubt, however, that the two astrologers feared God, and therefore he had a good opinion of them. Lilly assured him that the art of astrology was quite consonant to the Scriptures; and confidently predicted from his knowledge of the stars, that the parliamentary army would overthrow all its enemies. In Oliver's Protectorate, this quack informs us that he wrote freely enough. He became an Independent, and all the soldiery were his friends. When he went to Scotland, he saw a soldier standing in front of the army with a book of prophecies in his hand, exclaiming to the several companies as they passed by him, "Lo! hear what Lilly saith: you are in this month promised victory! Fight it out, brave boys! and then read that month's prediction!"

After the great fire of London, which Lilly said he had foretold, he was sent for by the committee of the House of Commons appointed to inquire into the causes of the calamity. In his *Monarchy or no Monarchy*, published in 1651, he had inserted an hieroglyphical plate representing on one side persons in winding-sheets digging graves; and on the other a large city in flames. After the great fire, some sapient member of the legislature bethought him of Lilly's book, and having mentioned it in the house, it was agreed that the astrologer should be summoned. Lilly attended accordingly, when Sir Robert Brook told him the reason of his summons, and called upon him to declare what he knew. This was a rare opportunity for the vainglorious Lilly to vaunt his abilities; and he began a long speech in praise of himself and his pretended science. He said that, after the execution of Charles I., he was extremely desirous to know what might from that time forth happen to the parliament and to the nation in general. He therefore consulted the stars, and satisfied himself. The result of his judgment he put into emblems and hieroglyphics, without any commentary, so that the true meaning might be concealed from the vulgar, and made manifest only to the wise; imitating in this the example of many wise philosophers who had done the like.

"Did you foresee the year of the fire?" said a member. "No," quoth Lilly, "nor was I desirous. Of that I made no scrutiny." After some further parley, the house found they could make nothing of the astrologer, and dismissed him with great civility. One specimen of the explanation of a prophecy given by Lilly, and related by him with much complacency, will be sufficient to shew the sort of trash by which he imposed upon the million. "In the year 1588," says he, "there was a prophecy printed in Greek characters, exactly deciphering the long troubles of the English nation from 1641 to 1660." And it ended thus: "And after him shall come a dreadful dead man, and with him a royal G, of the best blood in the world; and he shall have the crown, and shall set England on the right way, and put out all heresies." The following is the explanation of this oracular absurdity:

*"Monkery being extinguished above eighty or ninety years, and the Lord General's name being Monk, is the dead man. The royal G or C [it is gamma in the Greek, intending C in the Latin, being the third letter in the alphabet] is Charles II., who for his extraction may be said to be of the best blood of the world."*

In France and Germany astrologers met even more encouragement than they received in England. In very early ages Charlemagne and his successors fulminated their wrath against them in common with sorcerers. Louis XI., that most superstitious of men, entertained great numbers of them at his court; and Catherine de Medicis, that most superstitious of women, hardly ever undertook any affair of importance without consulting them. She chiefly favoured her own countrymen; and during the time she governed France, the land was overrun by Italian conjurors, necromancers, and fortune-tellers of every kind. But the chief astrologer of that day, beyond all doubt, was the celebrated Nostradamus, physician to her husband, King Henry II. He was born in 1503 at the town of St. Remi, in Provence, where his father was a notary. He did not acquire much fame till he was past his fiftieth year, when his famous *Centuries*, a collection of verses, written in obscure and almost unintelligible language, began to excite attention. They were so much spoken of in 1556, that Henry II. resolved to attach so skilful a man to his service, and appointed him his physician. In a biographical notice of him, prefixed to the edition of his *Vraies Centuries*, published at Amsterdam in 1668, we are informed that he often discoursed with his royal master on the secrets of futurity, and received many great presents as his reward, besides his usual allowance for medical attendance. After the death of Henry he retired to his native place, where Charles IX. paid him a visit in 1564; and was so impressed with veneration for his wondrous knowledge of the things that were to be, not in France only, but in the whole world for hundreds of years to come, that he made him a counsellor of state and his own physician, besides treating him in other matters with a royal liberality. "In fine," continues his biographer, "I should be too prolix were I to tell all the honours conferred upon him, and all the great nobles and learned men that arrived at his house from the very ends of the earth, to see and converse with him as if he had been an oracle. Many strangers, in fact, came to France for no other purpose than to consult him."

*Nostradamus. — from the frontispiece to a collection of his prophecies, published at amsterdam, a.d. 1666.*

The prophecies of Nostradamus consist of upwards of a thousand stanzas, each of four lines, and are to the full as obscure as the oracles of old. They take so great a latitude, both as to time and space, that they are almost sure to be fulfilled somewhere or other in the course of a few centuries. A little ingenuity, like that evinced by Lilly in his explanation about General Monk and the dreadful dead man, might easily make events to fit some of them.[58]

He is to this day extremely popular in France and the Walloon country of Belgium, where old farmer-wives consult him with great confidence and assiduity.

Catherine di Medicis was not the only member of her illustrious house who entertained astrologers. At the beginning of the fifteenth century there was a man, named Basil, residing in Florence, who was noted over all Italy for his skill in piercing the darkness of futurity. It is said that he foretold to Cosmo di Medicis, then a private citizen, that he would attain high dignity, inasmuch as the ascendant of his nativity was adorned with the same propitious aspects as those of Augustus Cæsar and the Emperor Charles V.[59] Another astrologer foretold the death of Prince Alexander di Medicis; and so very minute and particular was he in all the circumstances, that he was suspected of being chiefly instrumental in fulfilling his own prophecy — a very common resource with these fellows to keep up their credit. He foretold confidently that the prince should die by the hand of his own familiar friend, a person of a slender habit of body, a small face, a swarthy complexion, and of most remarkable taciturnity. So it afterwards happened, Alexander having been murdered in his chamber by his cousin Lorenzo, who corresponded exactly with the above description.[60] The author of *Hermippus Redivivus*, in relating this story, inclines to the belief that the astrologer was guiltless of any participation in the crime, but was employed by some friend of Prince Alexander to warn him of his danger.

A much more remarkable story is told of an astrologer who lived in Romagna in the fifteenth century, and whose name was Antiochus Tibertus.[61] At that time nearly all the petty sovereigns of Italy retained such men in their service; and Tibertus, having studied the mathematics with great success at Paris, and delivered many predictions, some of which, for guesses, were not deficient in shrewdness, was taken into the household of Pandolfo di Malatesta, the sovereign of Rimini. His reputation was so great, that his study was continually thronged either with visitors who were persons of distinction, or with clients who came to him for advice; and in a short time he acquired a considerable fortune. Notwithstanding all these advantages, he passed his life miserably, and ended it on the scaffold. The following story afterwards got into circulation, and has been often triumphantly cited by succeeding astrologers as an irrefragable proof of the truth of their science. It was said that, long before he died, he uttered three remarkable prophecies — one relating to himself, another to his friend, and the third to his patron, Pandolfo di Malatesta. The first delivered was that relating to his friend Guido di Bogni, one of the greatest captains of the time. Guido was exceedingly desirous to know his fortune, and so importuned Tibertus, that the latter consulted the stars and the lines on his palm to satisfy him. He afterwards told him with a sorrowful face, that, according to all the rules of astrology and palmistry, he should be falsely suspected by his best friend, and should lose his life in consequence. Guido then asked the astrologer if he could foretell his own fate; upon which Tibertus again consulted the stars, and found that it was decreed from all eternity that he should end his days on the scaffold. Malatesta, when he heard these predictions, so unlikely, to all present appearance, to prove true, desired his astrologer to predict his fate also, and to hide nothing from him, however unfavourable it might be. Tibertus complied, and told his patron, at that time one of the most flourishing and powerful princes of Italy, that he should suffer great want, and die at last like a beggar in the common hospital of Bologna. And so it happened in all three cases. Guido di Bogni was accused by his own father-in-law, the Count di Bentivoglio, of a treasonable design to deliver up the city of Rimini to the papal forces, and was assassinated afterwards, by order of the tyrant Malatesta, as he sat at the supper-table, to which he had been invited in all apparent friendship. The astrologer was at the same time thrown into prison, as being concerned in the treason of his friend. He attempted to escape, and had succeeded in letting himself down from his dungeon-window into a moat, when he was discovered by the sentinels. This being reported to Malatesta, he gave orders for his execution on the following morning.

Malatesta had, at this time, no remembrance of the prophecy; and his own fate gave him no uneasiness; but events were silently working its fulfilment. A conspiracy had been formed, though Guido di Bogni was innocent of it, to deliver up Rimini to the pope; and all the necessary measures having been taken, the city was seized by the Count de Valentinois. In the confusion, Malatesta had barely time to escape from his palace in disguise.

He was pursued from place to place by his enemies, abandoned by all his former friends, and, finally, by his own children. He at last fell ill of a languishing disease, at Bologna; and, nobody caring to afford him shelter, he was carried to the hospital, where he died. The only thing that detracts from the interest of this remarkable story is the fact, that the prophecy was made after the event.

For some weeks before the birth of Louis XIV., an astrologer from Germany, who had been sent for by the Marshal de Bassompierre and other noblemen of the court, had taken up his residence in the palace, to be ready, at a moment's notice, to draw the horoscope of the future sovereign of France. When the queen was taken in labour, he was ushered into a contiguous apartment, that he might receive notice of the very instant the child was born. The result of his observations were the three words, *diu, durè, feliciter*; meaning, that the new-born prince should live and reign long, with much labour, and with great glory. No prediction less favourable could have been expected from an astrologer, who had his bread to get, and who was at the same time a courtier. A medal was afterwards struck in commemoration of the event; upon one side of which was figured the nativity of the prince, representing him as driving the chariot of Apollo, with the inscription "Ortus solis Gallici," — the rising of the Gallic sun.

The best excuse ever made for astrology was that offered by the great astronomer, Kepler, himself an unwilling practiser of the art.

He had many applications from his friends to cast nativities for them, and generally gave a positive refusal to such as he was not afraid of offending by his frankness. In other cases he accommodated himself to the prevailing delusion. In sending a copy of his *Ephemerides* to Professor Gerlach, he wrote, that *they were nothing but worthless conjectures*; but he was obliged to devote himself to them, or he would have starved. "Ye overwise philosophers," he exclaimed, in his *Tertius Interveniens*; "ye censure this daughter of astronomy beyond her deserts! *Know ye not that she must support her mother by her charms?* The scanty reward of an astronomer would not provide him with bread, if men did not entertain hopes of reading the future in the heavens."

Necromancy was, next to astrology, the pretended science most resorted to, by those who wished to pry into the future. The earliest instance upon record is that of the witch of Endor and the spirit of Samuel. Nearly all the nations of antiquity believed in the possibility of summoning departed ghosts to disclose the awful secrets that God made clear to the disembodied. Many passages in allusion to this subject will at once suggest themselves to the classical reader; but this art was never carried on openly in any country. All governments looked upon it as a crime of the deepest dye. While astrology was encouraged, and its professors courted and rewarded, necromancers were universally condemned to the stake or the gallows. Roger Bacon, Albertus Magnus, Arnold of Villeneuve, and many others, were accused by the public opinion of many centuries, of meddling in these unhallowed matters. So deep-rooted has always been the popular delusion with respect to accusations of this kind, that no crime was ever disproved with such toil and difficulty. That it met great encouragement, nevertheless, is evident from the vast numbers of pretenders to it; who, in spite of the danger, have existed in all ages and countries.

Geomancy, or the art of foretelling the future by means of lines and circles, and other mathematical figures drawn on the earth, is still extensively practised in Asiatic countries, but is almost unknown in Europe.

Augury, from the flight or entrails of birds, so favourite a study among the Romans, is, in like manner, exploded in Europe. Its most assiduous professors, at the present day, are the abominable Thugs of India.

Divination, of which there are many kinds, boasts a more enduring reputation. It has held an empire over the minds of men from the earliest periods of recorded history, and is, in all probability, coeval with time itself. It was practised alike by the Jews, the Egyptians, the Chaldeans, the Persians, the Greeks, and the Romans; is equally known to all modern nations, in every part of the world; and is not unfamiliar to the untutored tribes that roam in the wilds of Africa and America. Divination, as practised in civilised Europe at the present day, is chiefly from cards, the tea-cup, and the lines on the palm of the hand. Gipsies alone make a profession of it; but there are thousands and tens of thousands of humble families in which the good-wife, and even the good-man, resort to the grounds at the bottom of their tea-cups, to know whether the next harvest will be abundant, or their sow bring forth a numerous litter; and in which the young maidens look to the same place to know when they are to be married, and whether the man of their choice is to be dark or fair, rich or poor, kind or cruel. Divination by cards, so great a favourite among the moderns, is, of course, a modern science; as cards do not yet boast an antiquity of much more than four hundred years. Divination by the palm, so confidently believed in by half the village lasses in Europe, is of older date, and seems to have been known to the Egyptians in the time of the patriarchs; as well as divination by the cup, which, as we are informed in Genesis, was practised by Joseph. Divination by the rod was also practised by the Egyptians. In comparatively recent times, it was pretended that by this means hidden treasures could be discovered. It now appears to be altogether exploded in Europe. Onomancy, or the foretelling a man's fate by the letters of his name, and the various transpositions of which they are capable, is a more modern sort of divination; but it reckons comparatively few believers.

The following list of the various species of divination formerly in use, is given by Gaule in his *Magastromancer*, and quoted in Hone's *Year-Book*, p. 1517.

- *Stereomancy*, or divining by the elements.
- *Aeromancy*, or divining by the air.
- *Pyromancy*, by fire,
- *Hydromancy*, by water.
- *Geomancy*, by earth.
- *Theomancy*, pretending to divine by the revelation of the Spirit, and by the Scriptures, or word of God.
- *Demonomancy*, by the aid of devils and evil spirits.

- *Idolomancy*, by idols, images, and figures.
- *Psychomancy*, by the soul, affections, or dispositions of men.
- *Anthropomancy*, by the entrails of human beings.
- *Theriomancy*, by beasts.
- *Ornithomancy*, by birds.
- *Ichthyomancy*, by fishes.
- *Botanomancy*, by herbs.
- *Lithomancy*, by stones.
- *Kleromancy*, by lots.
- *Oneiromancy*, by dreams.
- *Onomancy*, by names.
- *Arithmancy*, by numbers.
- *Logarithmancy*, by logarithms.
- *Sternomancy*, by the marks from the breast to the belly.
- *Gastromancy*, by the sound of, or marks upon the belly.
- *Omphalomancy*, by the navel.
- *Chiromancy*, by the hands.
- *Podomancy*, by the feet.
- *Onchyomancy*, by the nails.
- *Cephaleonomancy*, by asses' heads.
- *Tephromancy*, by ashes.
- *Kapnomancy*, by smoke.
- *Knissomancy*, by the burning of incense.
- *Ceromancy*, by the melting of wax.
- *Lecanomancy*, by basins of water.
- *Katoptromancy*, by looking-glasses.
- *Chartomancy*, by writing in papers, and by Valentines.
- *Macharomancy*, by knives and swords.
- *Crystallomancy*, by crystals.
- *Dactylomancy*, by rings.
- *Koskinomancy*, by sieves.
- *Axinomancy*, by saws.
- *Chalcomancy*, by vessels of brass, or other metal.
- *Spatilomancy*, by skins, bones, &c.
- *Astromancy*, by stars.

- *Sciomancy*, by shadows.
- *Astragalomancy*, by dice.
- *Oinomancy*, by the lees of wine.
- *Sycomancy*, by figs.
- *Tyromancy*, by cheese.
- *Alphitomancy*, by meal, flour, or bran.
- *Krithomancy*, by corn or grain.
- *Alectromancy*, by cocks.
- *Gyromancy*, by circles.
- *Lampadomancy*, by candles and lamps.

Oneiro-Criticism, or the art of interpreting dreams, is a relic of the most remote ages, which has subsisted through all the changes that moral or physical revolutions have operated in the world. The records of five thousand years bear abundant testimony to the universal diffusion of the belief, that the skilful could read the future in dreams. The rules of the art, if any existed in ancient times, are not known; but in our day, one simple rule opens the whole secret. Dreams, say all the wiseacres in Christendom, are to be interpreted by contraries. Thus, if you dream of filth, you will acquire something valuable; if you dream of the dead, you will hear news of the living; if you dream of gold and silver, you run a risk of being without either; and if you dream you have many friends, you will be persecuted by many enemies. The rule, however, does not hold good in all cases. It is fortunate to dream of little pigs, but unfortunate to dream of big bullocks. If you dream you have lost a tooth, you may be sure that you will shortly lose a friend; and if you dream that your house is on fire, you will receive news from a far country. If you dream of vermin, it is a sign that there will be sickness in your family; and if you dream of serpents, you will have friends who, in the course of time, will prove your bitterest enemies; but, of all dreams, it is most fortunate if you dream that you are wallowing up to your neck in mud and mire. Clear water is a sign of grief; and great troubles, distress, and perplexity are predicted, if you dream that you stand naked in the public streets, and know not where to find a garment to shield you from the gaze of the multitude.

In many parts of Great Britain, and the continents of Europe and America, there are to be found elderly women in the villages and country-places whose interpretations of dreams are looked upon with as much reverence as if they were oracles. In districts remote from towns it is not uncommon to find the members of a family regularly every morning narrating their dreams at the breakfast-table, and becoming happy or miserable for the day according to their interpretation. There is not a flower that blossoms, or fruit that ripens, that, dreamed of, is not ominous of either good or evil to such people. Every tree of the field or the forest is endowed with a similar influence over the fate of mortals, if seen in the night-visions. To dream of the ash, is the sign of a long journey; and of an oak, prognosticates long life and prosperity. To dream you stript the bark off any tree, is a sign to a maiden of an approaching loss of a character; to a married woman, of a family bereavement; and to a man, of an accession of fortune. To dream of a leafless tree, is a sign of great sorrow; and of a branchless trunk, a sign of despair and suicide. The elder-tree is more auspicious to the sleeper; while the fir-tree, better still, betokens all manner of comfort and prosperity. The lime-tree predicts a voyage across the ocean; while the yew and the alder are ominous of sickness to the young and of death to the old.[62] Among the flowers and fruits charged with messages for the future, the following is a list of the most important, arranged from approved sources, in alphabetical order:

- *Asparagus*, gathered and tied up in bundles, is an omen of tears. If you see it growing in your dreams, it is a sign of good fortune.
- *Aloes*, without a flower, betokens long life; in flower, betokens a legacy.
- *Artichokes*. This vegetable is a sign that you will receive, in a short time, a favour from the hands of those from whom you would least expect it.
- *Agrimony*. This herb denotes that there will be sickness in your house.
- *Anemone* predicts love.

- *Auriculas*, in beds, denote luck; in pots, marriage; while to gather them, foretells widowhood.
- *Bilberries* predict a pleasant excursion.
- *Broom-flowers* an increase of family.
- *Cauliflowers* predict that all your friends will slight you, or that you will fall into poverty and find no one to pity you.
- *Dock-leaves*, a present from the country.
- *Daffodils*. Any maiden who dreams of daffodils is warned by her good angel to avoid going into a wood with her lover, or into any dark or retired place where she might not be able to make people hear her if she cried out. Alas for her if she pay no attention to the warning!
- "Never again shall she put garland on;

Instead of it she'll wear sad cypress now,
And bitter elder broken from the bough."

- *Figs*, if green, betoken embarrassment; if dried, money to the poor, and mirth to the rich.
- *Hearts-ease* betokens heart's pain.
- *Lilies* predict joy; *water-lilies*, danger from the sea.
- *Lemons* betoken a separation.
- *Pomegranates* predict happy wedlock to those who are single, and reconciliation to those who are married and have disagreed.
- *Quinces* prognosticate pleasant company.
- *Roses* denote happy love, not unmixed with sorrow from other sources.
- *Sorrel*. To dream of this herb is a sign that you will shortly have occasion to exert all your prudence to overcome some great calamity.
- *Sunflowers* shew that your pride will be deeply wounded.
- *Violets* predict evil to the single, and joy to the married.
- *Yellow-flowers* of any kind predict jealousy.
- *Yew-berries* predict loss of character to both sexes.

It should be observed that the rules for the interpretation of dreams are far from being universal. The cheeks of the peasant girl of England glow with pleasure in the morning after she has dreamed of a rose, while the *paysanne* of Normandy dreads disappointment and vexation for the very same reason. The Switzer who dreams of an oak-tree does not share in the Englishman's joy; for he imagines that the vision was a warning to him that, from some trifling cause, an overwhelming calamity will burst over him. Thus do the ignorant and the credulous torment themselves; thus do they spread their nets to catch vexation, and pass their lives between hopes which are of no value and fears which are a positive evil.

Omens. Among the other means of self-annoyance upon which men have stumbled, in their vain hope of discovering the future, signs and omens hold a conspicuous place. There is scarcely an occurrence in nature which, happening at a certain time, is not looked upon by some persons as a prognosticator either of good or evil. The latter are in the greatest number, so much more ingenious are we in tormenting ourselves than in discovering reasons for enjoyment in the things that surround us. We go out of our course to make ourselves uncomfortable; the cup of life is not bitter enough to our palate, and we distil superfluous poison to put into it, or conjure up hideous things to frighten ourselves at, which would never exist if we did not make them. "We suffer," says Addison,[63] "as much from trifling accidents as from real evils. I have known the shooting of a star spoil a night's rest, and have seen a man in love grow pale and lose his appetite upon the plucking of a merrythought. A screech-owl at midnight has alarmed a family more than a band of robbers; nay, the voice of a cricket has struck more terror than the roaring of a lion. There is nothing so inconsiderable which may not appear dreadful to an imagination that is filled with omens and prognostics. A rusty nail or a crooked pin shoot up into prodigies."

The century and a quarter that has passed away since Addison wrote has seen the fall of many errors. Many fallacies and delusions have been crushed under the foot of Time since then; but this has been left unscathed, to frighten the weak-minded and embitter their existence. A belief in omens is not confined to the humble and uninformed. A general who led an army with credit has been known to feel alarmed at a winding-sheet in the candle; and learned men, who had honourably and fairly earned the highest honours of literature, have been seen to gather their little ones around them, and fear that one would be snatched away, because,

> *"When stole upon the time the dead of night,*
> *And heavy sleep had closed up mortal eyes,"*

a dog in the street was howling at the moon. Persons who would acknowledge freely that the belief in omens was unworthy of a man of sense, have yet confessed at the same time that, in spite of their reason, they have been unable to conquer their fears of death when they heard the harmless insect called the death-watch ticking in the wall, or saw an oblong hollow coal fly out of the fire.

Many other evil omens besides those mentioned above alarm the vulgar and the weak. If a sudden shivering comes over such people, they believe that, at that instant, an enemy is treading over the spot that will one day be their grave. If they meet a sow when they first walk abroad in the morning, it is an omen of evil for that day. To meet an ass, is in like manner unlucky. It is also very unfortunate to walk under a ladder; to forget to eat goose on the festival of St. Michael; to tread upon a beetle, or to eat the twin nuts that are sometimes found in one shell. Woe, in like manner, is predicted to that wight who inadvertently upsets the salt; each grain that is overthrown will bring to him a day of sorrow. If thirteen persons sit at table, one of them will die within the year; and all of them will be unhappy. Of all evil omens this is the worst. The facetious Dr. Kitchener used to observe that there was one case in which he believed that it was really unlucky for thirteen persons to sit down to dinner, and that was when there was only dinner enough for twelve. Unfortunately for their peace of mind, the great majority of people do not take this wise view of the matter. In almost every country of Europe the same superstition prevails, and some carry it so far as to look upon the number thirteen as in every way ominous of evil; and if they find thirteen coins in their purse, cast away the odd one like a polluted thing. The philosophic Beranger, in his exquisite song, *Thirteen at Table*, has taken a poetical view of this humiliating superstition, and mingled, as is his wont, a lesson of genuine wisdom in his lay. Being at dinner, he overthrows the salt, and, looking round the room, discovers that he is the thirteenth guest. While he is mourning his unhappy fate, and conjuring up visions of disease and suffering and the grave, he is suddenly startled by the apparition of Death herself, not in the shape of a grim foe, with skeleton-ribs and menacing dart, but of an angel of light, who shews the folly of tormenting ourselves with the dread of her approach, when she is the friend, rather than the enemy, of man, and frees us from the fetters which bind us to the dust.

If men could bring themselves to look upon death in this manner, living well and wisely till her inevitable approach, how vast a store of grief and vexation would they spare themselves!

Among good omens, one of the most conspicuous is to meet a piebald horse. To meet two of these animals is still more fortunate; and if on such an occasion you spit thrice, and form any reasonable wish, it will be gratified within three days. It is also a sign of good fortune if you inadvertently put on your stocking wrong side out. If you wilfully wear your stocking in this fashion, no good will come of it. It is very lucky to sneeze twice; but if you sneeze a third time, the omen loses its power, and your good fortune will be nipped in the bud. If a strange dog follow you, and fawn on you, and wish to attach itself to you, it is a sign of very great prosperity. Just as fortunate is it if a strange male cat comes to your house and manifests friendly intentions towards your family. If a she cat, it is an omen, on the contrary, of very great misfortune. If a swarm of bees alight in your garden, some very high honour and great joys await you.

Besides these glimpses of the future, you may know something of your fate by a diligent attention to every itching that you may feel in your body. Thus, if the eye or the nose itches, it is a sign you will be shortly vexed; if the foot itches, you will tread upon strange ground; and if the elbow itches, you will change your bedfellow. Itching of the right hand prognosticates that you will soon have a sum of money; and, of the left, that you will be called upon to disburse it.

These are but a few of the omens which are generally credited in modern Europe. A complete list of them would fatigue from its length, and sicken from its absurdity. It would be still more unprofitable to attempt to specify the various delusions of the same kind which are believed among oriental nations. Every reader will remember the comprehensive formula of cursing preserved in *Tristram Shandy* — curse a man after any fashion you remember or can invent, you will be sure to find it there. The oriental creed of omens is not less comprehensive. Every movement of the body, every emotion of the mind, is at certain times an omen. Every form and object in nature, even the shape of the clouds and the changes of the weather; every colour, every sound, whether of men or animals, or birds or insects, or inanimate things, is an omen. Nothing is too trifling or inconsiderable to inspire a hope which is not worth cherishing, or a fear which is sufficient to embitter existence.

From the belief in omens springs the superstition that has, from very early ages, set apart certain days, as more favourable than others, for prying into the secrets of futurity. The following, copied verbatim from the popular *Dream and Omen Book* of Mother Bridget, will shew the belief of the people of England at the present day. Those who are curious as to the ancient history of these observances, will find abundant aliment in the *Every-day Book*.

"*The 1st of January. — If a young maiden drink, on going to bed, a pint of cold spring water, in which is beat up an amulet, composed of the yolk of a pullet's egg, the legs of a spider, and the skin of an eel pounded, her future destiny will be revealed to her in a dream. This charm fails of its effect if tried any other day of the year.*

"*Valentine Day. — Let a single woman go out of her own door very early in the morning, and if the first person she meets be a woman, she will not be married that year; if she meet a man she will be married within three months.*

*"Lady Day. – The following charm may be tried this day with certain success: String thirty-one nuts on a string, composed of red worsted mixed with blue silk, and tie it round your neck on going to bed, repeating these lines:*

> *"Oh, I wish! oh, I wish to see*
> *Who my true love is to be!*

*Shortly after midnight, you will see your lover in a dream, and be informed at the same time of all the principal events of your future life.*

*"St. Swithin's Eve. – Select three things you most wish to know; write them down with a new pen and red ink on a sheet of fine wove paper, from which you must previously cut off all the corners and burn them. Fold the paper into a true lover's knot, and wrap round it three hairs from your head. Place the paper under your pillow for three successive nights, and your curiosity to know the future will be satisfied.*

*"St. Mark's Eve. – Repair to the nearest churchyard as the clock strikes twelve, and take from a grave on the south side of the church three tufts of grass (the longer and ranker the better), and on going to bed place them under your pillow, repeating earnestly three several times,*

> *'The Eve of St. Mark by prediction is blest,*
> *Set therefore my hopes and my fears all to rest:*
> *Let me know my fate, whether weal or woe;*
> *Whether my rank's to be high or low;*
> *Whether to live single, or be a bride,*
> *And the destiny my star doth provide.'*

*Should you have no dream that night, you will be single and miserable all your life. If you dream of thunder and lightning, your life will be one of great difficulty and sorrow.*

*"Candlemas Eve. – On this night (which is the purification of the Virgin Mary), let three, five, seven, or nine young maidens assemble together in a square chamber. Hang in each corner a bundle of sweet herbs, mixed with rue and rosemary. Then mix a cake of flour, olive-oil, and white sugar; every maiden having an equal share in the making and the expense of it. Afterwards it must be cut into equal pieces, each one marking the piece as she cuts it with the initials of her name. It is then to be baked one hour before the fire, not a word being spoken the whole time, and the maidens sitting with their arms and knees across. Each piece of cake is then to be wrapped up in a sheet of paper, on which each maiden shall write the love part of Solomon's Songs. If she put this*

under her pillow she will dream true. She will see her future husband and every one of her children, and will know besides whether her family will be poor or prosperous, a comfort to her or the contrary.

"*Midsummer.* – Take three roses, smoke them with sulphur, and exactly at three in the day bury one of the roses under a yew-tree; the second in a newly-made grave, and put the third under your pillow for three nights, and at the end of that period burn it in a fire of charcoal. Your dreams during that time will be prophetic of your future destiny, and, what is still more curious and valuable, says Mother Bridget, the man whom you are to wed will enjoy no peace till he comes and visits you. Besides this, you will perpetually haunt his dreams.

"*St. John's Eve.* – Make a new pincushion of the very best black velvet (no inferior quality will answer the purpose), and on one side stick your name at full length with the very smallest pins that can be bought (none other will do). On the other side make a cross with some very large pins, and surround it with a circle. Put this into your stocking when you take it off at night, and hang it up at the foot of the bed. All your future life will pass before you in a dream.

"*First New Moon of the year.* – On the first new moon in the year take a pint of clear spring water, and infuse into it the white of an egg laid by a white hen, a glass of white wine, three almonds peeled white, and a tablespoonful of white rose-water. Drink this on going to bed, not making more nor less than three draughts of it; repeating the following verses three several times in a clear distinct voice, but not so loud as to be overheard by any body:

'If I dream of water pure
Before the coming morn,
'Tis a sign I shall be poor,
And unto wealth not born.
If I dream of tasting beer,
Middling then will be my cheer –
Chequer'd with the good and bad,
Sometimes joyful, sometimes sad;
But should I dream of drinking wine,
Wealth and pleasure will be mine.
The stronger the drink, the better the cheer –
Dreams of my destiny, appear, appear!'

*"Twenty-ninth of February. — This day, as it only occurs once in four years, is peculiarly auspicious to those who desire to have a glance at futurity, especially to young maidens burning with anxiety to know the appearance and complexion of their future lords. The charm to be adopted is the following: Stick twenty-seven of the smallest pins that are made, three by three, into a tallow candle. Light it up at the wrong end, and then place it in a candlestick made out of clay, which must be drawn from a virgin's grave. Place this on the chimney-place, in the left-hand corner, exactly as the clock strikes twelve, and go to bed immediately. When the candle is burnt out, take the pins and put them into your left shoe; and before nine nights have elapsed your fate will be revealed to you."*

We have now taken a hasty review of the various modes of seeking to discover the future, especially as practised in modern times. The main features of the folly appear essentially the same in all countries. National character and peculiarities operate some difference of interpretation. The mountaineer makes the natural phenomena which he most frequently witnesses prognosticative of the future. The dweller in the plains, in a similar manner, seeks to know his fate among the signs of the things that surround him, and tints his superstition with the hues of his own clime. The same spirit animates them all — the same desire to know that which Infinite Mercy has concealed. There is but little probability that the curiosity of mankind in this respect will ever be wholly eradicated. Death and ill fortune are continual bugbears to the weak-minded, the irreligious, and the ignorant; and while such exist in the world, divines will preach upon its impiety and philosophers discourse upon its absurdity in vain. Still it is evident that these follies have greatly diminished. Soothsayers and prophets have lost the credit they formerly enjoyed, and skulk in secret now where they once shewed their faces in the blaze of day. So far there is manifest improvement.

# Chapter 7.

The Magnetisers.

*Some deemed them wondrous wise, and some believed them mad.*
**Beattie's Minstrel.**

The wonderful influence of imagination in the cure of diseases is well known. A motion of the hand, or a glance of the eye, will throw a weak and credulous patient into a fit; and a pill made of bread, if taken with sufficient faith, will operate a cure better than all the drugs in the pharmacopœia. The Prince of Orange, at the siege of Breda, in 1625, cured all his soldiers, who were dying of the scurvy, by a philanthropic piece of quackery, which he played upon them with the knowledge of the physicians, when all other means had failed.[64] Many hundreds of instances, of a similar kind, might be related, especially from the history of witchcraft. The mummeries, strange gesticulations, and barbarous jargon of witches and sorcerers, which frightened credulous and nervous women, brought on all those symptoms of hysteria and other similar diseases, so well understood now, but which were then supposed to be the work of the Devil, not only by the victims and the public in general, but by the operators themselves.

In the age when alchymy began to fall into some disrepute, and learning to lift up its voice against it, a new delusion, based upon this power of imagination, suddenly arose, and found apostles among all the alchymists. Numbers of them, forsaking their old pursuits, made themselves magnetisers. It appeared first in the shape of mineral, and afterwards of animal, magnetism, under which latter name it survives to this day, and numbers its dupes by thousands.

The mineral magnetisers claim the first notice, as the worthy predecessors of the quacks of the present day. The honour claimed for Paracelsus, of being the first of the Rosicrucians, has been disputed; but his claim to be considered the first of the magnetisers can scarcely be challenged. It has been already mentioned of him, in the part of this work which treats of alchymy, that, like nearly all the distinguished adepts, he was a physician; and pretended, not only to make gold and confer immortality, but to cure all diseases. He was the first who, with the latter view, attributed occult and miraculous powers to the magnet. Animated apparently by a sincere conviction that the magnet was the philosopher's stone, which, if it could not transmute metals, could soothe all human suffering and arrest the progress of decay, he travelled for many years in Persia and Arabia, in search of the mountain of adamant, so famed in oriental fables. When he practised as a physician at Basle, he called one of his nostrums by the name of azoth — a stone or crystal, which, he said, contained magnetic properties, and cured epilepsy, hysteria, and spasmodic affections. He soon found imitators. His fame spread far and near; and thus were sown the first seeds of that error which has since taken root and flourished so widely. In spite of the denial of modern practitioners, this must be considered the origin of magnetism; for we find that, beginning with Paracelsus, there was a regular succession of mineral magnetisers until Mesmer appeared, and gave a new feature to the delusion.

Paracelsus boasted of being able to *transplant* diseases from the human frame into the earth, by means of the magnet. He said there were six ways by which this might be effected. One of them will be quite sufficient as a specimen. "If a person suffer from disease, either local or general, let the following remedy be tried. Take a magnet, impregnated with mummy,[65] and mixed with rich earth. In this earth sow some seeds that have a congruity or homogeneity with the disease; then let this earth, well sifted and mixed with mummy, be laid in an earthen vessel; and let the seeds committed to it be watered daily with a lotion in which the diseased limb or body has been washed. Thus will the disease be transplanted from the human body to the seeds which are in the earth. Having done this, transplant the seeds from the earthen vessel to the ground, and wait till they begin to sprout into herbs; as they increase, the disease will diminish; and when they have arrived at their full growth, it will disappear altogether."

Kircher the Jesuit, whose quarrel with the alchymists was the means of exposing many of their impostures, was a firm believer in the efficacy of the magnet. Having been applied to by a patient afflicted with hernia, he directed the man to swallow a small magnet reduced to powder, while he applied at the same time to the external swelling, a poultice made of filings of iron. He expected that by this means the magnet, when it got to the corresponding place inside, would draw in the iron, and with it the tumour; which would thus, he said, be safely and expeditiously reduced.

As this new doctrine of magnetism spread, it was found that wounds inflicted with any metallic substance could be cured by the magnet. In process of time, the delusion so increased, that it was deemed sufficient to magnetise a sword, to cure any hurt which that sword might have inflicted! This was the origin of the celebrated "weapon-salve," which excited so much attention about the middle of the seventeenth century. The following was the recipe given by Paracelsus for the cure of any wounds inflicted by a sharp weapon, except such as had penetrated the heart, the brain, or the arteries. "Take of moss growing on the head of a thief who has been hanged and left in the air; of real mummy; of human blood, still warm — of each, one ounce; of human suet, two ounces; of linseed oil, turpentine, and Armenian bole — of each, two drachms. Mix all well in a mortar, and keep the salve in an oblong, narrow urn." With this salve the weapon, after being dipped in the blood from the wound, was to be carefully anointed, and then laid by in a cool place. In the mean time, the wound was to be duly washed with fair clean water, covered with a clean, soft, linen rag, and opened once a day to cleanse off purulent or other matter. Of the success of this treatment, says the writer of the able article on Animal Magnetism, in the twelfth volume of the *Foreign Quarterly Review*, there cannot be the least doubt; "for surgeons at this moment follow exactly the same method, *except* anointing the weapon!"

The weapon-salve continued to be much spoken of on the Continent, and many eager claimants appeared for the honour of the invention. Dr. Fludd, or A. Fluctibus, the Rosicrucian, who has been already mentioned in a previous part of this volume, was very zealous in introducing it into England. He tried it with great success in several cases, and no wonder, for while he kept up the spirits of his patients by boasting of the great efficacy of the salve, he never neglected those common, but much more important remedies, of washing, bandaging, &c. which the experience of all ages had declared sufficient for the purpose. Fludd moreover declared, that the magnet was a remedy for all diseases, if properly applied; but that man having, like the earth, a north and a south pole, magnetism could only take place when his body was in a boreal position! In the midst of his popularity, an attack was made upon him and his favourite remedy, the salve; which, however, did little or nothing to diminish the belief in its efficacy. One "Parson Foster" wrote a pamphlet, entitled *Hyplocrisma Spongus; or, a Spunge to wipe away the Weapon-Salve*; in which he declared, that it was as bad as witchcraft to use or recommend such an unguent; that it was invented by the Devil, who, at the last day, would seize upon every person who had given it the slightest encouragement. "In fact," said Parson Foster, "the Devil himself gave it to Paracelsus; Paracelsus to the emperor; the emperor to the courtier; the courtier to Baptista Porta; and Baptista Porta to Dr. Fludd, a doctor of physic, yet living and practising in the famous city of London, who now stands tooth and nail for it." Dr. Fludd, thus assailed, took up the pen in defence of his unguent, in a reply called *The Squeezing of Parson Foster's Spunge; wherein the Spunge-bearer's immodest carriage and behaviour towards his brethren is detected; the bitter flames of his slanderous reports are, by the sharp vinegar of truth, corrected and quite extinguished; and lastly, the virtuous validity of his spunge in wiping away the-weapon-salve, is crushed out and clean abolished.*

Shortly after this dispute a more distinguished believer in the weapon-salve made his appearance in the person of Sir Kenelm Digby, the son of Sir Everard Digby, who was executed for his participation in the Gunpowder Plot. This gentleman, who, in other respects, was an accomplished scholar and an able man, was imbued with all the extravagant notions of the alchymists. He believed in the philosopher's stone, and wished to engage Descartes to devote his energies to the discovery of the elixir of life, or some other means by which the existence of man might be prolonged to an indefinite period. He gave his wife, the beautiful

Venetia Anastasia Stanley, a dish of capons fed upon vipers, according to the plan supposed to have been laid down by Arnold of Villeneuve, in the hope that she might thereby preserve her loveliness for a century. If such a man once took up the idea of the weapon-salve, it was to be expected that he would make the most of it. In his hands, however, it was changed from an unguent into a powder, and was called the *powder of sympathy*. He pretended that he had acquired the knowledge of it from a Carmelite friar, who had learned it in Persia or Armenia, from an oriental philosopher of great renown. King James, the Prince of Wales, the Duke of Buchingham, and many other noble personages, believed in its efficacy. The following remarkable instance of his mode of cure was read by Sir Kenelm to a society of learned men at Montpellier. Mr. James Howell, the well-known author of the *Dendrologia*, and of various letters, coming by chance as two of his best friends were fighting a duel, rushed between them and endeavoured to part them. He seized the sword of one of the combatants by the hilt, while, at the same time, he grasped the other by the blade. Being transported with fury one against the other, they struggled to rid themselves of the hindrance caused by their friend; and in so doing, the one whose sword was held by the blade by Mr. Howell, drew it away roughly, and nearly cut his hand off, severing the nerves and muscles, and penetrating to the bone. The other, almost at the same instant, disengaged his sword, and aimed a blow at the head of his antagonist, which Mr. Howell observing, raised his wounded hand with the rapidity of thought to prevent the blow. The sword fell on the back of his already wounded hand, and cut it severely. "It seemed," said Sir Kenelm Digby, "as if some unlucky star raged over them, that they should have both shed the blood of that dear friend for whose life they would have given their own, if they had been in their proper mind at the time." Seeing Mr. Howell's face all besmeared with blood from his wounded hand, they both threw down their swords and embraced him, and bound up his hand with a garter, to close the veins which were cut and bled profusely. They then conveyed him home, and sent for a surgeon. King James, who was much attached to Mr. Howell, afterwards sent his own surgeon to attend him. We must continue the narrative in the words of Sir Kenelm Digby: "It was my chance," says he, "to be lodged hard by him; and four or five days after, as I was making myself ready, he came to my house, and prayed me to view his wounds. 'For I understand,' said he, 'that you have extraordinary remedies on such occasions; and my surgeons apprehend some fear that it may grow to a gangrene, and so the hand must be cut off.' In effect, his countenance discovered that he was in much pain, which, he said, was insupportable in regard of the extreme inflammation. I told him I would willingly serve him; but if, haply, he knew the manner how I could cure him, without touching or seeing him, it might be that he would not expose himself to my manner of curing; because he would think it, peradventure, either ineffectual or superstitious. He replied, 'The many wonderful things which people have related unto me of your way of medicinement makes me nothing doubt at all of its efficacy; and all that I have to say unto you is comprehended in the Spanish proverb, *Hagase el milagro y hagalo Mahoma* — Let the miracle be done, though Mahomet do it.'

*"I asked him then for any thing that had the blood upon it: so he presently sent for his garter, wherewith his hand was first bound; and as I called for a basin of water, as if I would wash my hands, I took a handful of powder of vitriol, which I had in my study, and presently dissolved it. As soon as the bloody garter was brought me, I put it in the basin, observing, in the interim, what Mr. Howell did, who stood talking with a gentleman in a corner of my chamber, not regarding at all what I was doing. He started suddenly, as if he had found some strange alteration in himself. I asked him what he ailed? 'I know not what ails me, but I find that I feel no more pain. Methinks that a pleasing kind of freshness, as it were a wet cold napkin, did spread over my hand, which hath taken away the inflammation that tormented me before.' I replied, 'Since, then, you feel already so much good of my medicament, I advise you to cast away all your plasters; only keep the wound clean, and in a moderate temper betwixt heat and cold.' This was presently reported to the Duke of Buckingham, and, a little after, to the king, who were both very curious to know the circumstances of the business; which was, that after dinner I took the garter out of the water,*

*and put it to dry before a great fire. It was scarce dry before Mr. Howell's servant came running, and saying that his master felt as much burning as ever he had done, if not more; for the heat was such as if his hand were betwixt coals of fire. I answered that, although that had happened at present, yet he should find ease in a short time; for I knew the reason of this new accident, and would provide accordingly; for his master should be free from that inflammation, it might be before he could possibly return to him. But, in case he found no ease, I wished him to come presently back again; if not, he might forbear coming. Thereupon he went, and, at the instant I did put the garter again into the water; thereupon he found his master without any pain at all. To be brief, there was no cense of pain afterwards; but within five or six days the wounds were sicatrised and entirely healed."*

Such is the marvellous story of Sir Kenelm Digby. Other practitioners of that age were not behind him in their pretensions. It was not always thought necessary to use either the powder of sympathy, or the weapon-salve, to effect a cure. It was sufficient to magnetise the sword with the hand (the first faint dawn of the *animal* theory), to relieve any pain the same weapon had caused. They asserted, that if they stroked the sword *upwards* with their fingers, the wounded person would feel immediate relief; but if they stroked it *downwards*, he would feel intolerable pain.[66]

Another very singular notion of the power and capabilities of magnetism was entertained at the same time. It was believed that a *sympathetic alphabet* could be made on the flesh, by means of which persons could correspond with each other, and communicate all their ideas with the rapidity of volition, although thousands of miles apart. From the arms of two persons a piece of flesh was cut, and mutually transplanted, while still warm and bleeding. The piece so severed grew to the new arm on which it was placed; but still retained so close a sympathy with its native limb, that its old possessor was always sensible of any injury done to it. Upon these transplanted pieces were tatooed the letters of the alphabet; so that, when a communication was to be made, either of the persons, though the wide Atlantic rolled between them, had only to prick his arm with a magnetic needle, and straightway his friend received intimation that the telegraph was at work. Whatever letter he pricked on his own arm pained the same letter on the arm of his correspondent.

Contemporary with Sir Kenelm Digby was the no less famous Mr. Valentine Greatraks, who, without mentioning magnetism, or laying claim to any theory, practised upon himself and others a deception much more akin to the animal magnetism of the present day than the mineral magnetism it was then so much the fashion to study. He was the son of an Irish gentleman, of good education and property, in the county of Cork. He fell, at an early age, into a sort of melancholy derangement. After some time he had an impulse, or strange persuasion in his mind, which continued to present itself, whether he were sleeping or waking, that God had given him the power of curing the king's evil. He mentioned this persuasion to his wife, who very candidly told him that he was a fool. He was not quite sure of this, notwith-standing the high authority from which it came, and determined to make trial of the power that was in him. A few days after-wards, he went to one William Maher, of Saltersbridge, in the parish of Lismore, who was grievously afflicted with the king's evil in his eyes, cheek, and throat. Upon this man, who was of abundant faith, he laid his hands, stroked him, and prayed fervently. He had the satisfaction to see him heal considerably in the course of a few days; and finally, with the aid of other remedies, to be quite cured. This success encouraged him in the belief that he had a divine mission. Day after day he had further impulses from on high that he was called upon to cure the ague also. In the course of time he extended his powers to the curing of epilepsy, ulcers, aches, and lameness. All the county of Cork was in a commotion to see this extraordinary physician, who certainly operated some very great benefit in cases where the disease was heightened by hypochondria and depression of spirits. According to his own account,[67] such great multitudes resorted to him from divers places, that he had no time to follow his own business, or enjoy the company of his family and friends. He was obliged to set aside three days in the week, from six in the morning till six at night, during which time only he laid hands upon all that came. Still the crowds which thronged around him were so great, that the neighbouring towns were not able to accommodate them. He thereupon left his house in the country, and went to Youghal, where the resort of sick people, not only from all parts of Ireland, but from England, continued so great, that the magistrates were afraid they would infect the place by their diseases. Several of these poor credulous people no sooner saw him than they fell into fits, and he restored them by waving his hand in their faces, and praying over them. Nay, he affirmed that the touch of his glove had driven pains away, and, on one occasion, cast out from a woman several devils, or evil spirits, who tormented her day and night. "Every one of these devils," says Greatraks, "was like to choke her when it came up into her throat." It is evident from this that the woman's complaint was nothing but hysteria.

The clergy of the diocese of Lismore, who seem to have had much clearer notions of Greatraks' pretensions than their parishioners, set their faces against the new prophet and worker of miracles. He was cited to appear in the Dean's Court, and prohibited from laying on his hands for the future: but he cared nothing for the Church. He imagined that he derived his powers direct from heaven, and continued to throw people into fits, and bring them to their senses again, as usual, almost exactly after the fashion of modern magnetisers. His reputation became, at last, so great, that Lord Conway sent to him from London, begging that he would come over immediately to cure a grievous headache which his lady had suffered for several years, and which the principal physicians of England had been unable to relieve.

Greatraks accepted the invitation, and tried his manipulations and prayers upon Lady Conway. He failed, however, in affording any relief. The poor lady's headache was excited by causes too serious to allow her any help, even from faith and a lively imagination. He lived for some months in Lord Conway's house, at Ragley, in Warwickshire, operating cures similar to those he had performed in Ireland. He afterwards removed to London, and took a house in Lincoln's-Inn Fields, which soon became the daily resort of all the nervous and credulous women of the metropolis. A very amusing account of Greatraks at this time

(1665) is given in the second volume of the *Miscellanies of St. Evremond*, under the title of the Irish prophet. It is the most graphic sketch ever made of this early magnetiser. Whether his pretensions were more or less absurd than those of some of his successors, who have lately made their appearance among us, would be hard to say.

"When M. de Comminges," says St. Evremond, "was ambassador from his most Christian majesty to the king of Great Britain, there came to London an Irish prophet, who passed himself off as a great worker of miracles. Some persons of quality having begged M. de Comminges to invite him to his house, that they might be witnesses of some of his miracles, the ambassador promised to satisfy them, as much to gratify his own curiosity as from courtesy to his friends; and gave notice to Greatraks that he would be glad to see him.

*"A rumour of the prophet's coming soon spread all over the town, and the hotel of M. de Comminges was crowded by sick persons, who came full of confidence in their speedy cure. The Irishman made them wait a considerable time for him, but came at last, in the midst of their impatience, with a grave and simple countenance, that showed no signs of his being a cheat. Monsieur de Comminges prepared to question him strictly, hoping to discourse with him on the matters that he had read of in Van Helmont and Bodinus; but he was not able to do so, much to his regret, for the crowd became so great, and cripples and others pressed around so impatiently to be the first cured, that the servants were obliged to use threats, and even force, before they could establish order among them, or place them in proper ranks.*

"The prophet affirmed that all diseases were caused by evil spirits. Every infirmity was with him a case of diabolical possession. The first that was presented to him was a man suffering from gout and rheumatism, and so severely that the physicians had been unable to cure him. 'Ah,' said the miracle-worker, 'I have seen a good deal of this sort of spirits when I was in Ireland. They are watery spirits, who bring on cold shivering, and excite an overflow of aqueous humours in our poor bodies.' Then addressing the man, he said, 'Evil spirit, who hast quitted thy dwelling in the waters to come and afflict this miserable body, I command thee to quit thy new abode, and to return to thine ancient habitation!' This said, the sick man was ordered to withdraw, and

*another was brought forward in his place. This new comer said he was*
*tormented by the melancholy vapours. In fact, he looked like a hypo-*
*chondriac; one of those persons, diseased in imagination, and who but*
*too often become so in reality. 'Aerial spirit,' said the Irishman, 'return,*
*I command thee, into the air; – exercise thy natural vocation of raising*
*tempests, and do not excite any more wind in this sad unlucky body!'*
*This man was immediately turned away to make room for a third*
*patient, who, in the Irishman's opinion, was only tormented by a little*
*bit of a sprite, who could not withstand his command for an instant. He*
*pretended that he recognised this sprite by some marks which were*
*invisible to the company, to whom he turned with a smile, and said,*
*'This sort of spirit does not often do much harm, and is always very*
*diverting.' To hear him talk, one would have imagined that he knew all*
*about spirits, – their names, their rank, their numbers, their employ-*
*ment, and all the functions they were destined to; and he boasted of*
*being much better acquainted with the intrigues of demons than he was*
*with the affairs of men. You can hardly imagine what a reputation he*
*gained in a short time. Catholics and Protestants visited him from every*
*part, all believing that power from heaven was in his hands."*

After relating a rather equivocal adventure of a husband and
wife, who implored Greatraks to cast out the devil of dissension
which had crept in between them, St. Evremond thus sums up
the effect he produced on the popular mind: "So great was the
confidence in him, that the blind fancied they saw the light
which they did not see – the deaf imagined that they heard – the
lame that they walked straight, and the paralytic that they had
recovered the use of their limbs. An idea of health made the sick
forget for a while their maladies; and imagination, which was not
less active in those merely drawn by curiosity than in the sick,
gave a false view to the one class, from the desire of seeing, as it
operated a false cure on the other from the strong desire of being
healed. Such was the power of the Irishman over the mind, and
such was the influence of the mind upon the body. Nothing was
spoken of in London but his prodigies; and these prodigies were
supported by such great authorities, that the bewildered multitude believed them almost without examination, while more
enlightened people did not dare to reject them from their own
knowledge. The public opinion, timid and enslaved, respected

this imperious and, apparently, well-authenticated error. Those who saw through the delusion kept their opinion to themselves, knowing how useless it was to declare their disbelief to a people filled with prejudice and admiration."

About the same time that Valentine Greatraks was thus *magnetising* the people of London, an Italian enthusiast, named Francisco Bagnone, was performing the same tricks in Italy, and with as great success. He had only to touch weak women with his hands, or sometimes (for the sake of working more effectively upon their fanaticism) with a relic, to make them fall into fits, and manifest all the symptoms of magnetism.

Besides these, several learned men, in different parts of Europe, directed their attention to the study of the magnet, believing that it might be rendered efficacious in many diseases. Van Helmont, in particular, published a work on the effects of magnetism on the human frame; and Balthazar Gracian, a Spaniard, rendered himself famous for the boldness of his views on the subject. "The magnet," said the latter, "attracts iron; iron is found every where; every thing, therefore, is under the influence of magnetism. It is only a modification of the general principle, which establishes harmony or foments divisions among men. It is the same agent that gives rise to sympathy, antipathy, and the passions."[68]

Baptista Porta, who, in the whimsical genealogy of the weapon-salve, given by Parson Foster, in his attack upon Dr. à Fluctibus, is mentioned as one of its fathers, had also great faith in the efficacy of the magnet, and operated upon the imagination of his patients in a manner which was then considered so extraordinary that he was accused of being a magician, and prohibited from practising by the court of Rome. Among others who distinguished themselves by their faith in magnetism, Sebastian Wirdig and William Maxwell claim especial notice. Wirdig was professor of medicine at the university of Rostock in Mecklenburg, and wrote a treatise called *The New Medicine of the Spirits*, which he presented to the Royal Society of London. An edition of this work was printed in 1673, in which the author maintained that a magnetic influence took place, not only between the celestial and terrestrial bodies, but between all living things. The whole world, he said, was under the influence of magnetism; life was preserved by magnetism; death was the consequence of magnetism!

Maxwell, the other enthusiast, was an admiring disciple of Paracelsus, and boasted that he had irradiated the obscurity in which too many of the wonder-working recipes of that great philosopher were enveloped. His works were printed at Frankfort in 1679. It would seem, from the following passage, that he was aware of the great influence of imagination, as well in the production as in the cure of diseases. "If you wish to work prodigies," says he, "abstract from the materiality of beings — increase the sum of spirituality in bodies — rouse the spirit from its slumbers. Unless you do one or other of these things — unless you can bind the idea, you can never perform any thing good or great." Here, in fact, lies the whole secret of magnetism, and all delusions of a similar kind: increase the spirituality — rouse the spirit from its slumbers, or, in other words, work upon the imagination — induce belief and blind confidence, and you may do any thing. This passage, which is quoted with approbation by M. Dupotet[69] in a work, as strongly corroborative of the theory now advanced by the animal magnetists, is just the reverse. If they believe they can work all their wonders by the means so dimly shadowed forth by Maxwell, what becomes of the universal fluid pervading all nature, and which they pretend to pour into weak and diseased bodies from the tips of their fingers?

Early in the eighteenth century the attention of Europe was directed to a very remarkable instance of fanaticism, which has been claimed by the animal magnetists as a proof of their science. The *Convulsionaries of St. Medard*, as they were called, assembled in great numbers round the tomb of their favourite saint, the Jansenist priest Paris, and taught one another how to fall into convulsions. They believed that St. Paris would cure all their infirmities; and the number of hysterical women and weak-minded persons of all descriptions that flocked to the tomb from far and near was so great as daily to block up all the avenues leading to it. Working themselves up to a pitch of excitement, they went off one after the other into fits, while some of them, still in apparent possession of all their faculties, voluntarily exposed themselves to sufferings which on ordinary occasions would have been sufficient to deprive them of life. The scenes that occurred were a scandal to civilisation and to religion — a strange mixture of obscenity, absurdity, and superstition. While some were praying on bended knees at the shrine of St. Paris, others were shrieking and making the most hideous noises. The women especially exerted themselves. On one side of the chapel there might be seen a score of them, all in convulsions; while at another as many more, excited to a sort of frenzy, yielded themselves up to gross indecencies. Some of them took an insane delight in being beaten and trampled upon. One in particular, according to Montégre, whose account we quote,[70] was so enraptured with this ill-usage, that nothing but the hardest blows would satisfy her. While a fellow of Herculean strength was beating her with all his might with a heavy bar of iron, she kept continually urging him to renewed exertion. The harder he struck the better she liked it, exclaiming all the while, "Well done, brother, well done! Oh, how pleasant it is! what good you are doing me! Courage, my brother, courage; strike harder, strike harder still!" Another of these fanatics had, if possible, a still greater love for a beating. Carré de Montgeron, who relates the circumstance, was unable to satisfy her with sixty blows of a large sledge-hammer. He afterwards used the same weapon with the same degree of strength, for the sake of experiment, and succeeded in battering a hole in a stone wall at the twenty-fifth stroke. Another woman, named Sonnet, laid herself down on a red-hot brazier without flinching, and acquired for herself the nickname of the *Salamander*; while others, desirous of a more illustrious martyrdom, attempted to crucify themselves. M. Deleuze, in his critical history of *Animal Magnetism*, attempts to prove that this fanatical frenzy was produced by magnetism, and that these mad enthusiasts magnetised each other without being aware of it. As well might he insist that the fanaticism which tempts the Hindoo bigot to keep his arms stretched in a horizontal position till the sinews wither, or his fingers closed upon his palms till the nails grow out of the backs of his hands, is also an effect of magnetism!

For a period of sixty or seventy years magnetism was almost wholly confined to Germany. Men of sense and learning devoted their attention to the properties of the loadstone; and one Father Hell, a Jesuit, and professor of astronomy at the University of Vienna, rendered himself famous by his magnetic cures. About the year 1771 or 1772 he invented steel-plates of a peculiar form, which he applied to the naked body as a cure for several diseases. In the year 1774 he communicated his system to Anthony Mesmer. The latter improved upon the ideas of Father Hell, constructed a new theory of his own, and became the founder of Animal Magnetism.

It has been the fashion among the enemies of the new delusion to decry Mesmer as an unprincipled adventurer, while his disciples have extolled him to the skies as a regenerator of the human race. In nearly the same words as the Rosicrucians applied to their founders, he has been called the discoverer of the secret which brings man into more intimate connexion with his Creator, the deliverer of the soul from the debasing trammels of the flesh, the man who enables us to set time at defiance, and conquer the obstructions of space. A careful sifting of his pretensions, and examination of the evidence brought forward to sustain them, will soon shew which opinion is the more correct. That the writer of these pages considers him in the light of a man who, deluding himself, was the means of deluding others, may be inferred from his finding a place in these volumes, and figuring among the Flamels, the Agrippas, the Borris, the Böhmens, and the Cagliostros.

He was born in May 1734, at Mersburg, in Swabia, and studied medicine at the University of Vienna. He took his degrees in 1766, and chose the influence of the planets on the human body as the subject of his inaugural dissertation. Having treated the matter quite in the style of the old astrological physicians, he was exposed to some ridicule both then and afterwards. Even at this early period some faint ideas of his great theory were germinating in his mind. He maintained in his dissertation "that the sun, moon, and fixed stars mutually affect each other in their orbits; that they cause and direct in our earth a flux and reflux not only in the sea, but in the atmosphere, and affect in a similar manner all organised bodies through the medium of a subtile and mobile fluid, which pervades the universe, and associates all things together in mutual intercourse and harmony." This influence, he said, was particularly exercised on the nervous system, and produced two states, which he called *intension* and *remission*, which seemed to him to account for the different periodical revolutions observable in several maladies. When in after-life he met with Father Hell, he was confirmed by that person's observations in the truth of many of his own ideas. Having caused Hell to make him some magnetic plates, he determined to try experiments with them himself for his further satisfaction.

He tried accordingly, and was astonished at his success. The faith of their wearers operated wonders with the metallic plates. Mesmer made due reports to Father Hell of all he had done, and the latter published them as the results of his own happy invention, and speaking of Mesmer as a physician whom he had employed to work under him. Mesmer took offence at being thus treated, considering himself a far greater personage than Father Hell. He claimed the invention as his own, accused Hell of a breach of confidence, and stigmatised him as a mean person, anxious to turn the discoveries of others to his own account. Hell replied, and a very pretty quarrel was the result, which afforded small talk for months to the literati of Vienna. Hell ultimately gained the victory. Mesmer, nothing daunted, continued to promulgate his views till he stumbled at last upon the animal theory.

One of his patients was a young lady, named Œsterline, who suffered under a convulsive malady. Her attacks were periodical, and attended by a rush of blood to the head, followed by delirium and syncope. These symptoms he soon succeeded in reducing under his system of planetary influence, and imagined he could foretell the periods of accession and remission. Having thus accounted satisfactorily to himself for the origin of the disease, the idea struck him that he could operate a certain cure if he could ascertain beyond doubt, what he had long believed, that there existed between the bodies which compose our globe an action equally reciprocal and similar to that of the heavenly bodies, by means of which he could imitate artificially the periodical revolutions of the flux and reflux before mentioned. He soon convinced himself that this action did exist. When trying the metallic plates of Father Hell, he thought their efficacy depended on their form; but he found afterwards that he could produce the same effects without using them at all, merely by passing his hands downwards towards the feet of the patient, even when at a considerable distance.

This completed the theory of Mesmer. He wrote an account of his discovery to all the learned societies of Europe, soliciting their investigation. The Academy of Sciences at Berlin was the only one that answered him, and their answer was any thing but favourable to his system or flattering to himself. Still he was not discouraged. He maintained to all who would listen to him that the magnetic matter, or fluid, pervaded all the universe — that every human body contained it, and could communicate the superabundance of it to another by an exertion of the will. Writing to a friend from Vienna, he said, "I have observed that the magnetic is almost the same thing as the electric fluid, and that it may be propagated in the same manner, by means of intermediate bodies. Steel is not the only substance adapted to this purpose. I have rendered paper, bread, wool, silk, stones, leather, glass, wood, men, and dogs — in short, every thing I touched, magnetic to such a degree, that these substances produced the same effects as the loadstone on diseased persons. I have charged jars with magnetic matter in the same way as is done with electricity."

Mesmer did not long find his residence at Vienna as agreeable as he wished. His pretensions were looked upon with contempt or indifference, and the case of Mademoiselle Œsterline brought him less fame than notoriety. He determined to change his sphere of action, and travelled into Swabia and Switzerland. In the latter country he met with the celebrated Father Gassner, who, like Valentine Greatraks, amused himself by casting out devils, and healing the sick by merely laying hands upon them. At his approach, delicate girls fell into convulsions, and hypochondriacs fancied themselves cured. His house was daily besieged by the lame, the blind, and the hysteric. Mesmer at once acknowledged the efficacy of his cures, and declared that they were the obvious result of his own newly-discovered power of magnetism. A few of the father's patients were forthwith subjected to the manipulations of Mesmer, and the same symptoms were induced. He then tried his hand upon some paupers in the hospitals of Berne and Zurich, and succeeded, according to his own account, but no other person's, in curing an opththalmia and a gutta serena. With memorials of these achievements he returned to Vienna, in the hope of silencing his enemies, or at least forcing them to respect his newly-acquired reputation, and to examine his system more attentively.

His second appearance in that capital was not more auspicious than the first. He undertook to cure a Mademoiselle Paradis, who was quite blind, and subject to convulsions. He magnetised her several times, and then declared that she was cured; at least, if she was not, it was her fault and not his. An eminent oculist of that day, named Barth, went to visit her, and declared that she was as blind as ever; while her family said she was as much subject to convulsions as before. Mesmer persisted that she was cured. Like the French philosopher, he would not allow facts to interfere with his theory.[71] He declared that there was a conspiracy against him; and that Mademoiselle Paradis, at the instigation of her family, feigned blindness in order to injure his reputation!

The consequences of this pretended cure taught Mesmer that Vienna was not the sphere for him. Paris, the idle, the debauched, the pleasure-hunting, the novelty-loving, was the scene for a philosopher like him, and thither he repaired accordingly. He arrived at Paris in 1778, and began modestly by making himself and his theory known to the principal physicians. At first, his encouragement was but slight; he found people more inclined to laugh at than to patronise him. But he was a man who had great confidence in himself, and of a perseverance which no difficulties could overcome. He hired a sumptuous apartment, which he opened to all comers who chose to make trial of the new power of nature. M. D'Eslon, a physician of great reputation, became a convert; and from that time, animal magnetism, or, as some called it, mesmerism, became the fashion in Paris. The women were quite enthusiastic about it, and their admiring tattle wafted its fame through every grade of society. Mesmer was the rage; and high and low, rich and poor, credulous and unbelieving, all hastened to convince themselves of the power of this mighty magician, who made such magnificent promises. Mesmer, who knew as well as any man living the influence of the imagination, determined that, on that score, nothing should be wanting to heighten the effect of the magnetic charm. In all Paris, there was not a house so charmingly furnished as Monsieur Mesmer's. Richly-stained glass shed a dim religious light on his spacious saloons, which were almost covered with mirrors. Orange-blossoms scented all the air of his corridors; incense of the most expensive kinds burned in antique vases on his chimney-pieces; æolian harps sighed melodious music from distant chambers; while sometimes a sweet female voice, from above or below, stole softly upon the mysterious silence that was kept in the house, and insisted upon from all visitors. *Was ever any thing so delightful!* cried all the Mrs. Wittitterleys of Paris, as they thronged to his house in search of pleasant excitement; *So wonderful!* said the pseudo-philosophers, who would believe anything if it were the fashion; *So amusing!* said the worn-out debauchés, who had drained the cup of sensuality to its dregs, and who longed to see lovely women in convulsions, with the hope that they might gain some new emotions from the sight.

The following was the mode of operation: In the centre of the saloon was placed an oval vessel, about four feet in its longest diameter, and one foot deep. In this were laid a number of wine-bottles, filled with magnetised water, well corked-up, and disposed in radii, with their necks outwards. Water was then poured into the vessel so as just to cover the bottles, and filings of iron were thrown in occasionally to heighten the magnetic effect. The vessel was then covered with an iron cover, pierced through with many holes, and was called the *baquet*. From each hole issued a long movable rod of iron, which the patients were to apply to such parts of their bodies as were afflicted. Around this *baquet* the patients were directed to sit, holding each other by the hand, and pressing their knees together as closely as possible, to facilitate the passage of the magnetic fluid from one to the other.

Then came in the assistant magnetisers, generally strong, handsome young men, to pour into the patient from their finger-tips fresh streams of the wondrous fluid. They embraced the patient between the knees, rubbed them gently down the spine and the course of the nerves, using gentle pressure upon the breasts of the ladies, and staring them out of countenance to magnetise them by the eye! All this time the most rigorous silence was maintained, with the exception of a few wild notes on the harmonica or the piano-forte, or the melodious voice of a hidden opera-singer swelling softly at long intervals. Gradually the cheeks of the ladies began to glow, their imaginations to become inflamed; and off they went, one after the other, in convulsive fits. Some of them sobbed and tore their hair, others laughed till the tears ran from their eyes, while others shrieked and screamed and yelled till they became insensible altogether. This was the crisis of the delirium. In the midst of it, the chief actor made his appearance, waving his wand, like Prospero, to work new wonders. Dressed in a long robe of lilac-coloured silk richly embroidered with gold flowers, bearing in his hand a white magnetic rod, and with a look of dignity which would have sat well on an eastern caliph, he marched with solemn strides into the room. He awed the still sensible by his eye, and the violence of their symptoms diminished. He stroked the insensible with his hands upon the eye-brows and down the spine; traced figures upon their breast and abdomen with his long white wand, and they were restored to consciousness. They became calm, acknowledged his power, and said they felt streams of cold or burning vapour passing through their frames, according as he waved his wand or his fingers before them.

"It is impossible," says M. Dupotet, "to conceive the sensation which Mesmer's experiments created in Paris. No theological controversy, in the earlier ages of the Catholic Church, was ever conducted with greater bitterness." His adversaries denied the discovery; some calling him a quack, others a fool, and others again, like the Abbé Fiard, a man who had sold himself to the Devil! His friends were as extravagant in their praise, as his foes were in their censure. Paris was inundated with pamphlets upon the subject, as many defending as attacking the doctrine. At court, the queen expressed herself in favour of it, and nothing else was to be heard of in society.

By the advice of M. D'Eslon, Mesmer challenged an examination of his doctrine by the Faculty of Medicine. He proposed to select twenty-four patients, twelve of whom he would treat magnetically, leaving the other twelve to be treated by the faculty according to the old and approved methods. He also stipulated that, to prevent disputes, the government should nominate certain persons who were not physicians, to be present at the experiments; and that the object of the inquiry should be, not how these effects were produced, but whether they were really efficacious in the cure of any disease. The faculty objected to limit the inquiry in this manner, and the proposition fell to the ground.

Mesmer now wrote to Marie Antoinette, with the view of securing her influence in obtaining for him the protection of government. He wished to have a château and its lands given to him, with a handsome yearly income, that he might be enabled to continue his experiments at leisure, untroubled by the persecution of his enemies. He hinted the duty of governments to support men of science, and expressed his fear, that if he met no more encouragement, he should be compelled to carry his great discovery to some other land more willing to appreciate him. "In the eyes of your majesty," said he, "four or five hundred thousand francs, applied to a good purpose, are of no account. The welfare and happiness of your people are every thing. My discovery ought to be received and rewarded with a munificence worthy of the monarch to whom I shall attach myself." The government at last offered him a pension of twenty thousand francs, and the cross of the order of St. Michael, if he had made any discovery in medicine, and would communicate it to physicians nominated by the king. The latter part of the proposition was not agreeable to Mesmer. He feared the unfavourable report of the king's physicians; and, breaking off the negotiation, spoke of his disregard of money, and his wish to have his discovery at once recognised by the government. He then retired to Spa, in a fit of disgust, upon pretence of drinking the waters for the benefit of his health.

After he had left Paris, the Faculty of Medicine called upon M. D'Eslon, for the third and last time, to renounce the doctrine of animal magnetism, or be expelled from their body. M. D'Eslon, so far from doing this, declared that he had discovered new secrets, and solicited further examination. A royal commission of the Faculty of Medicine was, in consequence, appointed on the 12th of March 1784, seconded by another commission of the Académie des Sciences, to investigate the phenomena and report upon them. The first commission was composed of the principal physicians of Paris; while, among the eminent men comprised in the latter, were Benjamin Franklin, Lavoisier, and Bailly the historian of astronomy. Mesmer was formally invited to appear before this body, but absented himself from day to day, upon one pretence or another. M. D'Eslon was more honest, because he thoroughly believed in the phenomena, which it is to be questioned if Mesmer ever did, and regularly attended the sittings and performed experiments.

Bailly has thus described the scenes of which he was a witness in the course of this investigation. "The sick persons, arranged in great numbers and in several rows around the *baquet*, receive the magnetism, by all these means: by the iron rods which convey it to them from the *baquet*—by the cords wound round their bodies—by the connexion of the thumb, which conveys to them the magnetism of their neighbours—and by the sounds of a piano-forte, or of an agreeable voice, diffusing the magnetism in the air. The patients were also directly magnetised by means of the finger and wand of the magnetiser moved slowly before their faces, above or behind their heads, and on the diseased parts, always observing the direction of the holes. The magnetiser acts by fixing his eyes on them. But above all, they are magnetised by the application of his hands and the pressure of his fingers on the hypochondres and on the regions of the abdomen; an application often continued for a long time — sometimes for several hours.

"Meanwhile the patients in their different conditions present a very varied picture. Some are calm, tranquil, and experience no effect. Others cough, spit, feel slight pains, local or general heat, and have sweatings. Others again are agitated and tormented with convulsions. These convulsions are remarkable in regard to the number affected with them, to their duration and force. As soon as one begins to be convulsed, several others are affected. The commissioners have observed some of these convulsions last more than three hours. They are accompanied with expectorations of a muddy viscous water, brought away by violent efforts. Sometimes streaks of blood have been observed in this fluid. These convulsions are characterised by the precipitous, involuntary motion of all the limbs, and of the whole body; by the contraction of the throat — by the leaping motions of the hypochondria and the epigastrium — by the dimness and wandering of the eyes — by piercing shrieks, tears, sobbing, and immoderate laughter. They are preceded or followed by a state of languour or reverie, a kind of depression, and sometimes drowsiness. The smallest sudden noise occasions a shuddering; and it was remarked, that the change of measure in the airs played on the piano-forte had a great influence on the patients. A quicker motion, a livelier melody, agitated them more, and renewed the vivacity of their convulsions.

"Nothing is more astonishing than the spectacle of these convulsions. One who has not seen them can form no idea of them. The spectator is as much astonished at the profound repose of one portion of the patients as at the agitation of the rest — at the various accidents which are repeated, and at the sympathies which are exhibited. Some of the patients may be seen devoting their attention exclusively to one another, rushing towards each other with open arms, smiling, soothing, and manifesting every symptom of attachment and affection. All are under the power of the magnetiser; it matters not in what state of drowsiness they may be, the sound of his voice — a look, a motion of his hand — brings them out of it. Among the patients in convulsions there are always observed a great many women, and very few men."[72]

These experiments lasted for about five months. They had hardly commenced, before Mesmer, alarmed at the loss both of fame and profit, determined to return to Paris. Some patients of rank and fortune, enthusiastic believers in his doctrine, had followed him to Spa. One of them named Bergasse, proposed to open a subscription for him, of one hundred shares, at one hundred louis each, on condition that he would disclose his secret to the subscribers, who were to be permitted to make whatever use they pleased of it. Mesmer readily embraced the proposal; and such was the infatuation, that the subscription was not only filled in a few days, but exceeded by no less a sum than one hundred and forty thousand francs.

With this fortune he returned to Paris, and recommenced his experiments, while the royal commission continued theirs. His admiring pupils, who had paid him so handsomely for his instructions, spread his fame over the country, and established in all the principal towns of France, "Societies of Harmony," for trying experiments and curing all diseases by means of magnetism. Some of these societies were a scandal to morality, being joined by profligate men of depraved appetites, who took a disgusting delight in witnessing young girls in convulsions. Many of the pretended magnetisers were asserted at the time to be notorious libertines, who took that opportunity of gratifying their passions.

At last the commissioners published their report, which was drawn up by the illustrious and unfortunate Bailly. For clearness of reasoning and strict impartiality it has never been surpassed. After detailing the various experiments made, and their results, they came to the conclusion that the only proof advanced in support of animal magnetism was the effects it produced on the human body—that those effects could be produced without passes or other magnetic manipulations—that all these manipulations and passes and ceremonies never produce any effect at all if employed without the patient's knowledge; and that therefore imagination did, and animal magnetism did not, account for the phenomena.

This report was the ruin of Mesmer's reputation in France. He quitted Paris shortly after, with the three hundred and forty thousand francs which had been subscribed by his admirers, and retired to his own country, where he died in 1815, at the advanced age of eighty-one. But the seeds he had sown fructified of themselves, nourished and brought to maturity by the kindly warmth of popular credulity. Imitators sprang up in France, Germany, and England, more extravagant than their master, and claiming powers for the new science which its founder had never dreamt of. Among others, Cagliostro made good use of the delusion in extending his claims to be considered a master of the occult sciences. But he made no discoveries worthy to be compared to those of the Marquis de Puysegur and the Chevalier Barbarin, honest men, who began by deceiving themselves before they deceived others.

The Marquis de Puysegur, the owner of a considerable estate at Busancy, was one of those who had entered into the subscription for Mesmer. After that individual had quitted France, he retired to Busancy, with his brother, to try animal magnetism upon his tenants, and cure the country people of all manner of diseases. He was a man of great simplicity and much benevolence, and not only magnetised but fed the sick that flocked around him. In all the neighbourhood, and indeed within a circumference of twenty miles, he was looked upon as endowed with a power almost divine. His great discovery, as he called it, was made by chance. One day he had magnetised his gardener; and observing him to fall into a deep sleep, it occurred to him that he would address a question to him, as he would have done to a natural somnambulist. He did so, and the man replied with much clearness and precision. M. de Puysegur was agreeably surprised: he continued his experiments, and found that, in this state of magnetic somnambulism, *the soul of the sleeper was enlarged, and brought into more intimate communion with all nature, and more especially with him, M. de Puysegur.* He found that all further manipulations were unnecessary; that, without speaking or making any sign, he could convey his will to the patient; that he could, in fact, converse with him, soul to soul, without the employment of any physical operation whatever!

Simultaneously with this marvellous discovery he made another, which reflects equal credit upon his understanding. Like Valentine Greatraks, he found it hard work to magnetise all that came—that he had not even time to take the repose and relaxation which were necessary for his health. In this emergency he hit upon a clever expedient. He had heard Mesmer say that he could magnetise bits of wood: why should he not be able to magnetise a whole tree? It was no sooner thought than done. There was a large elm on the village green at Busancy, under which the peasant girls used to dance on festive occasions, and the old men to sit, drinking their *vin du pays*, on the fine summer evenings. M. de Puysegur proceeded to this tree and magnetised it, by first touching it with his hands, and then retiring a few steps from it; all the while directing streams of the magnetic fluid from the branches toward the trunk, and from the trunk toward the root. This done, he caused circular seats to be erected round it, and cords suspended from it in all directions. When the patients had seated themselves, they twisted the cords round the diseased parts of their bodies, and held one another firmly by their thumbs to form a direct channel of communication for the passage of the fluid.

M. de Puysegur had now two "hobbies"—the man with the enlarged soul and the magnetic elm. The infatuation of himself and his patients cannot be better expressed than in his own words. Writing to his brother, on the 17th of May 1784, he says, "If you do not come, my dear friend, you will not see my extraordinary man, for his health is now almost quite restored. I continue to make use of the happy power for which I am indebted to M. Mesmer. Every day I bless his name; for I am very useful, and produce many salutary effects on all the sick poor in the neighbourhood. They flock around my tree; there were more than one hundred and thirty of them this morning. It is the best *baquet* possible; *not a leaf of it but communicates health!* all feel, more or less, the good effects of it. You will be delighted to see the charming picture of humanity which this presents. I have only one regret — it is, that I cannot touch all who come. But my magnetised man — my intelligence — sets me at ease. He teaches me what conduct I should adopt. According to him, it is not at all necessary that I should touch every one; a look, a gesture, even a wish, is sufficient. And it is one of the most ignorant peasants of the country that teaches me this! When he is in a crisis, I know of nothing more profound, more prudent, more clearsighted (*clairvoyant*) than he is."

In another letter, describing his first experiment with the magnetic tree, he says, "Yesterday evening I brought my first patient to it. As soon as I had put the cord round him he gazed at the tree; and, with an air of astonishment which I cannot describe, exclaimed, 'What is it that I see there?' His head then sunk down, and he fell into a perfect fit of somnambulism. At the end of an hour, I took him home to his house again, when I restored him to his senses. Several men and women came to tell him what he had been doing. He maintained it was not true; that, weak as he was, and scarcely able to walk, it would have been scarcely possible for him to have gone down stairs and walked to the tree. To-day I have repeated the experiment on him, and with the same success. I own to you that my head turns round with pleasure to think of the good I do. Madame de Puysegur, the friends she has with her, my servants, and, in fact, all who are near me, feel an amazement, mingled with admiration, which cannot be described; but they do not experience the half of my sensations. Without my tree, which gives me rest, and which will give me still more, I should be in a state of agitation, inconsistent, I believe, with my health. I exist too much, if I may be allowed to use the expression."

In another letter, he descants still more poetically upon his gardener with the enlarged soul. He says, "It is from this simple man, this tall and stout rustic, twenty-three years of age, enfeebled by disease, or rather by sorrow, and therefore the more predisposed to be affected by any great natural agent, — it is from this man, I repeat, that I derive instruction and knowledge. When in the magnetic state, he is no longer a peasant who can hardly utter a single sentence; he is a being, to describe whom I cannot find a name. I need not speak; *I have only to think before him, when he instantly understands and answers me.* Should any body come into the room, he sees him, if I desire it (but not else), and addresses him, and says what I wish to say; not indeed exactly as I dictate to him, but as truth requires. When he wants to add more than I deem it prudent strangers should hear, I stop the flow of his ideas, and of his conversation in the middle of a word, and give it quite a different turn!"

Among other persons attracted to Busancy by the report of these extraordinary occurrences was M. Cloquet, the Receiver of Finance. His appetite for the marvellous being somewhat insatiable, he readily believed all that was told him by M. de Puysegur. He also has left a record of what he saw, and what he credited, which throws a still clearer light upon the progress of the delusion.[73] He says that the patients he saw in the magnetic state had an appearance of deep sleep, during which all the physical faculties were suspended, to the advantage of the intellectual faculties. The eyes of the patients were closed, the sense of hearing was abolished; and they awoke only at the voice of their magnetiser. "If any one touched a patient during a crisis, or even the chair on which he was seated," says M. Cloquet, "it would cause him much pain and suffering, and throw him into convulsions. During the crisis, they possess an extraordinary and supernatural power, by which, on touching a patient presented to them, they can feel what part of his body is diseased, even by merely passing their hand over the clothes." Another singularity was, that these sleepers who could thus discover diseases, see into the interior of other men's stomachs, and point out remedies, remembered absolutely nothing after the magnetiser thought proper to disenchant them. The time that elapsed between their entering the crisis and their coming out of it was obliterated. Not only had the magnetiser the power of making himself heard by the somnambulists, but he could make them follow him by merely pointing his finger at them from a distance, though they had their eyes the whole time completely closed.

Such was animal magnetism under the auspices of the Marquis de Puysegur. While he was exhibiting these phenomena around his elm-tree, a magnetiser of another class appeared in Lyons, in the person of the Chevalier de Barbarin. This gentleman thought the effort of the will, without any of the paraphernalia of wands or *baquets*, was sufficient to throw patients into the magnetic sleep. He tried it and succeeded. By sitting at the bedside of his patients, and praying that they might be magnetised, they went off into a state very similar to that of the persons who fell under the notice of M. de Puysegur. In the course of time a very considerable number of magnetisers, acknowledging Barbarin for their model, and called after him Barbarinists, appeared in different parts, and were believed to have effected some remarkable cures. In Sweden and Germany this sect of fanatics increased rapidly, and were called *spiritualists*, to distinguish them from the followers of M. de Puysegur, who were called *experimentalists*. They maintained that all the effects of animal magnetism, which Mesmer believed to be producible by a magnetic fluid dispersed through nature, were produced by the mere effort of one human soul acting upon another; that when a connexion had once been established between a magnetiser and his patient, the former could communicate his influence to the latter from any distance, even hundreds of miles, by the will. One of them thus described the blessed state of a magnetic patient: "In such a man animal instinct ascends to the highest degree admissible in this world. The *clairvoyant* is then a pure animal, without any admixture of matter. His observations are those of a spirit. He is similar to God: his eye penetrates all the secrets of nature. When his attention is fixed on any of the objects of this world — on his disease, his death, his well-beloved, his friends, his relations, his enemies — in spirit he sees them acting; he penetrates into the causes and the consequences of their actions; he becomes a physician, a prophet, a divine!"[74]

Let us now see what progress these mysteries made in England. In the year 1788 Dr. Mainauduc, who had been a pupil, first of Mesmer, and afterwards of D'Eslon, arrived in Bristol, and gave public lectures upon magnetism. His success was quite extraordinary. People of rank and fortune hastened from London to Bristol to be magnetised, or to place themselves under his tuition.

Dr. George Winter, in his *History of Animal Magnetism*, gives the following list of them: "They amounted to one hundred and twenty-seven, among whom there were one duke, one duchess, one marchioness, two countesses, one earl, one baron, three baronesses, one bishop, five right honourable gentlemen and ladies, two baronets, seven members of parliament, one clergyman, two physicians, seven surgeons, besides ninety-two gentlemen and ladies of respectability." He afterwards established himself in London, where he performed with equal success.

He began by publishing proposals to the ladies for the formation of a Hygeian Society. In this paper he vaunted highly the curative effects of animal magnetism, and took great credit to himself for being the first person to introduce it into England, and thus concluded: "As this method of cure is not confined to sex or college education, and the fair sex being in general the most sympathising part of the creation, and most immediately concerned in the health and care of its offspring, I think myself bound in gratitude to you, ladies, for the partiality you have shewn me in midwifery, to contribute, as far as lies in my power, to render you additionally useful and valuable to the community. With this view I propose forming my Hygeian Society, to be incorporated with that of Paris. As soon as twenty ladies have given in their names, the day shall be appointed for the first meeting at my house, when they are to pay fifteen guineas, which will include the whole expense."

Hannah More, in a letter addressed to Horace Walpole in September 1788, speaks of the "demoniacal mummeries" of Dr. Mainauduc, and says he was in a fair way of gaining a hundred thousand pounds by them, as Mesmer had done by his exhibitions in Paris.

So much curiosity was excited by the subject, that, about the same time, a man named Holloway gave a course of lectures on animal magnetism in London, at the rate of five guineas for each pupil, and realised a considerable fortune. Loutherbourg the painter and his wife followed the same profitable trade; and such was the infatuation of the people to be witnesses of their strange manipulations, that at times upwards of three thousand persons crowded around their house at Hammersmith, unable to gain admission. The tickets sold at prices varying from one to three guineas. Loutherbourg performed his cures by the touch, after the manner of Valentine Greatraks, and finally pretended to a divine mission. An account of his miracles, as they were called, was published in 1789, entitled *A List of New Cures performed by Mr. and Mrs. de Loutherbourg, of Hammersmith Terrace, without Medicine; by a Lover of the Lamb of God. Dedicated to his Grace the Archbishop of Canterbury.*

This "Lover of the Lamb of God" was a half-crazy old woman, named Mary Pratt, who conceived for Mr. and Mrs. de Loutherbourg a veneration which almost prompted her to worship them. She chose for the motto of her pamphlet a verse in the thirteenth chapter of the Acts of the Apostles: "Behold, ye despisers, and wonder and perish! for I will work a work in your days which ye shall not believe, though a man declare it unto you." Attempting to give a religious character to the cures of the painter, she thought a *woman* was the proper person to make them known, since the apostle had declared that a *man* should not be able to conquer the incredulity of the people. She stated, that from Christmas 1788 to July 1789, De Loutherbourg and his wife had cured two thousand people, "having been made *proper recipients to receive divine manuductions*; which heavenly and divine influx, coming from the radix *God*, his Divine Majesty had most graciously bestowed upon them to diffuse healing to all, be they deaf, dumb, blind, lame, or halt."

In her dedication to the Archbishop of Canterbury she implored him to compose a new form of prayer, to be used in all churches and chapels, that nothing might impede this inestimable gift from having its due course. She further entreated all the magistrates and men of authority in the land to wait on Mr. and Mrs. de Loutherbourg, to consult with them on the immediate erection of a large hospital, with a pool of Bethesda attached to it. All the magnetisers were scandalised at the preposterous jabber of this old woman, and De Loutherbourg appears to have left London to avoid her, — continuing, however, in conjunction with his wife, the fantastic tricks which had turned the brain of this poor fanatic, and deluded many others who pretended to more sense than she had.

From this period until 1798 magnetism excited little or no attention in England. An attempt to revive the belief in it was made in that year, but it was in the shape of mineral rather than of animal magnetism. One Benjamin Douglas Perkins, an American, practising as a surgeon in Leicester Square, invented and took out a patent for the celebrated "Metallic Tractors." He pretended that these tractors, which were two small pieces of metal strongly magnetised, something resembling the steel plates which were first brought into notice by Father Hell, would cure gout, rheumatism, palsy, and, in fact, almost every disease the human frame was subject to, if applied externally to the afflicted part, and moved about gently, touching the surface only. The most wonderful stories soon obtained general circulation, and the press groaned with pamphlets, all vaunting the curative effects of the tractors, which were sold at five guineas the pair. Perkins gained money rapidly. Gouty subjects forgot their pains in the presence of this new remedy; the rheumatism fled at its approach; and toothache, which is often cured by the mere sight of a dentist, vanished before Perkins and his marvellous steel-plates. The benevolent Society of Friends, of whose body he was a member, warmly patronised the invention. Desirous that the poor, who could not afford to pay Mr. Perkins five guineas, or even five shillings for his tractors, should also share in the benefits of that sublime discovery, they subscribed a large sum, and built an hospital, called the "Perkinean Institution," in which all comers might be magnetised free of cost. In the course of a few months they were in very general use, and their lucky inventor in possession of five thousand pounds.

Dr. Haygarth, an eminent physician at Bath, recollecting the influence of imagination in the cure of disease, hit upon an expedient to try the real value of the tractors. Perkins's cures were too well established to be doubted; and Dr. Haygarth, without gain-saying them, quietly, but in the face of numerous witnesses, exposed the delusion under which people laboured with respect to the curative medium. He suggested to Dr. Falconer that they should make wooden tractors, paint them to resemble the steel ones, and see if the very same effects would not be produced. Five patients were chosen from the hospital in Bath, upon whom to operate. Four of them suffered severely from chronic rheumatism in the ankle, knee, wrist, and hip; and the fifth had been afflicted for several months with the gout. On the day appointed for the experiments Dr. Haygarth and his friends assembled at the hospital, and with much solemnity brought forth the fictitious tractors. Four out of the five patients said their pains were immediately relieved; and three of them said they were not only relieved but very much benefited. One felt his knee warmer, and said he could walk across the room. He tried and succeeded, although on the previous day he had not been able to stir. The gouty man felt his pains diminish rapidly, and was quite easy for nine hours, until he went to bed, when the twitching began again. On the following day the real tractors were applied to all the patients, when they described their symptoms in nearly the same terms.

To make still more sure, the experiment was tried in the Bristol infirmary, a few weeks afterwards, on a man who had a rheumatic affection in the shoulder, so severe as to incapacitate him from lifting his hand from his knee. The fictitious tractors were brought and applied to the afflicted part, one of the physicians, to add solemnity to the scene, drawing a stop-watch from his pocket to calculate the time exactly, while another, with a pen in his hand, sat down to write the change of symptoms from minute to minute as they occurred. In less than four minutes the man felt so much relieved, that he lifted his hand several inches without any pain in the shoulder!

An account of these matters was published by Dr. Haygarth, in a small volume entitled, *Of the Imagination, as a Cause and Cure of Disorders, exemplified by fictitious Tractors*. The exposure was a *coup de grace* to the system of Mr. Perkins. His friends and patrons, still unwilling to confess that they had been deceived, tried the tractors upon sheep, cows, and horses, alleging that the animals received benefit from the metallic plates, but none at all from the wooden ones. But they found nobody to believe them; the Perkinean institution fell into neglect; and Perkins made his exit from England, carrying with him about ten thousand pounds, to soothe his declining years in the good city of Pennsylvania.

Thus was magnetism laughed out of England for a time. In France the revolution left men no leisure for studying it. The *Sociétés de l'Harmonie* of Strasbourg, and other great towns lingered for a while, till sterner matters occupying men's attention, they were one after the other abandoned, both by pupils and professors. The system, thus driven from the first two nations of Europe, took refuge among the dreamy philosophers of Germany. There the wonders of the magnetic sleep grew more and more wonderful every day; the patients acquired the gift of prophecy; their vision extended over all the surface of the globe; they could hear and see with their toes and fingers, and read unknown languages, and understand them too, by merely having the book placed on their stomachs. Ignorant peasants, when once entranced by the grand mesmeric fluid, could spout philosophy diviner than Plato ever wrote, descant upon the mysteries of the mind with more eloquence and truth than the profoundest metaphysicians the world ever saw, and solve knotty points of divinity with as much ease as waking men could undo their shoe-buckles!

During the first twelve years of the present century little was heard of animal magnetism in any country of Europe. Even the Germans forgot their airy fancies, recalled to the knowledge of this every-day world by the roar of Napoleon's cannon and the fall or the establishment of kingdoms. During this period a cloud of obscurity hung over the science, which was not dispersed until M. Deleuze published, in 1813, his *Histoire Critique du Magnétisme Animal*. This work gave a new impulse to the half-forgotten fancy. Newspapers, pamphlets, and books again waged war upon each other on the question of its truth or falsehood; and many eminent men in the profession of medicine recommended inquiry with an earnest design to discover the truth.

The assertions made in the celebrated treatise of Deleuze are thus summed up:[75] "There is a fluid continually escaping from the human body," and "forming an atmosphere around us," which, as "it has no determined current," produces no sensible effects on surrounding individuals. It is, however, "capable of being directed by the will;" and, when so directed, "is sent forth in currents," with a force corresponding to the energy we possess. Its motion is "similar to that of the rays from burning bodies;" "it possesses different qualities in different individuals." It is capable of a high degree of concentration, "and exists also in trees." The will of the magnetiser, "guided by a motion of the hand, several times repeated in the same direction," can fill a tree with this fluid. Most persons, when this fluid is poured into them from the body and by the will of the magnetiser, "feel a sensation of heat or cold" when he passes his hand before them, without even touching them. Some persons, when sufficiently charged with this fluid, fall into a state of somnambulism, or magnetic ecstasy; and when in this state, "they see the fluid encircling the magnetiser like a halo of light, and issuing in luminous streams from his mouth and nostrils, his head and hands, possessing a very agreeable smell, and communicating a particular taste to food and water."

One would think that these "notions" were quite enough to be insisted upon by any physician who wished to be considered sane; but they form only a small portion of the wondrous things related by M. Deleuze. He further said, "When magnetism produces somnambulism, the person who is in this state acquires a prodigious extension of all his faculties. Several of his external organs, especially those of sight and hearing, become inactive; but the sensations which depend upon them take place internally. Seeing and hearing are carried on by the magnetic fluid, which transmits the impressions immediately, and without the intervention of any nerves or organs directly to the brain. Thus the somnambulist, though his eyes and ears are closed, not only sees and hears, but sees and hears much better than he does when awake. In all things he feels the will of the magnetiser, although that will be not expressed. He sees into the interior of his own body, and the most secret organisation of the bodies of all those who may be put *en rapport*, or in magnetic connexion, with him. Most commonly, he only sees those parts which are diseased and disordered, and intuitively prescribes a remedy for them. He has prophetic visions and sensations, which are generally true, but sometimes erroneous. He expresses himself with astonishing eloquence and facility. He is not free from vanity. He becomes a more perfect being of his own accord for a certain time, if guided wisely by the magnetiser, but wanders if he is ill-directed."

According to M. Deleuze, any person could become a magnetiser and produce these effects, by conforming to the following conditions, and acting upon the following rules:

*"Forget for a while all your knowledge of physics and metaphysics.*

*"Remove from your mind all objections that may occur.*

*"Imagine that it is in your power to take the malady in hand, and throw it on one side.*

*"Never reason for six weeks after you have commenced the study.*

*"Have an active desire to do good; a firm belief in the power of magnetism, and an entire confidence in employing it. In short, repel all doubts; desire success, and act with simplicity and attention."*

That is to say, "be very credulous; be very persevering; reject all past experience, and do not listen to reason," and you are a magnetiser after M. Deleuze's own heart.

Having brought yourself into this edifying state, "remove from the patient all persons who might be troublesome to you; keep with you only the necessary witnesses — a single person if need be; desire them not to occupy themselves in any way with the processes you employ and the effects which result from them, but to join with you in the desire of doing good to your patient. Arrange yourself so as neither to be too hot nor too cold, and in such a manner that nothing may obstruct the freedom of your motions; and take precautions to prevent interruption during the sitting. Make your patient then sit as commodiously as possible, and place yourself opposite to him, on a seat a little more elevated, in such a manner that his knees may be betwixt yours, and your feet at the side of his. First, request him to resign himself; to think of nothing; not to perplex himself by examining the effects which may be produced; to banish all fear; to surrender himself to hope, and not to be disturbed or discouraged if the action of magnetism should cause in him momentary pains. After having collected yourself, take his thumbs between your fingers in such a way that the internal part of your thumbs may be in contact with the internal part of his, *and then fix your eyes upon him*! You must remain from two to five minutes in this situation, or until you feel an equal heat between your thumbs and his. This done, you will withdraw your hands, removing them to the right and left; and at the same time turning them till their internal surface be outwards, and you will raise them to the height of the head. You will now place them upon the two shoulders, and let them remain there about a minute; afterwards drawing them gently along the arms to the extremities of the fingers, touching very slightly as you go. You will renew this pass five or six times, always turning your hands, and removing them a little from the body before you lift them. You will then place them above the head; and after holding them there for an instant, lower them, passing them before the face, at the distance of one or two inches, down to the pit of the stomach. There you will stop them two minutes also, putting your thumbs upon the pit of the stomach and the rest of your fingers below the ribs. You will then descend slowly along the body to the knees, or rather, if you can do so without deranging yourself, to the extremity of the feet. You will repeat the same processes several times during the remainder of the sitting. You will also occasionally approach your patient, so as to place your hands behind his shoulders, in order to descend slowly along the spine of the back and the thighs, down to the knees or the feet. After the first passes, you may dispense with putting your hands upon the head, and may make the subsequent passes upon the arms, beginning at the shoulders, and upon the body, beginning at the stomach."

Such was the process of magnetising recommended by Deleuze. That delicate, fanciful, and nervous women, when subjected to it, should have worked themselves into convulsions will be readily believed by the sturdiest opponent of animal magnetism. To sit in a constrained posture—be stared out of countenance by a fellow who enclosed her knees between his, while he made *passes* upon different parts of her body, was quite enough to throw any weak woman into a fit, especially if she were predisposed to hysteria, and believed in the efficacy of the treatment. It is just as evident that those of stronger minds and healthier bodies should be sent to sleep by the process. That these effects have been produced by these means, there are thousands of instances to shew. But are they testimony in favour of animal magnetism?—do they prove the existence of the magnetic fluid? It needs neither magnetism, nor ghost from the grave, to tell us that silence, monotony, and long recumbency in one position, must produce sleep; or that excitement, imitation, and a strong imagination acting upon a weak body, will bring on convulsions.

M. Deleuze's book produced quite a sensation in France; the study was resumed with redoubled vigour. In the following year, a journal was established devoted exclusively to the science, under the title of *Annales du Magnétisme Animal*; and shortly afterwards appeared the *Bibliothèque du Magnétisme Animal*, and many others. About the same time, the Abbé Faria, "the man of wonders," began to magnetise; and the belief being that he had more of the mesmeric fluid about him, and a stronger will, than most men, he was very successful in his treatment. His experiments afford a convincing proof that imagination can operate all, and the supposed fluid none, of the results so confidently claimed as evidence of the new science. He placed his patients in an arm-chair; told them to shut their eyes; and then, in a loud commanding voice, pronounced the single word, "Sleep!" He used no manipulations whatever—had no *baquet*, or conductor of the fluid; but he nevertheless succeeded in causing sleep in hundreds of patients. He boasted of having in his time produced five thousand somnambulists by this method. It was often necessary to repeat the command three or four times; and if the patient still remained awake, the abbé got out of the difficulty by dismissing him from the chair, and declaring that he was incapable of being acted on. And it should be especially remarked that the magnetisers do not lay claim to universal efficacy for their fluid; the strong and the healthy cannot be magnetised; the incredulous cannot be magnetised; those who reason upon it cannot be magnetised; those who firmly believe in it can be magnetised; the weak in body can be magnetised, and the weak in mind can be magnetised. And lest, from some cause or other, individuals of the latter classes should resist the magnetic charm, the apostles of the science declare that there are times when even *they* cannot be acted upon; the presence of one scorner or unbeliever may weaken the potency of the fluid and destroy its efficacy. In M. Deleuze's instructions to a magnetiser, he expressly says, "Never magnetise before inquisitive persons!"[76]

Here we conclude the subject, as it would serve no good purpose to extend to greater length the history of Animal Magnetism; especially at a time when many phenomena, the reality of which it is impossible to dispute, are daily occurring to startle and perplex the most learned, impartial, and truth-loving of mankind. Enough, however, has been stated to shew, that if there be some truth in magnetism, there has been much error, misconception, and exaggeration. Taking its history from the commencement, it can hardly be said to have been without its uses. To quote the words of Bailly, in 1784, "Magnetism has not been altogether unavailing to the philosophy which condemns it: it is an additional fact to record among the errors of the human mind, and a great experiment on the strength of the imagination." Over that vast inquiry of the influence of mind over matter, — an inquiry which the embodied intellect of mankind will never be able to fathom completely, — it will at least have thrown a feeble and imperfect light. It will have afforded an additional proof of the strength of the unconquerable will, and the weakness of matter as compared with it; another illustration of the words of the inspired Psalmist, that "we are fearfully and wonderfully made."

# Chapter 8.

Influence Of Politics And Religion On The Hair And Beard.

*Speak with respect and honour*
*Both of the beard and the beard's owner.*

**Hudibras.**

The famous declaration of St. Paul, "that long hair was a shame unto a man," has been made the pretext for many singular enactments, both of civil and ecclesiastical governments. The fashion of the hair and the cut of the beard were state questions in France and England, from the establishment of Christianity until the fifteenth century.

We find, too, that in much earlier times, men were not permitted to do as they liked with their own hair. Alexander the Great thought that the beards of the soldiery afforded convenient handles for the enemy to lay hold of, preparatory to cutting off their heads; and, with a view of depriving them of this advantage, he ordered the whole of his army to be closely shaven. His notions of courtesy towards an enemy were quite different from those entertained by the North American Indians, and amongst whom it is held a point of honour to allow one "chivalrous lock" to grow, that the foe, in taking the scalp, may have something to catch hold of.

At one time, long hair was the symbol of sovereignty in Europe. We learn from Gregory of Tours, that, among the successors of Clovis, it was the exclusive privilege of the royal family to have their hair long and curled. The nobles, equal to kings in power, would not shew any inferiority in this respect, and wore not only their hair, but their beards of an enormous length. This fashion lasted, with but slight changes, till the time of Louis the Debonnaire; but his successors, up to Hugh Capet, wore their hair short, by way of distinction. Even the serfs had set all regulation at defiance, and allowed their locks and beards to grow.

At the time of the invasion of England by William the Conqueror, the Normans wore their hair very short. Harold, in his progress towards Hastings, sent forward spies to view the strength and number of the enemy. They reported, amongst other things, on their return, that "the host did almost seem to be priests, because they had all their face and both their lips shaven." The fashion among the English at the time was to wear the hair long upon the head and the upper lip, but to shave the chin. When the haughty victors had divided the broad lands of the Saxon thanes and franklins among them, when tyranny of every kind was employed to make the English feel that they were indeed a subdued and broken nation, the latter encouraged the growth of their hair, that they might resemble as little as possible their cropped and shaven masters.

This fashion was exceedingly displeasing to the clergy, and prevailed to a considerable extent in France and Germany. Towards the end of the eleventh century, it was decreed by the pope, and zealously supported by the ecclesiastical authorities all over Europe, that such persons as wore long hair should be excommunicated while living, and not be prayed for when dead. William of Malmesbury relates, that the famous St. Wulstan, Bishop of Worcester, was peculiarly indignant whenever he saw a man with long hair. He declaimed against the practice as one highly immoral, criminal, and beastly. He continually carried a small knife in his pocket, and whenever any body offending in this respect knelt before him to receive his blessing, he would whip it out slily, and cut off a handful, and then, throwing it in his face, tell him to cut off all the rest, or he would go to hell.

But fashion, which at times it is possible to move with a wisp, stands firm against a lever; and men preferred to run the risk of damnation to parting with the superfluity of their hair. In the time of Henry I., Anselm, Archbishop of Canterbury, found it necessary to republish the famous decree of excommunication and outlawry against the offenders; but, as the court itself had begun to patronise curls, the fulminations of the Church were unavailing. Henry I. and his nobles wore their hair in long ringlets down their backs and shoulders, and became a *scandalum magnatum* in the eyes of the godly. One Serlo, the king's chaplain, was so grieved in spirit at the impiety of his master, that he preached a sermon from the well-known text of St. Paul before the assembled court, in which he drew so dreadful a picture of the torments that awaited them in the other world, that several of them burst into tears, and wrung their hair, as if they would have pulled it out by the roots. Henry himself was observed to weep. The priest, seeing the impression he had made, determined to strike while the iron was hot, and pulling a pair of scissors from his pocket, cut the king's hair in presence of them all. Several of the principal courtiers consented to do the like, and for a short time long hair appeared to be going out of fashion. But the courtiers thought, after the first glow of their penitence had been cooled by reflection, that the clerical Delilah had shorn them of their strength, and in less than six months they were as great sinners as ever.

Anselm, the Archbishop of Canterbury, who had been a monk of Bec, in Normandy, and who had signalised himself at Rouen by his fierce opposition to long hair, was still anxious to work a reformation in this matter. But his pertinacity was far from pleasing to the king, who had finally made up his mind to wear ringlets. There were other disputes, of a more serious nature, between them; so that when the archbishop died, the king was so glad to be rid of him, that he allowed the see to remain vacant for five years. Still the cause had other advocates, and every pulpit in the land resounded with anathemas against that disobedient and long-haired generation. But all was of no avail. Stowe, in writing of this period, asserts, on the authority of some more ancient chronicler, "that men, forgetting their birth, transformed themselves, by the length of their haires, into the semblance of woman kind;" and that when their hair decayed from age, or other causes, "they knit about their heads certain rolls and braidings of false hair." At last accident turned the tide of fashion. A knight of the court, who was exceedingly proud of his beauteous locks, dreamed one night that, as he lay in bed, the devil sprang upon him, and endeavoured to choke him with his own hair. He started in affright, and actually found that he had a great quantity of hair in his mouth. Sorely stricken in conscience, and looking upon the dream as a warning from heaven, he set about the work of reformation, and cut off his luxuriant tresses the same night. The story was soon bruited abroad; of course it was made the most of by the clergy, and the knight, being a man of influence and consideration, and the acknowledged leader of the fashion, his example, aided by priestly exhortations, was very generally imitated. Men appeared almost as decent as St. Wulstan himself could have wished, the dream of a dandy having proved more efficacious than the entreaties of a saint. But, as Stowe informs us, "scarcely was one year past, when all that thought themselves courtiers fell into the former vice, and contended with women in their long haires." Henry, the king, appears to have been quite uninfluenced by the dreams of others, for even his own would not induce him a second time to undergo a cropping from priestly shears. It is said, that he was much troubled at this time by disagreeable visions. Having offended the Church in this and other respects, he could get no sound, refreshing sleep, and used to imagine that he saw all the bishops, abbots, and monks of every degree, standing around his bedside, and threatening to belabour him with their pastoral staves; which sight, we are told, so frightened him, that he often started naked out of his bed, and attacked the phantoms sword in hand. Grimbalde, his physician, who, like most of his fraternity at that day, was an ecclesiastic, never hinted that his dreams were the result of a bad digestion, but told him to shave his head, be reconciled to the Church, and reform himself with alms and prayer. But he would not take this good advice, and it was not until he had been nearly drowned a year afterwards, in a violent storm at sea, that he repented of his evil ways, cut his hair short, and paid proper deference to the wishes of the clergy.

In France, the thunders of the Vatican with regard to long curly hair were hardly more respected than in England. Louis VII., however, was more obedient than his brother-king, and cropped himself as closely as a monk, to the great sorrow of all the gallants of his court. His queen, the gay, haughty, and pleasure-seeking Eleanor of Guienne, never admired him in this trim, and continually reproached him with imitating, not only the head-dress, but the asceticism of the monks. From this cause a coldness arose between them. The lady proving at last unfaithful to her shaven and indifferent lord, they were divorced, and the kings of France lost the rich provinces of Guienne and Poitou, which were her dowry. She soon after bestowed her hand and her possessions upon Henry Duke of Normandy, afterwards Henry II. of England, and thus gave the English sovereigns that strong footing in France which was for so many centuries the cause of such long and bloody wars between the nations. When the Crusades had drawn all the smart young fellows into Palestine, the clergy did not find it so difficult to convince the staid burghers who remained in Europe, of the enormity of long hair. During the absence of Richard Cœur de Lion, his English subjects not only cut their hair close, but shaved their faces. William Fitz-osbert, or Long-beard, the great demagogue of that day, reintroduced among the people who claimed to be of Saxon origin the fashion of long hair. He did this with the view of making them as unlike as possible to the citizens and the Normans. He wore his own beard hanging down to his waist, from whence the name by which he is best known to posterity.

The Church never shewed itself so great an enemy to the beard as to long hair on the head. It generally allowed fashion to take its own course, both with regard to the chin and the upper lip. This fashion varied continually; for we find that, in little more than a century after the time of Richard I., when beards were short, that they had again become so long as to be mentioned in the famous epigram made by the Scots who visited London in 1327, when David, son of Robert Bruce, was married to Joan, the sister of King Edward. This epigram, which was stuck on the church-door of St. Peter Stangale, ran as follows:

> *"Long beards heartlesse,*
> *Painted hoods witlesse,*
> *Gray coats gracelesse,*
> *Make England thriftlesse."*

When the Emperor Charles V. ascended the throne of Spain he had no beard. It was not to be expected that the obsequious parasites who always surround a monarch, could presume to look more virile than their master. Immediately all the courtiers appeared beardless, with the exception of such few grave old men as had outgrown the influence of fashion, and who had determined to die bearded as they had lived. Sober people in general saw this revolution with sorrow and alarm, and thought that every manly virtue would be banished with the beard. It became at the time a common saying, —

> *"Desde que no hay barba, no hay mas alma."*
> *We have no longer souls since we have lost our beards.*

In France also the beard fell into disrepute after the death of Henry IV., from the mere reason that his successor was too young to have one. Some of the more immediate friends of the great Béarnais, and his minister Sully among the rest, refused to part with their beards, notwithstanding the jeers of the new generation.

Who does not remember the division of England into the two great parties of Roundheads and Cavaliers? In those days every species of vice and iniquity was thought by the Puritans to lurk in the long curly tresses of the monarchists, while the latter imagined that their opponents were as destitute of wit, of wisdom, and of virtue, as they were of hair. A man's locks were the symbol of his creed, both in politics and religion. The more abundant the hair, the more scant the faith; and the balder the head, the more sincere the piety.

*Peter the Great.*

But among all the instances of the interference of governments with men's hair, the most extraordinary, not only for its daring, but for its success, is that of Peter the Great, in 1705. By this time fashion had condemned the beard in every other country in Europe, and with a voice more potent than popes or emperors, had banished it from civilised society. But this only made the Russians cling more fondly to their ancient ornament, as a mark to distinguish them from foreigners, whom they hated. Peter, however, resolved that they should be shaven. If he had been a man deeply read in history, he might have hesitated before he attempted so despotic an attack upon the time-hallowed customs and prejudices of his countrymen; but he was not. He did not know or consider the danger of the innovation; he only listened to the promptings of his own indomitable will, and his fiat went forth, that not only the army, but all ranks of citizens, from the nobles to the serfs, should shave their beards. A certain time was given, that people might get over the first throes of their repugnance, after which every man who chose to retain his beard was to pay a tax of one hundred roubles. The priests and the serfs were put on a lower footing, and allowed to retain theirs upon payment of a copeck every time they passed the gate of a city. Great discontent existed in consequence, but the dreadful fate of the Strelitzes was too recent to be forgotten, and thousands who had the will had not the courage to revolt. As is well remarked by a writer in the *Encyclopædia Britannica*, they thought it wiser to cut off their beards than to run the risk of incensing a man who would make no scruple in cutting off their heads. Wiser, too, than the popes and bishops of a former age, he did not threaten them with eternal damnation, but made them pay in hard cash the penalty of their disobedience. For many years, a very considerable revenue was collected from this source. The collectors gave in receipt for its payment a small copper coin, struck expressly for the purpose, and called the "*borodováia*," or "the bearded." On one side it bore the figure of a nose, mouth, and moustaches, with a long bushy beard, surmounted by the words, "*Deuyee Vyeatee*," "money received;" the whole encircled by a wreath, and stamped with the black eagle of Russia. On the reverse, it bore the date of the year. Every man who chose to wear a beard was obliged to produce this receipt on his entry into a town. Those who were refractory, and refused to pay the tax, were thrown into prison.

Since that day, the rulers of modern Europe have endeavoured to persuade, rather than to force, in all matters pertaining to fashion. The Vatican troubles itself no more about beards or ringlets, and men may become hairy as bears, if such is their fancy, without fear of excommunication or deprivation of their political rights. Folly has taken a new start, and cultivates the moustache.

Even upon this point governments will not let men alone. Religion as yet has not meddled with it; but perhaps it will; and politics already influence it considerably. Before the revolution of 1830, neither the French nor Belgian citizens were remarkable for their moustaches; but, after that event, there was hardly a shopkeeper either in Paris or Brussels whose upper lip did not suddenly become hairy with real or mock moustaches. During a temporary triumph gained by the Dutch soldiers over the citizens of Louvain, in October 1830, it became a standing joke against the patriots, that they shaved their faces clean immediately; and the wits of the Dutch army asserted that they had gathered moustaches enough from the denuded lips of the Belgians to stuff mattresses for all the sick and wounded in their hospital.

The last folly of this kind is still more recent. In the German newspapers, of August 1838, appeared an ordonnance, signed by the king of Bavaria, forbidding civilians, on any pretence whatever, to wear moustaches, and commanding the police and other authorities to arrest, and cause to be shaved, the offending parties. "Strange to say," adds *Le Droit*, the journal from which this account is taken, "moustaches disappeared immediately, like leaves from the trees in autumn; every body made haste to obey the royal order, and not one person was arrested."

The king of Bavaria, a rhymester of some celebrity, has taken a good many poetical licences in his time. His licence in this matter appears neither poetical nor reasonable. It is to be hoped that he will not take it into his royal head to make his subjects shave theirs; nothing but that is wanting to complete their degradation.

*Bayeux Tapestry.*[77]

**Footnotes.**

1. Miss Elizabeth Villiers, afterwards Countess of Orkney.

2. The wits of the day called it a *sand-bank*, which would wreck the vessel of the state.

3. This anecdote, which is related in the correspondence of Madame de Bavière, Duchess of Orleans and mother of the Regent, is discredited by Lord John Russell in his *History of the principal States of Europe from the Peace of Utrecht*; for what reason he does not inform us. There is no doubt that Law proposed his scheme to Desmarets, and that Louis refused to hear of it. The reason given for the refusal is quite consistent with the character of that bigoted and tyrannical monarch.

4. From *maltôte*, an oppressive tax.

5. This anecdote is related by M. de la Hode, in his *Life of Philippe of Orleans*. It would have looked more authentic if he had given the names of the dishonest contractor and the still more dishonest minister. But M. de la Hode's book is liable to the same objection as most of the French memoirs of that and of subsequent periods. It is sufficient with most of them that an anecdote be *ben trovato*; the *vero* is but matter of secondary consideration.

6. The French pronounced his name in this manner to avoid the ungallic sound, *aw*. After the failure of his scheme, the wags said the nation was *lasse de lui*, and proposed that he should in future be known by the name of Monsieur He*las*!

7. The curious reader may find an anecdote of the eagerness of the French ladies to retain Law in their company, which will make him blush or smile according as he happens to be very modest or the reverse. It is related in

the *Letters of Madame Charlotte Elizabeth de Bavière, Duchess of Orleans*, vol. ii. p. 274.

8.   The following squib was circulated on the occasion:
"Foin de ton zèle séraphique,
Malheureux Abbé de Tencin,
Depuis que Law est Catholique,
Tout le royaume est Capucin!"
Thus somewhat weakly and paraphrastically rendered by Justandsond, in his translation of the *Memoirs of Louis XV.*:
"Tencin, a curse on thy seraphic zeal,
Which by persuasion hath contrived the means
To make the Scotchman at our altars kneel,
Since which we all are poor as Capucines!"

9.   From a print in a Dutch collection of satirical prints relating to the Mississippi Mania, entitled "Het groote Tafereel der Dwaasheid;" or, The great picture of Folly. The print of Atlas is styled, "L'Atlas actieux de Papier." Law is calling in Hercules to aid him in supporting the globe. Quoted in Wright's *England under the House of Hanover*.

10. The Duke de la Force gained considerable sums, not only by jobbing in the stocks, but in dealing in porcelain, spices, &c. It was debated for a length of time in the parliament of Paris whether he had not, in his quality of spice-merchant, forfeited his rank in the peerage. It was decided in the negative. A caricature of him was made, dressed as a street-porter, carrying a large bale of spices on his back, with the inscription, "Admirez La Force."

11. "Lucifer's New Row-Barge" exhibits Law in a barge, with a host of emblematic figures representing the Mississippi follies. — *From a Print in Mr. Hawkins' Collection*.

12. Duclos, *Memoires Secrets de la Régence.*

13. The Duchess of Orleans gives a different version of this story; but whichever be the true one, the manifestation of such feeling in a legislative assembly was not very creditable. She says that the president was so transported with joy, that he was seized with a rhyming fit, and, returning into the hall, exclaimed to the members:
    *"Messieurs! Messieurs! bonne nouvelle!*
    *Le carrosse de Lass est reduit en cannelle!"*

14. Law in a car drawn by cocks; from *Het groote Tofereel der Dwaasheid.*

15. Neck or nothing, or downfall of the Mississippi Company. — *From a Print in Mr. Hawkins' Collection.*

16. *A South-Sea Ballad; or, Merry Remarks upon Exchange-Alley Bubbles. To a new Tune called "The Grand Elixir; or, the Philosopher's Stone discovered."*

17. Coxe's *Walpole,* Correspondence between Mr. Secretary Craggs and Earl Stanhope.

18. Stock-jobbing Card, or the humours of Change Alley. Copied from a print called *Bubblers' Medley,* published by Carrington Bowles.

19. Tree, surrounded by water; people climbing up the tree. One of a series of bubble cards, copied from the *Bubblers' Medley,* published by Carrington Bowles.

20. Gay (the poet), in that disastrous year, had a present from young Craggs of some South-Sea stock, and once supposed himself to be master of twenty thousand pounds. His friends persuaded him to sell his share, but he dreamed of dignity and splendour, and could not

hear to obstruct his own fortune. He was then importuned to sell as much as would purchase a hundred a year for life, "which," says Fenton, "will make you sure of a clean shirt and a shoulder of mutton every day." This counsel was rejected; the profit and principal were lost, and Gay sunk under the calamity so low that his life became in danger. — *Johnson's Lives of the Poets*

21. Smollett.

22. Caricature, copied from *Bubblers' Medley*, published by Carrington Bowles.

23. Britannia stript by a South-Sea Director. From *Het groote Tafereel der Dwaasheid*.

24. "'God cannot love,' says Blunt, with tearless eyes,
    'The wretch he starves, and piously denies.' …
    Much-injur'd Blunt! why bears he Britain's hate?
    A wizard told him in these words our fate:
    'At length corruption, like a gen'ral flood,
    So long by watchful ministers withstood,
    Shall deluge all; and av'rice, creeping on,
    Spread like a low-born mist, and blot the sun;
    Statesman and patriot ply alike the stocks,
    Peeress and butler share alike the box,
    And judges job, and bishops bite the Town,
    And mighty dukes pack cards for half-a-crown:
    See Britain sunk in Lucre's forbid charms,
    And France reveng'd of Ann's and Edward's arms!'
    'Twas no court-badge, great Scriv'ner! fir'd thy brain,
    Nor lordly luxury, nor city gain:
    No, 'twas thy righteous end, asham'd to see
    Senates degen'rate, patriots disagree,
    And nobly wishing party-rage to cease,
    To buy both sides, and give thy country peace."
    *Pope's Epistle to Allen Lord Bathurst.*

25. The Brabant Screen. This caricature represents the Duchess of Kendal behind the "Brabant Screen," supplying Mr. Knight with money to facilitate his escape; and is copied from a rare print of the time, in the collection of E. Hawkins, Esq. F.S.A.

26. Emblematic print of the South-Sea Scheme. By W. Hogarth.

27. The South-Sea project remained until 1845 the greatest example in British history of the infatuation of the people for commercial gambling. The first edition of these volumes was published some time before the outbreak of the Great Railway Mania of that and the following year.

28. *Biographie Universelle.*

29. His sum "of perfection," or instructions to students to aid them in the laborious search for the stone and elixir, has been translated into most of the languages of Europe. An English translation, by a great enthusiast in alchymy, one Richard Russell, was published in London in 1686. The preface is dated eight years previously from the house of the alchymist, "at the Star, in Newmarket, in Wapping, near the Dock." His design in undertaking the translation was, as he informs us, to expose the false pretences of the many ignorant pretenders to the science who abounded in his day.

30. Article, Geber, *Biographie Universelle.*

31. Naudé, *Apologie des Grands Hommes accusés de Magie,* chap. xviii.

32. Lenglet, *Histoire de la Philosophie Hermétique*. See also Godwin's *Lives of the Necromancers*.

33. Naudé, *Apologie des Grands Hommes accusés de Magie*, chap. xvii.

34. Vidimus omnia ista *dum ad Angliam transiimus, propter intercessionem domini Regis Edoardi illustrissimi.*

35. Converti una vice in aurum ad L millia pondo argenti vivi, plumbi, et stanni. — *Lullii Testamentum.*

36. These verses are but a coarser expression of the slanderous line of Pope, that "every woman is at heart a rake."

37. Fuller's *Worthies of England*.

38. *Biographie Universelle.*

39. For full details of this extraordinary trial, see Lobineau's *Nouvelle Histoire de Bretagne*, and D'Argentré's work on the same subject. The character and life of Gilles de Rays are believed to have suggested the famous Blue Beard of the nursery tale.

40. See the article "Paracelsus," by the learned Renaudin, in the *Biographie Universelle*.

41. The "crystal" alluded to appears to have been a black stone, or piece of polished coal. The following account of it is given, in the supplement to Granger's *Biographical History*. "The black stone into which Dee used to call his spirits was in the collection of the Earls of Peterborough, from whence it came to Lady Elizabeth Germaine. It was next the property of the late Duke of Argyle, and is now Mr. Walpole's. It appears upon examination to be noth-

ing more than a polished piece of cannel coal; but this is what Butler means when he says,
'Kelly did all his feats upon
The devil's looking-glass — a stone.'"

42. Lilly the astrologer, in his *Life*, written by himself, frequently tells of prophecies delivered by the angels in a manner similar to the angels of Dr. Dee. He says, "The prophecies were not given vocally by the angels, but by inspection of the crystal in types and figures, or by apparition the circular way; where, at some distance, the angels appear, representing by forms, shapes, and creatures, what is demanded. It is very rare, yea even in our days," quoth that wiseacre, "for any operator or master to hear the angels speak articulately: when they do speak, *it is like, the Irish, much in the throat!*"

43. Albert Laski, son of Jaroslav, was Palatine of Siradz, and afterwards of Sendomir, and chiefly contributed to the election of Henry of Valois, the Third of France, to the throne of Poland, and was one of the delegates who went to France in order to announce to the new monarch his elevation to the sovereignty of Poland. After the deposition of Henry, Albert Laski voted for Maximilian of Austria. In 1583 he visited England, when Queen Elizabeth received him with great distinction. The honours which were shewn him during his visit to Oxford, by the especial command of the Queen, were equal to those rendered to sovereign princes. His extraordinary prodigality rendered his enormous wealth insufficient to defray his expenses, and he therefore became a zealous adept in alchymy, and took from England to Poland with him two known alchymists. — Count Valerian Krasinski's *Historical Sketch of the Reformation in Poland*.

44. The following legend of the tomb of Rosencreutz, written by Eustace Budgell, appears in No. 379 of

the *Spectator*:—"A certain person, having occasion to dig somewhat deep in the ground where this philosopher lay interred, met with a small door, having a wall on each side of it. His curiosity, and the hope of finding some hidden treasure, soon prompted him to force open the door. He was immediately surprised by a sudden blaze of light, and discovered a very fair vault. At the upper end of it was a statue of a man in armour, sitting by a table, and leaning on his left arm. He held a truncheon in his right hand, and had a lamp burning before him. The man had no sooner set one foot within the vault, than the statue, erecting itself from its leaning posture, stood bolt upright; and, upon the fellow's advancing another step, lifted up the truncheon in his right hand. The man still ventured a third step; when the statue, with a furious blow, broke the lamp into a thousand pieces, and left his guest in sudden darkness. Upon the report of this adventure, the country people came with lights to the sepulchre, and discovered that the statue, which was made of brass, was nothing more than a piece of clock-work; that the floor of the vault was all loose, and underlaid with several springs, which, upon any man's entering, naturally produced that which had happened.

"Rosicreucius, say his disciples, made use of this method to shew the world that he had re-invented the ever-burning lamps of the ancients, though he was resolved no one should reap any advantage from the discovery."

45. No. 574. Friday, July 30th, 1714.

46. "Vitulus Aureus quem Mundus adorat et orat, in quo tractatur de naturæ miraculo transmutandi metalla." *Hagæ*, 1667.

47. *Voyages de Monconis*, tome ii. p. 379.

48. See the Abbé Fiard, and *Anecdotes of the Reign of Louis XVI.* p. 400.

49. *Biographie des Contemporains*, article "Cagliostro." See also *Histoire de la Magie en France*, par M. Jules Garinet, p. 284.

50. The enemies of the unfortunate Queen of France, when the progress of the Revolution embittered their animosity against her, maintained that she was really a party in this transaction; that she, and not Mademoiselle D'Oliva, met the cardinal and rewarded him with the flower; and that the story above related was merely concocted between her La Motte, and others to cheat the jeweller of his 1,600,000 francs.

51. See Gibbon and Voltaire for further notice of this subject.

52. *Charlemagne: Poëme épique par Lucien Buonaparte.*

53. This prophecy seems to have been that set forth at length in the popular *Life of Mother Shipton*:
"When fate to England shall restore
A king to reign as heretofore,
Great death in London shall be though,
And many houses be laid low."

54. The *London Saturday Journal* of March 12th, 1842, contains the following: — "An absurd report is gaining ground among the weak-minded, that London will be destroyed by an earthquake on the 17th of March, or St. Patrick's day. This rumour is founded on the following ancient prophecies: one professing to be pronounced in the year 1203; the other, by Dr. Dee the astrologer, in 1598:
"In eighteen hundred and forty-two
Four things the sun shall view;

London's rich and famous town
Hungry earth shall swallow down.
Storm and rain in France shall be,
Till every river runs a sea.
Spain shall be rent in twain,
And famine waste the land again.
So say I, the Monk of Dree,
In the twelve hundredth year and three."
*Harleian Collection (British Museum)*, 800 b, fol. 319.
"The Lord have mercy on you all —
Prepare yourselves for dreadful fall
Of house and land and human soul —
The measure of your sins is full.
In the year one, eight, and forty-two,
Of the year that is so new;
In the third month of that sixteen,
It may be a day or two between —
Perhaps you'll soon be stiff and cold.
Dear Christian, be not stout and bold —
The mighty, kingly-proud will see
This comes to pass as my name's Dee."
1598. *Ms. in the British Museum.*
The alarm of the population of London did not on this occasion extend beyond the wide circle of the uneducated classes, but among them it equalled that recorded in the text. It was soon afterwards stated that no such prophecy is to be found in the Harleian Ms.

55. *Chronicles of England*, by Richard Grafton; London, 1568, p. 106.

56. *Faerie Queene*, b. 3, c. 3, s. 6-13.

57. Although other places claim the honour(!) of Mother Shipton's birth, her residence is asserted, by oral tradition, to have been for many years a cottage at Winslow-cum-Shipton, in Buckinghamshire, of which the above is

a representation. We give the contents of one of the popular books containing her prophecies:

*The Strange and Wonderful History and Prophecies of Mother Shipton, plainly setting forth her Birth, Life, Death, and Burial.* 12mo. Newcastle. Chap. 1. — Of her birth and parentage. 2. How Mother Shipton's mother proved with child; how she fitted the justice, and what happened at her delivery. 3. By what name Mother Shipton was christened, and how her mother went into a monastery. 4. Several other pranks play'd by Mother Shipton in revenge of such as abused her. 5. How Ursula married a young man named Tobias Shipton, and how strangely she discovered a thief. 6. Her prophecy against Cardinal Wolsey. 7. Some other prophecies of Mother Shipton relating to those times. 8. Her prophecies in verse to the Abbot of Beverly. 9. Mother Shipton's life, death, and burial.

58. Let us try. In his second century, prediction 66, he says:
"From great dangers the captive is escaped.
A little time, great fortune changed.
In the palace the people are caught.
By good augury the city is besieged."
"What is this," a believer might exclaim, "but the escape of Napoleon from Elba — his changed fortune, and the occupation of Paris by the allied armies?"
Let us try again. In his third century, prediction 98, he says:
"Two royal brothers will make fierce war on each other;
So mortal shall be the strife between them,
That each one shall occupy a fort against the other;
For their reign and life shall be the quarrel."
Some Lillius Redivivus would find no difficulty in this prediction. To use a vulgar phrase, it is as clear as a pikestaff. Had not the astrologer in view Don Miguel and Don Pedro when he penned this stanza, so much less obscure and oracular than the rest?

59. *Hermippus Redivivus*, p. 142.

60. *Jovii Elog.* p. 320.

61. *Les Anecdotes de Florence, ou l'Histoire secrète de la Maison di Medicis*, p. 318.

62. It is quite astonishing to see the great demand there is, both in England and France, for dream-books, and other trash of the same kind. Two books in England enjoy an extraordinary popularity, and have run through upwards of fifty editions in as many years in London alone, besides being reprinted in Manchester, Edinburgh, Glasgow, and Dublin. One is *Mother Bridget's Dream-book and Oracle of Fate*; the other is the *Norwood Gipsy*. It is stated, on the authority of one who is curious in these matters, that there is a demand for these works, which are sold at sums varying from a penny to sixpence, chiefly to servant-girls and imperfectly-educated people, all over the country, of upwards of eleven thousand annually; and that at no period during the last thirty years has the average number sold been less than this. The total number during this period would thus amount to 330,000.

63. *Spectator*, No. 7, March 8, 1710-11.

64. See Van der Mye's account of the siege of Breda. The garrison, being afflicted with scurvy, the Prince of Orange sent the physicians two or three small phials, containing a decoction of camomile, wormwood, and camphor, telling them to pretend that it was a medicine of the greatest value and extremest rarity, which had been procured with very much danger and difficulty from the East; and so strong, that two or three drops would impart a healing virtue to a gallon of water. The soldiers had faith in their commander; they took the medicine

with cheerful faces, and grew well rapidly. They afterwards thronged about the prince in groups of twenty and thirty at a time, praising his skill, and loading him with protestations of gratitude.

65. Mummies were of several kinds, and were all of great use in magnetic medicines. Paracelsus enumerates six kinds of mummies; the first four only differing in the composition used by different people for preserving their dead, are the Egyptian, Arabian, Pisasphaltos, and Libyan. The fifth mummy of peculiar power was made from criminals that had been hanged; "for from such there is a gentle siccation, that expungeth the watery humour, without destroying the oil and spirituall, which is cherished by the heavenly luminaries, and strengthened continually by the affluence and impulses of the celestial spirits; whence it may be properly called by the name of constellated or celestial mummie." The sixth kind of mummy was made of corpuscles, or spiritual effluences, radiated from the living body; though we cannot get very clear ideas on this head, or respecting the manner in which they were caught. — *Medicina Diatastica; or, Sympathetical Mummie, abstracted from the Works of Paracelsus, and translated out of the Latin,* by Fernando Parkhurst, Gent. London, 1653, pp. 2, 7. Quoted by the *Foreign Quarterly Review*, vol. xii. p. 415.

66. Reginald Scott, quoted by Sir Walter Scott, in the notes to the *Lay of the last Minstrel,* c. iii. v. xxiii.

67. Greatraks' Account of himself, in a letter to the Honourable Robert Boyle.

68. *Introduction to the Study of Animal Magnetism,* by Baron Dupotet de Sennevoy, p. 315.

69. *Introduction to the Study of Animal Magnetism,* p. 318.

70. *Dictionaire des Sciences Médicales* — Article *Convulsionnaires*, par Montégre.

71. An enthusiastic philosopher, of whose name we are not informed, had constructed a very satisfactory theory on some subject or other, and was not a little proud of it. "But the facts, my dear fellow," said his friend, "the facts do not agree with your theory." — "Don't they?" replied the philosopher, shrugging his shoulders, "then, *tant pis pour les faits;*" — so much the worse for the facts!

72. *Rapport des Commissaires*, rédigé par M. Bailly. Paris, 1784.

73. *Introduction to the Study of Animal Magnetism*, by Baron Dupotet, p. 73.

74. See *Foreign Review and Continental Miscellany*, vol. v. p. 113.

75. See the very clear, and dispassionate article upon the subject in the fifth volume (1830) of *The Foreign Review*, p. 96 et seq.

76. *Histoire Critique du Magnétisme Animal*, p. 60.

77. The above engraving, shewing two soldiers of William the Conqueror's army, is taken from the celebrated Bayeux Tapestry. — See *ante*, p. **297**.

**END OF VOL. I.**

www.ingramcontent.com/pod-product-compliance
Lightning Source LLC
Chambersburg PA
CBHW032341280326
41935CB00008B/407